Assessment IS Instruction: Reading, Writing, Spelling, and Phonics for ALL Learners

Assessment IS Instruction: Reading, Writing, Spelling, and Phonics for ALL Learners

Susan Mandel Glazer
Rider University

Christopher-Gordon Publishers, Inc.
Norwood, Massachusetts

Credits

Christopher-Gordon Publishers, Inc.
1502 Providence Highway, Suite #12
Norwood, MA 02062
(800) 934-8322

Printed in the United States of America

10 9 8 7 6 5 4 3 2   02 01 00 99

Library of Congress Catalog Card Number: 98-071294
ISBN: 0-926842-77-3

Dedication

This book is dedicated to those whose CONSISTENT support and friendship have given new life and animation to my endeavors.

Lyn and Les

Jane, Peg, Marie

Phyllis, Gail, Carol

Carl and Arthur

Gloria and Alma

Loni and Harry

Jerry and Mort

Kathy and Roger

Sandy and Steve

Margot and Nancy

Hank and Gerry

Daisy and Henry

Mary and Milton

Rick

My students of all ages, and Colleagues at Rider University

How fortunate I am!

Applause

Books "acknowledge"; audiences "applaud." I've chosen to be an applauding audience for the many who have been part of the development of this book. There are my graduate students Sue Aurin, Robin Hepp, Kim Wagner, Danyell Clark, Alissa Daniel, Mia Hyde, Debbie Luckey, Bridgette Nevola, Sue Downs, Barbara Hidalgo, Brooke Turner, Amy Kroberger, Ronda Lomberg, Fran Imperato, Ruth O'Keefe, Chris Rice, Rhonda Slawinski, Barbara Bauman, Michele Anderson, JoAnn Harris, Anne Molle, Lorraine Reynolds, Aimee Patti, Diane Curry, Lynn Oleyar, Elena Bruno, Ingrid Graff, Kristine Daufman, Amy Bowers, Lynn Rubin, Vicky Cox, Laura Milo, Tracy Rossi, Patti Conboy, Judy Dill, Christine Sweeney Skinner, Karen Steele, Caren De Sanctis, Mary Beth Kitson, Katrin-Kaja Roomann, Juli Leen, Gloria Smith, Janet Freidman, and Margaret VanSteinwyk.

To the children, thank you for your products, dialogue, and ideas about literacy learning. Thank you to the parents for the confidence in our practices and belief in the philosophies of learning supporting them.

Thank you to my friend Pehr-Olof Rönnholm, his teachers and staff, Anne-Fofie Lyytinen-Lund, Liliane Kjellman, Mikael Fröjdö, Linda Fagerström, Maria Laurén-Lindholm, Annika Kinnari, Jalonene Anita, and Marika Jakobsson who have demonstrated that the ideas in this text work across continents, cultures, and languages. Gratitude to Susan Alton and Tad Schmidt of Staff Development Resources for providing the workshop venue for me to confirm the ideas by sharing them with teachers.

I am grateful for Gail Turner's loyalty, understanding of the importance of literacy, and respect for my desire to "get-it-done-yesterday." To Phyllis Fantauzzo, thank you for knowing the children who produced the products that illustrate the ideas. I am humbled by Phyllis's unconditional nurturing and support in all of my endeavors. Carol Satz's creative, up-beat disposition, and "detective-like" mind for details have helped to refine the important issues.

Bouquets to Arnold, Alice, Lee, Bobbye, Sherri, Alan, and Marcia, whose compassion provides strength to continue. To Pat Broderick and Alan Raymond of *Teaching, K–8,* gratitude for believing in the ideas. To Hiram Howard and especially Sue Canavan, respect and praise for producing the best there is for professionals, and including my work. Special acknowledgment to Katrin-Kaja Roomann for the critiquing and editing I find so frustrating.

To my fabulous mother, Mary Mandel, and my charismatic father-in-law, Hank Glazer, how grateful I am for the parental audience so few of my generation are still fortunate to have.

A standing ovation to you all. How blessed I am!

SMG
3/98

vi

Contents

Prologue

Each morning, when I awake, I ask myself, "Which shoes shall I wear today?" The answer to my question is found by looking out of my apartment window. One particular day I observed New Yorkers carrying umbrellas, and I was able to answer my question. I knew I'd wear my old faithful brown pumps, reserved for rainy days. As I prepared to go to the university, I recalled the meetings, classes, and writing assignments scheduled, and asked myself, "Should I wear a business suit, or can I comfortably put on casual slacks and a sweater?" My appointment book provided me with the necessary data to conclude that the suit was in order. My first look in the mirror that morning frightened me. "What in the world are the red blotches under my eyes?" I asked myself. "Is this another sign of the aging process? If they don't go away by this afternoon I'll call Michael, my physician," was the answer. "He'll steer me in the right direction."

I recall entering a large ballroom recently. The gathering was a reception where I was supposed to know many people. As I glanced around the room, I asked myself, "Who do I know here?" I moved my eyes, systematically scanning the room from left to right looking for something familiar—a face, piece of furniture, the sound of a voice. I spotted a tall, gray-haired gentleman. He looked like my dentist, George. "I wonder what he's doing here?" I thought. "He's probably interested in the speaker's topic," I responded. How good I felt when I thought I knew someone in this audience. The physical characteristics of this man across the 30-foot room certainly did resemble those of George. As I moved closer, the new data at closer range confirmed that I'd made an error. It was not my dentist.

It seems that we are always "testing." We ask questions and then answer them. We categorize our predictions and our responses. If you monitor your behaviors, you will realize that you do this in every activity. This "testing" is satisfying when answers come easily, but frustrating when solutions to questions are difficult to find.

Knowing how to find answers to questions and categorizing responses is the key to passing the "tests" of daily living.

We question and then answer ourselves continuously in order to make meaning of situations and events in our lives. Many questions are answered immediately without thinking about how to respond. We ask, then search for data that provide the clues for answers to our self-questioning. We ask, then answer, we ask, then answer, we ask again, and then answer. We "flip-flop" back and forth between questions and answers in all of our daily endeavors. When questions can't be answered easily, we attempt to unlock their mysteries by seeking appropriate resources. In a sense, we seek instruction that guides us to the answers.

As in life, learning in school is always tested. Teachers and peers spontaneously ask each other questions. They ask and answer, ask and answer again, "flipping" and "flopping" between assessment and instruction instantly. The processes—flipping and flopping between assessing and then instructing ourselves to respond—are integrated.

This book is about managing and balancing the merging of literacy assessment and instruction in classrooms. The activities have been used again and again by students ages 5 to 18 in integrated literacy environments. Assessment and instructional activities are managed by students so that they realize the logical relationship between "what they know" and "what they need to learn." The instructional strategies easily adapt to self-monitoring activities. Many of these self-monitoring tools were developed in the Center for Reading and Writing at Rider University. They have been revised many times based on their effectiveness with students. The tools are generic to age, abilities, and content area studies. They, therefore, become frameworks for managing knowledge and experience gained from student interactions in and out of the classroom.

Ask yourself, as you read this book, "Am I creating an environment in such a way that students realize authentic functions and purposes for learning? Am I creating learning situations where students take risks, responsibility, and control of their own learning?" May the ideas in this text be integrated with yours. May assessment and instruction merge in your classrooms, as they do "naturally" in daily living.

Susan

CHAPTER 1

A Rationale for Change in Literacy Classrooms

Our nation is test crazy. We test everything. We test babies' blood type, eye color, height, and weight at birth. We even test these before they are born. We test preschoolers' intelligence before they enter nursery school. If intelligent "enough," some go to a school that is academically focused. Others are enrolled in those schools concerned with social development. We taste test food in supermarkets; rate hotel rooms, responding to the service, decor, heat, light, and more. We do this because we believe that "the solution to all our problems is to give more tests" (A. Farstrup, personal communication, June 3, 1996). Students' achievement test scores are so important that these dominate the media. The "poorer" the scores, the larger the headlines.

Unfortunately, test scores have guided the public to scrutinize and form inappropriate perceptions of our nation's schools. "Bashing our public schools is a national pastime . . . ," says Regie Routman (1996). "Because we in society pay for public schools and most of us send our children to them, schools are constantly being scrutinized" (p. 3). "The trouble with the endless concern over 'problems in education,'" says Frank Smith (1995, April), "is that many well-meaning but often misguided and sometimes meddlesome people believe that solutions must exist . . . (p. 584)." So educators now, as in the past, respond to the "bashing" by trying to fix things. What usually happens, says Smith, is that "typically, [we] try harder to do more of something that is already being done although what is being done is probably one of the problems" (p. 585). The "more of something" that continues is more tests and more scores and grade equivalents. Therein lies the problem.

As educators we have made great strides in our field, and learned how to use the updated alternatives to standardized tests that complement updated instructional procedures. We still, however, permit standardized tests to flourish. Many staunch opposers of testing administer these very tests to children, thereby supporting ignorant public agendas concerned with testing. Two front page *New York Times* (June 7, 1995) headlines, "Math Survey in Public Schools Shows No State Is 'Cutting It'," and (August 23, 1996) "S.A.T. Scores Rise, College Board Says," exemplify the population's perceptions of test scores as indicators of failures and successes of our public educational systems. An in-depth public opinion study, designed to find out what Americans expect from public schools, indicates strong public endorsement for raising academic standards (Johnson & Immerwahr, 1994). Confirmation of this public agenda resides in many surveys conducted in the last decade that have repeatedly illustrated that Americans insist it is important for students to pass a qualifying examination before receiving a high school diploma (Gallup Organization, 1984, 1988, 1994).

This same set of surveys questioned the general public concerning the form of assessment used to illustrate achievement. The response indicated that 70 percent of the parent population in the United States believes that promoting students to the next grade should be based on performance on a traditional (i.e., multiple-choice) test (Johnson & Immerwahr, 1994). Fifty-four percent of the same parent sample felt that essays could replace multiple-choice type tests. Surveys, public opinion polls, and politics play an important role in keeping our testing system in the forefront of the media.

Reading is one of the most frequently measured abilities (F. Smith, 1983). The lack of change in reading assessment can probably be attributed to confused public perceptions about innovative approaches to teaching and learning. Changes come so quickly, that "sticking" with the familiar—the test—is one way to keep change from being painfully disruptive. The test is familiar, and therefore balances the confusion. Peggy VanLeirsburg's (1993, p. 33) summary of reading and achievement tests, which includes subtests in reading for elementary students, indicates the growth of the importance of tests since 1900 to 1989.

Tests In Print, published every five years, is a comprehensive listing of all current tests. Linda Murphy, managing editor (February, 1997) of the Buros Institute at the University of Nebraska, publishers of *Tests In Print,* indicates that although firm numbers are not available, the number of tests included in the 1999 *Tests In Print, V* is expected to increase from 300 to 400. This information and the figures in Figure 1-1 confirm and support the need for the familiar.

Historically, schools and societies have changed. Instructional procedures have certainly changed. My "a-bit-more-than" three decades in education have brought me full circle from basal text reading series to individualized instruction in the 1960s, and now to holistic teaching with consideration for the individual child. Trends have resulted in turmoil, with scholars debating sight-word learning versus phonics, basal reading series versus literature, formal grammar instruction versus the "natural approach," to name only a few. Commonly used professional terms have gone from politically correct to incorrect overnight. The popular phrase "whole language" is now politically subservient to "phonics/skill-based reading program." "Child-centered"

Decade	Number	Cumulative Number
1910–1919	5	5
1920–1929	21	26
1930–1939	33	59
1940–1949	12	71
1950–1959	21	92
1960–1969	28	120
1970–1979	20	140
1980–1989	8	148

Figure 1-1. Standardized Reading Tests and Achievement Test Batteries for Elementary Students Published in the United States by Decade

is "out" and "curriculum driven" in. "Literature-based reading programs" are being shelved for "basal reading series." "Beginning reader" has once again surfaced, replacing the popular "emergent reader" designation. The tumultuous controversies have come and gone, and come and gone twice in my career. They have, however, not been all bad, for they've spurred the development of wonderful resources. Marilyn Jager Adams (1991), Nancie Atwell (1987), Walter Barbe (1961), Morton Botel (1973), Alvina Treut Burrows (1965), Lucy Calkins (1994), Jean Chall (1967), Marie Clay (1975), Ken Goodman (1986), Donald Graves (1983), Bill Martin Jr. (1974), Margaret Meek (1982), James Moffett (1968), Regie Routman (1988), Frank Smith (1978), James Smith (1967), and Jeanette Veatch (1966) are among many who've responded to the changes, producing professional references and instructional materials commensurate with the times. The marvelous insights provided by these leaders in literacy education over the past several decades have altered the faces of instruction. School bashing continues based on continued presentations of test scores.

Aired public opinions and meek educators are strong contributing factors to "school bashing." Educators continue to permit those who are not members of our profession to inappropriately criticize. More rather than fewer of us continue to cower to political powers fueling government intervention in educational reform. Evidence of these intrusions resides in projects and governmental actions such as:

- a national voluntary 4th-grade reading test developed by a committee appointed by a government agency (National Test Panel, 1997) designed to assess all U.S. fourth graders' reading abilities;

- The National Education Goals Report (1997) citing national progress, thus reporting:
  — reading achievement at grade 12 has declined;
  — the percentage of secondary school teachers who hold a degree in their main teaching assignment has decreased;
  — student drug use and attempted sales of drugs at school have increased;
  — more teachers are reporting that disruptions in their classrooms interfere with their teaching. (National Goals Panel, 1997)

The Reading Excellence Act H. R. 2614 (1997) and other bills have caused mass media publicity concerning literacy education resulting in misunderstandings about how and what we teach. Reading, writing, phonics, and spelling research is misinterpreted, and those misinterpretations are used to support local, state, and national candidates for office. Bills at state (Arizona, California, etc.) levels are facilitating the passage of laws that tell teachers precisely how and what to teach and what not to teach. These also include laws that require university professors and classroom teachers to teach about "phonics." The purpose of these laws is to eliminate instruction based on specific learning theories. At the present time, it's the "whole language philosophy" that's the focus of bashing. David Berliner (personal communication, 1997), a college dean in the state of Arizona, writes:

> The state[s] simply should not tell professionals what treatments are appropriate. Would the state[s] demand that surgeons perform by-pass surgery instead of angioplastys? Would it demand that psychologists treat clients by Skinnerian procedures instead of psychodynamic approaches? We think not. But somehow the state[s] seems to think it is all right to tell teachers to teach one way and not another. . . . Legislators act legitimately when they take reasonable steps to insure public safety and protect the rights of . . . citizens— particularly . . . children. Legislators exceed their responsibilities, if not their competence, when they attempt to micro-manage professionals' activities.

Until we take charge, stop politicians from controlling our profession, and make our own decisions about assessment and instruction, **standardized tests are here to stay.** Outside influences have played a major role in the growth and format of tests since their beginnings. The events that led us to our "test mania" are important to know in order for change to occur.

The Beginning—1900s

The quantification of educational abilities can be attributed to the work of Binet and Simon (1905), who developed a test to determine intelligence for draftees for the armed forces. They created the test in order to eliminate the unscientific approach of counting the number of lumps on one's head to determine intelligence. A specific number and size of lumps was supposed to be an indicator of academic ability. The standardized test, created in England, had great influence in the United States at the beginning of the 20th century.

Values in the United States changed during the first 25 years of the century due to the large numbers of immigrants who came to this country yearly. In 1905, for example, more than one million people, mostly Europeans, left their birthplaces to make their home in the United States (N. B. Smith, 1963). Poverty coupled with illiteracy were emerging problems that had to be solved. Settlement houses, which fed, clothed, sheltered, and educated the people, were created in the hope that these would improve conditions. By 1918, each state passed compulsory education laws (Rippa, 1988). Emigration served to raise social awareness on issues of inequity of opportunity, as well. The 19th Amendment to the Constitution, passed by Congress in 1920, provided women with the right to be educated and to vote. The abolition of slavery also led to increased school populations in the years between 1900 and 1929 (Glaser, 1981). School attendance rose dramatically from 18 to 25 million because of mandatory school attendance, but also in part because of the inclusion of kindergarten and the passage of child labor laws (Rippa, 1988). Diversities presented challenges to educators, and they attempted to solve problems by using standardized tests to determine abilities.

The tests, as they were originally conceived, were not meant to assess achievement. They were designed to separate those who were deficient mentally—those who were feebleminded (or retarded)—from those who were not. However, these tests became popular in the United States, especially for the purpose of testing the intelligence of Army recruits in World War I (Yerkes, 1921).

— The 1960s

The '60s decade was when I began my career, and it was also a time of massive interest in the reading process. While linguists began to study the process, Nila Banton Smith (1963), among others (DeBoer & Dallmann, 1965; Dechant, 1964; McKee, 1948; Tinker & McCullough, 1952), wrote texts about the teaching of reading. These usually divided instruction into four parts: (1) word identification, (2) meanings, (3) study skills and, (4) fluency and speed, and referred to these parts as the "large skill areas . . . generalities" (N. B. Smith, 1963, p. 165). Lessons dealing with each of the subskills dominated instruction. Children learned, in word recognition lessons, how to identify words by looking at picture clues. Another word recognition skill included identifying the sounds created by a spelling pattern in order to figure out the word ("at" as in "cat"). One hundred pages of the Smith text were devoted to word recognition. A forty-five-page chapter addressed the meaning-making clearly, indicating that word recognition skills were more important. Strategies for teaching meaning lacked theoretical bases. The suggestion that the way to teach ". . . meaning in reading is through discussion in which the teacher makes a special contribution by **throwing in questions here and there**" (p. 268), indicates a lack of attention to scientific knowledge.

Surveying the texts forced me to realize that the early authors paid little or no attention to Edmund Burke Huey, who wrote in his book, originally published in 1908:

> And so to completely analyze what we do when we read would almost be the acme of a psychologist's achievements, for it would be to describe very many of the most intricate workings of the human mind, as well as to unravel the tangled story of the most remarkable specific performance that civilization has learned in all its history. (1968, p. 6.)

Texts of the 1960s defined reading as the translation of graphic symbols (the letters) into an oral code, the sounds corresponding to those letters. This was far more sophisticated, implied Nila Bantam Smith, than the early notions about the teaching of reading which centered on ". . . spelling and pronunciation . . . [as] the concept of reading instruction for several centuries" (N. B. Smith, 1963, p. 165). A worksheet fashioned after those most often used is one of the components of a reading instructional series of the early 1960s. It illustrates how the philosophy about learning to read was carried out. (See Figure 1-2.) Children were expected to match items, one to the other, as part of their learning.

Assessment in the 1960s

The 1960s was a time when laypersons grew concerned about reading achievement in school. Rudolf Flesch (1956) capitalized on the public's concern. His book, *Why Johnny Can't Read* (1955) was received by the American public with open arms. He had found a way to convince his followers that he had the answer to America's failing readers. Dr. Flesch said, in that book:

> The teaching of reading—all over the United States, in all the schools, in all the textbooks—is totally wrong and flies in the face of all logic and common sense. [Johnny can't read because] he was unfortunately exposed to an ordinary American school. (p. 9)

The notion that ALL American schools were to blame for poor reading was an inappropriate conclusion accepted widely by the public. It put the blame on the educa-

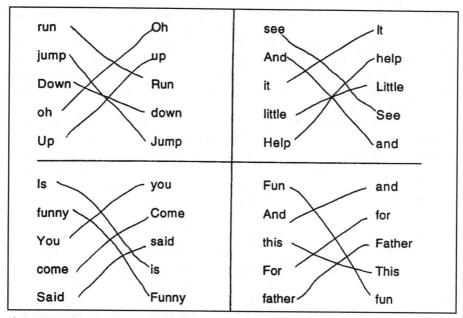

Figure 1-2. Beginning Reader Worksheet

tors, taking all responsibility for learning out of the hands of parents and caregivers. Dr. Flesch said, "[Teaching reading] is very simple. Teach the child what each letter stands for and he can read. The method used in our schools does not work" (p. 10). Dr. Flesch's book *Teaching Johnny to Read* (1956) was promoted as a practical way to develop a child's reading ability. The book stipulates that teaching reading starts with the sounds of letters. The adult points to a letter, and then to the picture whose name includes the sound of that letter. A format somewhat like Flesch's is shown in Figure 1-3. The book consists of 72 lessons, one page introducing the sound of the

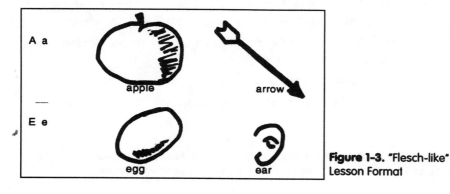

Figure 1-3. "Flesch-like" Lesson Format

letter(s); the second, a review page. The adult is to teach "Johnny" (who represents both boys and girls) the sound, and then the child is expected to make that sound when the adult points to the letter. Directions to "repeat, repeat, repeat" the exercises are provided, "until Johnny can read and write each word in [the exercise] without the slightest hesitation" (p. 7). Flesch's final recommendation was to forbid the student to read anything else, including stories, until he'd completed 50 of the 72 exercises in the book.

In all of the materials the child was to select and match. The select and match instructional format, much like the workbooks* (Figure 1-2), paralleled the activities of most tests (Figure 1-4). Selecting and matching were the formats for both instructional and assessment activities. The content is poor, for it asks children to match sounds by looking at pictures. Sounds need to be matched with sounds, and pictures with pictures in order to provide consistency for both teaching and testing.

The 1970s and New Research

The study of the reading process exploded in the 1960s with linguists, sociolinguists, psychologists, and psycholinguists all jumping on the reading research bandwagon. This probably occurred because reading was, and still is considered to be the foundation for all success in and out of school. The linguists were the first to make reading the focus of their research. Their studies resulted in a theory supporting the notion that reading is related to other language processes, specifically, writing, listening, and speaking. One of the major insights provided by linguists was that all literate societies try to represent features of their oral language in writing (Pearson & Stephens, 1994). We might, for example, use underlining, *italics*, **boldface** type, or ALL CAPS to represent stress in written form. The linguists also supported the notion that reading could no longer stand as an isolated activity, but rather was an interdisciplinary one. This theory drove the development of instructional materials written by the linguists themselves. The materials were based on the following principles:

- one needs knowledge of the major spelling patterns of the English language in order to learn to read (cat and fat = Consonant Vowel Consonant pattern);

- instructional materials must include minimal contrasts between these spelling patterns (cat-fat, took-tool, etc.);

- beginning readers need to read stories;

- pictures must be avoided so beginning readers can attend to words;

---

*The *Think-and-Do Books,* by William S. Gray, Marion Monroe, and Sterl Artley (1956), New York: Scott, Foresman, bring back vivid memories of seatwork activities.

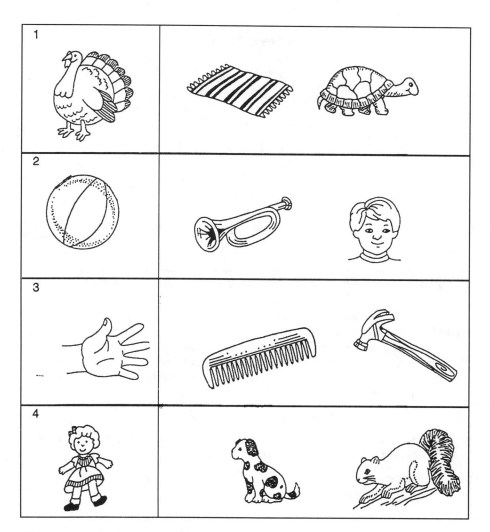

Figure 1-4. Testing Formats for Assessing Ability to Comprehend Beginning Sounds

- teaching procedures must permit daily evaluation of reading progress. (Fries, Wilson, & Rudolph, 1966)

Linguists believed that all of the elements necessary to learn to read were included in the materials (Figure 1-5). Repeated spelling patterns, minimal contrasts in these spellings, and short (choppy) sentences make up the story. Although boring and con-

---

Sid and the Lid

Sid and the lid.

The lid and Sid.

Sid wanted a lid.

But the lid was hid.

Sid looked for the lid.

But Sid slid.

"Whoops!" said Sid.

"I slid on the lid."

Figure 1–5.   Sample of Instructional Materials Based on Linguistic Theory

trived, it is in fact a story. Unlike earlier materials where the teaching of sounds were isolated, the teaching of sounds and symbols were within the context of the passage.

Testing children's reading after using these materials was easy. The same sort of activities were included in test formats. The format shown in Figure 1-6 certainly resembles the linguist's focus. The responses are predictable and expected. The answer can be determined by the way the language is used.

Directions: Read the riddle. Print an answer for each one on the line. Your teacher will do the first one with you.

It is gray.

It is big.

It has wrinkled skin.

It is an _____.

It is yellow.

It swims.

It says, "Quack, quack."

It is a _____.

It has four wheels.

You can ride in it.

It is big and yellow.

It is a _____.

It is black and white.

It has soft fur.

It barks, "Bow wow."

It is a _____.

Figure 1–6.   Skill/Sound Discrimination

The 1970s also brought Ken Goodman and Frank Smith, and they led the field of inquiry. Goodman's (1965) study of cues and miscues enlightened educators to realize that errors children make while reading out loud should be viewed as "windows" into how children process information in order to comprehend what they read. The child who reads the word "cop," for example, when "policeman" is written, permits us to see that he understands the concept and is "translating" the ideas into his own language. Goodman found that students were using cues from the text in order to "predict" about the content. His work also convinced educators that students are able to read many more words in the context of passages than when they are presented in isolated lists. Goodman's mark has been felt in most classrooms in the United States and in many countries abroad. The fact that errors are thought of as clues to the way students think about text changed the teaching of reading.

Frank Smith's (1971) idea that reading cannot be taught, but rather is something that one learns to do, was revolutionary. Like speaking or walking, one learns to read by reading. "From the point of view of language, reading makes no demands that the brain does not meet in the comprehension of speech" (p.1), says Smith. According to Smith, reading is ONLY incidentally visual. The eyes view the visual information but, says Smith, "that information disappears when the light goes out. Nonvisual information is in your head already, behind the eyes" (p.13). Smith and other psycholinguists believe that the more nonvisual information one has stored in one's memory, the less visual information one needs to read.

The work of Goodman and Smith guided professionals to believe that:

- meaning-making experiences are more important than recognizing words in isolation;

- text provides readers with the impetus to make meaning of words;

- errors provide information about students' thinking about text;

- past experiences (information in one's head) are essential in order to read successfully.

What About the Tests?

A 1989 version of a standardized test of reading ability used in classrooms today illustrates that students, even in the prereading stage, are expected to match, and also to select one item in four. The multiple-choice format requiring the child to select from a list of items denies all good learning theory (Figure 1-7). Students, in order to demonstrate abilities, need to demonstrate logical relationships (Fantauzzo, 1996). The format of the test seems illogical. Responses provide no information about the processes the students used to acquire their responses. The focus is on the answer with the purpose of securing a score and grade equivalent. The work of Goodman

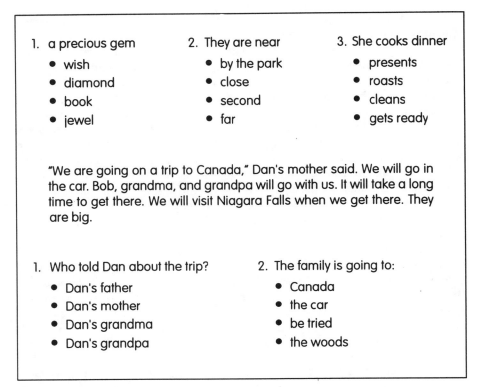

1. a precious gem
   - wish
   - diamond
   - book
   - jewel

2. They are near
   - by the park
   - close
   - second
   - far

3. She cooks dinner
   - presents
   - roasts
   - cleans
   - gets ready

"We are going on a trip to Canada," Dan's mother said. We will go in the car. Bob, grandma, and grandpa will go with us. It will take a long time to get there. We will visit Niagara Falls when we get there. They are big.

1. Who told Dan about the trip?
   - Dan's father
   - Dan's mother
   - Dan's grandma
   - Dan's grandpa

2. The family is going to:
   - Canada
   - the car
   - be tried
   - the woods

Figure 1-7. Vocabulary and Comprehension Test Format

and Smith and other professionals in the field (Halliday, 1975; Heath, 1983; Wells, 1986) impacted on the field of literacy education. The research, however, seemed to have little effect on reading assessment practices.

From the brief review, it's easy to see that standardized tests have been around for a while and have made their mark.

Why Tests Are Here to Stay

The complex nature of the political issues surrounding testing has coerced the public's continued demand for using these tools. Public confidence in test results have "boggled" the task of finding alternatives that are accepted by educational communities, as well as communities of laypersons, parents, and politicians. The nature of developing and then validating alternative tools is a barrier. Salary and tenure issues, parental pressures, and demands for high test scores for prep school and college admissions rely, in great part, on standardized test scores. Teacher effectiveness is often based on observations of direct instruction (Searfoss & Enz, 1996).

Tests seem to provide the stability and control factor that the ever-changing instructional paradigms don't. Tests have become a yardstick for the public to use as a measure of success (or failure) for both students and teachers. The homogeneous barometer preserves a desire for conformity and the expectation that ALL children perform similarly. When all students—the general population, gifted and talented, dysgraphic, perceptually impaired, even those who are ADD (attention deficit disorder)—are expected to take the same tests and read and learn from the same textbooks inadequate and distorted educational outcomes are inevitable.

These, and other difficult issues are often challenged by laypersons in meddlesome ways. Noneducators have interfered in professional areas in which they have no right or business to. Yet, it continues. Outsiders must stop interfering, and it is up to educators to stop them. The overemphasis placed on scores must change to reflect the ideals and cultural standards—the social influences of our times (Archbald & Newmann, 1988). Many have attempted to make changes. All sorts of alternative assessment procedures have and are still being "concocted" by school and district assessment committees. The teachers on these committees are expected to develop alternatives in short, precisely defined periods of time. Some of the committees are provided with professional development activities. They attend workshops and meetings, listening to consultants brought in for a day or two to educate the participants. And then these good teachers are expected to "create" alternatives including checklists, rubrics, and portfolios. Several things, however, have happened.

1. Checklists of skills have been created for teachers to use to "check off" student knowledge. Checklists often include rating categories. "All of the time," "Some of the time," "Not at all"; "Mastered," "Progressing," "Introduced"; "has accomplished," "has not fully accomplished," or "needs work accomplishing," are only some of the alternative assessment designations found on forms.

    A Minneapolis father expresses the ideas of many parents concerning this alternative form of assessment.

    > . . . When I got my son's report card, I was fully confused. It just had columns and check marks of "has not fully accomplished" or "needs work accomplishing." I had no idea where he was at, what level he was at. What *was* he accomplishing? It was a real arbitrary thing—the opinion of the teacher. *She* couldn't even tell us where he was at. It was real vague, without those boundaries and concrete measures that say, "Yes, he can do fractions, or he knows his multiplication tables." All of that was totally lost.

    Alternative procedures that replace letter and number grades with vague and superficial designations lack specificity. The lack of clarity results in inadequate descriptions of achievement, resulting in negative public reactions to alternative trends. People often don't understand why newer trends are considered better, especially when they are unclear. Groups of laypersons (especially parents who need specific descriptions of their children's growth) often become unnerved by what is perceived as "fuzziness" and lack of precision.

2.   Many talented teachers have developed alternative assessment tools that emerged from their instructional activities. Their successful creations have often resulted in school and district-wide mandates to implement their specific systems in ALL classrooms. The specificity of specific classroom management and content may mean that the system may not work in other classes. Harp (1996) cites one teacher who developed a checklist based on helping readers learn to ask themselves critical questions about strategies they use to help them read. It was evident that the children had learned to use the strategies included on the list. The tool could not be used in other classrooms, for these strategies were not taught by other teachers.

It is important that teachers share successful alternative assessment strategies they've developed with peers. When, however, administrators mandate that all teachers use these specific tools, the personalized nature of the instruments is lost. It is, in a sense, standardizing the alternative.

There needs to be some standardization for reporting progress in schools. It seems reasonable, therefore, to adopt an organizational structure and format for reporting purposes (see Chapter 5). Truly authentic assessment practices are those paralleling instructional procedures in each classroom. If they don't, the authenticity is dissolved and the "matching" obliterated. The purpose, to "mirror 'real' as opposed to artificial literacy events" (Hill & Ruptic,1994) is defeated. Hill and Ruptic (1994) cite Meyer (1992) who states:

> In . . . authentic assessment [and instruction], the student not only completes or demonstrates the desired behavior[s], but also does it in a real-life context. "Real life" may be in terms of the student . . . or an adult expectation. The significant criterion for the authenticity of [an] . . . assignment might be that the locus of control rests with the student; that is, the student determines the topic, the time allocated, the pacing, and the conditions under which the . . . [product] is generated. (p. 40)

So, How Can Change Occur?

The inferiority complex that seems to exist among teachers perpetuates the use of standardized tests, textbook series, and other homogenizing components of teaching and learning. The lack of self-confidence in our knowledge and low self-esteem invites laypersons to criticize. We need to "pull up" our self-esteem and inform the public that we KNOW what to do and how. Communities need to know that (1) testing requires time, (2) there are differences between teaching and learning, and testing procedures, (3) testing often infringes upon academic activities, (4) tests impose infringement on academic freedom, and (5) tests are often not appropriate tools for measuring achievement for many of the diverse student populations in classrooms.

Time and Testing

It is estimated that each child in the United States encounters 2,000 test items yearly (Tierney, Carter, & Desai, 1991). Teacher surveys reveal that children, in addition to the tests, spend an average of fourteen hours of school time during one year preparing to take standardized tests (Tierney, Carter, & Desai, 1991, p. 22). While most students spend two to six hours yearly taking tests, special education students (the hard-to-teach) spend 4 to 18 hours during the same time period taking tests (VanLeirsburg, 1993). Classroom time is spent in preparing students for the testing. The time would be better spent on activities that involve student interaction; collaboration; action; reactions; and responses to reading, listening, viewing, and experiencing.

Teaching and Learning. and Testing

Standardized tests have been developed without considering the research that explains language learning processes and its relationship to learning to read.

Because the differences in how children learn and how they are assessed are so vast, test-taking activities are confusing. There is a poor alignment of testing activities with classroom instructional activities (Hiebert, Valencia, & Afflerbach, 1994). Of additional significance is the realization that traditional norm-referenced test items are unable, because of their format, to capture the extent of higher-level literacy abilities needed for daily living.

Infringement on Academic Activities

An unfortunate residual effect of tests is their influence on the content of instruction. In conversations with teachers, I've often heard, "The test content isn't covered in our school curriculum." Teachers, in order to help their students pass the tests, have reviewed test contents, and revised their curriculum. They have used the content of tests, rather than their curriculum or student interests, in order to decide what to teach (Koretz, 1991; Shepard, 1990).

Publishers, too, have complied with test content. This is noticeable in textbooks where end-of-the-book tests simulate standardized test formats (Hiebert, Valencia, & Afflerbach, 1994; Pearson & Valencia, 1987; Stallman & Pearson, 1990; Valencia & Pearson, 1987). When test contents and formats drive instruction, the results are reductions in the quality of teaching and learning.

Infringement on Academic Freedom

An abominable effect of standardized, norm-referenced tests is their infringement on academic freedom. Teachers have, for a long time, been subservient to public opinion polls concerning the importance of tests. Teachers often say, "I must give that test, it's mandated by the district. Parents want to know how well their children are doing." Realtors use test scores as indicators of "desirable" real estate. If scores are high, the school district is a good one. My understanding of these mandates is realistic. My tolerance for public responses to the "ups" and "down" of scores is minimal.

Diverse Classroom Populations

Populations in our classrooms have changed. Public Law Number 92-142, the Education for All Handicapped Children Act of 1975, has altered classroom populations probably more than any other factor.

All of the support for alternatives to standardized tests has and will not stop test makers from creating traditional tests, teachers from administering them, and parents from desiring the results. The results, however, should not be used as *the* indicator of ability, achievement, or for grade placement. The results are better used to determine instruction and other needs (Fantauzzo, 1996). Test scores must become one of many indicators of growth. Once scores are immersed with other variables, they become part of a greater system of assessment. That "greater" system includes finding ways to describe student products, so that the students and adults see growth and change.

"Performance-based assessment" has become a commonly used phrase to represent assessment tools that illustrate growth (Harris & Hodges, 1995, p. 182). Responses produced by students in performance assessment resemble those expected in instructional activities. The various responses and products, compiled, are the materials collected over time to illustrate trends in growing and learning. "Portfolios" have, therefore, gained most support.

A Statement to Educators

We are a nation that prides itself on diversity. Our cultures, customs, and social values are diverse. We celebrate Christmas, Chanukah, and Kwanzaa at just about the same time yearly in our schools, illustrating the respect for differences among us. Yet the bottom lines are test scores and content knowledge, and these, regretfully, remain homogeneous.

Although most teachers, especially those in literacy education, seem to abhor standardized tests, the majority are still administering them. Large numbers are involved in textbook adoptions for entire school districts. The delicate balance between the wonderful classroom environments, curricula, and testing remains. When test scores control a nation's educational system, the thrust toward respect for diversity is diminished, and consideration for individual differences seems to wash away in stanine scores and test results. It is time that tests be put in their proper place. It is time, too, that classrooms support appropriate alternatives to tests that affect the lives of students more positively than they have in the past.

CHAPTER 2

Portfolios—The Alternative "Trend"

The word "portfolio" has been used nationally and internationally to define changes in classroom assessment practices. Lack of clarity concerning the meaning of the word, however, has resulted in lack of preciseness concerning what portfolios are supposed to be, and how they are to be used. Confusion has surpassed cognizability because educators have attempted to use it to replace or interchange it with words like "assess," "evaluate," and "critique." The word "authentic" has found its way into the pool of descriptors, and has become a charged alternative for describing portfolio activities. This, too, causes some misunderstandings. One teacher, when speaking about the school's alternatives to tests said, "We do portfolios in our school. That's the 'authentic' assessment part of report cards. But we give tests and do grades on report cards, too."

Are We Selecting and Using Terms Appropriately?*

Simply stated, "no." The trendy use of terms has been functioning as a marketing device for "selling" ideas to audiences of parents and educators. The desire to find some consistent definition of the word led me to search for the meaning of the word "assess," since it seems to be used more often than others. Several educators have agreed that this term is "safe" and sounds friendly. I used three dictionaries to find definitions. All three defined the word as follows:

> *assess*: to set an estimated value on (property, etc.) for taxation.

---

*This section was first published in *Reading Today*, August/September, 1994.

Imagine using the word "assess," as defined by Webster, Roget, and Oxford to describe activities that demonstrate a student's growth and needs! If interpreted correctly, the definition means to decide the value of things numerically. The purpose is to determine a fee based on the worth of the property. Since property is a "thing" that we use, the fee is determined by supply and demand, quality, and location.

I suppose that if we are going to "assess" a child's growth, we need, according to the definition, to determine how popular the child is according to personality, religion, race, or sex. We would consider the cultural, social, and academic factors because these, according to the definition, depict quality. Then we need to consider where the student goes to school, since location is a factor in assessing estimated values. Last, but not least, the assessed value needs to be translated into a numerical value—a price—for the assessment is the "tax" we pay based on that value.

Do you, based on the definition and the rationale, feel comfortable using the term "assess" as an alternative for describing academic progress? Since this definition seemed inappropriate, a definition of "evaluate" was sought. Webster, Roget, and Oxford defined this word as follows:

> *evaluate:* To find the value or amount of; to judge or determine the worth or quality of an article.

This definition is not much different from the first. Value implies numbers; judgments indicate standards; and worth or quality of an article says, "Student, you're not much different from a piece of property. Your value, or worth, or grade depends on how you perform based on adult expectations." How startling to think that student academic worth is based not only on quantitative scores (values) but adult expectations. It is difficult to recall what adult expectations feel like when one is grown. For most children, they are devastating. One ten-year-old youngster suffering with Tourette's Syndrome begged his mother to answer affirmatively when he asked, "Did I do good, Mom? Did I?"

The word "authentic" was my next challenge. "Authentic" implies that approaches to assessment genuinely resemble learning experiences. This means that what students do to learn is similar to what they do to assess, evaluate, and test that learning. The word, according to the dictionaries, is defined as follows:

> *authentic:* can be believed; trustworthy; genuine.

Dancers are tested by performing at a recital, a ballet, or in a review. Students rehearse the steps, again and again, in a studio environment similar to one in which they will perform. A similar, but hypothetical situation familiar to the classroom is the multiple-choice test format. Let's pretend, for a moment, that you believe (heaven forbid) that a multiple-choice test format is the best way to determine student achievement. If you believe this, then you are obligated to prepare children for that testing format. You would have multiple-choice learning experiences daily. Children would be asked, for example, to play games where they would be expected to select the correct answer from a group of possible responses. They would have worksheets and discussions that included selecting the best answer from a group of situations.

The rehearsal—the practice period—would familiarize students with the multiple-choice test format. As a result, they would feel more comfortable during the performance session—the test. Classroom activities simulate the multiple-choice testing session, making the test itself "authentic."

Do the definition and example imply that tests used in the past have been "unauthentic"? Does using the term "authentic assessment" indicate that the value or worth, the judgments and evaluations of student performance have been incorrect and improper?

As I searched, I'd hoped that the word "portfolio" would be just the right term to describe what is happening in some classrooms. This definition posed questions, as well. The dictionaries defined the term as follows:

> *portfolio:* a flat, portable case, usually of leather, for carrying loose
> sheets of paper, manuscripts, drawings; a list of stocks and com-
> mercial paper owned by a bank, an investor, etc.

Fashion models have portfolios. The contents reflect and support the abilities of the individual to take part in fashion photography and runway modeling. Photographs from several settings are included and selected by the model him/herself, but also by that individual's agent and coach. Based on the contents, the model is an investment, much like stock, that has potential for earning money. The investors—those who benefit from the encased demonstrations of modeling performances—fund publicity and other activities. The model is merely their commodity.

Many samples included in artists' portfolios are self-selected. Realistically, however, artists, writers, and performers usually put ONLY the very best examples of their work in these folders. The best are those that will sell, not necessarily their favorite productions.

Defining Portfolios in This Text

The portfolios in this text have evolved over a period of nineteen years. They began as a place to gather products, sort them, and make decisions about what was best for demonstrating progress. After several years they became cumbersome and ambiguous when discussing purpose, almost in the way. Students enjoyed handling them, for as one nine-year-old shared, "I feel grown up like my dad. He keeps his stuff in a portfolio, too." The thought of referring to responses to reading, original stories, biographies, and dialogues as "stuff" forced me to think about what a portfolio ought to be in classrooms. After twenty years, the portfolio has evolved into a management system for classroom work. It defines categories, keeps products systematically sorted, and guides the daily work schedule. It is truly a collection of products, but the products in each of its four sections are accompanied by a self-monitoring tool. These tools guide students to understand "what they know" and "what they need to learn." A progress report form is also fastened to the product and self-evaluation tool providing students with a way to systematically record daily what they learned, what each needs to learn, and teachers' roles. This businesslike, logical arrangement of work products provides students with consistent ways to describe their activities so that everyone—students, parents, teachers, and administrators—thinks about the works in progress and the products in similar ways.

This systematized portfolio guides organization of time. It is concrete, with definitive guidelines for classifying and acknowledging growth and needs. It can be used across grade, age, and ability levels. It is also appropriate for organizing classes in all content areas, as well. Our portfolios, developed in the Center for Reading and Writing over time, have become tools for guiding learning and teaching. They have been an ideological means for guiding learners of all ages to become independent learners. The students know what to do, when to do it, and how to assess their productions.

The rest of this text expands on this portfolio system. The arrangement, strategies, and instructional guidelines are categorized like our portfolios. The management system is precise, clearly defined, and permits students to take control of their learning.

Summary

The diverse nature of communities, particularly in the United States, has resulted in diverse cultures and values, diverse learning abilities, and diverse learning styles. The assessment procedures have been insensitive to the diversities in classrooms. This seems to be the result of communities', laypersons', and some educators' understanding of evaluation and assessment. For most, tests, testing, and the resulting test scores prevail as indicators of achievement. Although changes in procedures in testing to match instruction have been attempted, assessment tools have generally remained the same.

In order for substantial changes to occur, precise definitions and use of terms for describing changes in educational practice must also be considered. The precise, consistent use of words defines and clarifies actions.

Each classroom, and each individual therein, has personal "real-life" experiences. Respect for individuality means electing characteristically appropriate assessment and instruction strategies to fit the originality each student brings to a classroom. Managing personalized integrated language arts instruction while observing differences is a challenge. Guiding others to understand that instruction IS assessment and assessment IS instruction is my goal. If "politically" correct words, phrases, and labels facilitate the process, use them, but ONLY if you provide students with healthy, productive classrooms for learning.

CHAPTER 3

The Children:
Our Populations, Our Future

"In one of my classrooms," shared Shelley Harwayne (1992), principal of the Manhattan New School in New York City, "there are twenty-seven children. Twenty-one of those children have a first language different than English."

"I have a child with cerebral palsy, one who is legally blind, and another who is ADHD, that's attention deficit hyperactive disorder," reported one teacher at a recent social gathering. "I've tried to teach them, but I need help," she continued.

"My weekends are spent going from one garage sale to the next. I need to get lots of cassette tape recorders. Lots of the kids in my room can't write stories, or even write about what they read. So if I have tape recorders, they can talk into them as an alternative," shared another teacher at the same social event.

Today's Classrooms Demand Alternative Procedures

Populations of today's classrooms are culturally, academically, physically, and socially diverse. The growth of diverse populations in classrooms can be attributed to society's mobility. A major reason for today's diversities, however, is attributed to the Individuals with Disabilities Education Act (IDEA). This congressional action provides that each state establish

> procedures to assure that, to the maximum extent appropriate, children with disabilities . . . are educated with children who are not disabled, and that . . . removal of children with disabilities from the regular education environment occurs only when . . . education in regular classes with the use of supplementary aids and services cannot be achieved satisfactorily.

This mandate, which is often referred to as the "least restrictive environment" (LRE), has been satisfied in the past by providing mainstreaming opportunities for many classified pupils who received academics in a self-contained special education classroom and were integrated with children who were not disabled in non-academic activities. These activities included such things as art, music, lunch, gym, and recess. Today, because of court proceedings (Daniel, 1989; Greer, 1991; Oberti, 1993; Roncker, 1983), mainstreaming means including those children in regular classrooms whose

- education cannot be met more effectively in a special education classroom;
- social, communications, and self-confidence skills are better met by interacting with ALL children;
- presence does not disrupt or distract from usual occurrences;
- needs do not demand more teacher time than other children;
- cost for placement in a regular classroom does not so burden a district's funds that services available to other children are adversely affected. (Holland, 1994)

The influences of the civil rights movement, particularly concerning social developments and court decisions, changed the face of American education. It was the 1954 case of *Brown versus the Board of Education* that challenged the practice of segregating students; in this case, segregating them according to race. In its ruling, the U.S. Supreme Court declared that education must be made available to ALL children on equal terms. The Brown decision, and the extension of public school education to black and white children on equal terms, began a period of intense concern and questioning among parents of handicapped children. These parents asked why the same principles of equal access to education did not apply to their children, and so Public Law 92-142 came into being. The law has resulted in much media attention to special needs learners. The attention has forced parents and educators to be sure that equal opportunities and the least restricted environments are carefully planned for special needs learners.

Equal opportunity for all students has resulted in inclusion. This means that all children, those gifted, those average, and those with special needs are placed together in classrooms. Issues surrounding inclusion have appeared to polarize the positions of advocates for different special populations. Whether to include or not to include all children in the same classroom spurs ongoing debates. While debates continue, teachers in classrooms are expected to work with all children, those who are ADD, ADHD, the bilingual/bicultural child, the communication handicapped, those dysgraphic, dyslexic, gifted and talented, those with neurological and perceptual impairments, those who are physically challenged, and some who are socially and emotionally maladjusted.

The Children "Included"

"It'll be done when you come home from work," assured Jason, when his wife requested that the bills be put in order. "Yeah, sure," she sputtered sarcastically, as she slammed the door shut. "You always say you'll get it done, but only the good Lord knows what that means." Jason knew the pattern. He didn't seem to be able to do anything in depth. When he was 13, he was supposed to write about the stories he read. "I just couldn't seem to write. By the time I got out my notebook, I forgot what I was supposed to do. Then when I started, I could only write a sentence or two." (See Figure 3-1.) Jason's intentions for completing projects were always there, but he could never seem to get things accomplished.

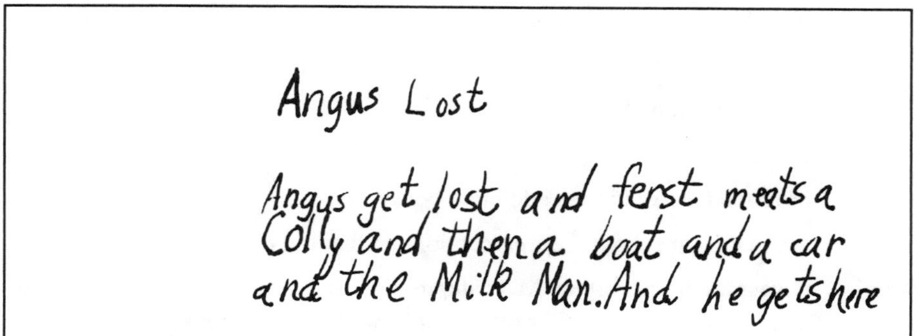

Angus Lost

Angus get lost and ferst meats a Colly and then a boat and a car and the Milk Man. And he gets here

OLIVER
I was O.R

The Runaway Bunny
I liked the picers
AMAZING BEARS
I liked the photes.

Figure 3-1. Jason's Literature Response Journal Entry

Jason has an **attention deficit disorder (ADD),** a neurological syndrome whose characteristics include impulsivity, distractibility, and possibly hyperactivity or excess energy. Jason, and others with ADD usually

- have difficulty getting organized;
- procrastinate and have chronic difficulties getting started;
- begin many projects, but have trouble following through;
- search for high stimulation;
- are often creative, intuitive, and highly intelligent;
- have difficulty following established procedures;
- have low tolerance for frustration;
- have a sense of insecurity;
- experience mood swings;
- are restless;
- have tendencies toward addictive behaviors;
- are inaccurate about their perceptions of themselves;
- have a family history of ADD, depression, substance abuse, or other disorders of impulse control or mood (Hallowell & Ratey, 1994).

Rachael couldn't sit still. She was always fidgeting. She never looked at you when you spoke with her. She seemed to always be somewhere else, and running there. Rachael was impulsive, easily aroused, and always needed immediate reinforcement for things she completed (Barkley, 1981). When stories were read, she never seemed to pay attention. She often shouted out of turn, offering responses to questions that were inappropriate. Rachael has an **attention deficit hyperactive disorder (ADHD).**

Damaris's parents were concerned with her ability to communicate in English in school. "Her mother and I talk to each other in Portuguese all the time. I don't know how she will talk in school." The child's father told me that he wanted both of his children to speak Portuguese, that is why Portuguese was the language spoken in the home.

Damaris was **bilingual.** She spoke Portuguese, but also English, the language never spoken by her parents, in the home. Portuguese, however, was her first language, the one she'd heard from infancy. Because customs at home were different than those practiced by most people in school, she was also bicultural. Damaris's teacher picked up on this after several days. Whenever she spoke to the child, Damaris's eyes turned down, and so did her head. "Look at me when I talk to you," said the teacher, but the child seemed to disobey. You see, the culturally correct way to respond to adults in Damaris's home was *not* to look at the adult. To look at the adult was considered impolite. In the American culture it is polite to look the adult right in the eye. How confused this **bicultural** child must have been! Damaris learned the appropriate school behavior by observing the teacher's responses to her peers, noticed their behaviors, and caught their habits. How nice it would have been if the cultural customs of her home were familiar to her teacher!

Jennifer's responses in conversations often led one to believe that she was talking to someone else. There was the time that the children were talking about oranges and their characteristics. Jennifer raised her hand during the discussion and said, "I saw a lemon once, and it was yellow." Her teacher noticed this type of response often. Jennifer would respond by staying within the category discussed, in this case fruit, but not with the object. This was puzzling and confusing. "Why," the teacher asked, "why does Jen talk about something other than the object?"

Jennifer has a **communication handicap.** Her ability to connect ideas appropriately seems to be impaired. Jennifer's handicap is only one of the many communication disorders that students exhibit. The disorders have many facets. Communication is the process that involves the transmission of thoughts and ideas between two or more individuals. People talk, express ideas, and someone listens. The listener receives the information. When one has difficuty making oneself understood, an expressive disorder may be the cause. Expressive disorders are often characterized by disorganized thoughts in both speaking and writing. Conversely, when one understands (or doesn't) an idea differently than expected, a receptive disorder may exist (See Appendix C). Communication handicaps are difficult to understand, and often difficult to notice. The difficulty is due, in part, to the fact that language involves several complex abilities. These include (1) making meaning of language, (2) understanding the rule systems governing language, and (3) comprehending and then using the sound sequences of language. Effective communicators have a command of these components and use them interactively.

Children with communication problems have difficulty sharing their thoughts and ideas effectively. The difficulty in identifying these children has caused much strife for teachers and learners. Children with severe communication disorders produce products that are significantly different from those of others in the classroom. Their excessive inability to remember stands out from others.

No one could understand Taisha's illegible handwriting. (See Figure 3-2.) She seemed to have a system, even though her writing looked like scribbles. There were spaces between the "squiggles." Some of her marks were repeated, and she used combinations of her squiggles systematically, indicating that her writing represented ideas. She also pointed to her words while reading her written text. Taisha suffers from **dysgraphia.** She has difficulty producing handwriting. No one knows exactly why this happens, but it is believed that either illness or injury to her brain causes the problem.

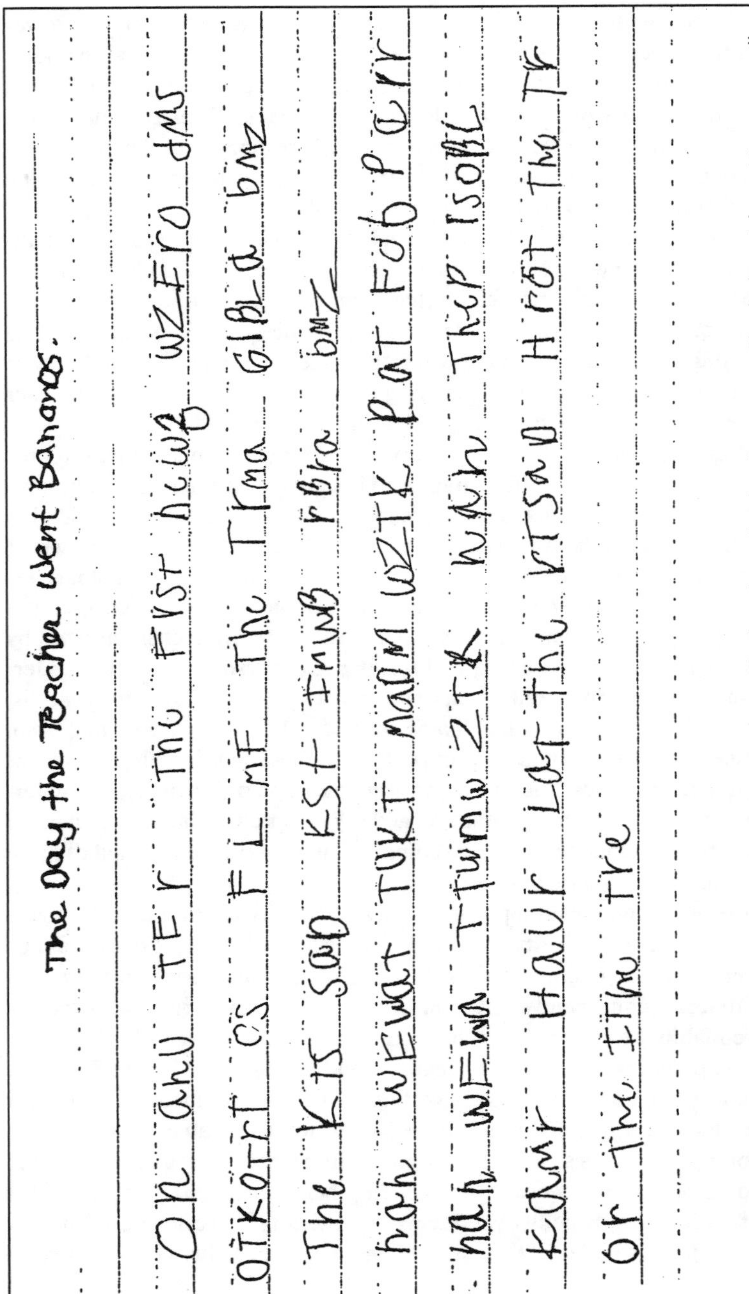

The Day the Teacher Went Bananas.

Oh ahù TEʳr Thu FYST hcwB wZEʳo dms
oTKoʳrl cʒ FLmE Thu Tʳma GlBLd bmz
Thu KIS soD KSt ɛruwB ʳBʳa bmz
hah WEwcT TUKT maDM wZIK RaT FdB PaYr
hah WEwh TTumw ZIK Wah ThuP TSoBL
KamʳHaUʳ LaT thu ʳTSaD HʳoT ThuTʸE
oʳ Tʳu ITʳhu TʸE

One day we had the teacher who taught us how to count for lunch we had 16 bananas. The kids said next time we will get bananas. Then we went to art and music. Then the principal came in and said you're not the teacher the next day that's where we went. The End.

Figure 3-2.   Taisha's Retelling

No matter how hard he tried, Jeremy couldn't read. "The words jump all over the page," he told me one day. "I look at them, but they just look jumbled up." Jeremy suffers from what is probably the most publicized learning disability, **dyslexia.** The term has had many definitions, both broad and narrow. It is defined in *The Literacy Dictionary* (Harris & Hodges, 1995) as "a developmental reading disability, presumably congenital and perhaps hereditary, that may vary in degree from mild to severe" (p. 63). Dyslexia, originally referred to as "word blindness," occurs in people whose vision, hearing, intelligence, and general language functions are adequate for normal functioning. Children and adults who are dyslexic often have difficulty spelling words and learning a second language. My experience with thousands of children and parents has led me to believe that dyslexia is how laypersons refer to most reading problems. "My son is dyslexic," one mother told me. "How do you know that?" I asked. "Well, he wrote an 's' backwards like this. And he says 'was' for 'saw'." The child was just six years old. The characteristics she mentioned can be symptoms of a learning disability, but they are developmentally appropriate behaviors quite common for children of this age. Lack of knowledge about early development, and a concern for her child, guided her to the conclusion. Dyslexia is a difficult disability to understand. Experts must be sought to guide those who work with dyslexic individuals to understand and deal with the disability.

My dear friends' son, much like a nephew to me, phoned me at the age of nine with a serious problem. "Aunt Susan," he said, "I took this test and got a high grade so my parents and the teacher decided I belonged in this special class. It is for kids who are smart." "So, Alan," I responded, "what's the problem?" "Well," he continued, "I want to be with my friends. They are all in the regular room, and I'm with these other kids. My friends call them the nerds." "Why?" I asked. "They're brainy and they act weird." "So how can I help, Alan?" "Well, how can I get them to send me back to my class?" My better judgment was overridden by a distressed young man whom I loved dearly. "Alan," I continued, "here's a plan." I suggested to this nine-year-old that he miss one word on his Friday spelling test. After the test, I asked if there were any residual effects from the error. "Oh, all my teacher said was, 'Alan, you must have been tired. You got one wrong'." My suggestion to miss three words on the test the next week, and three the following week as well, proved successful. "My Mom got a note from the teacher that said that I needed to go back to my old classroom. There must have been a mistake in putting me in the gifted class to begin with."

That amusing story tells the tale of many who are **gifted and talented.** They are kids like any others who happen to have "special talents or skills, . . . superior intellectual functioning or potential, . . . so much demonstrated or potential talent as to need distinctive educational programs or services" (Harris & Hodges, 1995, p. 97) that attendance in regular classrooms has not met their needs. Unfortunately, options usually vary about how superior a child needs to be in order to be "gifted." It is usually determined, however, by a standardized test score. The lower limit for the gifted may be considered the top 10 percent, the top 2 percent, more than 2 standard deviations above the mean, or at the same specific IQ score (sometimes as low as 130). When test scores determine giftedness, there is little chance for some who do not test well to be thought of as such. All students have gifts. Identifying and guiding them to use those gifts in socially appropriate ways is essential. Alan's isolation from his peers, because of his gifts, became detrimental to his social development, and he let me know that.

Simon had difficulty holding a pencil. Often he'd sort of slump in his seat. At the beginning of the school year, the teacher thought he was "goofing off." You see, Simon was born with cerebral palsy. Although a mild case, his **neurological impairment** resulted from damage to his nervous system. Often, Simon was not able to control his fingers or that part of his spine that helped him to sit up straight. They moved involuntarily because of injury to his brain. Other impairments that occur in children include amputations, arthritis, spina bifida, muscular dystrophy, scoliosis, and hip disorders.

Perceptual impairment has served as a "catchall" phrase for students whose characteristic behaviors don't seem to fit easily into other categories. Understanding what makes it difficult for children with this syndrome to learn is the key. A look at the word "perception" provides insight.

Perception, according to *The Literacy Dictionary* (Harris & Hodges, 1995), is the "extraction of information from sensory stimulation" (p. 181). One understands the reality of situations by perceiving it. If you are attending a lecture given by a well-known person whom you know *only* by reputation, but have never seen, you most likely will be able to recognize that person. You are able to do this because you know, from past experience, that lecturers usually wear suits, act assertive, position themselves in the front of the lecture hall, prepare the podium in advance, and more. You notice a person, whom you've never seen before, and she possesses the characteristics mentioned above. Your *perception* is that she must be the person who will give the lecture.

Think what you might *perceive* if the person in front of the lecture hall arrived in a bikini bathing suit. What, based on your knowledge and past experiences with lectures, would you do and think? You'd probably laugh, think you were in the wrong place, or assume that the lecturer just took a swim and stopped in to check things out before changing. Your *perception* of this situation is that things just don't fit.

Perceptions are one's reality. What is realistic to one is not necessarily realistic to another. There is, however, general agreement concerning appropriate and expected realities in the world. There is a moon in the sky. The fact that it is small and gold-like to one, and large and granite-like to another is a matter of experience and *perception*. Wearing a bikini bathing suit to present an academic seminar is *perceptually* inappropriate. But it might be appropriate if the seminar dealt with lifesaving, swimming, scuba diving, or other water-related activities. If you are a person who loves water sports, you just might think of that.

Children's *perceptions* about things they read are based on past experiences, as well as their sense of reality. Children who *perceive* ideas like most others do well in school. Children, however, whose ideas and responses to the things they read about and learn in school are different than expected, are often said to have a **perceptual impairment.** When a visual perceptual impairment exists, the child views and sees things on a page in a distorted manner. If the impairment is auditory, she hears sounds in unexpected and unusual ways. The sound that is created, and the way the child hears that sound may be quite different. The perceptually impaired child usually misses the crucial link that permits him/her to respond meaningfully. Jeremy has a visual perceptual disorder classified as a communications handicap. Figure 3-3 and 3-4 shows that he was able to copy words and figures.

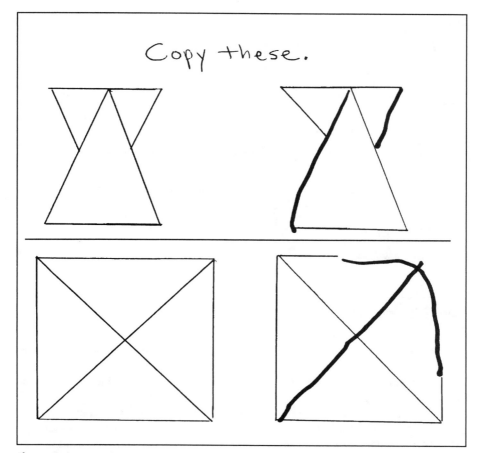

Figure 3-3.   Copying

Figure 3-4. Jeremy's Copying

Jeremy's problem occurs when he's asked to write something on his own. "Something happens in my brain," he said. "I can't remember what the letters look like. That's why I have to copy." Jeremy was able to write "is a dog" in Figure 3-5 because he asked his teacher to write the words so he'd have them to copy.

Although Jeremy's problem was severe, many children suffer from milder yet similar perceptual handicaps. Jeremy's disability resulted in the inability to remember how letters look. His visual short-term memory couldn't help him recall the images necessary to write them.

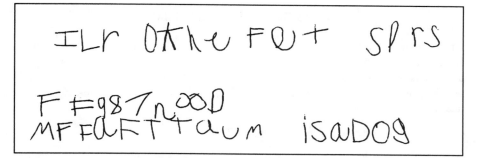

Figure 3-5. Jeremy's Handwritten Story

A woman, passing a wheelchair-bound woman, asked in a loud voice, "Do you need help opening the door?" "Thank you, no," she said. "I can hear you," she continued. "It's my legs that don't work, not my ears!" It's interesting how many people respond to the **physically challenged.** For some unexplainable reasons, many who interact with people with these anomalies raise their voices when talking to them.

There is general agreement that a condition relating to **emotional** and **social disorders** exists. There is, however, no definition satisfactory to all (Gearheart, Weishahn, & Gearheart, 1992). According to P.L. 94-142, the phrase *serious emotional disturbance* means

- an inability to learn which cannot be explained by intellectual, sensory, or health factors;

- an inability to build or maintain satisfactory relationships with peers and teachers;

- inappropriate types of behavior or feelings under normal circumstances;

- a general pervasive mood of unhappiness or depression;

- a tendency to develop physical symptoms or fears associated with personal or school problems.

According to Public Law 101-476, the terms include children who are schizophrenic or autistic (Federal Register, August 23, 1977, p. 42478).

While many debate definitions, teachers find it easy to identify children with emotional and social problems (McDowell, Adamson, & Wood, 1982). All students experience emotional and social problems at times, but they are transitory. Severe problems, however, are indicated by the frequency of occurrence of atypical behaviors, the duration of a particular behavior, and the degree of severity from the experienced teacher's point of view. When behaviors are so severe that they are disruptive, the student should probably be placed in a special class.

How Do Many Refer to These Children?

Unfortunately, few teachers have had the education necessary to teach ALL children. Behaviors, therefore, are often misunderstood. Unknowledgeable teachers, as well as parents, often make comments about diverse learners' behaviors. Comments are usually unscientific and demonstrate little knowledge about differences. Some I've heard are:

- If he'd only listen, he'd be able to follow the directions.
- His problem is that he's lazy.
- He only wants to talk about what he is interested in.
- She always pays attention to something other than the topic. That's why the work isn't done.
- She talks a lot on purpose at quiet times just to get my attention.
- He could write neatly if he took his time.
- She can't possibly understand what she's reading. Just listen to how choppy she sounds.
- He's so inconsistent. He's very verbal, but his writing is minimal. He's not creative when it comes to writing.
- He's in another world; that's why he doesn't pay attention.
- She learned inappropriate responses. That's why she acts funny at times.
- He manipulates in order to get what he wants.
- If he can be so precise when he plays football, then he certainly can hand in a presentable paper.
- If he can play championship chess, then he can stop himself from bumping into desks all the time.
- He knows how to spell, but he's so slow. If he'd stop being so meticulous, he'd be able to get his work done.
- If he doesn't learn to spell, he will fail the writing class.
- She doesn't know grammar. She uses words incorrectly in sentences.

Sound familiar? These statements, although commonly heard, are unjust, unfounded, and discriminatory. There is no such thing as a lazy, uncreative, or dumb child. There isn't a child who doesn't want to learn. What there are, are adults who call children "lazy," "uncreative," and "dumb." These damaging labels, coupled with a lack of knowledge, hurt the children and our professional reputations. I've never heard a lawyer or physician speak negatively about their clients. If WE speak negatively about ours, we are acting in an unprofessional manner and admitting failure. We are also influencing these students' perceptions of themselves as readers and writers, as learners, in general.

Self-Perception and Success in Reading and Writing

There are some who believe that reading problems are based on emotional disorders (Eisenberg, 1962). It is obvious that students who have problems reading and writing are bound to become emotionally distraught about their progress. Emotional problems are probable when continuous and repeated frustrations result from learning to read and write. The frustrations also cause negative attitudes about school and learning. Student's perceptions of the reading and writing process, and themselves as learners–particularly as readers and writers—suffers in these incidents, and growth is deterred.

In 1989 we began to survey children in the Center for Reading and Writing to determine their perceptions of themselves as readers. We used our "Good Reader Sheet" to collect data concerning children's perceptions of the reading/writing process as well as their ideas about themselves. We found that children new to the Center hesitated to commit themselves to being either a poor or good reader. The students, probably concerned with teacher expectations, avoided self-assessment. Ninety-three percent of 1500 youngsters ages 6 to 17 "sat on the fence," offering comments such as:

- I'm a good reader, but I mess up sometimes;

- Sometimes I'm good, but I can be better;

- I'm not good, just a little good;

- I get tired when I read and then the words get jumbled. Then I almost fall asleep so I don't know what its about. So I guess I can be a good reader, but I'm not.

Fear of contradicting or disagreeing with teachers' viewpoints infringed on students' freedom to share their ideas about themselves.

Students' perceptions about the reading process varied. Response seemed to reflect the students' instructional activities in reading in school.

Eight-year-old Sebastian (Figure 3-6) sees reading as a spelling process. In a discussion with him I discovered that his teacher told him to spell words that he did not know when he read stories. "This," she said, "will help you read the words." Sebastian informed me that he was "a nice reader" because he always spelled words he couldn't read.

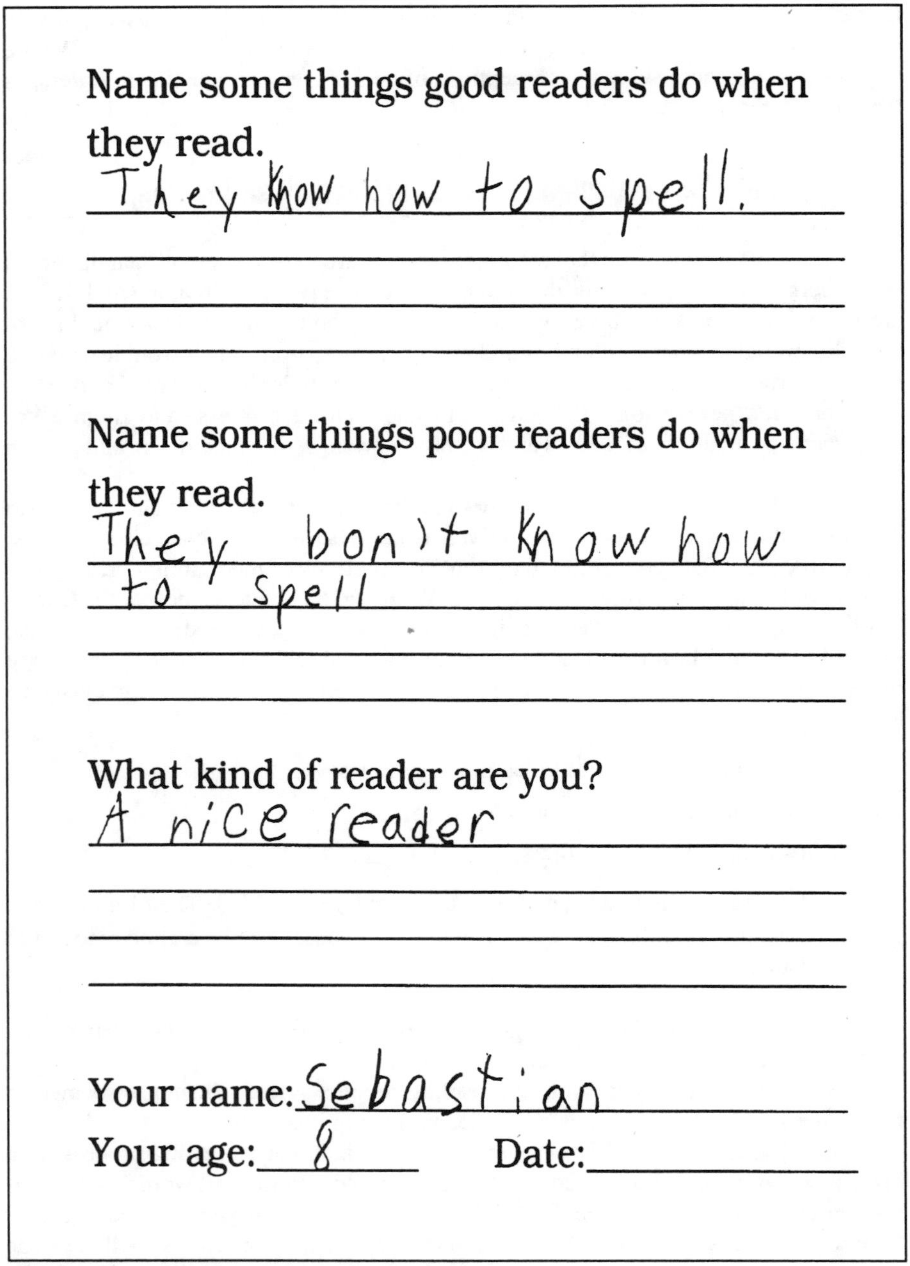

Name some things good readers do when they read.

They know how to spell.

Name some things poor readers do when they read.

They don't know how to spell

What kind of reader are you?

A nice reader

Your name: Sebastian

Your age: 8   Date:

Figure 3-6.   Sebastian's Good Reader Sheet

Twelve-year-old Jared (Figure 3-7) seems to perceive reading as an attention-to-task process. Attention seems to include working alone and not interfering with the others when they read. Attention, therefore, could be perceived by this student as lack of peer interaction.

Name some things good readers do when they read.

They keep their eyes on the book
a good reader does not distract others
pays attention to only the book.
reads alone

Name some things poor readers do when they read.

Poor readers do not keep their eyes on the book.
Read a little bit and stop
Never keep their eyes on the book

What kind of reader are you?

I am a reader who likes to read alot of scary stories and I always read alone and do not bother other people.

Your name: Jared Huttner

Your age: 12   Date: 5-26-96

Figure 3-7.   Jared's Good Reader Sheet

Eleven-year-old Heather (Figure 3-8) believes that phonics play a major role in the reading process. She understands the embarrassment that poor readers must feel as indicated by her response, "poor readers don't like to raise their hands to read things." The response indicates, too, that reading, for Heather, is an oratorical process. She confirms her notions about fluency with word recognition in her definition of her reading ability.

Heather

Name some things good readers do when they read.

Sometimes if they don't know a word they sound it out the read fluwently

Name some things poor readers do when they read.

Poor readers don't like to raise thire hands to read things and and if they don't know. a word they'll skip it

What kind of reader are you?

I'm a reader that is not fluwent that I sometimes get stuch on words but when I get the words I'm a very good reader

Your name: Heather Helble

Your age: 11   Date: June 0d

Figure 3-8.   Heather's Good Reader Sheet

Research (Michael, 1990; Swanson, 1985; Templeton, 1986; Weiss & Hagen, 1988) suggests that children's perceptions of reading are important for better understanding of the reading process. By listening carefully to what children say about reading and writing, and by observing what they do when they read, professionals can understand things about students that can be learned no other way. When we observe, we see the "interplay between how [students] come to define reading in the specific situations in which they find themselves" (Bogdan, 1982, pp. 7–8).

Herbert Blumer (1969) says,

> . . . human beings act toward things on the basis of the meanings that things have for them . . . the meaning of such things is derived from, or arises out of, the social interaction that one has with one's fellows, . . . these meanings are handled in, and modified through, an interpretive process used by the person in dealing with the things he encounters. (p. 2)

Students learn about themselves from the interactions they encounter in all situations. They learn about how others think of them and their products. They develop images of themselves, and theories about living based on responses from people in each situation in their lives. Children who have been unsuccessful with literacy activities will probably develop poor feelings about themselves and their interactions with written text. It is our obligation as professionals to find a way for each of our children to learn. It is our obligation, too, to make every child feel successful so that self-esteem soars. It is important for us to realize that standardized tests do NOT provide much information about why students achieve or don't. They provide even less information about students' self-esteem. All people are different. It is important to respect the differences, see them as treasures, and nurture the very best in each person.

Summary

The transitory nature of our populations and the existence of public laws mandating that all children be treated equally in schools have increased the diversity of learners in classrooms. Children gifted, average, and those with special needs are learning together in the same classroom. Understanding and recognizing who these children are is a prerequisite for guiding their ability to learn. Understanding the importance of students' perceptions of themselves as learners, and the effect of these perceptions on self-esteem is paramount. Since it is the obligation of all teachers to find a way for all children to learn, knowing how each child processes information is essential.

CHAPTER 4

Effective Classrooms for All Children: What Are They?

"There must be substantial shifts in what [and how our children are] commonly taught," says Richard Allington (1994, p. 14). We must stop confusing children's lack of experience with lack of ability. When this occurs, it is assumed that deficiencies are due to low intelligence rather than lack of opportunities to interact with stories, and other literacy activities. We need to cease slowing down instruction for diverse learners, rather than accelerating it. Slowing down suggests that a delaying rather than a different approach to learning is necessary to meet special needs. Educators must stop testing for the purpose of categorizing children and then labeling them. It is more productive to use funds to support professionals to find ways to instruct these students. Teachers must find effective teaching strategies for each child and spend less time on creating and using test-like, fill-in-the-blank seat work. Assignments can no longer replace teaching. Emphasis must focus on shifting from "getting the right answer" to discovering what students understand as they engage in activities (Allington, 1994).

What Do Schools Need to do to Integrate Assessment and Instruction?

I agree with Dick Allington (1994) who says that we need to stop the segmentation of teaching, sending children to one teacher or specialist for one thing, and to someone else for another thing. Rather than spending excess funds securing specialists, monies should be invested in enhancing classroom instruction. The school day needs to be reorganized, so that teachers have uninterrupted blocks of time to teach, and children have uninterrupted blocks of time to learn. One-hour periods just don't make sense in order for students to discuss, interpret, and find ways to connect their knowledge to mandated curriculum. Of utmost importance are provisions for ongoing professional development to guide teachers to weather the difficult task of meeting the needs of ALL learners.

When these changes occur, we can focus on (1) developing self-confidence, (2) coaching students to take responsibility, and (3) establishing courage to take risks in learning situations in order to take control of their lives. I have found in my experiences that these goals facilitate collegiality and develop the rapport necessary to create independent learners. Nineteen years in the Center for Reading and Writing at Rider University have also taught me that self-monitoring strategies provide students with devices that call for students and teachers to take responsibility for, risks with, and ultimately control of activities.

Creating Collegially Collaborative Learning Communities

Consistency is the key to collegially healthy environments. Consistency provides the stability necessary for students to develop realistic expectations and understand constraints in their daily work. Consistency brings an element of safety to those involved. Everyone knows what to do, when to do it, and what must be accomplished in order to succeed.

Consistent times to learn, consistent forms of praise, consistent use of language, consistent daily routines, and consistent frameworks and strategies for assessing and learning about ideas and concepts are the components that build collaborative classrooms.

Consistent Time Frames

Setting time limits establishes classroom management practices. Two-and-one-half hours of uninterrupted time provides teachers with the time to teach and children with time to learn. It is ideal to schedule a time daily, but if that is unrealistic, a morning or afternoon once or twice weekly is a way to begin. The 2½ hour block provides time for:

- reading and retelling in individual or small groups about what is read;

- engaging in guided and unguided reading and writing activities;

- interacting with literature and content materials, fiction and nonfiction;

- working with peers, exchanging and sharing ideas and products;

- carrying out long-term research projects in content area studies;

- editing, revising, and publishing stories, research reports, poems, etc.;

- engaging in creative play;

- completing daily routine writing activities (see page 45), and lots more.

The time block encourages spontaneous, realistic literacy experiences between children and their teacher. It permits teachers to teach concepts by "seizing appropriate moments" as they arise. Scheduled conferences based on individual and small group instructional needs also take place during this time. The block of time MUST be scheduled and kept regularly in order for assessment and instruction to come together in classrooms.

Consistent Praise

Numerical and letter grades have been and continue to be used to inform children about their performance. Letters, including A, B, C, D, or F, and "pass" or "fail" are popular designations. As alternative assessment procedures emerge, other techniques are slowly gaining in popularity. The letter grades, A, B, C, or D have been discarded in some instances and replaced with S (superior), VG (very good), G (good), and F (fair). A line drawing of a happy face has been used instead of "pass," and a sad-faced line drawing substitutes for "fail." (See Figure 4-1.)

Figure 4-1. Camouflage Grading System

Vague, unspecific oral praise is also frequently used to assess. Words and phrases such as "very good, terrific, I love it, great job, wonderful," are supposed to tell learners about their achievements. These designations lack consistency and reference points for students to gauge their progress. The words are personal, and therefore, biased. Children who have several teachers learn quickly the assessment value each assigns to the language. "Very good" for the math teacher might mean an "A." But it could designate "B" for the science teacher, because she says "really good" for the "A." Children learn that happy faces mean "pass," and that sad ones mean "fail." They also know that superior is an "A," very good a "B," and so on. When designations like these are used to replace grades, educators are merely substituting new symbols for older ones. This antiquated, unproductive, socially-biased grading system that categorizes and labels learners is still intact in many schools.

The best way for teachers to provide assessment guides is to inform students about their abilities. Wallace and Kaufman (1986) support this notion and suggest that teachers tell students about their performance. Direct praise tells students what they can do, and also provides them with a "yardstick" for repeating the mentioned task. Using phrases such as "I like . . . ", or "You did it right for me," suggest to students that they are performing for you, their teacher, rather than for themselves. Using direct praise diminishes the use of subjective grades and praise. This type of praise provides language that defines children's successes. The following statements illustrate direct praise:

- It's really important that you organized your work into categories like you did. That helps you know what to do next.

- It's good to see you reading out loud to yourself. You remember the information when you hear yourself read.

- It's important that you point like you did when you use the dictionary. Pointing helps you keep your place.

- It's wonderful that you reread your first draft. That will help you decide what you need to add or take out of your story.

Direct praise calls attention to the specific action, strategy, or product in focus. Knowing specifically what and why the activities are productive supports the student's actions, and provides motivation to repeat the activity again.

Consistent Language

"Language is . . . powerful," writes Frank Smith (1995). "Language permits one to make pronouncements of needs and feelings and to acquire and exchange information" (p. 15). Oral language is a major vehicle for sharing ideas and feelings in most classrooms. Nonverbal signals, facial expressions, eye contact, use of hands, and other body parts, also impart information. Adults' use of oral and nonverbal (kinesic) language defines for children meanings of situations and ideas (Halliday, 1975).

Often oral and kinesic language are used spontaneously and frivolously. The carefree language is wonderful when casual communications are in order. But, when language is used to instruct, regulate, and inform, the impulsive nature of spontaneous language can be destructive. An incident with a first-grade student illustrates how oral language without thought can affect children's behavior.

Seven-year-old Josh had been misbehaving during lunch. His teacher told him to "calm down, and sit in the lunchroom for the present." Josh sat, and sat, and sat, even after the rest of his classmates had been back in their classrooms for over an hour. A teacher's aide, while walking in the hall, spotted Josh sitting in the very spot where he'd been eating his lunch. She noticed Josh sobbing. She put her arms around him and asked, "Josh, why are you crying?" "I, I," he sputtered between sobs, "My teacher told me if I was good I'd get a present but, she musta forgot, cause I'm still here."

Poor Josh! His teacher used the word "present," which has a double meaning. She used it during a stressful, busy time, never thinking about how the child would interpret its meaning. The child explained, "When I'm good, my grandma gives me a present! I'm being good, and my teacher forgot." Sitting still is being good, and Josh's past experiences in similar situations meant a reward.

This teacher used "oral codes" for explaining, rather than demonstrating expectations. Have your own folders and projects so that you become part of the community of learners. Model for students by doing it WITH, not for children. **The modeling is TEACHING, not the explaining.**

Using language thoughtfully and systematically is important. Using the language consistently when it fills a need (for example: using language to control, as with Josh), or to communicate information (to inform) is essential. Being aware of your oral and kinesic language, and how it affects your students, is the first step to becoming consistent.

Guidelines for Becoming Aware of Your Language

1. Use the same arrangements of words, especially when you use language to regulate activities. When giving directions, you might say to the student, **"Write your name on your paper and begin working."** Many students may begin, while others need several reminders. Often teachers remind students of directions, and use similar, but not the same words and syntactic sentence arrangements. The rearranged sentence, **"Be sure you do your work after you write your name on the paper,"** was said by one teacher with the intention that it mean the same as the **bolded directions** above. The sentence arrangement and added words make the ideas new and different to many children, especially those who may have receptive communication problems.

   Guideline: Carefully plan your instructions and directions for children. Repeat the instructions, when necessary, using the SAME words. If you find that they don't work, change the syntax and words, after carefully planning again. It is important to say to children, "I will try another way to say that." This informs them that language can be used in many ways, and each of us understands differently. *Have the child to whom you give the directions repeat them immediately after you provide them.* If they need help, coach them, providing the words they do not repeat, one at a time. Asking children to repeat the language helps them to remember the instructions.

Providing the language again, if necessary, gives the student the individual support he/she might need to succeed.

2. Be careful when using words with double meanings. They are confusing to many, especially students with receptive communication disorders and limited vocabularies.

   Guideline: When you use words with double meanings, use a synonym for that word in the same sentence to clarify the language. The following examples can serve as a guide for using words with double meanings:

   - "Put the dishes on the **buffet.** It is the **cabinet** that I use to keep them in."

   - "I am going to **fast** for Lent. I **will not eat** any chocolate candy until Lent is over."

   - "She is waiting for the **present.** The **present is a** wonderful **gift.** It is a new bicycle."

3. Some words sound alike but are spelled differently. Students who have difficulty spelling will find these words extremely difficult to process.

   Guideline: Use the word and supply a synonym to explain the concept. Use its homophone (the word that is spelled differently but sounds the same) and supply a synonym for that as well.

   - "He's really **fair** all of the time. This **honest** trait makes him a special person."

   - "The bus **fare** is $1.50. The **cost of traveling** on a bus used to be only $.75."

4. Children with receptive language differences may have trouble with similes, figures of speech that use the word "as" or "like" to describe something.

   Guideline: Use similes with discretion. When they are used, explain the meaning of each immediately.

   - "He cries **like a baby.** Grown-ups don't usually cry a lot. Babies do."

   - "Her hands are **as rough as sandpaper.** They feel scratchy when you touch them."

   - "Jim **runs like a deer.** Deer really run fast, and so does Jim."

Precise, consistent use of language is important. Consistency helps children learn the concepts of language, and also provides the stability they need to build self-confidence.

Consistent Routines

Knowing what's going to happen first, next, and last in classrooms supports independence. The ability to know (predict by taking an educated guess) is possible only when routines exist. Routine activities during designated time blocks must be specific for all students in order for them to engage in tasks on their own. The activities must have realistic purposes for students, and they must facilitate interactions between those who live and work together in classrooms. I suggest six routine activities for all students of all abilities and all ages: (1) contracts, (2) dialogue journals, (3) literature journals, (4) content journals, (5) mail, and (6) a reading log.

Contracts

Self-monitoring and management begin by "contracting" activities with children. Agreements about work and workloads are made and recorded on a "contract" for each student in the classroom. (See Figure 4-2.) Included on the contracts are the daily routines as well as personalized activities for students to carry out independently. Small group work, collaborative peer activities, and activities with the teacher are listed for each student. These contracts become a self-monitoring tool for assessing progress.

Some children need to discuss contract agreements with teachers daily. Others may need to contract for two or more days. Some children will complete their assignments "instantly." Others will never finish. The "instanters" need to show what they've done. The "never finishers" need time modifications in order to complete tasks. One of our teachers wears a timer on a string around her neck for several students. They each try to time themselves to see if they can beat their own previous time. She also uses egg timers (those that use sand) for individuals to monitor their time. Respect each student's ability to manage time and activities and alter the contractual agreements based on each one's need.

Dialogue Journals

Dialogue journals offer students daily opportunities to communicate with their teachers informally, as if in conversation. Dialogues between the student and the teacher build rapport, provide experiences with written language, and increase the student's vocabulary for writing. The bonding built between students and teachers through written dialogues supports positive self-esteem. The format permits students to share ideas, events, and feelings (Stanton, 1980).

Danny and his teacher, Judy, were perfectly matched. They both liked the water, and they both scuba dived, especially on old wrecks. Judy knew this, and her first communication with Danny was focused on their common interest. (See Figure 4-3.) She wrote to Danny in an attempt to "catch" his interest and spur a real reason to

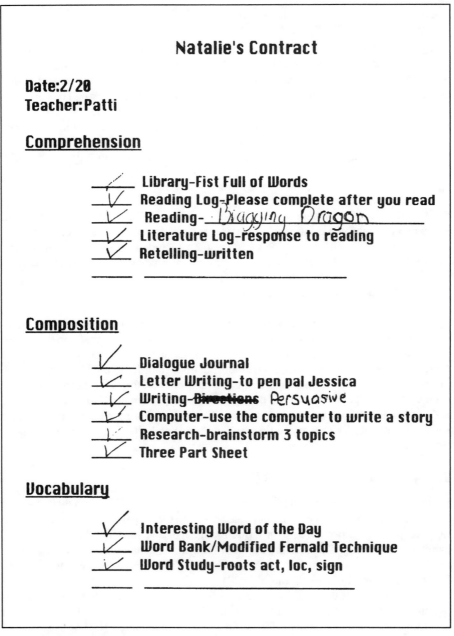

Figure 4-2.   Natalie's Contract

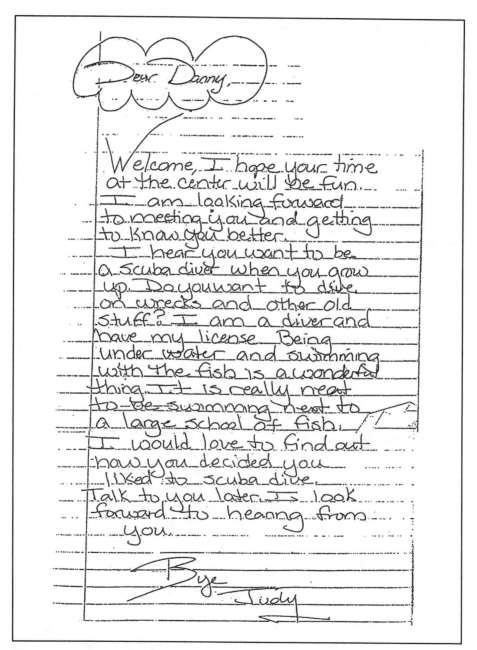

Figure 4-3. Judy's First Dialogue Journal Entry to Danny

write, and she did. Danny focused on Judy's questions, and responded to these in his dialogue responses. (See Figures 4-4 and 4-5.) Asking Danny questions seemed to be the strategy that got him going. He continued conversations emulating his teacher's format. Although asking questions doesn't work for all children, the exchange illus-

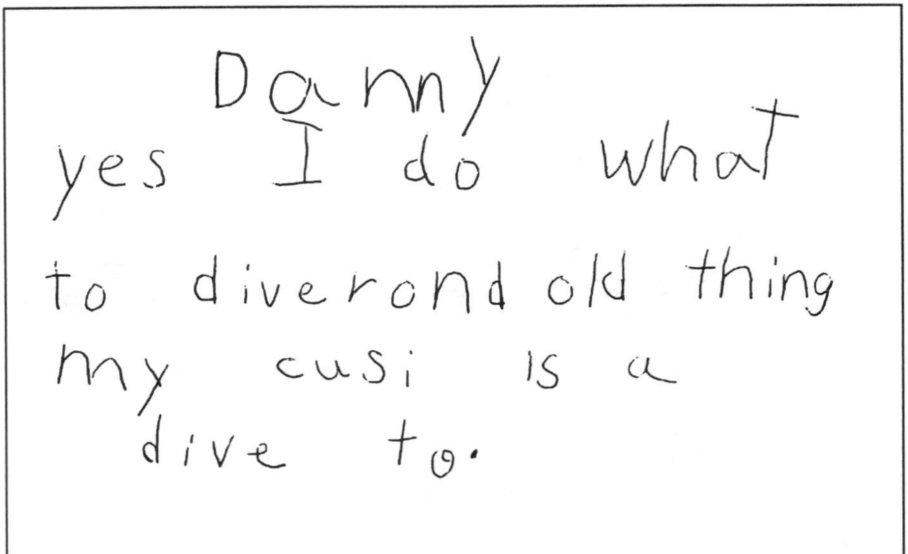

Danny
yes I do what
to diverond old thing
my cusi is a
dive to.

Dear Damy
    Diving on an old wreck is
great fun My dad and I
dove on an old boat and
found a cannon ball and
old gun shot pellets. It
was very creepy but exciting
Have you gone driving with your cousin
                    —Bye
                        Judy

Figure 4-4.   Danny's Dialogue Journal Response to Judy

no, and will you
bring in the
pali's. and did you
see the can in and
the gun. and I
wish I have the
bulis and the cahto
ball.

Figure 4-5. Danny's Dialogue Journal Entry

trates how interest and appropriate format motivated this child to exchange ideas by writing.

Thirteen-year-old Kai's journal illustrates the importance of appropriate teacher responses to students' problems. Kai was able to share habits, feelings, and even confidentialities by writing to her teacher, Gloria (Figure 4-6). Gloria's response (Figure 4-7) reveals that she is able to parallel the student's response. She lets Kai know that she has similar feelings. The last line, "Anyway, I hope our class here is fun and not boring," represents the teacher's voice, which is a shift from the other sections of this response. As days progressed, Gloria became more "teacherish," and often counseled. Kai's plea for help came easily, and blatantly. The trust built between Gloria and her student through the dialogue journal permitted this openness. Gloria's response (Figure 4-9) to Kai's plea (Figure 4-8) dramatically changes tone, causing Kai to close down (Figure 4-10). The plea for collegial companionship had gone unnoticed. It is easy for adults to find appropriate words to teach, counsel, and parent. It's difficult, but essential to find language that empathizes and supports.

Dialogue journals are important for developing written language. They are also vehicles crucial for building self-confidence and the ability to reflect on one's emotions, experiences, and reactions to both.

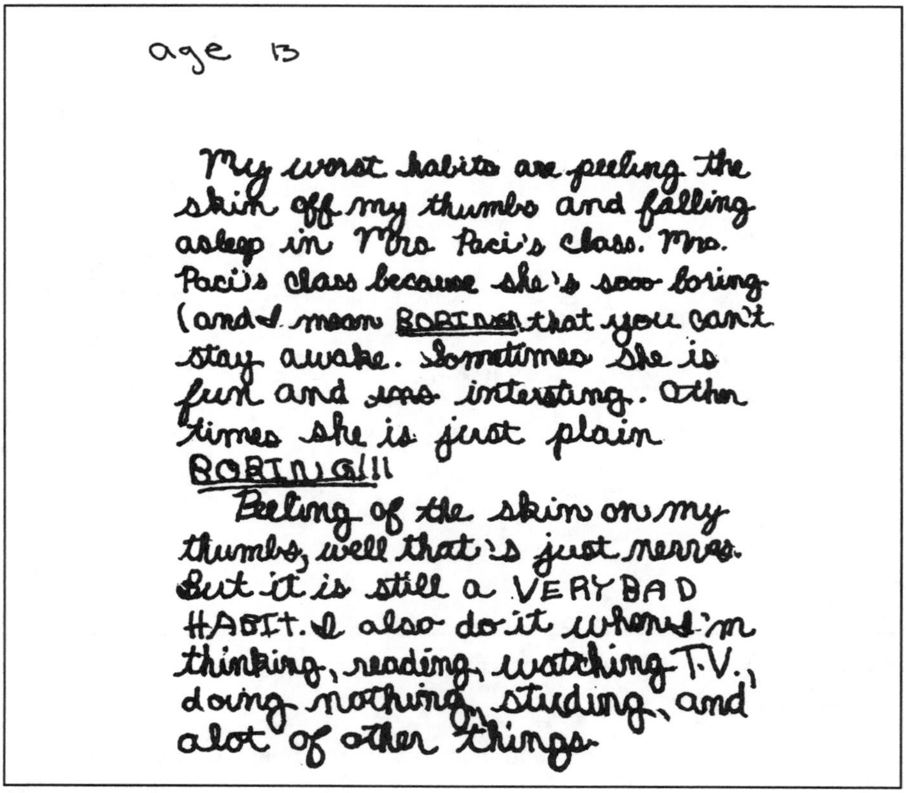

age 13

My worst habits are peeling the skin off my thumbs and falling asleep in Mrs Paci's class. Mrs. Paci's class because she's sooo boring (and I mean BORING that you can't stay awake. Sometimes She is fun and soo intersting. Other times she is just plain BORING!!!

Peeling of the skin on my thumbs, well that is just nerves. But it is still a VERY BAD HABIT. I also do it when I'm thinking, reading, watching T.V., doing nothing, studing, and alot of other things.

Figure 4-6.   Kai's Dialogue Journal Entry

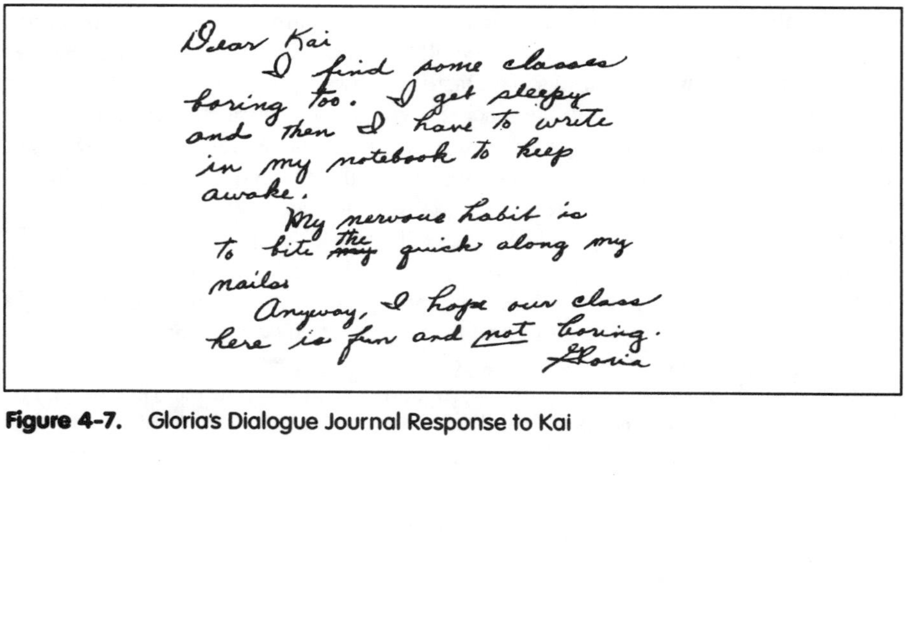

Dear Kai
  I find some classes boring too. I get sleepy and then I have to write in my notebook to keep awake.
  My nervous habit is to bite the quick along my nails
  Anyway, I hope our class here is fun and not boring.
                Gloria

Figure 4-7.   Gloria's Dialogue Journal Response to Kai

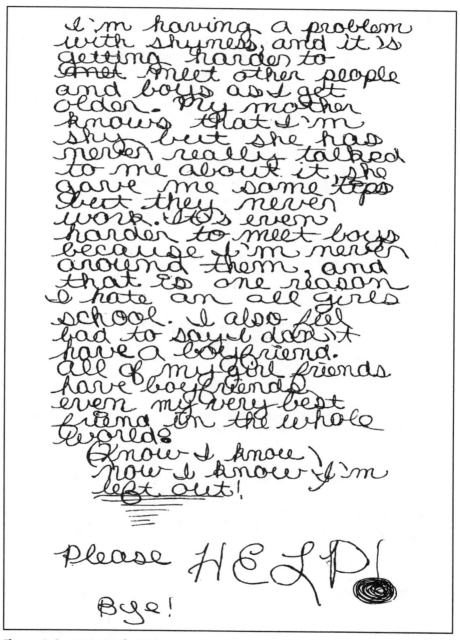

I'm having a problem with shyness, and it is getting harder to meet meet other people and boys as I get older. My mother knows that I'm shy but she has never really talked to me about it, she gave me some tips but they never work. It's even harder to meet boys because I'm never around them, and that is one reason I hate an all girls school. I also feel bad to say I don't have a boyfriend. All of my girl friends have boyfriends, even my very best friend in the whole world.

(know I know)

Now I know I'm left out!

Please HELP!

Bye!

Figure 4-8. Kai's Cry for Help

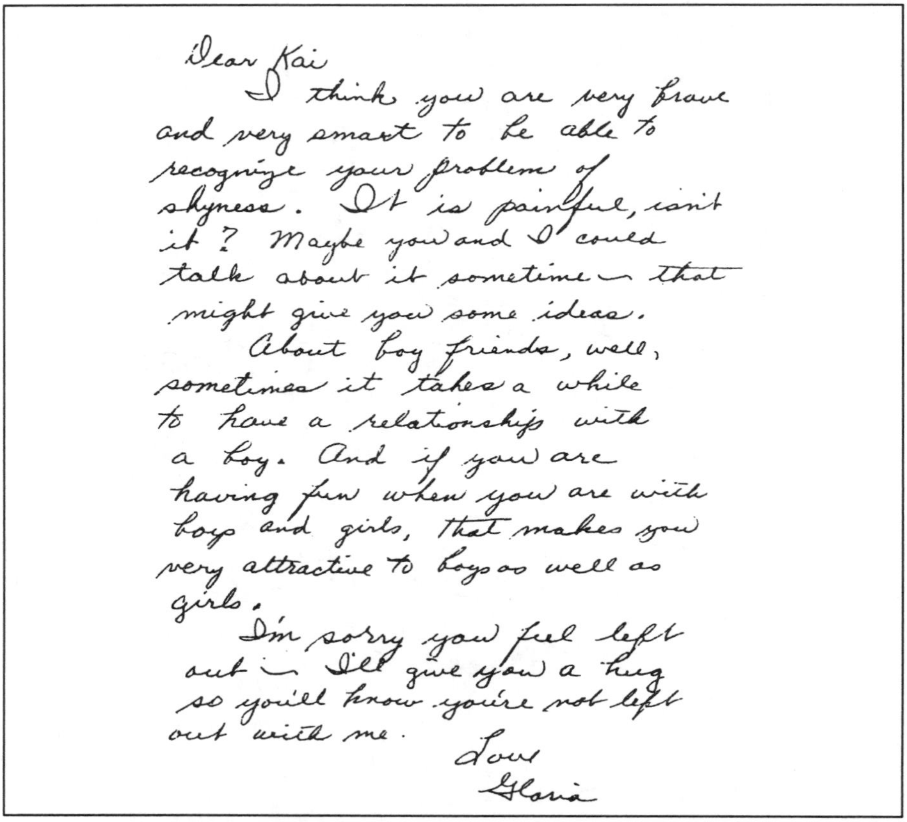

Dear Kai

I think you are very brave and very smart to be able to recognize your problem of shyness. It is painful, isn't it? Maybe you and I could talk about it sometime — that might give you some ideas.

About boy friends, well, sometimes it takes a while to have a relationship with a boy. And if you are having fun when you are with boys and girls, that makes you very attractive to boys as well as girls.

I'm sorry you feel left out — I'll give you a hug so you'll know you're not left out with me.

Love
Gloria

Figure 4-9. Gloria's Dialogue Response to Kai's Cry

Gloria, every thing is fine. Nothing has happened and nothing is wrong so far.

Bye!

Figure 4-10. Kai's Final Cry

Guidelines for Journal Responses

1. Parallel children's concerns empathetically, don't give advice. If, for example, the child writes,

   Dear Phyllis,

   My Mom was mean to me today. I hate her. Sometimes I feel like killing her.

   Love, Joan

   Respond by accepting, not denying the emotions. Reflect on your own experiences when answering. For example:

   Dear Joan,

   Sometimes I feel like I hate my Mom, too. But then, I get over it, and give her a hug. I love her all the time even though I feel angry sometimes.

   Love, Phyllis

2. Dialogue journals are private correspondences between student and teacher. They should not be shared with others, including students' parents. The trust built by the privacy facilitates the bond and openness needed in order for children to reflect on their lives.

3. Consult mental health professionals for advice concerning difficult issues revealed in journal dialogues. Serious confidential matters (a teen is pregnant, a child is taking drugs, another is abused, or secretly married) go beyond the domain of classroom teachers.

Literature and Content Journals

Almasi, McKeown, and Beck (1996) confirm earlier notions (Jagger, Carrara, & Weiss, 1986; Tierney & Leys, 1984) that discussions, both oral and written, play a major role in aiding students' comprehension. Discussions permit students to construct meaningful interpretations. Literature and content journals serve as wonderful vehicles for developing the ability to discuss fiction and nonfiction materials. Two different types of literature journal entries follow: (1) student entries without teacher responses and, (2) student entries and teacher dialogue responses.

The first discussion is twelve-year-old Natalie's independent conceptual ideas about sections of Lois Lowry's *The Giver* (1993). Each of the three responses were written during the time she read the text. The depth of her responses increases as she "self-discusses" the author's ideas.

> *The Giver* is a book that I will definitely read again. It was a greatly
> written story and I really enjoyed it. As soon as I forget the story, I
> will reread it. I really liked it.

The shallow response lacks reference to ideas in the story indicating inexperience with the information, with the dialoguing process, or with skills necessary to reflect on ideas. Although the student expresses enjoyment, there is no justification for the feelings. She never tells "why" she really likes the book. Her next response displays some connection to the text. She wrote:

> The ending made me think of celebrating. I like to think that the
> kids found a safe home. I think . . .

Natalie's response of happiness reflects the freedom the characters experienced in the story. Her hope for good fortune for the characters reveals her ability to use her prior knowledge of similar experiences and empathize with the situation. The incomplete sentence (I think . . .) demonstrates her conceptual understanding of the story's open, unfinished ending. Her freedom to include more of herself in the response is probably due, in part, to her short, but solid prior experience with the literature journal activity.

Her third entry uses the main character's memory of "the warm sun" to make a connection with it based on her own experience. She wrote:

> I think my favorite memory from the book is . . . the warm sun . . .
> My favorite true life memory is when I was riding my horse and
> my best friend was with me. I've never felt so happy or peaceful
> since. I think the character in the book could feel this way, too.

The peaceful calm projected by warm sun rays and Lois Lowry's words inspired an aesthetic reaction from this child. This encouraged her to connect herself to the author's words in *The Giver*.

Literature journals are important for developing other points of view. Discussions, however, are paramount for expanding students' ideas about authors' writing, and about readers' changing interpretations. A dialogue between Natalie and her teacher, Mrs. Bruno, illustrates how one response facilitates another. The book, *The Man Who Was Poe* (1989) by AVI was the topic of the following written dialogue.

The teacher wrote, to begin the interactive process, "I had to join your writing. Why? I wanted to be part of all the fun!"

Natalie: *The Man Who Was Poe* is a weird book. It is exciting and scary together creating a funny feeling. I'm wondering what that note meant, if it was his aunt that was dead and if so how did she die? I am also wondering where his sister went. I can't wait to finish it and find out what happened!!

Mrs. Bruno: Just you wait and see! I read a few chapters and you will soon find out about Sis. Do you trust Mr. Dupin? I don't. I wonder what Edmund will do? I feel sorry for him . . . he desperately needs help. Do you think Sis is alive? Respond . . .

Natalie: Mrs. Bruno, I think Mr. Dupin is a little weird, but he will solve the mystery so he can write a good book, not to help Edmund. I think Sis is alive in some alleyway tied up and being used. It's so good so far. I can't really understand who Mrs. Whitman is but I think it might be his mom or his sis.

Mrs. Bruno: Nat, Mrs. Whitman is Mr. Dupin's love. She is not Edmund's mom. He only wants to marry her and write his story his way. What do you think will happen next?

Natalie: Mrs. Bruno, I think that Dupin will solve the mystery, leave the boy when he is drunk, and then come back with a change of heart.

Mrs. Bruno: Nat, you seem to trust Mr. Dupin. I still don't. I think he'll trick Edmund somehow. I just don't like him!

Natalie: Mrs. Bruno, that was a great book! Mr. Dupin was weird, but I trusted him. Do you think that the boy will meet Mr. Dupin in the future? That would be so cool!

Mrs. Bruno, in a letter to Natalie, assessed her responses when she wrote:

Once again, so much can be observed from this written dialogue. You were a strategic reader because you:

- used an emotional equation to identify your initial feelings about the plot (exciting + scary = a funny feeling);

- recognized the confusion over the initial note and realized even though you could read it, you couldn't understand it;

- constantly asked questions as you read which forced you to make sense of the story;

- made predictions based on the characters' actions and personalities;

- documented your enthusiasm by saying how much you wanted to finish because you couldn't wait to find out what happened (as I mentioned in the beginning of this letter, reading for you is the breath of life);

- recognized the characters' motives and justified them (I found it amazing that you supported your trust of Mr. Dupin even after I doubted it!);

- indirectly asked for help in identifying a character's relationship to Mr. Dupin (Mrs. Whitman). Asking for help is certainly a strategy to use if all else fails;

- put all the pieces together and made a final prediction that made perfect sense;

- asked if there could possibly be a chance for a future sequel. (This made sense coming from you. After all, you need to breathe!) (Bruno, 1996)

Mrs. Bruno's assessment informed rather than evaluated her student. She told Natalie what she did, and the strategies she used to do it. Focusing on strategies informed the student about the importance of using those strategies again in similar activities. The teacher's involvement with the text, the personalization of her responses, and the prompts to "push" the student just a bit further all illustrate the power of literature journals for incorporating instruction with assessment. The student responded, the teacher elaborated on the response in the student's journal, prompting the student to respond some more. The student reacted and responded in each new entry with greater detail and clarity.

Maloney demonstrated her observational skills by watching ants in their farm. She watched them every morning and wrote what she saw in her **content journal** (Figure 4-11). She also loved to watch the caterpillars grow and spin their cocoons.

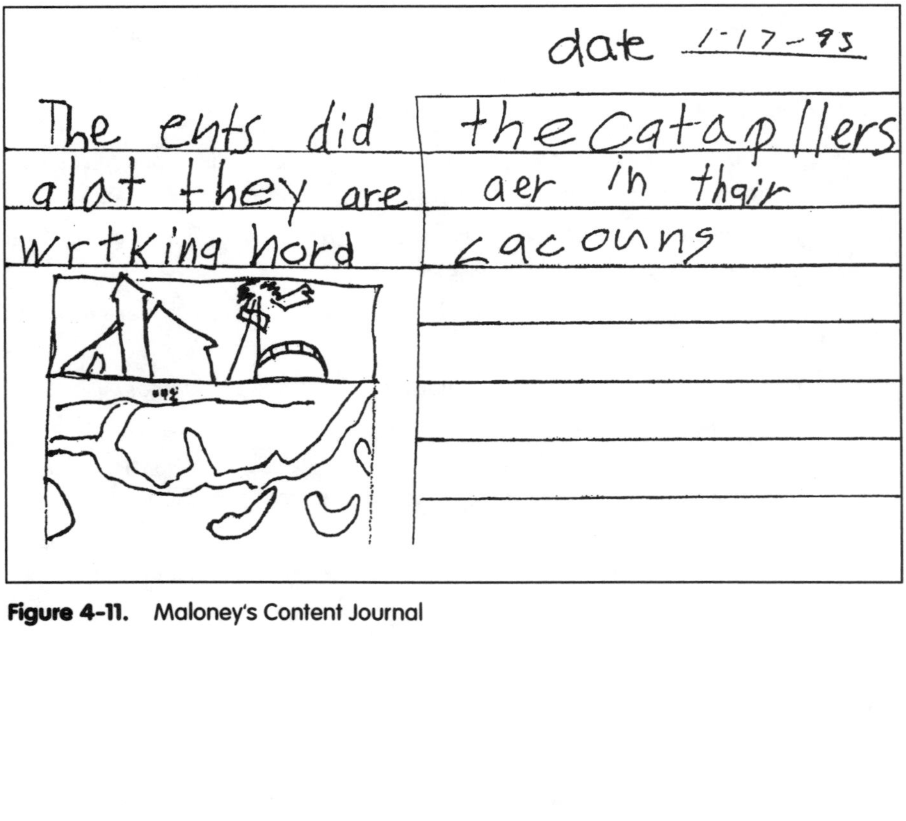

date 1-17-95

The ents did | the catapllers
alat they are | aer in thair
wrtking hord | cacouns

Figure 4-11. Maloney's Content Journal

She drew a line down the middle of the page in her **content journal** (Figure 4-11). This permitted her to observe and make comparisons of the simultaneous work of both groups of insects. Content journals are wonderful for recording observations of experiments, animal life, plant and animal growth, and more.

They are also vehicles for organizing, writing, and reflecting on content area studies. Natalie chose to do a research project about horses. Her discussion with her teacher and two other students whose interests were similar helped her formulate several questions about horses (Figure 4-12). She gathered several reference books about horses and answered her questions (Figure 4-13). She refers to page numbers in her text that correspond with the pages in the book from which she gathered the information.

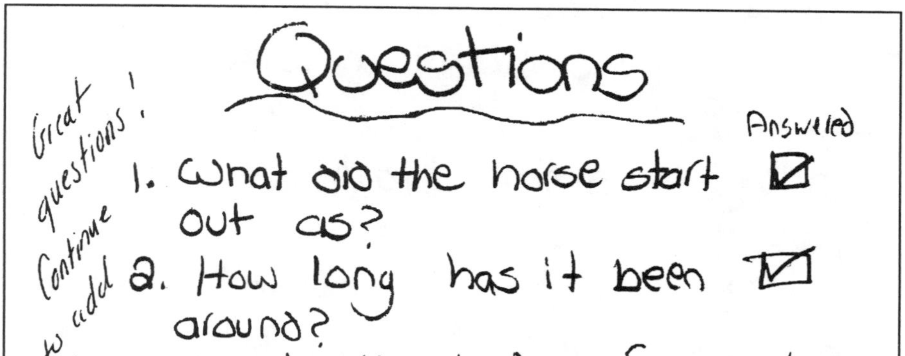
Questions

Answered

1. What did the horse start out as? ☑
2. How long has it been around? ☑
3. What other kinds of animals are related to the horse? ☐
4. How many different stages did it go through before it got to what it is? ☐
5. How many different breeds are there? ☑
6. What are some myths about magic horses? ☑

BIBLIOGRPHY ON Page 45

Great questions! Continue to add and research your answers using ReQuest!

Figure 4-12. Natalie's Content Journal (Page 1 of 4)

12-18

ANSWERS

1. The horse started out as "EOHIPPUS" which means dawn horse. The dawn horse was about the size of a fox with big eyes and a small brain. It had teeth so soft it couldn't chew grass. In sted of hoofs it had 4 big, clumsey feet that looked like paws. Each "PAW" had 3 front toes and 1 at the back, at the tip of each there was a tiny hoop. It took 47 million year for its brain to grow bigger, its teeth to get plat3₃

Figure 4-13. Natalie's Content Journal (Page 2 of 4)

stronger, and theif "PAWS" to become a single hoof. P.13

The first true horse was born in NA 3 million years ago. They were no bigger then ponies but were like the modern horse. Some migrated over the landbrige that once connected NA and Asia and others to S.A. Soon after 11,000 BC all N.A. & S.A horses disappered for an unknown reason.

P15

P.22 The horse 1st seved humans on a farm in Southern Rusia & western Asia around 4000 BC.

For thousands of years their only important joh was in battle

p.32

Figure 4-13. Natalie's Content Journal (Page 3 of 4)

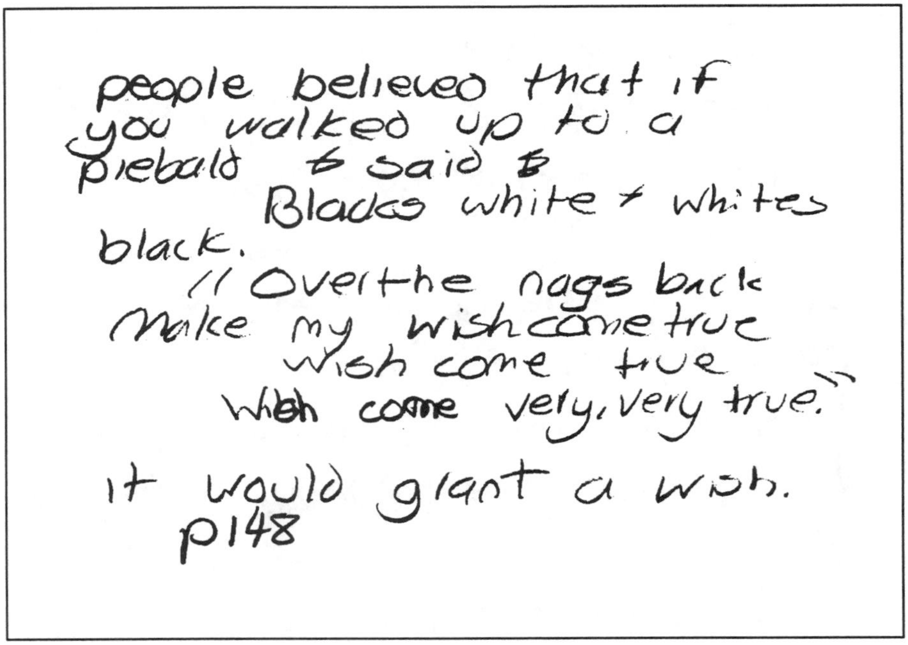
people believeo that if
you walkeo up to a
piebald & said &
Blacks white + whites
black.
"Over the nags back
Make my wish come true
wish come true
wish come very, very true."
it would glant a wish.
p148

Figure 4-13. Natalie's Content Journal (Page 4 of 4)

The content journal is a resource for helping children remember what they've read, how to paraphrase information from texts, and how to write and respond to social studies, science, math, art, and other content area subjects.

Mail

Everyone in a school building—teachers, administrators, custodians, crossing guards, education specialists, volunteers—ought to have a mailbox. Teachers begin the mail writing process by putting a personal note in each student's mailbox on the first day of school. I first learned about mailboxes from Vera Milz (1980) and learned even more from Regie Routman (1988). We all suggest that they can be made of shoeboxes, a legal-sized envelope, or other containers that can be kept in a permanent spot, one for each person in the school building. Children, especially those in elementary and middle schools, love to get mail. The first thing many of them do in the morning is check their mailbox. Letters, during the early part of the school year, are short, but as time progresses the content is more detailed, and text is longer and more specific. (See Figures 4-14 and 4-15.)

Dear ingrit I
hope you
have a
gret time
went it is
theKgiveing
Alex

Figure 4-14.   Alex's Letter to Ingrid

Different paper and stationery as well as writing tools (pens, markers, pencils, etc.) should be placed in spaces easily accessible to the children. Some teachers label the storage area, "Mail paper." This is especially helpful for younger children. Self-selecting the paper and tools is important and facilitates feelings of control over learning.

Reading Log

Keeping records teaches organizational skills. They teach youngsters to routinely log what they read. (See Figure 4-16.) Some children use the log after they read a chapter, an article, or an editorial. Keeping a literature log alerts students to the different genres available for their reading pleasure. The teachers in our Center post the genre names at eye level in their classrooms or in the halls. Conversations, casual and formal, include discussions of genres.

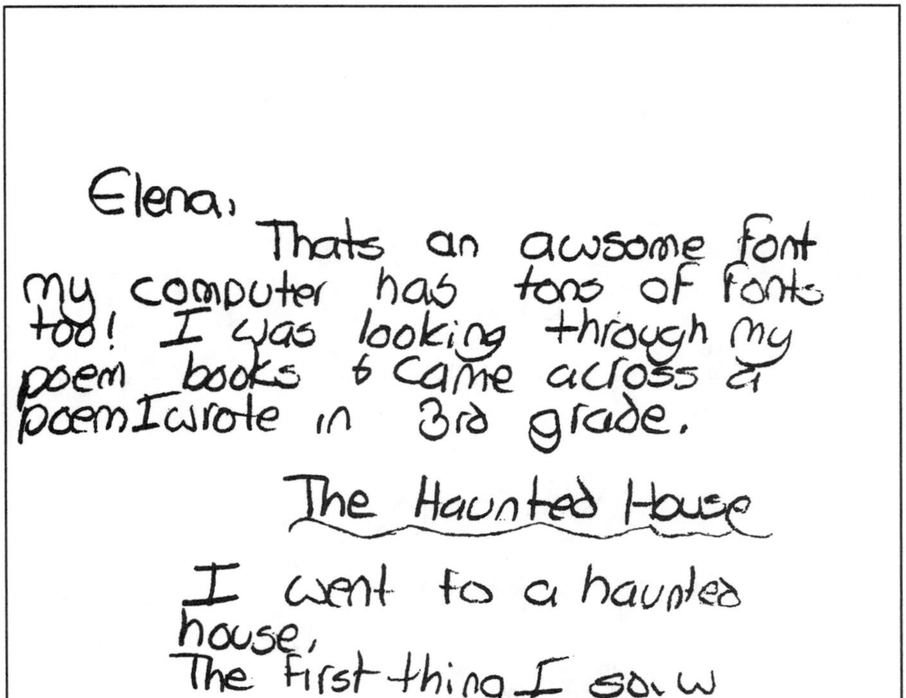

Elena,
   Thats an awsome font
my computer has tons of fonts
too! I was looking through my
poem books & came across a
poem I wrote in 3rd grade.

   The Haunted House

I went to a haunted
house,
The first thing I saw
was a mouse.
I looked behind a post & saw
a ghost,
I looked in a pen & saw a hen,
I'm never going there again!!

Like it? I was my fav!!!!

                    Nat

Figure 4-15.   Nat's Message to Elena

READING LOG

Name _Rahul_

Date	Title/Author	Genre	Notes
7-7	Nate The Great And The Snowy Trail	Mystery	Good Reading size book
7-7	Nate The Great & The Boring Beach Bag	Mystery	Good Reading Book
7-10	Nate The Great And the Sticky Case	Mystery	Good Reading size
7-12	Nate the Great And the Lost List	Mystery	Good Reading Book

Figure 4-16.   Rahul's Reading Log

Summary

Great classrooms have scheduled blocks of uninterrupted time so teachers are able to teach and children have time to talk about ideas in order to learn. Strategies effective for guiding children to become independent learners include self-monitoring tools that provide students with frameworks for assessing their own products. Self-monitoring is assessment and also instruction. Time blocks and consistent formats for praise, use of language, and vehicles for communicating in writing guide learners to take control and responsibility for learning. The activities, goals, and strategies that encourage self-monitoring are applicable for all children and all content area subjects. Teacher responses to students must be personalized, honest, and consistent. Consistent classroom formats permit children to predict what is expected of them, thus building self-confidence and a desire for learning.

CHAPTER 5

Organizing, Managing, and Merging Assessment and Instruction

So often I've been asked, "How do you manage to guide individual children to self-monitor and learn at the same time?" "How do you personalize instruction for twenty-five or more in the classroom?" The most pressing challenge is authenticizing school activities and at the same time integrating the teaching and learning of literacy skills within literature and content area studies.

Authenticizing and personalizing both instruction and assessment, and integrating the teaching of language arts skills, is the essence of this chapter. The challenge of managing and coordinating these elements in precise, well-defined, and functional ways for students can be awesome, even devastating at first. There are just some situations where explaining (heaven forbid) and assigning (oh no) seem to work well. Explanations and assignments can never replace student-executed hands-on activities or self-monitoring activities. Although it sounds impossible, with appropriate professional development, classrooms, like life itself, can become a "hustle and bustle" of healthy, ongoing, authentic learning.

Instructional Formats

Two frequently used instructional formats dominate today's classrooms: (1) teacher-centered instruction (curriculum-driven), and (2) student-centered (student-driven) instruction.

Teacher-Centered (curriculum-driven) Formats

The most frequently used format for classroom instruction is teacher-centered activity. Teachers, in this model, are actively involved in delivering and explaining **about** ideas to students. The characteristics of this instructional format usually include:

- requiring specific answers to questions;

- selecting a correct response from a multiple of choices;

- expecting students to know specific kinds and amounts of materials in content and skill area studies.

When teachers explain with only verbal or written directions, students are working without models. Words, written and spoken, are not the actions, but representations for the actions. They are coded messages for the "real thing." Explanations without models require students to translate the code (words) into the actions themselves. We are, in a sense, testing children to see if they are able use a code to represent a reality.

Ms. Star explained to her third-grade students how to write descriptive text. "Today, boys and girls," she began, "we are going to make our stories interesting. In order to do this, we need to use words that make the story fun to read. Adjectives do that. These are descriptive words." Ms. Star paused for a moment, and then asked, "Who can tell me some?" Children raised their hands, and several provided examples. One youngster responded, "It's an adjective when you say, today is a very bad, rainy day." Ms. Star responded, "That's right, Paul, 'very' and 'bad' and 'rainy' are adjectives. They tell about the day." The elated teacher praised the child for his answer. What she didn't realize is that she had tested and given a verbal "grade" for the correct response. It was the child who provided the examples—the appropriate information— for his peers.

The assumption made by teachers who explain is that learners are able to transform words into actions. If, for example, a student hears, "Create a story and include all of the story elements," it is assumed that the youngster knows the elements, and how to assemble them to construct a story. Most of us, when provided with an explanation or directions, create a picture in our minds about what the product is supposed to be. That picture is based on one's perception and knowledge of the concepts. If students are unable to form that picture, they are usually unable to provide teachers with the expected, specific answers to questions. In order to "save their pride," students use guessing as a strategy to find the answer. If incorrect, disillusionments and confusions result.

Teacher-centered instructional paradigms parallel the activities of a pea shooter. The information (the pea) is popped into the straw (the shooter), and then blown out of the other end. For centuries, information has been popped in, and requests to "blow" it out the other end have been made of students. The "blow out" approach to teaching and testing students' learning parallels the structure of most standardized tests. In these tools, fact and information are important. The processes students use to discover "how" to get answers are not considered.

Student-Centered (student-driven) Formats

In student-centered classrooms, teachers guide students to manage their own learning. The guidance and content of learning are based on teachers' observations of students and their interactions in the classroom. The curriculum is driven by student needs. Children understand and can explain:

- what they know, and what they need to learn;
- when they need their teachers;
- when they are able to solve problems themselves;
- how to access and acquire resources;
- who and what they need in order to grow and learn.

Students in classrooms centered around their needs realize that they are as responsible for their learning as is their teacher. This was well illustrated when Kathy, a ten-year-old, approached the principal who was observing the lesson, and said, "Mr. Buzz, my teacher needs help teaching me about 'think and search' questions." "Tell me about 'think and search' questions, Kathy," responded the principal. "I can't, Mr. Buzz," she continued, "that's how I know my teacher needs help." The principal, with the teacher's consent, continued the instruction. After several minutes, Kathy stood up and said, "Mr. Buzz, I still don't understand it. You do it the same as Mrs. Skinner." The principal agreed, and he and the child decided that he needed to find another strategy to guide her. After spending twenty minutes preparing an alternative lesson, he returned, and continued the lesson with eight children who'd been involved earlier. Four minutes into the lesson, in a loud voice Kathy said, "I got it Mr. Buzz. You find a 'think and search' answer by searching for the answers. And, there's more than one. You're a good teacher after all. You found a way to teach me."

The most effective student-centered classrooms are those whose rapport invites students to discover what they must do in order to comprehend ideas. When adults believe that children are able to take charge of their learning, feelings of collegiality emerge in both teachers and students. Most literacy skills are developed within the context of the curriculum. Content area subjects become functionally meaningful because activities resemble "real life."

The physical arrangement of classrooms affects children's performance (Weinstein, 1977). Classrooms that accommodate individual and group needs encourage choices and include specific activities and locations for working in content areas. Content-specific items, such as dry leaves during the fall season and living bugs in jars during spring, provide "food for thought" that coerces children to create language (Glazer & Burke, 1994). Storage areas, work spaces for specific activities, and personal spaces for each student set the tone for tailoring instruction to each child (Figure 5-1). Managing an integrated language arts classroom, where teachers

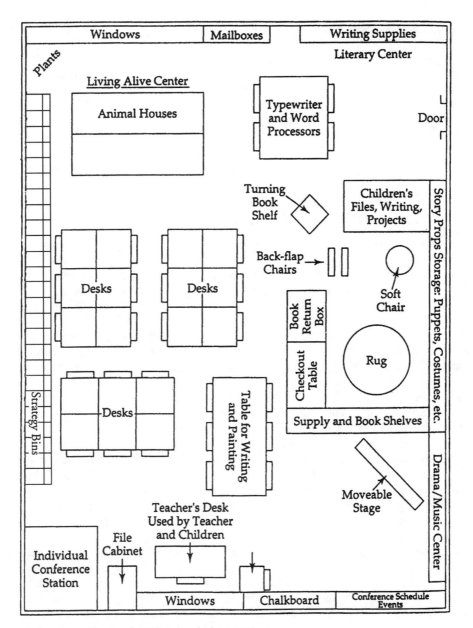

Figure 5-1. The Student-Centered Classroom

From S. M. Glazer & E. M. Burke, *An Integrated Approach to Early Literacy: Literature to Language* (p. 173). Copyright © (1994) by Allyn & Bacon. Reprinted/Adapted by permission.

observe behaviors in order to discover strengths and needs, is a big concern of teachers. How do we manage a classroom of twenty-four so that children thrive as individuals as well as members of a learning community? How can we observe and take notes about each child with twenty-four present? Is it really possible to use forms of alternative assessment in a class of twenty-four?

The intricacies of managing an integrated language arts classroom are best described by visiting a classroom. Since that is not possible, I've created a video with words, describing one teacher's procedures for engaging students. The description attempts to describe one-on-one, small- and whole-group learning experiences. It also illustrates how observations and note taking about strengths and needs occurs in classrooms. Let me invite you to spend a morning in Ms. Turner's primary class of ten girls and fourteen boys. It is October and most of the children have learned the daily routine. Many are able to manage their own time. Some are dependent upon their teacher or peers for guidance.

The Day Begins*

(In an elementary school, somewhere in America)

7:30 A.M.
Ms. Turner's classroom was organized into four clusters of tables with places for six children at each. Six- and seven-year-old children were mixed. Changes were made when several children had to be together to work on a specific project or when new friendships were established.

Ms. Turner had arrived at 7:30 to put the new books on display in the library corner. The books *Duck* by David Lloyd, *Father Fox's Pennyrhymes* by Clyde Watson, *What's in the Cave?* by Peter Seymour, and *Wake Up, William!* by Anita Riggio had limited vocabularies and repeated sentence patterns that rhymed. Ms. Turner knows that Derick and Melissa remember words best when they are in contexts written with repeated sentence patterns and rhymes. Both children read and reread these books. This helped them build their sight vocabularies. Ms. Turner took out the contracts for the two children and wrote the day's assignment under the category "reading." It said:

> There are new books in the book rack for you.
>
> Use the fist-full-of-words rule to pick one.
>
> Sign up for a conference.

There were always several books available so each child was able to carry out the fist-full-of-words self-selection strategy. The risk of failing was minimized by Ms. Turner's careful planning. The conference sign up chart was posted on the wall near the classroom entrance. Next to it, hanging from a hook, was a pencil on a string. Each child's name was listed down the left side of the chart. The days of the week were written across the top. Children could check the day on which they would have a private conference with their teacher to retell stories they had read or heard. Ms. Turner looked over the names of the children who had signed up for conferences. She assigned the time each conference was to take place next to the child's name. Children checked this chart first thing in the morning and wrote the time on their contracts. Ms. Turner went to the library center. She had gotten books from the municipal library that had been requested by individual children. She put them in a basket labeled, "You asked for it." The appropriate child's name was attached to each book. She put prediction monitoring sheets in an envelope marked, "Predict About Your Book." She also put one inside the cover of each book. She put a new supply of lined and unlined writing paper in the library and writing centers. Sharpened pencils were placed into a canister, and erasers in an empty "eraser box" which had been full the day before. Winnie the Pooh, a toy bear that had fallen, was placed upright next to a book of the same name. Ms. Turner tidied the bed made from a bathtub, fluffed the several pillows on the floor, and placed some empty audio cassettes in a box near several tape recorders for children to use to record their story retellings. She stopped to read Tanya's written retelling of *Cloudy with a Chance of Meatballs,* which was fastened to the wall. Ms. Turner found that Tanya recalled one story episode out of more than ten. She needed a guided retelling session to help her recall more episodes. She read Eric's spontaneous story about his grandfather who was in the hospital. It included a vivid description of the hospital room. She noted a pattern in Eric's invented spellings and planned to make this part of his next conference with her. She was distracted by Charlie, the classroom gerbil, who was running around in his cage. Ms. Turner looked up at the clock. She realized that she had only thirty minutes to complete her preparations for her children. Charlie's food tray was empty. Ms. Turner wrote a note to Vincent, this week's caretaker, and tacked it onto the bulletin board in the living-alive center. It read:

> Dear Vincent,
>
> Charlie's food tray is empty. I think he needs more food.
>
> > Love,
> > Ms. Turner

The ant farm, which was observed daily by seven-year-old Alicia and Gail, seemed exceptionally busy. Several children wrote daily about the changes they observed using a story map. Ms. Turner discovered that the box of maps was empty. She dashed to the copy machine in the office to reproduce more for the children. Observational notes hung all around the ant farm. Alicia had not hung her notes. Ms. Turner thought that she might not have written them. Gail's notes hung on the wall. Ms. Turner wrote the following note to both girls and placed it next to the ant farm.

> Dear Alicia and Gail,
>
> Wow! What is going on in the ant farm? Alicia, I missed reading your ant farm observations today. Please sign up for a conference to share them with me.
>
> > Love,
> > Ms. Turner

Three books about plants were put next to the blooming cactus on the plant table. They were about desert plant life and written with limited vocabularies. Ms. Turner was drawn to Crocky's cage. He seemed to be hopping around more than usual. She opened the top of the can, labeled "Meal Worms for Crocky," spooned out some, and placed them in the frog's feeding tray. Crocky, in his frog-like way, lapped up the worms with his long, sticky tongue. Ms. Turner wrote on the chart posted next to his cage, "One spoonful of meal worms, 8:21 A.M." Writing a note to Habbiba, Solomon, Fred, and Anita—Crocky's caregivers—encouraged collaborative learning. The note read:

> Dear Habbiba, Solomon, Fred, and Anita,
>
> Crocky was hopping around the cage. He looked hungry. So, I took one spoonful of meal worms. I put it in his cage. Guess what! He gobbled it up! The worms smell! Crocky eats them anyway.
>
> > Love,
> > Ms. Turner

A copy of the note was left in each child's mailbox. A second copy of the letter was placed on top of an easy-to-read book about frogs.

Ms. Turner hurried to the writing center: She had had dialogues with ten of the twenty-four children in their journals. It was important for her responses to be in the children's writing folders when they arrived. Several new writing ideas on strips of paper were put into the "Writing Idea Box." These included:

- retell your favorite story by writing it
- retell your favorite story by talking it onto a tape
- make a rhyme using these words:
  cat rat sat hat pat fat
  mat bat that vat

Ms. Turner put several blank story writing booklets on the shelf. Some were cut in the shape of pumpkins. These were fastened with a staple, with orange construction paper used to cover the blank writing paper inside. She placed each child's daily contract in his or her work basket. It was almost 8:30. Ms. Turner had prepared more than nineteen different integrated reading/language arts activities for the children. That meant that each had choices. The children knew that the classroom was prepared for them to begin activities on their own. Books were always changing. Animals were added and some taken away. Story props and dress-up clothing were rearranged and changed regularly. But contracts, retelling monitoring sheets, prediction sheets, and other tools for recording and observing were always the same. So were the time blocks. Children knew the routines and expected changes. They were able, therefore, to take control of their learning in this risk-free classroom setting.

Ms. Turner had prepared for almost an hour, and there were still things to be done. She moved quickly to the door area, to greet each youngster as they "popped" into the classroom. Children moved to their tables, and Ms. Turner to hers. Some had begun to take a daily paper from the pile left on her desk. This morning she put an article about Michigan in Tommie's basket. Tommie had told Ms. Turner that he was going to visit his relatives in that state during vacation. She remembered that she had forgotten to put the readers' theater version of Dr. Seuss's *Horton Hatches the Egg* in the music and drama center. Ms. Turner felt that Alicia, Fred, Antonio, and Eshee needed to rehearse stories by reading them out loud. She knew that Eshee and Alicia would look for the script. They had been selecting dialogue plays, consistently, for three weeks. The readers' theater activity was perfect for these reluctant readers.

ATTENTION

New readers' theater play

Horton Hatches the Egg by *Dr. Seuss.*

The Children Arrive and Language Activities Begin

8:30 A.M. to approximately 9:50 A.M.
"Hi, Ms. Turner." "Morning Tommie. I left you an article from my paper about Michigan. It's in your basket. Since you're going to visit your Grandma in Lansing in two weeks, you might find it interesting." Ms. Turner peered beyond her newspaper to observe children's activity. She was torn, however, between reading the newspaper and observing youngsters to assess their strengths and needs. She put down the paper and pulled out her note pad and wrote some observations. She also made notes for herself, directing her observations.

Notes

8:40 A.M.   *Fred walked to table. He "threw" down his book, sat in chair; and put chin on his hands. Took journal out of his work basket. Seemed to read my response. He took a pencil and began to write. Pressed hard on the point. Erased several times.*

Today—watch Fred's behavior in other situations. Read his journal. I wonder why Fred seems angry?

8:42 A.M.   *Habbiba went directly to Crocky. Looked in cage and wrote on chart. Put worms in cage. Took paper and wrote.*

Today—read writing. Use direct praise to let Habbiba know that she's been an independent learner. Milestone—She went on her own and completed task.

8:45 A.M.

Ms. Turner went back to her table and to looking at the newspaper. She also listened to the activity in the room to assess children's self-direction. Sometimes she wished that she had eyes all around her head. She thought she heard Vincent talking to the gerbil. "Here's some food for you, Charlie. No wonder you're hungry. You're always running on your wheel." Several children, including Derick, signed up for a retelling conference. Derick noticed that all seven spaces, the total number of conferences in one day, were now taken. "It's a good thing I got here fast. I would have missed a time," said Derick to a classmate. Derick noticed the book *What's in the Cave*. He took it and proceeded to turn the pages, reading and feeling the pop-up characters on each. Ms. Turner noticed that he did not use the fist-full-of words rule. It seems, she thought, that he was sure that he could read it without checking. Derick and the four other children took their work baskets and went to their tables. Derick stood in the living alive corner beside Melissa.

Derick: I got a book already, so I can check one thing on my contract.

Melissa: What book did you get?

Derick: See. It's a pop-up book.

Melissa: What's it about?

Derick: (Shrugging his shoulders) I don't know. (As he turns the pages, he shares what is on the page.) It's about a, ah, a . . . What's this?

Melissa: A lazy lizard.

Derick: It's about a l-a-z-y lizard, and a fat bat, and a green snake.

Melissa: That says, "a sneaky snake."

Derick:　And a sneaky snake and a . . . what's this word?

Melissa:　Friendly.

Derick:　A friendly frog. He's orange. I never saw an orange frog before (as he shrugs shoulders and turns the page). And a s-s-s-s

Melissa:　Sly.

Derick:　Sly spider and . . .

Derick and
Melissa:　A broody bird.

Melissa:　(Derick looks on and holds book) A busy beetle. What else is in the cave?

Derick:　A MONSTER.

Derick turned back to the beginning of the book and began to read again. Melissa took her work basket and walked to her table. Ms. Turner scribbled in her notebook:

> Melissa—a natural peer tutor for Derick. She used "echo reading."
> Derick completed the book. Began to read it a second time—natural rehearsal. Milestone—Derick accepted peer guidance. He selected a book he was able to read. Stayed with it to the end and then reread, independently.

Ms. Turner was so absorbed in watching Derick that she failed to note the activities of other children. It was such an active child-centered classroom.

Several children had gone to the library center, selected a book, and took a prediction sheet. Others took one of the several guided retelling sheets. Ms. Turner made note of the strategy sheets each child took. She would watch for the rest of the week to see if children selected the same worksheets daily. Matthew and Keiko found the plant books in the living alive corner.

Matthew:　Is this for us?

Keiko:　(Shrugging her shoulders) I don't know. But it's not our corner this week. So it's probably not. But I'm reading it anyway.

Matthew:　Me too.

Ms. Turner had hoped that Derick and Brian would have taken them. The boys needed peer interaction to build confidence in their abilities to read.

By 8:50 the room was a hustle and bustle with language activities. Some children had begun to read self-selected books; others were reading the teacher's response in their dialogue journals, while others wrote in the journal. Several were cleaning animal cages and recording their activities on charts and in notebooks. More seven- than six-year-old children were completing oral and written retellings that were begun the day before. Contracts were reviewed by most of the children within the first twenty minutes of the school day. Some children left them on the tables to use as a reference. Others seemed to review the contract and put it back into the work basket. Several appeared to be staring into space. Ms. Turner moved to the library center. This was where the morning get-together took place. It usually began at 9:00 and lasted for approximately fifteen minutes. The morning's activity included the usual "news and notes." Children who had special events in their lives shared them. It was also the time to review the day's events. Preplans for some of these get-togethers included story reading time. Gail was this morning's story reader. She clutched her James Stevenson's *That Terrible Halloween Night*. She would read it to the class this morning. She had taken the book home to rehearse reading it out loud. She looked up at the clock. Then she looked at Ms. Turner, who was already seated in the library center. A second chair was beside Ms. Turner. Gail sat in the chair. The children knew that it was time to come together, stopped what they were doing and came to the center. Ms. Turner smiled and bid the group, "Good morning." Ben told the class that he was going to get a new baby. Sarah confirmed the news by saying, "Yeah, it's coming in April." Derick reminded the class that there would be a book fair next month. He was the class messenger and had received a note from the principal's office asking him to remind everyone about the date. A sign "Today's story reader is Gail." was hanging on the chart next to the child. Ms. Turner smiled at her and she began:

> Gail: Today, I am going to read *That Terrible Halloween Night* by James Stevenson. What do you think it's about (as she held the cover of the book toward the children)?

Gail began by asking children to predict. She had learned this from her teacher, who did it all the time. She read a page and then shared the picture. She did this until the book was completed. She announced that she would share the book and that she would write a retelling and make it into a book for the classroom library. After the morning get-together, Ms. Turner noticed that Jason seemed to be staring at the ant farm, and Kevin took his book out of his work basket.

> Jason: Hey, what are ya doin with my book?

> Kevin: I want to finish it. I only have a little left. You let me read it yesterday.

> Jason: O.K. Finish it. But I want it soon!

Ms. Turner thought about all of the things that occurred during the first forty-five minutes. She watched children:

- select a book

- read and respond to a journal entry
- care for a living thing and record some of the visible changes in the animals' behaviors
- read a book
- engage in collaborative learning
- sign up for conferences
- attend to other children's reading and writing
- respond to her modeling behaviors by reading her journal entry to them
- write a letter in response to hers
- make decisions about which activities to complete even though a group activity was occurring

Ms. Turner noticed individual strengths and needs during the forty-five minute period and recorded them whenever she found time in order to plan for the next day's activities. She learned from the morning's observations and recorded the notes.

Discussion

Ms. Turner had, indeed, created an environment for observing children. She kept goals in her mind and took quick objective notes. She was careful not to be subjective and not use words like shy, lazy, lackadaisical, or daydreamer. These were evaluative, relative terms and, therefore, inappropriate. Ms. Turner had data that helped her to provide the intervention necessary for further development.

9:20 to 11:30 A.M.
Two hours were blocked for independent work, small group activities, and individual conferences. By this time of year, mid-October, most children could manage their own time using their contract as a guide. During this time, Ms. Turner acted as a model, exhibiting desired behaviors as a nurturing caregiver and as a consultant to the children. Walking to each of the four table areas while children were working let them know that she was available for consulting. She became their audience ready to listen to their creative stories, their retellings, and their experiences. Ms. Turner knew that the children believed that their work and even their attempts were valued. The classroom was a bustle of activity. Children seemed to know what to do and so did their teacher. A sketch of the activities follows.

Child	Behaviors	Teacher's Notes
Tommie	Took Michigan article. Adult input provides motivation. Did not see him read it.	Follow up to encourage reading. Say, "I'll talk to you about the article later. I am going to Michigan"; or "Let me know when you've read the article. I have something to share about Michigan, with you."
Fred	Began journal writing independently. Seemed to respond to dialogue in journal—he wrote back.	Look for other settings where anger occurs. Find strategy to relieve anger. If a pattern, talk to school psychologist for suggestions.
Habbiba	Milestone day—she fed the frog without direction from peer or teacher. She also wrote her activities on her own. Hurrah!!!	Praise behavior. ("Habbiba, it's really important the way you came to school, fed Crocky, and wrote what you did. That's very independent behavior.") Provide additional care-tending activities.
Derick	Demonstrated independence and enthusiasm about reading. Got involved with stories that have limited vocabularies and interesting formats (pop-up books yesterday, and *Rebus Bears* today). Solved problems—got help with word identification, spontaneously. Seemed to have need to read. Liked books with surprises in them.	Create success. Make books available daily. Be sure he knows how to get help. Will say, "Derick, it's really important the way you read with Melissa. Because you read with her, both of you knew all of the words." Provide books with surprises like, *Where's Spot,* and Bank Street "Ready-to-Read" Rebus Series. Needs prediction activities.

Child	Behaviors	Teacher's Notes
Melissa	As usual, independent. Fit in with most children. Took opportunity to interact with story, no matter who is involved. Seemed to have a natural way of guiding peers, and making herself and others feel good about it.	Continue as is. Be careful not to overuse as helper.
Cindy Allison John Shamir	All selected retelling guide sheet for first time.	Note if child completes the elements included, if each works alone or with another, and the effects of peer interaction on recall using guided retelling sheet.
Kevin	Loves to read anything. If interested, finds way to "skin the cat" and get the book. Stays by himself most of the time.	Share some of the reading.

Children's Activities	Ms. Turner's Activities
Table I: Derick, Melissa, Fred, Habbiba, Randy and Allison Children each took their work baskets from the cubbies. Derick, Habbiba, and Randy found their journals and read and responded on their own. Melissa put the work basket on the table and went to the library. She was carrying one book. Fred, after completing journal writing, sat with chin in hands and looked around at others. He took paper out of the basket and fastened it onto a clipboard. He got up and left the classroom with the clipboard and pencil. He was correcting data about	Ms. Turner took notes about as many children as she could. She wrote: "Derick, Habbiba, Randy—took journals first. Wrote for twenty minutes. Habbiba got up three times and sharpened pencil twice. Randy erased her first sentence three times. Fred wrote for three minutes. Read paper and also looked around. He said to Allison, 'Want to do this with me?' Ms. Turner remembered that Allison scheduled a conference. She got her retelling evaluation sheet. She took a copy of the transcription of Allison's retelling and the guide sheet she had completed at home. She would guide Allison to moni-

Children's Activities	Ms. Turner's Activities
things on the bulletin board in the hall. The purpose was to become a better descriptive writer. His goal was to use at least two adjectives to describe each object. Allison went to get a retelling monitoring sheet. She took her book, her transcription which Ms. Turner had placed in her work basket, and her tape recorder to the table that said, "Conference! Do Not Disturb."	tor her own comprehension and then compare both evaluations. She noticed Melissa sitting and drawing. She went to her and said, 'Melissa, I left your contract in your work basket. Look at it. If you have questions, I will answer them before the retelling conference."
Table II: Keiko, Kevin, Shamir, Gail, John, and Anita Gail read *That Terrible Halloween Night* by Stevenson to these children on Halloween. They decided to retell it in writing. Every child has a copy of the book. Each read it at least once on their own. Keiko was rereading, and so were Kevin and Shamir. Gail had already taken out her pencil and Retelling Journal and placed the book at the top of the table. John took his Retelling Journal and began to write immediately, Anita took her contract and read and reread it. She looked about the table at peer activities. She seemed to be undecided about what to do. "Are you writing about the monster story?" "Yeah, I'm retelling it. Don't bother me!" grunted Kevin. Kevin wrote for fifteen minutes without stopping. During that time he stood up, sat down, took the paper under the table, sharpened his pencil twice, but continued to write for that period.	She continued note taking. Keiko, Kevin, and Shamir independently took the book and reread. They seem to like to reread stories, especially before a written retelling. Gail had taken the book and began to retell by looking at the pages. (Will review rules for unguided retellings at her next conference.) Keiko read the story and immediately began retelling. Shamir and Kevin read and then went to the library for a new book. Ms. Turner interacts: "Keiko, I like the way you reread, put away the book, and began to retell." Shamir and Kevin: "I'm glad you are picking a new book. Show me your retelling when it's done." To Anita, who seems to need to confirm what is to be done by talking about it, "I'm glad you use your contract to find out what to do. It's good to see what your friends are doing, too." Ms. Turner provided direct praise and told each child that he or she was engaging in appropriate behavior. Inappropriate behaviors, because they did not interfere with others, were ignored. Note: Story reading to group seemed to build Gail's confidence. She read easily, began written retelling, and smiled.

Children's Activities	Ms. Turner's Activities
Table III: Matthew, Solomon, Eshee, Cindy, Tanya, and Alicia	Ms. Turner noticed that Matthew took books after Solomon did. He watched Solomon pick up a book about crabs. Matthew picked up a science book too. Solomon noticed, and said, "Your topic is sports. Here are three books on that." Matthew took the *Pete Rose* book. He looked at the cover, then opened the book and held up his hand to use the fist-full-of-words rule. Solomon opened his notebook. He read the book and began to do a written retelling. Eshee found both books about China. "These are stories," he said to himself. As he got up he opened *Tales from Gold Mountain.* He stood at his table and read. A minute of reading went by and he sat down and continued. Tanya sat in her chair. She looked about, played with a toy bear, and scratched her eye. Alicia took *Newsweek,* and said, "Cindy, there's TV stuff in here." Cindy took *USA Today* after Alicia selected it, and said, "Stuff is in here too." Alicia seemed to use the index. She turned to a page and looked at pictures. Cindy turned each page of the paper, talking about the photos. Her talk did not seem to relate to TV. Solomon read and wrote. Tanya sat. Cindy seemed to read pictures in the newspaper. Alicia seemed to read the magazine. Matthew needed direction and then found a book. He demonstrated his knowledge of the self-selection strategy.
Newspaper "copy," as the children referred to it, was placed on the table. The group newspaper project was on its way. Copies of children's work were on the table. Each child was responsible for a topic. "Chinatown" was Eshee's topic. This would be the social studies column. Science was Solomon's favorite. He was not specific about his topic. Tanya could not decide. She chose *My Doctor* from the selection Ms. Turner presented. Alicia and Cindy decided they liked TV, and Matthew would write about sports. Ms. Turner put several books in the middle of the table. She had not marked each with a child's name. She hoped that each would seek one pertinent to the topic. Some of the books were: *Tales from Gold Mountain,* and *Mei Li* both for Eshee; *My Doctor* for Tanya; *Is This a House for a Hermit Crab?, Nessa's Fish, Under Your Feet,* and *The Story of The Seashore* were earmarked for Solomon. He could read these and a variety of science topics were represented by the titles. For Matthew Ms. Turner included, *How to Be a Good Basketball Player, I Can Read about Racing Cars, Pete Rose,* and the poetry book *Sports Pages.* She also left a *New York Times, USA Today, Newsweek,* and *Time Magazine.* Several copies of *Chickadee* were put with the newspapers. Children got their work baskets. Paper and pencils were put on the table by Ms. Turner. Some had their own project notebooks and pencil. Others took paper from the pile on the table.	

Children's Activities	Ms. Turner's Activities
Table IV: Antonio, Vincent, Eric, Brian, Tommie, Jason, and Michael	Ms. Turner knew that she could not observe and record the behaviors of this group today. She had only two eyes, one hand for writing and one brain for thinking about the children. She watched in-between the note taking for the other three groups. She remembered that:
Michael, Tommie, and Brian, upon entering the room, went for their work baskets. Antonio, Vincent, and Jason went to see Charlie, the gerbil. Antonio opened a notebook and began to talk and write. "Today, Charlie is still running on the wheel. He is running 10 times." The other two boys watched and talked about the gerbil. Jason moved to his work table. Vincent followed within two minutes. Antonio stayed for ten minutes and watched. He wrote and watched and wrote and watched for the entire time. Tommie and Brian took out their "Word Envelope." "I'll hold your word cards first, Brian," said Tommie. "Okay, but do them slow. Yesterday you went so fast I could hardly read them." Tommie put Brian's words on the table. He took one and "flashed" it toward him. "Spaghetti. Next one, please. Tuesday, Holy Communion, suit, splashed, dirty," etc. "Now it's my turn, Brian. You hold my cards." Tommie read words, and upon seeing one said, "I don't know that. Do you?" "Cracker Jacks." "Oh," said Tommie. "I don't like them even though I wrote it. I'm gonna throw it away." "I'll take it," said Brian. "I love them," he said, as he began to trace the letters and say the word simultaneously. The boys put the word cards down and found their section of the board, labeled with each of their names, to write their words. They wrote as many as they could before returning to their stacks to reread to recall the rest for writing. Vincent took his contract and wrote under "reading"— "Two chapters today." He picked up his *Encyclopedia Brown* book, took a pillow, propped it up against the corner wall, and began to read.	• Jason, for the first time, directed his behavior. • Tommie began working without teacher motivation as previously noted. • Antonio's notes should be checked. Did he really look and write about it? • Vincent needed prompts to begin to retell independently.

Modified from Glazer, S. M., & Burke, E. M. (1994). *An integrated approach to early literacy: Literature to language.* Boston, MA: Allyn & Bacon, Reprinted with permission.

Ms. Turner had walked through the room, talking—nurturing her children into literacy. Some were immersed; others were not. Some stayed on task for long periods of time; others did not. Some children sat at their tables and wrote; others sat on the floor. Some sharpened pencils three times before beginning their written retelling; others wrote immediately. Children worked individually; others worked in pairs. There was a low even humming of children's voices throughout the two-hour period. Shamir told Habbiba about his birthday party as he wrote his retelling. Gail showed Anita the "big girl" book that she could read. Anita continued to draw her picture, almost ignoring Gail's show-and-tell. Kevin skipped over to Derick's table three times to ask him how to spell the word *frog*. Derick finally took a 4- by 7-inch word card and wrote it for him. Keiko and Melissa read the words in their word bank envelope to each other. Keika wrote hers on the chalkboard and Melissa checked to see if they were written correctly. Matthew and Solomon took a prop bag and the *Berenstein Bears* book that was inside. Both put on the bear hat and mittens. Matthew read one page while Solomon read the other. Both boys check the box on their contract that indicated that they had engaged in reading that morning. Ms. Turner began individual conferences. She carried out three oral retelling sessions. Children told, and she recorded their retellings on tape. She would transcribe them that evening and carry out a self-monitoring conference before the end of the week. Ms. Turner gathered five of the children together who needed guidance in understanding how to create words using a spelling pattern. A seven-minute spelling game helped these youngsters add words to their word banks. Each wrote at least five new words that rhymed. Shamir called them "it" words. He wrote four. They were "fit," "sit," "kit" and "bit." Randy read a story to her doll in the drama center. It was one she had written herself. Solomon used the fist-full-of-words rule, selected a book, and, for the first time, attempted to use the prediction sheet. Ms. Turner saw this and, when she was free, went over to him and said, "Solomon, how wonderful! You selected your book using the rule and wrote a prediction sheet." Allison disagreed with Sarah about which Halloween costume would be the best. Twenty-four six- and seven-year-old children knew how to proceed at the beginning of the school day. They learned from modeled behavior and direct instruction. Ms. Turner understood the characteristics of six- and seven-year-olds. She knew six-year-olds were more fun but went to opposite extremes. They loved one moment and hated the next. They would cooperate at times, but hated to be wrong. Her seven-year-olds were a bit more reserved. They had quieted down after their first year. While six-year-olds were the focus of their world and active—sometimes aggressive, her seven-year-olds tended to be thoughtful, sensitive to the needs of others, and even withdrawn. More seven-year-olds used the "places to be alone with books" than six-year-olds. Sometimes the teacher was concerned but remembered that next year would bring more expansive behaviors. Six-year-olds were eager for all of the new experiences provided in this wonderful classroom. Their warm expressions of affection demonstrated their delight. Seven-year-olds were more serious in their approach to activities.

And growth continues . . .

A Model of Learning Supporting Student-Centered Classrooms

Teachers, eager to create student-centered classrooms, need knowledge of human development and learning processes in order to support curriculum decisions (Glazer & Burke, 1994). Teachers who understand developmental theory view their role as being much like that of a coach. They provide opportunities for students to—(1) observe models of desired behaviors and, (2) partially participate in the activity with guidance. The partial participation results from the learner's requests to be involved. After the instruction (modeling and partial participation), (3) rehearsal in an attempt to achieve some mastery occurs, and (4) performing the skills is the end result. The four-stage learning process—(1) observation, (2) partial participation, (3) rehearsal or role play, and (4) performance—created by Don Holdaway (1979) replicates, as much as possible, the natural learning processes of most humans. An illustration follows of how this model functions in a journal writing activity.

Stage 1.   You want your children to keep journals. So each morning when they arrive you model the behavior. You sit at a table and write in your journal. You greet the children, but you continue to write and they **observe** your actions. The continued behavior models for the children the actions that you hope they will be inspired to follow.

Stage 2.   One morning, a youngster approaches and says, "What are you doing?" "Come over here, and see my journal. I write in it every day. Look (as you flip to a specific page), I went to my cousin's house and she baked a cake that reminded me of my grandmother's. Here's what I wrote." The teacher puts her arm around the child's shoulder as she reads her journal aloud:

> I got these funny feelings that reminded me of my grandma when I tasted my cousin's cake. It almost tasted like my grandmother's. The taste of the cake reminded me of my grandmother's hair. It was long, and very thin. She braided it every morning. When she stayed at home and baked, she let the braid hang down her back. But, when she went out, she rolled the braid into a knot and pinned it at the base of her neck. The smell of my cousin's cake made me sad, because I miss my grandmother and the smell reminded me of her.

"I want to write in a journal too," remarks the child. This is the time to engage the youngster by guiding her into **partially participating** in the journal writing experience. "Here's a journal with your name on it, Lisa," might be one way to facilitate the activity. Providing the child with the journal and then sitting next to her coaches Lisa into the activity. "What should I write about?" might be answered with, "Well, on another page I wrote about my friend who came to visit me the other day. See, here it is." The teacher reads to the child:

> Sandy came to visit me. I hadn't seen her in twenty years. I remember all of the good times we had when we shared a room in college. She was the smart one, and she helped me with all of my papers. We talked about the time that I got an A on my paper and thought that the teacher made a mistake. We laughed and realized how much fun we had and how wonderful it was seeing each other again.

Modeling journal writing or any other activity invites involvement. When she asks for assistance, for example, "How do you spell" a specific word, you write it on a word card, a paper four by seven inches, and hand it to her. You are providing instruction when it is needed. When a child points to a word during reading a text and you tell it to him, you are coaching while both of you partially participate in the actions. The desire to learn, the coaching, and the interactions "hook" the children into journal writing, and reading more.

Stage 3.   This is the time that youngsters role play or rehearse without adult intervention. The adult may be in the room, but the child is engaged independently, as if the adult (the bonded mentor-teacher or parent) were not present. Time for rehearsal needs to be built into class schedules. Journal writing can be scheduled during the language arts time block (Chapter 4, p. 40). It might also occur first thing in the morning and also when time permits.

Stage 4.   This is **performance.** The youngster may say, when she reaches this stage, "Mrs. Turner, listen to what I wrote in my journal." Seize the moment, and attend to the child's performance. Performance times can be spontaneous or scheduled. When children share productions, learning comes full circle. The youngster assumes the role of the teacher, modeling for others the desired behavior.

The student-centered, student-driven learning model demands that educators create environments conducive to alternatives—alternative use of time, learning abilities and styles, learning strategies, and more. When students (rather than mandated content) are the focus of instruction, the desire to learn about anything is intense and powerful.

Managing Alternative Classroom Assessment as Instruction

Twenty years of development in our Center for Reading and Writing at Rider University has resulted in a management system that seems to work for all students. It evolved after eleven years of experimentation, and many failures. Our definitive management system has changed local public perceptions about the validity of alternative assessments, and student-driven curriculum. Students and their parents observe vividly illustrated, well-defined accounts of their children's academic growth, self-esteem, and desire to read and write. Our small group setting is perfect for developing the portfolio management system that is now used by hundreds of teachers with twenty-five (25) and more students. It functions exceptionally well in departmentalized situations where classes are often limited to forty minutes. It's successful because students know how to organize, discuss, and manage their work and work habits systematically.

Portfolio systems have become popular supplements, and in some places alternatives, to traditional grades, test scores, and report cards. The attempt to personalize and make displays of growth realistic have inspired a nation to include them in classrooms. These hands-on illustrations of products collected over time demonstrate changes and growth in skills.

The portfolios developed in our Center are different than most, for they function as an organizing agent for students. We have found that our system works because the portfolios are:

- systematic collections of student work;

- vehicles for ongoing assessment managed by students;

- self-evalution tools for students to discover "what they've learned," and "what they need" to learn;

- self-management vehicles for literacy and all content area studies;

- easy to explain and understand for laypersons as well as professional educators.

The portfolios are explicit, specific, and connected to instructional procedures. They provide descriptive pictures and interpretations of children's growth. They "paint" a realistic picture of children's interactions in school. Students are able to describe their accomplishments and provide the data to support the descriptors.

Standardized test scores provide comparative information in ways descriptive data cannot. The results of *a* single test can be pieces of the data that make up a portfolio. This is important in many places, for tests and their scores satisfy a portion of the population whose notions about these instruments remain firm. The descriptive data from portfolios often helps to confirm test scores. Confirming test scores with "seeable, touchable, hands-on" products supports the use of student work as proof of achievement. The reduced importance of scores to connote achievement will continue as systemic, sophisticated alternative assessment procedures develop.

A Management System for Assessment That IS Instruction

Our management system arms students with the tools needed to observe their growth and manage the content of learning simultaneously. The tools provide language for discussions and descriptions of student products and knowledge of processes they use in order to produce these. The portfolio (often referred to as "my folder") is divided into four categories: (1) comprehension, (2) composition, (3) vocabulary and language study, and (4) independence.

Comprehension

Comprehension is defined by Durkin (1993) as "the essence of reading." It is, however, much more. "Comprehension is a process in which a reader constructs meaning [by] interacting with text . . . through a combination of prior knowledge and previous experiences; information available in text; the essence [taken] in relationship to the text; and immediate, remembered, or anticipated social interactions and communications" (Ruddell, Ruddell, & Singer, 1994, p. 93). "The click of comprehension occurs only when the reader evolves a schema [an organized structure, or plan] that explains the whole message" (Anderson, 1994, p. 473). So readers who "click" know something about the content they read so they can fit it into their own structure. One seven-year-old defined comprehension as, "That's the things I can tell you that I know about."

Students get information when they read, and also when they hear and view texts, events, and experiences. They respond to the data, often producing oral, written, two- or three-dimensional products that identify what is learned (their comprehension), and what is needed. So comprehension, a term generally associated with literacy learning, applies to all activities.

The first section originally labeled "Reading" is now "Comprehension." Included are those products related to things students read. The name of this section of the portfolio emerged after eleven years, for we discovered that anything one reads, sees, hears, or touches and tastes must be understood. If it is not, there is little evidence that effective reading is occurring. As our knowledge of children's interactions with text grew, the section became known as "comprehension." This seemed to encompass a broader meaning of the activities—the "essence" of all activity. Children began to include written retellings of a book chapter. Our teachers also discovered that children included tape recordings of their response to data collected on a field trip. Science projects, which included observations of plants growing, ants building their tunnels in an ant farm, and observations of aspects of the solar system were also appropriately placed in this portfolio section by the children themselves. Students' perceptions of the "reading comprehension" process resulted in ideas extending beyond their teachers' perceptions. The untainted, unencumbered responses to their actions guided the students' definition of their actions.

The comprehension section of our literacy portfolio includes current works in progress, all of which are responses to things students hear, see, and read about. The section also includes student responses to comprehension strategies they learned to use in functional settings. Most unique about our portfolios is the fact that there are self-monitoring tools for every type of comprehension activity. Students produce the products using learning strategies, and learn what they know and need to learn. They find out about their strengths and needs using self-assessment strategies. Learning how to understanding is a byproduct of self-monitoring strategies. It is an integral part of our actions, and is organized in the "comprehension" section of the folders.

Composition

"In the beginning" we named this section "writing." Like most people, we used this word to define text as it appeared in print. Over time the label changed to "composition" to encompass all products. The desire to confirm the appropriateness of the label led me to review the definitions of both terms.

According to *The Literacy Dictionary* (Harris & Hodges, 1995) "writing" is defined as "the process or result of recording language graphically by hand or other means, as by letters, logograms, and other symbols" (p. 284). Composition is "the structure or organization of a work of art, music, or literature" (p. 38). A second definition, "the process or result of arranging ideas to form a clear and unified impression in order to create an effective message" (p. 39), describes what we want students to be able to accomplish when they compose.

Students demonstrate their learning when creating text. Often the text is written using conventional print—letters and words. But ideas are arranged and delivered orally, in graphically artistic forms, and musically. A choreographer delivers her creative composition through dance, and a painter uses canvas. An argument for self-monitoring is to provide students with alternative ways for each to demonstrate accomplishments effectively. The "composition" section of the literacy portfolio includes "writing," and also productions that are "composed" by students in response to reading. This means that students often decide to have a copy of a product in both the composition and comprehension sections. The focus of the self-monitoring activities helps students decide where products belong. An original story written by and modeled after one the student has read are often in both portfolio sections. When in the composition section, the focus is generally on assessing the effectiveness of the student's writing efforts. When placed in the comprehension side of the folder, the focus is based on how many of the story elements there are and how well they are include the story.

A nine-year-old defined the products in the composition section as "the stuff I write myself. Sometimes I tell the stuff, but that's writing too. When you think of it on your own and don't copy it from anybody, it's a composition." Products in this section include original stories or poems and research reports, but also a symphony, a story told through pictures, a slide presentation, and more. Consideration for the major forms of composition—argumentation, description, exposition, and narration—are suggested as subcategories within this section.

Vocabulary and Language Study

Understanding the elements of language can be awesome. Semantics (the meanings), syntax (the grammatical rules that govern sentences), and phonology (the study of the sounds of language) all come together when we speak. Understanding how this happens, however, requires the study of language itself, as content. Moffett and Wagner (1992) say, "You don't have to 'teach' these kinds of discourse [in the usual way]. They will teach themselves if you lay them out as a repertory of activities and materials, as a cornucopia to feast upon" (p. 263). Children need to play with letters and words, creating and manipulating combinations of these in order to understand how words, phrases, and sentences are made. Students need to play with sentence constructions so they can use these units to create larger language units.

When we study how letters make words, we study the spellings and punctuations of language. We study the derivations of words. We guide youngsters to understand homophones and homographs, portmanteau words, compound words, onomatopoeia, prefixes and suffixes, phonograms, clipped words, synonyms, collective nouns, and more. Language study involves learning vocabulary associated with content areas, including mathematics, science, social studies, health and safety, to name a few. Children need to learn that there are certain words that create exciting descriptions. They benefit from learning how words are derived. Using idiomatic expressions, contractions, words derived from Greek and Latin roots, and other word categories, they find ways to write, spell, talk, and type text that emulates their knowledge about language. The goal for students, when they play with and manipulate these word forms, is language creativity. The skilled "player" becomes a skilled "wordsmith," crafting language for effective communication.

Tools for self-monitoring knowledge of spelling, punctuation, word usage, and meanings guide children to assess and rework those aspects of vocabulary and language study necessary to craft quality text. This section of the portfolio guides students to self-monitor, and then "clean-up," create, and revise aspects of language important for sharing composed products with audiences of peers and adults.

Independence (Self-Monitoring)

Among the biggest challenges are (1) managing the paper work, and (2) scheduling individual conferences with children in classes of twenty-five or more. Teachers often ask, "How can I meet individual needs and also get through 'required curriculum'?"

Concerns about personalizing instruction are important, for quality education is that which accommodates each child's needs. In order for teachers to accommodate each child, the student must provide the energy necessary for learning. Moffett and Wagner (1992) refer to that energy as will. "Will is the energy that drives learning. It is personal force taking the direction of some intent" (p. 21).

A young man who had been to our Center for more than a year was unable to either read written text or write it. He had many syndromes associated with dyslexia, and the condition frustrated and disillusioned his thoughts about school and learning. "I really like to learn stuff," he shared, "but I give up because it's so hard." The boy's teacher realized that although he couldn't write, he was able to retell stories he'd seen on television. He also retold and interpreted ideas that had been read to him. The student was able to listen to and retain information. His will to learn, however, was diminished because of the demand to demonstrate learning in written form, and to get information through print. The child's motivation just disappeared.

I have learned that motivation is a driving force for learning. When impediments stand in its way, the will to labor to learn is destroyed. Without will, the need that forces each of us to achieve doesn't exist.

The teacher discovered that reading books onto tape, and providing the youngster with the tape and a copy of the book was successful. It seemed that when he heard the language and followed along in the text, he was able to demonstrate what he knew. Text production through dictation proved to be the spark that enticed the boy back to learning. The teacher's ability to find a way to empower the student with the will to learn illustrates the accommodation of individual differences.

Advocates of alternative assessment plead for individualization (accommodating differences) for learners. Individualization seems to guide students to understand that they have the power to make decisions in classrooms. Not only did the youngster struggling with dyslexia become empowered with a way to respond, but he began to make his own decisions about what to learn, justifying each decision. The ability to make decisions depends on a need to take responsibility for actions. In the past, textbook authors have made decisions concerning what students will read and learn. When adult authors and teachers decide the contents of learning, standardized tests can easily be used as vehicles for illustrating student performance. This paradigm—adult-selected materials and assessment tools—however, creates dependent learners. These learners strive to please adults, not themselves. The activities and the will to learn do not belong to them, making the entire learning and assessment system arbitrary.

"The argument against student choice is usually that youngsters don't know what there is to choose from or how to make wise decisions" (Moffett & Wagner, 1992, p. 22). The result of any system where people choose for others is the inability of a large part of the population to make wise decisions. If "practice makes perfect," then making productive decisions requires rehearsal.

Portfolio management requires decision making. Contracts between children and teachers, and reading logs (see Chapter 4, p. 46) are self-monitoring tools where individual and joint decisions are made. These guides, used routinely by students, support self-regulation of activities and time. Reviewing and recording daily progress also develops self-monitoring skills. The Progress Report Form in Figure 5-2 has been successfully used with children and adults—those who are average, gifted, and

Progress Report Form

Your Name:_____Today's Date:_____

Your Teacher's Name:_____Your Age:_____

Comprehension____Composition___Vocabulary____Independence_____

What I Can Do	What I Need	My Teacher's Job

Figure 5-2. Progress Report Form

those with special needs. Guiding children to learn to keep records of their progress, "what they know," and "what they need to learn," can be tedious and time consuming, but the results are rewarding.

Beginning to Use the Progress Report Form

Ms. Rossi habitually reviewed with her class what the children learned from an activity. She'd prepare an easel at childrens' eye-level and gather the children together at the completion of each activity to summarize and review learnings. Each youngster was provided with a copy of the Progress Report Form posted on the easel. The teacher knew the importance of providing a model for children to observe. She also realized that it was important to encourage the children, as suggested by Holdaway (1979), to partially participate in the process. The following conversation occurred after the children had released butterflies that were nurtured from the caterpillar stage to the mature butterfly state.

Ms. Rossi: Gosh, it was exciting to see the butterflies fly away. I was really surprised at how they fluttered their wings.

Tim: Yeah! It looked like they were clapping, like you clap your hands.

Ms. Rossi: Oh, that's a wonderful observation, Tim. You were able to describe, in words, what you saw. I am going to write this on your Progress Report Form (writes as she says), What did you learn about the butterflies' wings, Tim?

Tim: I learned that—

Ms. Rossi: Slowly, so that I can write it down.

Tim: I learned that the butterfly claps his wings when he flies away.

Ms. Rossi: You can write it down on your Progress Report Form when I write, if you'd like. What else did you all learn?

Theresa: I learned that they stay in the box a long time before they get out.

Ms. Rossi: Slowly, Theresa, so I can write it all down.

Theresa: They stay in the box a long time before they get away (Ms. Rossi writes "get away," rather than "get out," since it's Theresa's last contribution).

Ms. Rossi: What else did you learn? (Calls on child who raises her hand) Sarah. (Ms. Rossi motions with hands to talk slowly)

Sarah: Well, I learned that it takes three weeks for the cocoons to open.

Ms. Rossi: You guys can write it on your Progress Report Form as I write on mine (she repeats Sarah's contribution slowly as she writes). It takes three weeks for the cocoons to open.

Tahisa: And they eat sugar water.

Ms. Rossi: (Talking as she writes), And they eat sugar water.

Ms. Rossi continued to take dictation. She used the form as she hoped the students would use it. She knew that she was modeling the use of the form, and that she was also guiding children to understand the relationship between speech and print.

How to Continue

Begin by reviewing regularly and asking students "what they learned." They ought to be recording achievements on personal Progress Report Forms. Be sure that each child has a copy of the form mounted on a clipboard or other hard surface to make writing easy.

The second step is to break the group into smaller units. The maximum number of children in these small units should not exceed six. Proceed by asking, "What did you learn today?" This time, move from child to child, encouraging each, one at a time to share specifically what was accomplished. When the child volunteers information, say, "Write it down on your progress report form." When a student hesitates, probe by asking questions that encourage answers. Say, for example, "Open your portfolio to the comprehension section. Take out today's retelling. Tell me what you retold." If the student cannot, for some reason, respond, coach the youngster by providing the words for him. You might say, for example, "You read." Slow down, and look at the child at eye level, coaching him to tell the name of the book, which ought to be in front of him. "What did you do?" If the child still does not say, "I read (says name of book)," tell him the name, and ask, "What did you read?" If he does not answer, say, "You read (insert name of the book). Say it with me . . ." Feed the words to the youngster, encouraging him to repeat each, almost as if you were a chorus. Continue to coach the child to echo your words, when necessary. Many teachers often begin by asking, "Do you remember when we did . . .?" DON'T begin by asking, "Do you remember . . .?" If a youngster remembered, or was able to contribute without the teacher's assistance, he would.

Christopher's teacher began by encouraging him to talk about the information. She wrote the first form, and after several tries, Chris began to write his own. His teacher assisted him and, eventually, with coaching he and others were able to complete forms on their own. Figures 5-3 to 5-5 illustrate growth from the first form completed by the teacher to one completed by the student.

Progress Report Form

Your Name: Christopher _____ Today's Date: Lissa

Your Teacher's Name: 10/14 _____ Your Age: _____

Comprehension ✓ Composition___Vocabulary____Independence___

What You Can Do	What You Need	My Teacher's Job
You can work in Your reading response journal about the things you feel when you read a story or chapter	You need to do this with books you read on your own, not just the ones I read to you.	I need to provide This as part of Your daily Contract
You can retell a story on paper and fill out a self-monitoring retelling guide sheet You can do this on your own.	You need to do This on your own. You need to get The retelling sheet Then you need to have a conference with me.	I need to be sure there are retelling sheets for you. I need to schedule a conference.

Figure 5-3. Christopher's Progress Report Form

Progress Report Form

Your Name: Christopher,   Today's Date: 7/13

Your Teacher's Name: Lissa   Your Age: _____

Comprehension____ Composition ✓ Vocabulary____ Independence ~~Writing~~

What I Can Do	What I Need	My Teacher's Job
write my report and print it out	topic pereid paper	
I can write about butterflies Lissa 7/13	caterpillar	We need to go over the writing process
You can write a rough draft by talking information that you wrote on your file cards, organize them and create paragraphs based on topics.	You need to begin to edit your writing. You begin filling out an about my writing sheet You need to finish filling it out.	I need to have a mini lesson about editing & your prior knowledge about editing

Figure 5-4.   Christopher's Progress Report Form

Progress Report Form   7/10/96

Student: Jessica Jones   Teacher: JoAnn

Time Period: From: _____ To: _____

Area (Check one or more)   Comprehension ✓   Composition ✓

Vocabulary ✓   Independence ✓   Other _____

What I can do	What I need	My teacher's job
Comprehension:		
- I previewed + predicted what would happen in my book using the back of it.	- Practice previewing more	- Remind me to use the sheet every time I start a new book.
Composition:		
- I put my work together + looked at what I was going to start with for my research project	- I need to start putting more things together + organize it better	- she can help me start organizing my project
- I can make up a story	- More guidlines on a creative story	- give me more guidlines for writing a story
- I can observe butterflys or ants	- I need to keep on reporting	
Vocabulary:		
- I used the spelling workshop	I need to practice the other words now	- give us new pgs. so we can do the other words
- I can also use Modified Fernald.		
Independence:		
- I can write up what I did each day	- I need to add more details sometime	- keep telling us to use the form

Figure 5-5. Jessica's Progress Report Form

Using the Portfolio to Merge Instruction and Assessment

In classrooms that support personalized, self-monitoring activities, students need tools for building independence and a sense of responsibility for their own learning. Children need to know (1) what they've learned, and (2) what they still need to learn. They need to be able to ascertain when they need their teacher, and when they are able to solve problems by themselves. There need to be places to work alone, with small and large groups, and spaces for displaying student products and information. There must be places for children to discuss ideas and observations. Easy-to-keep pets—ant and butterfly farms, gerbils, turtles, frogs, and garden snakes—are important for guiding the development of both self-monitoring and observational skills. Children as caregivers to these pets have a functional reason to learn how to observe likenesses and differences. They also learn how to use descriptors to define these in written form. Most important, youngsters learn responsibility by acting as parents, caregivers, and nurturing supporters of living things. Growing crystals, plants, roots, moss, and other plant life also provides reasons to learn observational and descriptive skills.

Materials must be available and easily accessible for students at all times. Learning strategy sheets need a permanent place for easy access. The four sections of the portfolio: (1) comprehension, (2) composition, (3) vocabulary and language study, and (4) independence and self-monitoring (or whatever you choose to name sections of the portfolio) are logical designations for filing student products and organizing strategy sheets. We created bin-like containers with Lucite fronts and hung them on the wall in the Center's halls and on walls in classrooms, at childrens' eye-level. We refer to these as "strategy bins." Each self-monitoring sheet has its own labeled slot. The sheets are grouped into sections as they are in the portfolio. Another less expensive but effective procedure for keeping sheets in the classroom is to post manila envelopes on a bulletin board or wall in the classroom. Attach a copy of the enclosed worksheets on the front, arranging the envelopes in categories as in the portfolio. The importance of consistent language and organizational procedures is paramount for guiding students to build schemata necessary for becoming independent learners. All student products, assignments, and strategy sheets are filed in the working portfolio. (See Figure 5-6.)

Constructing and Storing Portfolios

Two-pocket folders fastened together with staples, or a plastic bookbinder are most versatile. They fit easily into desks, bookbags, and lay flat on tabletops. Accordion folders also make wonderful portfolios, especially when students choose to add subsections. Often teachers prepare the portfolio for each student before school begins. Included in the portfolio, even before the student uses it, are the following:

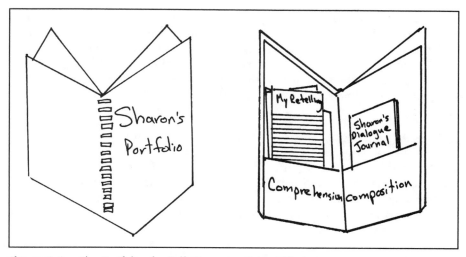

Figure 5-6.   The Portfolios for Self-Managing School Work

Comprehension section—a notebook labeled "literature journal," a reading log, a progress report form, and a poem or short story that will be of particular interest to that child. The content journal can also be filed in this section, especially if students use it to retell and reflect about what they've read in their content area subjects (Chapter 6).

Composition section—the dialogue journal, formula poetry strategy sheets, creative writing journals, working drafts of science and social studies projects, as well as other original texts are included here. Letters to be sent or those received might also be filed here. Individual mailboxes or slots, however, are suggested for each student in the classroom.

Vocabulary and word and language study—spelling; word study including prefixes, suffixes, or word roots belong in this section. An envelope labeled "My Word Bank" for younger children and a notebook titled "Spelling Assignments" for older students is needed for collecting spelling words. Phonics, content vocabulary study, punctuation, editing—any content dealing with the study of language—ought to be categorized in the vocabulary and language study of the portfolio (Chapter 8).

Independence and self-monitoring pocket—a daily schedule, a contract prepared for the student, a reading log sheet, and a personal schedule (see pp. 40–63).

Many students create subdivisions in each section. Some have several sections under vocabulary and language study labeled, for example, "spelling words," "roots," "prefixes and suffixes." Others include several sections in the comprehension section as well. Comprehension materials for science, social studies, as well as literature belong here, since students respond to things they read and hear. When students subdivide portfolio categories, they demonstrate their ability to take a system and make it their own.

Introducing the Portfolio

You can arrange the students' portfolios in a box in alphabetical order. The portfolios may also be placed at each student's desk. Whichever way you choose, have the folders ready when students come into your classroom the very first morning of the school year. Create one for yourself and put it with the students'—in the box of portfolios—or on your desk.

The First Day of School*

Ms. Rossi had prepared a name tag for each youngster. She put them on a table in alphabetical order according to each child's first name, near the door. As the third graders came into the room, she sat at the conference table, writing in her dialogue journal. The table was visible from the corridor. She continued to write as each youngster approached, glancing, however, at each student. Her actions informed them that she was doing something important, but that they were important too. "Good morning. So glad we're in the same class. I'm just about finished writing in my dialogue journal. There is a box of portfolios on the shelf," she continued, pointing to the portfolios filed alphabetically. "They are in alphabetical order. Look for yours alphabetically, using your first name. There's a note for you in your dialogue journal." She closed her journal when half of the children had been seated, and most of the others were in the classroom. She filed her journal in the appropriate portfolio section and closed it. She began to move around the room from student to student. "Oh, I'm glad to see that you found your portfolio. Here is your dialogue journal, Jim. It's in the composition section of the portfolio. I wrote something in it for you." "Tiffany," she said as she put her arm on the child's shoulder, "there is a letter for you in your mailbox." Ms. Rossi knew, from reading a note in Tiffany's records that she owned a horse. "I know that you love horses, so I clipped an article about Shetland ponies and

---

*If teachers meet children at the door of the auditorium or any place other than the classroom, have name tags with you, and give one to each student. Have portfolios on tables, and direct children to get theirs. Model an activity (dialogue journal, if you choose), and continue as Ms. Rossi does, once children settle in their seats.

put it in your letter, too." Ms. Rossi put Cynthia McFarland's *Hoofbeats: The Story of a Thoroughbred* and *Album of Horses* by Marguerite Henry (both preteen novels) in her classroom library. Her note to Tiffany in the dialogue journal referred to those books, and where to find them.

Personally directed comments and suggestions were provided for each student and continued until all of the children were seated and involved with the portfolio, the mailbox, and other individual activities. Ms. Rossi moved about the room, observing the children in an attempt to get to know each a little bit better. When she talked to a child, she tried to personalize her conversations based on their specific interests. As she passed them in the classroom, she'd often talk about an activity, mentioning the section in the portfolio in which it was filed. This continuously brought the management system to the children's attention. Her technique, guiding children into functional activities when there was a purpose, was always successful. She used the time to assess student needs. She always asked herself questions about childrens' behaviors as she moved about the room. This first day, she asked:

- How long will it take for Billy to begin to use his portfolio?

- I wonder if Chloe always gets down to work immediately?

- I wonder what strategy will keep Brian from poking his pencil on other childrens' desks?

She'd answer these questions by writing observational notes about what she saw. After fifteen minutes of hustle and bustle of language activity, Ms. Rossi noticed that some children were reading the message she'd written in their dialogue journals. Others were asking peers to identify words that they didn't know. Some children found their mailboxes, their letter, and were reading it. Others found the stationery on the supply shelf, and responded to the note on their letters which said, "Please write back." Tiffany approached Ms. Rossi about horse books. The child was immediately directed to the classroom library, which included 75 books, three per child. The book selections were made based on children's interests, reading ability, content area studies, and genre. Poetry, mystery, nonfiction (information books), fairy tales, short chapter books (including the *Babysitter's Club* series and *Something Queer* series of books) were also included. All of the children adored the *Goosebumps* books by R. L. Stine, so Ms. Rossi put at least ten of these on the library shelves. Ms. Rossi enticed other children into books in ways similar to those used by Ms. Turner (see pp. 77–81).

Twenty minutes had passed since school began. Ms. Rossi moved herself to a carpeted area prepared for class conversations. She sat in a chair, and motioned to the children to come to the rug. Several responded, and within minutes all the children had gathered.

Ms. Rossi's (1) personalized preparation, (2) modeled activities, and (3) walking from child to child facilitating activity helped her assess student needs. Her walks around the classroom exemplify one way to begin personalized instruction and assessment. From the beginning of the school year, she illustrated, through actions, the value of the individual. She also demonstrated the importance of group management and organization by putting the portfolio into the hands of each youngster immediately. The frameworks for learning—contracts, progress report forms, reading log sheets—were the same for all, but messages were specific to each student. She was able to do this because she carefully reviewed each child's records from previous teachers, spoke to people in the children's lives (the school custodian, nurse, cook, athletic teachers, art, music, drama teachers, and parents, siblings, etc.) in order to learn relevant specifics about each.

A poster labeled "Conference Sign Up" hung at student eye-level in a central location in the room. A photocopy of the sign-up form was reproduced and placed in the independence section of the portfolio. The routine activities were listed on the form for each of the children. Also scheduled were special small group work times for certain boys and girls. Ms. Rossi pointed out the chart to children as they walked by. She mentioned, casually, that there was one just like it in the portfolio.

Her casual, yet deliberate delivery guided students individually to take responsibility for their actions. Repeating the same information (i.e., "there's a letter for you in your mailbox") to many children in a short period of time, helped many of them to remember, understand, and get involved. Repetition informed children of the importance of messages. Ms. Rossi began each of her days in a similar fashion. She would

- be involved with an activity in order to *model* behavior

- invite children to *partially participate* as she modeled

- circulate through the room, as children *rehearsed* activities

- provide time for them to get together to *share, collaborate,* and *confirm* learning

Next Step to Begin

Continue to personalize the morning activities. Then identify, with children, those routines that they can carry out daily on their own. These include the dialogue journals, content and literature journals, the reading log, the progress report forms, and letter writing. Remind children when they say, "What can I do now?" to "Look at your contract," or say, "What do you think you can do?" If hesitant, coach by saying, "You can write in your dialogue journal, or read your book and retell what you remember, and then respond to the story in your literature journal." Review these and other options routinely. The important thing is that the same activities are engaged in routinely so independence and confidence can be built.

Some Principles So Basic, We Never Think About Them

There are some language behaviors that we take for granted. They are the routine things—the mortar or glue—that connect one activity to the next in classrooms. Our very "self" and the interactions we facilitate with children ARE a significant aspect of "the mortar or glue" of instruction. Our tone of voice and physical gestures make a difference in students' feelings about school and learning. The way we carry ourselves from one area of the room to another inscribes the classroom with expectations. Students have access to learning based on their feelings and sense of security about the environment. Each student keeps a record in his/her mind about adult responses to behaviors, building personal schemata and self-expectations. Each student's schemata determine each's accessibility to learning. If they understand expectations, they acquire the power to make choices.

Imagine, for example, that a teacher raises her voice each time a child responds spontaneously. The child who is stressed by the raised voice knows to speak only when raising her hand. The child predicts the expected teacher behavior and avoids the discomfort it presents. Although negative, the student can expect a specific behavior because it is consistently predictable. Although this situation may be alarming, more alarming are inconsistent teacher behaviors.

Ms. McLore's classroom behaviors were inconsistent. She wasn't cognizant of the fact that she responded differently in similar situations. Sometimes, when a child left her seat without asking permission, it seemed fine. At other times, this same behavior resulted in punishment. "I told you," she shouted to one boy, "never to leave your chair without raising your hand." When the child said, "But, Theresa just got up!" Ms. McLore responded, "Don't talk back to me." Her response indicated that she viewed the child's observation as threatening. Although all of the interactions were unhealthy and unproductive, the inconsistency was most damaging. Children are unable to develop schemata for behaviors when teacher responses are inconsistent.

Building Healthy Environments to Facilitate Literacy Learning

Building trust in the environment is the backbone for healthy classrooms. Students gain access to trusting feelings when access to any activity, book, person, materials, or method is available at all times. The routine activities discussed in Chapter 4 are accessible. Children know when they may engage in them, how to proceed, and also know the sort of response they can expect for their efforts. The consistency built through daily routine activities empowers students. Students learn the constraints they are expected to live by in the classroom. Constraints include the use of direct praise (p. 41); consistent time schedules (p. 40); consistent use of language (p. 42); and the consistent use of contracts and progress report forms to regulate, review, and record strengths and needs. Important, too, is for teachers to become aware of the oral language used when:

- we ask children to begin work or stop working;
- we seek information from youngsters;
- children attempt to interrupt to meet a need;
- we praise or reprimand children for their actions;
- children negotiate with each other to solve problems.

Asking Children to Begin or Stop Working

Make a date with yourself to listen to an adult ask a child to carry out an activity. Most of the time you will probably hear, "Jennifer, do you want to come over here and read with me?" Jennifer has the option of saying either "yes" or "no" to this question. She was presented with an option that was really not an option at all. For some unknown reasons, adults often ask questions that suggest an option is available when students have no choice. Quizzical investigation among teachers into this behavior led me to believe that many do this because it sounds polite. Others noted their hesitation to "teacher-direct" children. This approach seemed less controlling. Students, especially those with special needs, must be told what to do, how to do it, and when it should be done (McDaniel, 1986). Ambivalent requests like the one above initiate feelings of dishonesty, resulting in distrust. Wallace and Kaufman (1986) support my findings. ALL children respond best when we are direct—we tell, don't ask. When you want a student to do something, tell him to do it. The statement, "John, come here for a retelling conference. Bring your retelling with you," is definitive and direct. There is no room for choice, and therefore, no room for confusion.

Seeking Information from Students

"Whenever I ask him what he did in school, he always says, nothing," remarked one parent. "When I ask a child to retell the story he read, I have a difficult time getting him started. Once he starts, I have a difficult time getting him to continue," said one of our teachers. Getting children to talk seems to be a concern. Once they begin, getting them to continue is also a puzzlement. Often we hear adults attempt to encourage youngsters to continue, and say, "What else do you have to say?" Sometimes I've heard, "Do you want to share anything else?" This type of question seems to encourage children to say "No." "What else," and "Do you want to share?" seem to be stoppers. They encourage negative responses rather than facilitate the creation of oral text. Phyllis Fantauzzo, the school psychologist in our Center, in her interactions with reluctant "talkers" discovered that

- repeating the last three words that a child said, and then saying, "a-n-d" with a raised voice acts as a catalyst for children, young and old, to continue talking.

Six-year-old Geoffrey brought a toy motorcycle to school for show and tell. His courage to get up in front of the group and share ideas orally took a long time to muster up. He lowered his head and, in a very timid-sounding voice, confirmed his hesitations about the situation. He began with, "This is a man on a motorcycle," and started moving away from the front of the room as if to go back to his seat. His teacher softly but with a firm voice said, "A man on a motorcycle, a-n-d . . . ?" Geoffrey stopped moving and continued, "A-n-d he has on a black suit." His teacher said, "A black suit, a-n-d . . . ?" "He has on a helmet," said the child. "Has on a helmet a-n-d . . . ?" repeated the teacher. "And he has black pants," Geoffrey said definitively. "He has black pants and . . . ?" said his teacher. "And," continued Geoffrey, "And, that's all!" Geoffrey overcame his reluctance because of the repetition of his own words, and the use of the word "and" with raised intonation. This technique, although simple in explanation, works magically in almost all situations.

When Children Interrupt

You're working individually with a student at a location designated as "the conference table." Another youngster comes over and whispers loudly, "Mrs. Rubin, can I go to the library?" Your immediate inclination is to answer the youngster, but then you remember the class rule, which is "no interruptions during individual conferences." The child persists and continues whispering. You and the child with whom you are working proceed without permitting the intrusion. Eventually, the interrupter stops whispering your name, but stays behind you. You bite your tongue, for it is difficult to ignore the youngster. Ignoring her, however, will give her the following messages:

1. conferences are personal, important, and cannot be interrupted;
2. when you have a conference, yours will be respected in the same way.

At the completion of the conference, the teacher turned to the child, put her arm around her, and said warmly, "Now that I'm finished, what do you need?" Children eventually stop requesting, and wait when they've learned that interruptions won't work. They learn, too, to approach the teacher when appropriate. A signal indicating that disturbances are taboo also helps to prevent interruptions. Some of our teachers wear a "conference hat." Others use finger signals (i.e., one or two fingers in the air) to guide children from interrupting. We have found that immediately following an individual conference or lesson, it is best for teachers to circulate around the classroom to provided needed attention. Making this a habit—working individually and then circulating—informs children that their needs will be met within a relatively reasonable time period.

Praising and Reprimanding Students: Conflict and Compromise

There is almost never a time when reprimand serves to reinforce behaviors. Direct praise, discussed in Chapter 4, does. Firm guidelines for expected actions must be enforced. We tell students what we expect, what is acceptable or unacceptable behavior for them as well as for ourselves. We will inform children about a rule when the necessity arises.

Josh ran furiously down the hall of the Center. I moved quickly, put my hands on his shoulders, bent down to his eye level and said in a firm, nurturing voice, "We have a rule here, and it is no running in the halls. If you run, you can fall and hurt yourself, and that would make me upset. What's the rule, Josh?" Whenever a child runs in the hall, we stop the youngster and say, "I'm upset because you are running. Why do you think I'm upset?" Once children know the rules, they should be encouraged to repeat a rule when they break it. Requesting children to repeat the rule and the reason for its existence is important. Justification for any action supports independence and responsibility.

Sometimes behavior is inappropriate and just needs to be stopped. If, for example, one child physically hurts another, reprimand is appropriate. Firm words like, "That behavior is never to occur in this classroom," are also appropriate.

Learning to be accountable for one's behavior instills a sense of responsibility. Adults can get sidetracked concerning issues of accountability. The who, what, and when things that happen often become the focus of conflict. Strategies for guiding the acquisition of integrity about "the truth" sometimes get repressed in favor of "blame." An issue with two eleven-year-olds and their teacher sets an example of how to strategically keep the focus where it belongs.

Courtney wrote in her journal daily. She wrote about the human body using slang and inappropriate references. This made it difficult for the teacher to respond, but with assistance from the school counselor, the teacher was able to find ways to dialogue with Courtney. The teacher handled the content scientifically, replacing slang with proper names of body parts, and often shared scientific information about their functions. The rule, to write in your journal and share it only with the teacher, was adhered to by the child. The teacher knew that Courtney focused on these issues to get her attention. Her role was to respond, keeping within the content area. Courtney usually received attention for inappropriate or startling behaviors. Her inability to receive the attention from the inappropriate language caused her to write even more profanity. When responses rather than reprimand persisted, Courtney's need for a negative response led her to share the journal with another child. The teacher's hesitation in stopping the transaction forced me, the principal, who just happened to see the interactions, to respond. "All of you, Miss Zimmerman, Courtney, and Alice come to my office, now!" The definitive tone and directive approach informed all three that something was important.

Principal: I've asked you to come in here, because a rule was broken. The rule is, no one is to read journals except the teacher and the student.

Alice: I read Courtney's journal, that's why you got mad.

Principal: That's right. What's the rule, Alice?

Alice: Only share the journal with the teacher. I wasn't supposed to read it.

Principal: Correct. Courtney, you were not supposed to share it. Miss Zimmerman, you are in charge of monitoring the privacy of journals. Sharing and reading another's journal is not permitted, except with the teacher. It is not to happen again.

In many instances the content of the journal would have been the subject of the dispute. There were, however, no rules concerning content, so reprimand for this would have been improper. The important aspects of this interaction were:

- rules were the guidelines for the actions;
- all of those involved were appropriated responsibility for the behaviors.

Often personal values, morals, and even religious beliefs come between students, teachers, and issues. The importance of separating personal values from school rules in order to be equitable is paramount. When rules for classroom communities are definitive, equitable human interactions are easier to achieve. Rules empower citizens of communities with constraints necessary for cooperation. Feedback, based on rules, supports actions. The rules furnish the consistent guidelines that empower students and teachers to take both risks and responsibilities that build communities of learners.

Negotiation Between Children

The power to negotiate—arrange, bargain, consult, parley, mediate, make peace, settle, adjust, accommodate, or moderate—are based on ground rules for conflict management. The development of listening skills and the language used for peace-making need to be part of classroom curriculums. Role-play situations are becoming popular strategies for teaching these skills to students. Dialogue is the basic tool used for negotiating conflict for a win/win scenario. Dialogue is "real-life" conversation that is spontaneous, ongoing, unpondered, and uncomposed. It is the major ingredient necessary for literacy skills. Moffett (1968) refers to dialogue as "verbal collaboration" that must be accompanied by "cognitive collaboration. A conversation is a dialogical—a meeting and fusion of minds even if speakers disagree" (p. 73). Using language to guide youngsters to meet the minds of other human beings is a challenge necessary for them to survive in classrooms. Seek the guidance of professionals— counselors, psychologists, social workers—familiar with instructional approaches, for such language behavior will enhance the development of literacy skills, as well.

Summary

Classroom formats determine the tone of the classroom environment. Student-centered classrooms where children are empowered with strategies in order to learn are desired. Don Holdaway's model of learning facilitates student-centered environments. Incorrect perceptions about student-centered environments have flourished in the public eye due to unsophisticated alternative methods for charting and reporting instruction and growth. A self-management model for arranging students to categorize products has evolved into a successful instructional tool. The system has "married" assessment and instruction, for strategies that determine growth are also the frameworks for literacy skills. Ideas for beginning to use the system to successfully manage alternative assessment and personalized instruction are suggested. Basic principles that help to create healthy classrooms can be used in all content areas with all ages of students.

CHAPTER 6

Comprehension:
Processing and Producing Text

"My daughter isn't very patient. I wish she'd enjoy reading, but she doesn't. I want her to improve her comprehension skills. She's very creative, but she's not disciplined in study habits. And, her teacher tells me that she won't talk about things in class," remarked one parent. Statements like these suggest confusion about comprehension. According to the parent's statement, the comprehension process can be interpreted as a series of discrete skills. If these are taught, one should be able to read. If, for example, a student was instructed to "infer" or "interpret," he/she could apply the skills when reading a text. But, there is more to comprehension than skills instruction.

The student described above is in the eighth grade. She's earned a grade equivalent score of 10.4 on a standardized reading comprehension test. This assessment tool required that she select a correct answer from multiple choices after reading several short passages. Inference skills were necessary in order to earn this high score. The score suggests that she is able to read almost two-and-one-half years above her current grade in school. If the teenager is able to score two-and-one-half grades above her actual grade in school, what, then, was the problem in class?

The student had made a prediction (Figure 6-1) prior to reading her selection, Stephen King's *The Tommyknockers* (1989). Her prediction and her first response in her literature response journal (Figure 6-2) are the antithesis of what was expected based on her high test results. The high score, but meager written response and minimal verbal contributions in class seem to be contradictory.

The literature response journal entries of July 2 and 3 are personalized (see Figure 6-2). The youngster seems to be able to transact with the text affectively (i.e., this book is . . . confusing; she does not seem to have . . . inner conflicts). The student's reflections on the ideas in the text, however, need justification. She needed to present the author's ideas that gave rise to her reactions. The differences between

Prediction

My name: _jessica jones_ _____ Date: _7/1/96_

Book: __The TommyKnockers_____
Author: _Stephen King_____

I predict the book is about--	I predict this because--
-A town + how there minds are controlled by Something inside their town - How outsiders are not invited to come	- It is on the back of the book

Book:_____
Author:_____

I predict the book is about--	I predict this because--

Figure 6-1.   Jessica's Prediction

<u>Literature Response Journal</u>   7/2

   This book is kind of confusing so far, but all of stephen king's are alittle. I'm not sure who's the main character is yet but I'll keep this updated. So far this book has made me feel like the surroundings are eerie.

                                                   7/3

   There is a girl Roberta Anderson. She seems to be pretty down to earth, so far But she does seem to have some inner conflicts. She seems to wonder off too much. She seems almost mad at herself. This book is different, but king always builds up suspense.

                                                   7/9

I started a new book by R.L. Stine, called the New boy. It's all about this girl & how she's shy. She saw this new boy that she wants to meet but her friends (who already have boyfriends) are all over him. Janie feels left out while Eve & Faith always make fun of her even though they say they are her B.F.

Figure 6-2.   Jessica's Literature Response Journal

her responses in this journal and on the test are affective. Personalizing information seems to guide her to make meaning of print. She needs more discussion, oral and written, in order to give meaning to support her feelings. The items on the test were probably informational (cognitively based) and, therefore, "cut and dried." There was no need or chance for the youngster to elaborate, respond personally, or interact with others in order to expand on comprehension of the words. There was little to infer about. The score reflected the nature of the requested information and the test format.

Knowledge about the comprehension process helps address issues dealing with the test scores, students' individual responses to, and reflections on texts.

When a Student Doesn't Comprehend

Recognizing words has a great impact on comprehension. Laypersons, especially, think of the ability to recognize words as *the* foundation for success in reading. The student who has the ability to speak words, but lacks the knowledge necessary to recognize them in print will certainly have difficulty reading. Sometimes students know how to use letters and their sounds to form, pronounce, and read words. Decoding is important, but without the knowledge of word meanings and concepts embedded in the print, meaning is missed, and comprehension suffers.

All readers, even skilled ones, at times fail to comprehend some text. This occurs because comprehension is not just a group of skills, but a series of complex processes that demand a reader's attention. When a student struggles with "sounding out" and recognizing words, there is generally no choice but for him/her to use all available attention to accomplish the task of pronouncing the words. Children are expected to gain information, but when they use all of their energy to decode, there is none left for making meaning of the text.

The importance of sounding out words for reading has been driven out of proportion. It is this visual, mechanical skill that nonprofessionals are able to understand and therefore control. Frank Smith (1975) said, "You can lead a child to a textbook, but you cannot make him see (p. 49). . . . Reading is only partially a visual activity . . . [A reader] must rely more on nonvisual information that he already has behind his eyeballs than on the visual information that comes to him from the printed page" (p. 179). James Moffett and Betty Jane Wagner (1992) identify three elements—(1) lack of motivation, (2) lack of experience, and (3) egocentricity—as nonvisual causes of poor comprehension.

Lack of Motivation

Some students are just not interested in reading. Others may not like the specific content they are expected to read in school. The challenge for teachers is to entice students' interest, motivation, and desire to read. Researchers have found that up to 44 percent of successful speed in reading is due to motivation and desire to read. They also found that 22 percent of power—the skills necessary to comprehend—relied on effort and desire to know about the information (Ruddell & Unrau, 1994; Singer, 1994). Human transactions, which include talking, stimulate ideas and interest, thus spurring excitement about text (Rosenblatt, 1978). The key to better readers is getting them immersed in materials that satisfy their interests.

Lack of Experience

A sufficient amount of prior knowledge (experience) about ideas has a bearing on interests and comprehension (Anderson & Freebody, 1981; Ruddell & Unrau, 1994). Everyone has difficulty understanding something because he/she lacks sufficient knowledge about it. If, for example, I were expected to read a book about finite differentials, my lack of interest and knowledge would certainly contribute to my failure to understand the information. My knowledge is less-than-adequate, my interest nil.

Prior knowledge about content is important, but not sufficient. Prior knowledge about emotional experiences is an essential element for facilitating comprehension (Covington, 1983; Slavin, 1991). The way we feel about content has an impact on how we understand it. Prior academic and affective knowledge determines how well one interacts with an author's writing.

Egocentricity

The phrases "scheme theory" (Rummelhart, 1980) and "theory of the world" (F. Smith, 1978) come to mind when thinking about egocentricity as it relates to text. One's interpretations of ideas are subjectively personal. These are based on each person's expectations about the meaning of content. A reader's expectations are supported by clues that permit him/her to interpret text. Readers' ideas about content (theory of the world), and ability or facility to connect their ideas to those proposed by an author (schema theory) provide clues that guide interpretations. When readers find nothing to which they can connect the new ideas, comprehension deficits result. Inadequate comprehension may sometimes be due to a conflict of ideas between author and reader. A reader's knowledge of strategies (the process) for connecting information in text to something known (prior knowledge and experiences) is essential for comprehension.

Often students fail to see beyond their own interpretations. Moffett and Wagner (1992) attribute this egocentricity to a lack of awareness that "any other interpretation is possible" (p. 145). This makes it impossible to see others' points of view, thus limiting thoughts about text.

The Changing Nature of Comprehension Assessment

Traditionally, standardized tests for measuring literacy skills included many subtests. The selection of skills resulted from research (Davis, 1944, 1968; Hunt, 1957; Kerfott, 1968) that isolated those believed to be components of the comprehension process. Several skills lists (Davis, 1944, 1968) resulted in the conclusion that "comprehension in reading involves two skills: word knowledge and paragraph comprehension" (Hunt, 1957, p. 508). Revised lists frequently decreased and then increased the numbers of skills included. The indecisiveness of the skill components of comprehension confused test consumers. Questions concerning the number and variety of sub-tests, whether the test should be timed or untimed, and the type of format in which the test was constructed sparked debates among professionals (Farr, 1969).

The student-centered movement and psycholinguistic research demonstrated that there is more to determining comprehension than a series of testable skills. Ken Goodman (1969) concluded that:

> Research has demonstrated that the reader does not process print sequentially, but rather in a manner which reflects his use of language at every opportunity. Expectancies about syntax and semantics within contexts lead to hypotheses which can be confirmed (or unconfirmed) with only a small portion of the cues available in the text. Thus, not all the information needed by the reader is on the printed page—nor are all the printed details needed by him. (p. 82)

And so alternative assessment procedures, especially portfolios, took the United States and other countries by storm. Researchers—including Collins, Brown, and Larkin (1980), K. Goodman (1969), and Rummelhart (1977), among others—looked beyond the assessment of student products to the assessment of the processes readers use to construct meanings (Beck & McKeown, 1989; Kintegen, 1985; Kucan & Beck, 1996; Lytle, 1982; Olshavsky, 1975; Scardamalia & Bereiter, 1984; Zabrucky & Ratner, 1992).

Comprehension Strategies: Assessment AS Instruction

"How do I begin to teach a student to learn to comprehend?" is frequently asked. Pearson and Spiro (1981) suggest, "Instead of asking the question, 'What does the student not know that I have to help him or her learn?', educators should be asking, 'What is it that the student does know that I can use as an anchor point—a bridge— to help develop the concepts that he or she needs?'" (p. 80).

Comprehension and concept development are impossible without the ability to attend to tasks. "If each student had unlimited quantities of attention there would be no problem" (Samuels, 1994, p. 821). All students have some limitations, but many with specific anomalies face problems when tasks require more attention than is available.

Arthur's difficulty in decoding words was solved using commercial home remedies that taught him the sounds of language. Arthur's attention to "sounding out" was so focused that he was unable to conserve enough energy to concentrate on content.

Managing Attention for Reading

Managing and holding attention is necessary in order to comprehend. Students are able to attend and comprehend best when (1) reading materials are systematically organized and structured, and (2) students know how to connect the ideas they already have with those they read and learn.

Organization, Structure, and Making Connections

In order to demonstrate the importance of structure, study each of the figures in Figure 6-3 for approximately thirty seconds. Then try to reproduce them from memory. You'd agree, the first would be difficult to remember, for there is no logical pattern or organization to help "the reader" recall. The second, however, is easier. The systematic placement of the figures provides you with the power to count, create a mnemonic, or a picture in your mind that helps you recall.

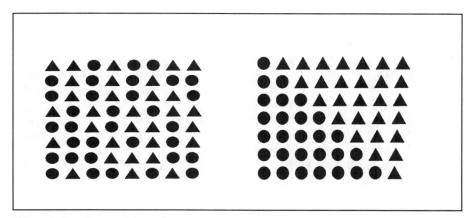

Figure 6-3.   Figures to Recall

The lists on the next page follow the same principle. The first has no well-defined order, and the second does. The categorized list provides a way for students, especially those who have difficulty creating categories themselves, to remember.

List 1	List 2
Norway	elephant
monkey	zebra
basketball	monkey
elephant	baseball
skiing	basketball
Finland	skiing
baseball	Norway
zebra	Iceland
Iceland	Finland

The frameworks in which the words are placed support comprehension. Dr. Seuss's books, and other books that frolic with rhythm and rhyme, are written with systematic structure and, therefore, provide frameworks that assist children's ability to comprehend. They are highly predictable, consistent, and also delightful to read and hear. The structures, once imaged in students' minds, guide them to remember, make connections, and understand. The voluminous amount of research supporting well-constructed text is sufficient evidence that well-organized texts are necessary for guiding students to attend and comprehend (Bartlett, 1932; Bower, 1976; Frederiksen, 1975; Kintsch, Mandel, & Kozminsky, 1977; Mandler & Johnson, 1977; Marshall & Glock, 1979; Pearson & Camperell, 1994; Reder, 1980; Rummelhart, 1977; Spiro, 1977; Stein & Nezworski, 1978; Thorndyke, 1977). Using frameworks repeatedly develops an automaticity with organizational skill, much like one developed for driving a car. When you first take the wheel, you think about everything—staying on the right side of the yellow line, signaling when making a turn, using the brake when you see an amber light. If you are about to make a turn and a green light turns to amber, you will most likely use your brake rather than your left-hand signal. With experience, activities become automatic and, except for extenuating circumstances, no thought is needed to execute action.

Frameworks provide students with the language and structure for learning and also assessing their growth, creating empowered students.

Frameworks for Comprehension

Strategies for guiding students to enhance comprehension have paralleled the skills required for test taking activities. Students are guided to respond to teacher-directed questions and test items. The recent deluge of professional literature about alternative assessment (Airasian, 1991; Belanoff & Dickson, 1991; Camp, 1992; Chittenden, 1991; Clay, 1993; Farr & Trumbull, 1997; Glazer & Brown, 1993; Goodman, 1986;

Graves, 1983; Harp, 1996; Hill & Ruptic, 1994; Meyer, 1992; Rhodes, 1993; Sharp, 1989; Valencia, 1990) confirms public and professional notions that changes in assessment practices in classrooms have become a reality because traditional procedures lack the depth of data secured by other means. Losing faith in the traditional assessment system in classrooms suggests that older practices for teaching comprehension must also change. The emphasis can now shift to alternative **instructional** practices that match, coordinate with, and double for the nontraditional assessment tools (Glazer, 1992; Glazer & Burke, 1994; Johns, VanLeirsburg, & Davis, 1994; Tierney, Readence, & Dishner, 1990). The frameworks supply strategies empowering students to understand the structure for learning. These strategies guide learning also by self-monitoring tasks.

The instruction AS assessment strategies selected for this text have demonstrated their effectiveness with all ages of students and most content areas. Frameworks for encouraging the development of

1. comprehension of story and story structure
2. comprehension of content area materials
3. comprehending the relationship of questions to text
4. strategies used by skilled readers to understand text

are included in this chapter. Although limited in number, these seem most appropriate for all ages and abilities. They are also appropriate to use in content area studies, as well. Conversations and discussions are essential for developing meaning using all of the strategies. Talk about "talk" will be included in discussions throughout.

Frameworks for Comprehending Story and Story Structure

Our teachers have found frameworks for (a) motivating interest, (b) picture reading, (c) retellings, and (d) graphic organizers especially helpful for guiding students to learn how to comprehend and assess (self-monitor) their knowledge of stories and their structure. The same frameworks used to learn these elements are used to assess. We emphasize the interdependent relationship between learning and assessing when using these procedures.

Motivating Interest

It's extremely difficult to read something that's boring. It's just as difficult to read something without purpose. Although I'd been familiar with research showing that motivation and interest are responsible 44 percent and 52 percent, respectively, for successful reading (Singer, 1994), I learned it best when my father died in May, 1984. It's the custom in the Jewish faith to say prayers of mourning for eleven months following a burial. I chose to follow the custom, but could not read the prayers, for they were written in Hebrew. I had little interest in or need to learn the language when attending religious school as a child. My very important mission coerced me to become familiar with the language in my middle age.

It's difficult to learn a new language, especially one whose phonological and orthographic systems are so alien. I found myself empathizing with youngsters whose reading problems helped them feel like I did the first time I attended the services. Although the sounds of the Hebrew language brought memories of my grandparents, I had no idea how to articulate or read the characters. Three elderly gentlemen who sat at the back of the synagogue seemed to be reading slowly enough for me to follow. I placed myself between two of them, and one placed my finger under a word in the Bible. He pushed my finger under the words, moving my hand from right to left, while coaching me to chorally say the words with him. I continued to read next to this empathic man, and finally learned the prayers.

Choral reading saved me from embarrassment, confusion, and loss of interest in honoring my beloved father. I felt successful because of the choral support. Even with support, without purpose and interest to learn the language, I would have failed.

Using Choral Reading in Classrooms   To begin, I suggest that you select a poem, fable, limerick, or song that will spur interest and enthusiasm. I sometimes use Jack Prelutsky's (1990), "Homework! Oh, Homework!" It begins,

> Homework! Oh Homework!
>
> I hate you! You stink!
>
> I wish I could wash you away in the sink (p. 54).*

It continues for three paragraphs of delightful rhyme to orthographically illustrate the apprehensions most children and adults feel about these tedious activities. This or other highly charged content that include predictable rhymes lure students to read the language. I move through the choral reading activity in the following order. The consistent routine guides students to learn the language and the words. Choral reading provides the support and confidence each needs to "read more!"

1.   Provide each student with a copy of the selection.

2.   Project the selection, using an overhead projector or write it on a large piece of easel paper and post for easy viewing.

3.   Say, "I am going to read this poem. You follow along as I read."

4.   Read the selection. When you finish say, "Read it with me."

5.   When finished say, "Now, let's reread it out loud together." Begin with them, and then drop your voice until you cannot be heard. If you think they need you, join in again.

---

*From: *New Kid on the Block,* Jack Prelutsky. Text copyright © 1990 by Jack Prelutsky. By permission of Greenwillow Books, A Division of William Morrow & Co., Inc.

Choral reading teaches and guides students to assess the following.

Teaches	Self-Assesses
• word recognition	• word recognition
• self-confidence	• needs concerning word recognition
• support is O.K.	• ideas concerned with learning to like to read
• about the genre used	• how different forms of writing create different feelings about reading

Choral reading and repetition guide students to recognize words. Choral reading is appropriate for all ages and stages of reading ability, especially when materials are concerned with highly charged topics of interest.

Picture Reading

Research in the 1970s (Denburg, 1976–1977; Levin, Bender, & Lesgold, 1976; Read & Barnsley, 1977; Rigney & Lutz, 1976; Rohwer & Harris, 1975; Samuels, 1970) concentrated on the positive effects of pictures on reading comprehension. It was discovered that longer text selections (Lesgold, DeGood, & Levin, 1977), basal text series (Read & Barnsley, 1977), learning and retaining information from more complicated text (Peeck, 1974), and understanding abstract concepts (Royer & Cable, 1975) were easier to understand when pictures were included in materials. Donald Graves wants children to read their own pictures as well as pictures in books, for picture reading helps them to understand stories (personal communication, September 17, 1997).

Reading Pictures before Reading Text   Reading pictures before reading text provides students with the opportunity to predict what the words in the book say. Prediction requires prior knowledge, illustrating for learners that picture reading is one way to connect what they know to what they will learn. It also provides an opportunity for students to use appropriate vocabulary to describe picture content. Using vocabulary before reading helps children recognize and read more words in the text. Listening to the vocabulary used permits professionals to assess students' knowledge of vocabulary and therefore their readiness for the content. The following table and vignette illustrate the importance of reading pictures for teaching and assessing growth.

Picture Reading

Teaches	Assesses
• Importance of prediction	• Knowledge of content vocabulary
• Hypothesizing through discussion	• Ability to connect prior knowledge to new data
• One way to connect prior knowledge to new data (through discussion)	• Use of words signaling the attempt to connect prior knowledge to new data (because; I think that; It goes with; I heard (saw, remember) about that before)
• Importance of observing details	• Students' attention to details as they are related to story and story structure

---

Ms. Clark selected Deborah Hopkinson's and James Ransome's *Sweet Clara and the Freedom Quilt.* This seemed like a wonderful book to share the day before the Martin Luther King, Jr., holiday. The story tells of Clara, a resourceful, courageous twelve-year-old who escapes slavery by sewing a map of the land—a freedom quilt—using scraps from her seamstress's bag. Illustrator James Ransome's vivid watercolors create well-organized, realistic images that describe and clarify facts. Clarity, logical organization, and realistic accounts of events are important criteria for quality illustrations in children's picture books, particularly in realistic fiction (Burke & Glazer, 1994). Ms. Clark had been talking about Dr. King, the great freedom worker, for several days. When she gathered the class on the rug and held the cover for all to see, one child asked, "Is this one for Martin Luther King's birthday?" "What do you think?" she responded. "Yeah, I think it is." "Why?" coached Ms. Clark, encouraging justification for the response. "I think it is because they are in the field. See this white stuff! I think it's cotton. And the slaves worked in cotton fields. And the boy and the girl are black. So I think it is about slaves." "It could be about slaves who got free!" remarked another child. "Why?" inquired Ms. Clark. "Well," the child continued, "they are running, and they are smiling, and they are carrying bags of stuff—it could be clothes—and maybe they just got out." Ms. Clark listened attentively, nodding her head affirmatively, indicating to the youngsters that all responses were appropriate when justified. She knew the importance of samples of children's spontaneous talk for assessing their knowledge of story structure, and their ability to use prior knowledge to make connections with the new text. She always had a pad of post-it notes handy to jot down observations of their oral language in order to appropriately plan for future instruction. "I've covered the print in the book with writing paper," she said. "We are going to read the pictures before we read the words in the story. Let's see if we can figure out what the story is about before we read it." "That's cool," remarked one boy. "It's like a puzzle." "It surely is," remarked Ms. Clark as she turned the book toward the children and opened to the title page. Several waved their hands. "I think it's about farming." "Why?" prompted Ms. Clark. "Well, see over there, the kids, they're riding in a wagon and there are people—it looks like people—slaves bending over. I think they are plant—, no, picking something." "So," commented Ms. Clark, "you think it's about slaves picking something. Let's see," she said as she turned to the first page in the story. "I told you they were slaves. And, that's cotton," remarked a boy. "How do you know?" requested Ms. Clark. "How do I know it's cotton?" "Yes," responded the teacher. "Well, it's white, and it's sunny, and cotton grows in the sun, and the sun is out and the cotton is on brown branches and I know that's how cotton grows because I saw it in the museum." Ms. Clark knew that this youngster had prior firsthand experience with the growth of the cotton plant and was using it to make connections to the story. "So this is the story of two slave teenagers who work in a cotton field," reviewed the teacher. "Yeah," said a child, "and they look happy because it's sunny." This was the first time a student had offered justification—a reason for her response—without prompts. "Maybe they're talking about getting free," predicted a youngster as Ms. Clark turned the page. "Now," she continued, "what do you think is happening next?" "She looks like she's sewing," said one child. Another continued, tagging her contribution onto the first. "And it looks like her mother is helping her." "Why do you say that?" asked the teacher. "Because the mother's hand is on the thing she's sewing, see!" responded the child pointing to the picture. "So," reviewed Ms. Clark, adding the new information, "the story's about two teenaged slaves who work in the cotton fields, and the girl also sews." "Yeah, but she may be sewing for fun," said a child. "Why?" coached Ms. Clark. "I don't know. It just looks that way," the child continued. Ms. Clark had decided to listen to the child as she turned to the next page to see if she spoke without regularly justifying answers. "Oh, I know. The mother is making a fire, and the girl is talking. Maybe she's saying she's hungry." "Why?" automatically came from Ms. Clark. "Because the mother is probably going to cook in the fire," replied the youngster. "Now she looks like she's sewing something different because the blue one is on the table and a white one is in her hand," commented another youngster. As the page turned, several youngsters' eagerness to see what came next was obvious. "I know, I know," shouted one, "that's the boss." "No," interjected another, "it's the slave owner. They owned the slaves." "Why do you think it's a slave owner?" asked the teacher. "Because she's white and she's looking at something," responded the child. "Maybe she's looking at the girls sewing," proposed another. "Why do you think that?" asked the teacher. "Because, look, she's holding the white thing that the girl sewed on this page," said the child as she moved toward the book, attempting to turn the page back.

Ms. Clark turned the page back, and the child said excitedly, "I'm right, see the thing is white here, too." "So," said Ms. Clark, "the story is about two young teens who are slaves and they work in the cotton field. And the girls' mother—we think she's the mother— teaches her to sew. Then she makes something that looks nice and the slave owner looks at it and . . . , from the picture, it seems that she is admiring it. So what do you think that means?" Ms. Clark continued to guide the children to read the pictures. The process involved:

1. selecting a book whose pictures "almost" tell the story;
2. fastening a piece of paper on each page to cover the print;
3. asking children to "predict," before reading, what the book was about;
4. asking the children to "tell what picture says is happening;"
5. asking "why" after each response for justification for the answer;
6. accepting all responses from children and their justifications;
7. repeating children's contributions after each page, followed by, "a-n-d?";
8. summarizing student contributions regularly during discussions and arranging them in story format.

The children's excitement over correct predictions support reading the pictures before reading the words in the text. This strategy was repeated often and actions became automatic for most of the children, providing them with the framework—respond and tell "why"—for strategically making meaning from text. As time moved on, Ms. Clark would say after children provided responses, "You shared your ideas and told why you chose them. Good readers create ideas and then tell why." She reminded children of their behavior for several days, and then asked a child, "What did you just do, Kim?" When children are able to repeat their actions and explain with language what they are doing, and then repeat their actions again, they demonstrate that they've learned.

A Natural Extension of the Activity That IS Assessment   Children usually emulate their teacher's behaviors. This was so evident when the teacher noticed that one youngster covered the words in Garth Williams's (1958) *The Rabbits' Wedding* and read the pictures. The teacher gave him a tape recorder, and as he spoke, the language of the story was recorded. Ms. Clark transcribed the child's picture reading to determine his knowledge of story structure. The information would permit her to plan instruction to meet the youngster's needs. She used the story retelling checklist to record the child's responses (Figure 6-4) and filed it in the comprehension section of the portfolio. She found it interesting to compare students' retellings who read the pictures before reading or listening to the text, to those whose prereading activities were limited to minimal talk about the book. The fact that more was recalled and language was richer confirmed the necessity for reading pictures before reading the text. The composition and retelling checklist provided the language necessary to

STUDENT'S COMPOSITION AND RETELLING CHECKLIST

NAME_____ DATE_____

NAME OF COMPOSITION OR BOOK _____

AUTHOR_____

	YES	NO
SETTING:		
I began my composition/ retelling with an INTRODUCTION	___	___
I told WHEN the story happened	___	___
I told WHERE the story happened	___	___
CHARACTERS:		
I told about the main character	___	___
I told about the other characters	___	___
PROBLEM:		
I told about the story problem or goal	___	___
EPISODES:		
I included episodes	___	___
SOLUTION:		
I told how the problem was solved or the goal was met	___	___
I told how the story ended	___	___
THEME:		
My story has a theme	___	___

When I compose/ retell on my own, I include:_____

_____

_____

The next time I compose/ retell, I need to remember to include these things:_____

_____

_____

©Susan Mandel Glazer
Rider University

Figure 6-4.   Student's Composition and Retelling Checklist

standardize descriptive reporting for all students. Ms. Clark used the language from the checklist in summarizing observations on the Progress Report Form (Figure 6-5). Her goal was for children to learn to record their actions using both forms independently. The self-monitoring provided feelings of empowerment. Students are not only proud of what they accomplish, but also proud of how they're able to discover what they need to learn.

Progress Report Form

Student: Sammie   Teacher: Ms. Satz
Time Period: From: Oct. 2, 1996   To: _____
Area (Check one or more)   Comprehension ✓   Composition ____
Vocabulary ____   Independence ____   Other _____

You What I can do	You What I need	My ▇▇▇▇ job
- You read the pictures and made them into a story. - You began with an introduction ("Two rabbits were outside in the grass on a sunny day.") Your introduction included WHERE the story happen and WHEN it happened.	- You need to talk about each episode in a story. - You need to sign up for a conference.	→ I need to write a story with you, and together we will make lots of episodes.

Figure 6-5. Sammie's Progress Report Form

Retellings

Researchers have demonstrated that reading stories to children before they come to school has a positive effect on learning to read (Cullinan, 1989; Durkin, 1966; Glazer & Searfoss, 1988; Teale, 1984; Wells, 1986). The language of story becomes part of the child's oral repertoire, providing him/her with the syntax, vocabulary, and organizational features necessary for understanding this genre (Feitelson, Kita, & Goldstein, 1986).

Children hear stories read and retold from birth. Humans read and retell, and also experience and retell about events almost as naturally as they breathe. Retelling has always been a way for people to recall, rehearse in order to remember, and share events in their lives (Glazer, 1992). It has always been the vehicle for preserving oral traditions of nations.

Retelling as Assessment   Reading teachers have been using retellings as an assessment tool since the late 1970s. We were less aware then of the wide scientific support for the procedure. It just happened naturally one day. A six-year-old child, who consistently scored poorly on comprehension tests, spontaneously retold a story after her teacher read it to the class. It was discovered that she recalled most of the story elements, so the teacher used retelling as a means to assess her comprehension. Many sources are available for guiding teachers as they use retelling as an assessment tool (Gambrell, Pfeiffer, & Wilson, 1985; Glazer, 1992; Glazer & Burke, 1994; Irwin & Mitchell, 1983; Mandler & Johnson, 1977; Marshall, 1983; Morrow, 1988). Frameworks for students' self-monitoring comprehension after retelling is a powerful instructional tool, as well. When used as a self-monitoring tool (Figure 6-4) the checklist provides indirect instruction for learners. By reviewing their retellings, students learn the names of story elements, and their meanings.

Direct interventions are guided retellings. Teachers prompt during retellings, guiding and coaching students to access specific information. Some teachers use specific questions to prompt students' recall (see Figure 6-6). Wording the prompts the same way each time they're used provides a framework for self-monitoring during retelling. Repeating, using exactly the same language, imprints the questions on students' minds. We have found that when students learn and ask themselves the questions, they understand how to construct and assess their knowledge. Retellings guide children to learn and assess as seen in the table on page 125.

Self-monitoring: Retellings as Instruction   Kevin read Margot Zemach's version of *The Three Wishes* (1986). This is the story of a poor couple whose attempt to use three granted wishes to satisfy their material desires brought unexpected events. When Kevin finished reading the story, he wrote his retelling (Figure 6-7) without prompting from his teacher. His teacher scheduled ten minutes for an individual conference. She tried to keep the conferences to less than ten minutes, for she knew that more than this is unproductive when carrying out direct instruction. Kevin sat next to his

Guided Retellings

Story Elements	Prompts/Questions
INTRODUCTION	Once upon a time . . . It happened this way . . . It all began . . .
SETTING	
Place	Where did the story take place?
Time	When did the story take place?
THEME	
Main character	Who is the story about?
Other characters	Who else is in the story?
PLOT	
Problem or goal	What is the main character's problem (or goal)?
EPISODES	
Events	What happened first? What happened next? (Use this prompt for each episode in the story, if necessary. Some children will need only one prompt to recall events.)
RESOLUTION	
Problem solver	How was the problem solved? or How did the main character achieve the goal?

Figure 6-6.　Story Structure Prompt Questions

Retelling

Teaches (Learning)	Assesses
• story elements	• recall of story elements
• organization of story	• ability to use story structure to organize recall
• names of stories and their authors	• knowledge of literature (fiction and nonfiction) and the authors
• the need to support one's responses (the "why" explanation after a response)	• one's ability to justify using appropriate support data
• the vocabulary of story structure	• the ability to use the vocabulary of story structure

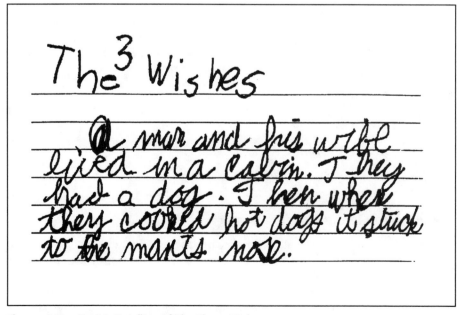

Figure 6-7.   Kevin's Retelling of *The Three Wishes*

teacher at the conference table and put his retelling in front of him. The following dialogue describes the first conference conversation.

Teacher: Kevin, I love the book *The Three Wishes*. I like it because it ends differently than I thought it would.

Kevin: Yeah. It was a good story.

Teacher: Why was it a good story for you, Kevin?

Kevin: I don't know, it was just good.

Teacher: What about it made it good?

Kevin: I don't know.

Teacher: Well, when you say that a story is good, you need to tell why.

Kevin: Well, uh, I guess the part where he made a wish and he got a sausage on his nose. Yeah, that was funny.

Teacher: Why was it funny, Kevin?

Kevin: Well, because, uh, (pauses) uh, it made me laugh.

Teacher: O.K. You remembered why. That's great! Now, Kevin, let's read your retelling together. (They read it chorally, together since it was dictated, to be sure that Kevin read all of his retelling. This was done because retellings are comprehension checks, not word recognition exercises.)

Teacher: (after reading the retelling out loud, together) Now, we're going to use this retelling sheet—I'll show you how—to help you discover what you remembered.

Kevin: O.K. But I didn't write so much.

Teacher: (putting a retelling checklist [Figure 6-8] next to Kevin's written retelling) Whatever you wrote is just fine. Are you ready?

Kevin: Yeah! (Kevin reads the retelling in Figure 6-7 independently)

Teacher: This retelling checklist (teacher points to the word "retelling" and crosses out the words "composition and") includes all the elements that make up a story. Now, all stories begin with an introduction. Here, (the teacher takes a ruler, and places it under the word on the first line) let's read the first one together. Kevin and the teacher: I began my retelling with an introduction (the teacher slowed down the reading as she echoed the

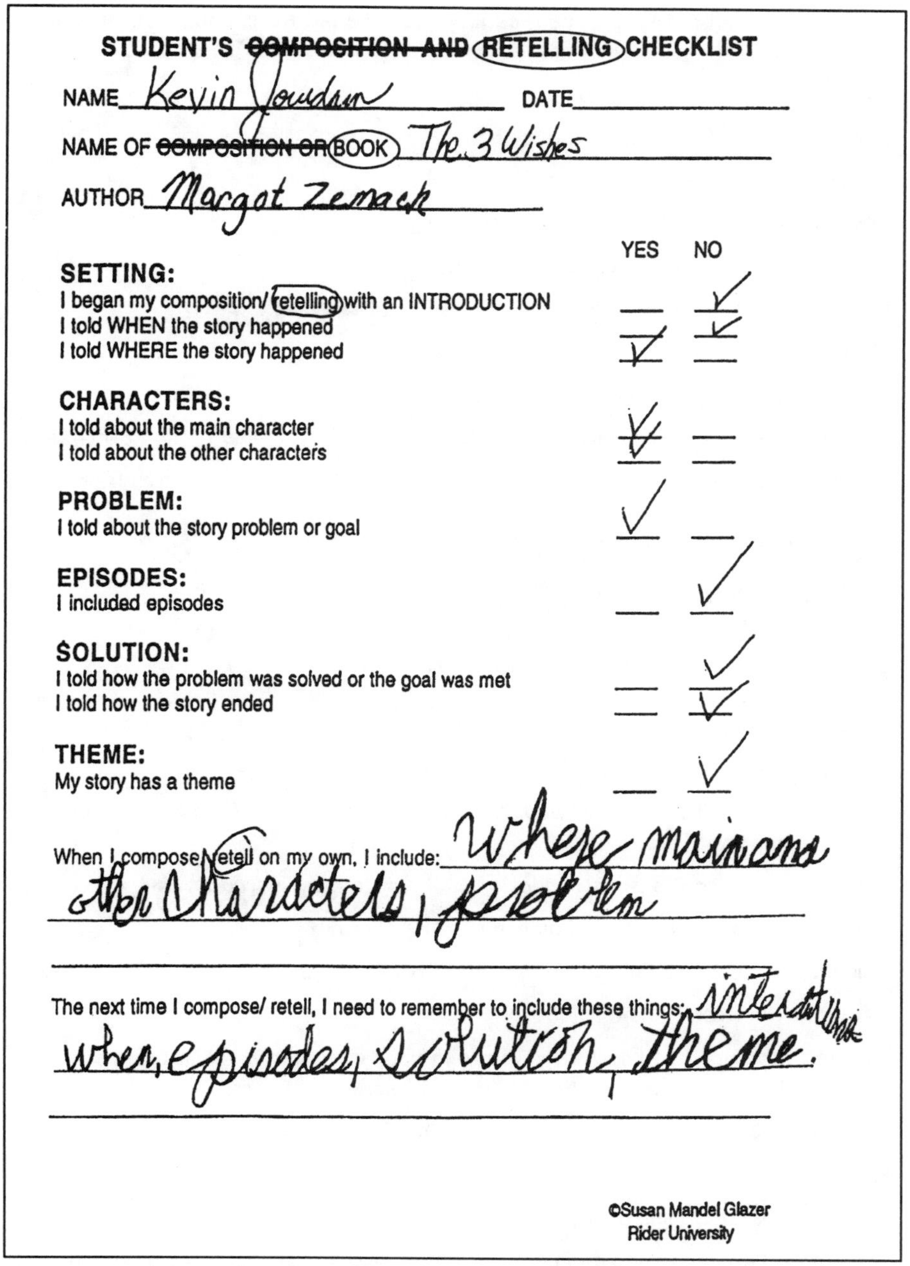

STUDENT'S ~~COMPOSITION AND~~ (RETELLING) CHECKLIST

NAME Kevin Jourdan DATE ____

NAME OF ~~COMPOSITION OR~~ (BOOK) The 3 Wishes

AUTHOR Margot Zemach

	YES	NO
SETTING:		
I began my composition/ (retelling) with an INTRODUCTION		✓
I told WHEN the story happened		✓
I told WHERE the story happened	✓	
CHARACTERS:		
I told about the main character	✓	
I told about the other characters	✓	
PROBLEM:		
I told about the story problem or goal	✓	
EPISODES:		
I included episodes		✓
SOLUTION:		
I told how the problem was solved or the goal was met		✓
I told how the story ended		✓
THEME:		
My story has a theme		✓

When I compose/ (retell) on my own, I include: where main and other characters, problem

The next time I compose/ retell, I need to remember to include these things: introduction when, episodes, solution, theme.

©Susan Mandel Glazer
Rider University

Figure 6-8. Kevin's Retelling Checklist

youngster. She stopped reading when she felt Kevin could continue on his own. She joined in when he needed the intervention).

Kevin: Yeah, I did.

Teacher: Kevin, find your introduction

Kevin: Here it is (pointing to the first line).

Teacher: Read your introduction, Kevin.

Kevin: A man and his wife lived in a cabin.

Teacher: So, the introduction is the first line of the story.

Kevin: Yeah, but it's not an introduction.

Teacher: What do you mean, it's not an introduction?

Kevin: Well, an introduction is, "Once upon a time . . . ," and I didn't do that.

Teacher: Lots of stories start with that introduction, but yours sounds like the beginning of a story too.

Kevin: Yeah, but I like "once upon a time" better!

Teacher: So, what about yours?

Kevin: I don't think it's a good one.

Teacher: Why?

Kevin: Because I didn't write "once upon a time," or something like that.

Teacher: What do you mean, "something like that?"

Kevin: Well, I like, uh—how about, "There was a man and a lady and they were married."

Teacher: Yeah, that's an introduction too. Why is it an introduction?

Kevin: Because it's a good opening to the story.

Teacher: What makes it a good opening, Kevin?

Kevin: Uh, I don't know. It just is.

Teacher: You need to know why. What's in your introduction (the teacher writes, "There was a man and a lady, and they were married")?

Kevin: It tells that there is a man and lady, and they are married.

Teacher: Right, and they are the story characters.

Kevin: Right. So the story is about them.

Teacher: Right, and that can be a good introduction; one that includes the main characters. So, you can write an introduction in the next retelling that includes the main characters. What about this retelling? What do you want to check on the checklist about your introduction (holding the ruler under the appropriate statement)?

Kevin: I didn't write an introduction, so I check "no."

Teacher: O.K. You checked "no" because . . . (raising her voice, and hesitating so that Kevin would respond, while putting the ruler under the next line).

Kevin: Because I didn't like what I wrote for an introduction.

Teacher: O.K.

Kevin: Right (reads), I told when the story happened. Well, let me see (taking his retelling and pointing his finger as he reads to himself). No, I didn't do that.

Teacher: You're right. When do you think the story happened?

Kevin: I don't know. Wait a minute, in the day, yeah, because I remember, the pictures look that way, see (opening the book to a page). And I didn't tell that.

Teacher: So (as she directs his attention with her finger to the checking column), so next to "I told when the story happened," what will you check?

Kevin: "No," again. I forgot both of them.

Teacher: What's important, Kevin, is that you know what you included and what you didn't.

(Kevin and his teacher continued until they completed checking all of the elements.)

Teacher: Now, let's read this together (putting her finger under the first word of the text).

Kevin and
Teacher: When I retell on my own, I include (Kevin looks at the teacher).

Teacher: Where can you find out what you included (putting her hand at the beginning of the checklist indicating where to find the answer)?

Kevin: Here? (points to the first element)

Teacher: You got it. Write here (points to the location on the checklist), all of the things you remembered to include.

Kevin: I included (as he began to write), where, main and other characters, (and he continued).

The teacher coached Kevin to write what he needed to remember next time, and he completed the sheet. Although the retelling was scanty, Kevin seemed to gain insight into how the self-monitoring process functioned. At the very end of the conference, the teacher discovered that both she and Kevin forgot about reviewing his prediction about the story before reading it.

Teacher: Oh my goodness, Kevin, we both forgot about your prediction.

Kevin: Yeah. Here it is (fumbling to get the paper shown in Figure 6-9).

Teacher: How close was your prediction to the real story?

Kevin: I guess pretty close, but I really didn't know what it was about.

Teacher: What helped you make the prediction?

Kevin: The name of the book, and uh, uh, the picture on the front.

Teacher: Titles and pictures are usually good helpers to use for predicting.

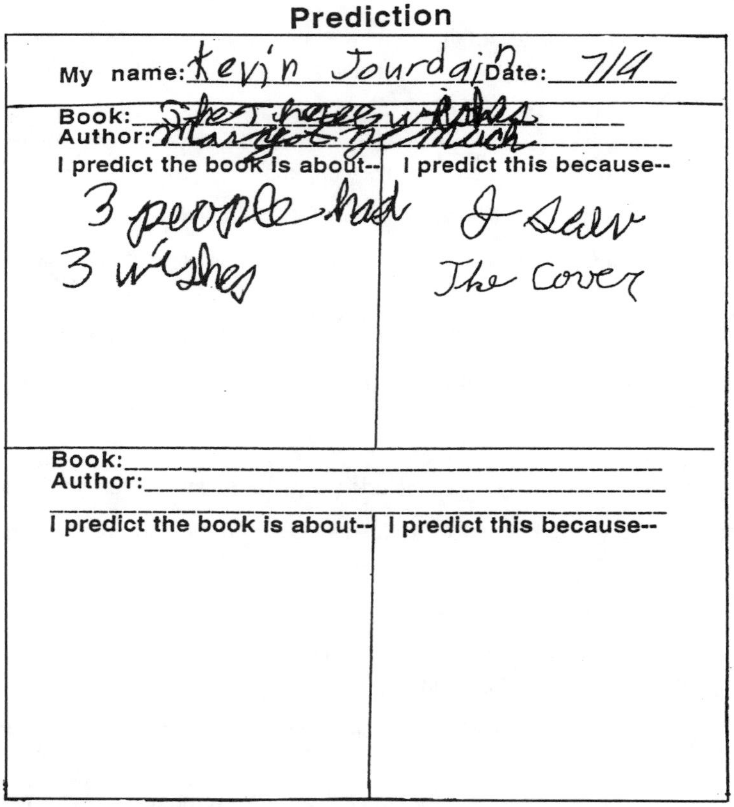

Prediction

My name: Kevin Jourdain   Date: 7/4

Book: _____

Author: _____

I predict the book is about--   I predict this because--

3 people had 3 wishes   I saw the Cover

Book: _____

Author: _____

I predict the book is about--   I predict this because--

Figure 6-9.   Kevin's Prediction

The teacher learned, after several conferences, that Kevin retold much more orally than when he wrote retellings. Dictating retellings onto tape proved more successful. After a volunteer, trained to transcribe children's oral text exactly as children spoke, transcribed Kevin's retelling (Figure 6-10), it demonstrated that this was the best way for him to show his comprehension. He was able to recall more elements this way (Figure 6-11). Handwriting seemed to be a barrier for producing text.

Kevin

This is Tikki Tikki Tembo. Its about a Kid who he was born first. this name was Tikki Tikki Tembo and the second child was Chang. The first child had, he was the honest one and the second child was a he had a hard name. One day they were flying a kite and Chang fell into a well. Then Tikki Tikki Tembo went to his mother and father and told her, Chang has fell into the well. "I can't hear you," she said. And then he said it louder. And the his mother said go to the old man who has the ladder. And then they quickly went to get Chang. Um. they had a big celebration after the old man got Chang.

And when Chang and Tikki Tikki Tembo were eating at the top of the well, Tikki Tikki Tembo tried to unknot the kite and he fell into the well and then Chang got the old man and he got. Chang got his ladder and he woke him up. And they all went to the well and the old man got Tikki Tikki Tembo. Then he was at the bottom so cold and he was sick. And thats the end.

Figure 6-10.   Kevin's Oral Retelling Transcription

STUDENT'S COMPOSITION AND RETELLING CHECKLIST

NAME *Kevin Jourdain*

DATE *7/22*

NAME OF COMPOSITION OR BOOK *Tikki Tikki Tembo*

AUTHOR *Arlene Mosel*

	YES	NO
SETTING:		
I began my composition/ (retelling) with an INTRODUCTION		✓
I told WHEN the story happened	✓	
I told WHERE the story happened	✓	
CHARACTERS:		
I told about the main character	✓	
I told about the other characters	✓	
PROBLEM:		
I told about the story problem or goal	✓	
EPISODES:		
I included episodes	✓	
SOLUTION:		
I told how the problem was solved or the goal was met	✓	
I told how the story ended	✓	
THEME:		
My story has a theme	✓	

When I compose/ (retell) on my own, I include: *when, where, main and other characters, problem, episodes, solution, theme*

The next time I compose/ (retell), I need to remember to include these things: *introduction*

Figure 6-11. Kevin's Retelling Checklist

Some students require a more structured framework for retelling a story. The map in Figure 6-12 is effective for students who have difficulty producing either narrative or handwritten text.

Setting	Character(s)	Problem	Episodes	Problem-Solution	Ending
a cabin	the man the wife	he was poor and wanted to be rich			

Figure 6-12. Story Retelling Map

Retellings are important vehicles for assessing students' recall of story. Self-monitoring retellings teaches students of all ages to identify and classify story elements. Further activities, however, to facilitate the development of interpretive and inferential skills related to ideas in stories are also necessary and important.

The Progress Report Form and Retellings   I recommend using the Progress Report Form to summarize all learning. Kevin was unable to comfortably write his own. His teacher, therefore, sat and discussed his activities, and included results of the discussion on the form (Figure 6-13). It becomes a teaching tool that also assesses the following skills.

Progress Report Form

Teaches	Assesses
• reviewing skills	• knowledge of content studied
• that additional reinforcement is provided by writing "what I learned"	• knowledge of review process
• spelling, handwriting, vocabulary	• spelling needs, productivity of handwriting, knowledge of specific vocabulary
• summarizing skills	• ability to summarize
• a way to manage and organize daily responses (products) to learning	• organizational and management skills
• an awareness of students' knowledge and abilities	• ability to use language to discuss their strengths and needs
• metacognitive practices	• metacognitive knowledge

The Progress Report Form is a wonderful vehicle for sharing accomplishments with parents.

Discussion, Conversations for Developing Concepts about Stories   Discussion, says Almasi (1996) "supposes cognitive engagement to the extent that the participants are actively involved in a dialogic conversation with one another rather than passively reciting answers to questions that may not be personally meaningful" (p. 2). Almasi, like many of us, derives her thoughts about discussion and conversation from the work of Rosenblatt (1978), who supports the notion that readers are not static. They continuously shape and reshape ideas about texts because of the transactions between themselves and the new information acquired from texts. Social interactions are necessary components of discussions and conversations. The reciprocal exchange of ideas through talk is influenced by each person involved and his/her interactions with a text (Gall & Gall, 1976). So text meanings are derived from environmental interactions with those who have had common literacy or other information-bearing experiences. Discussions, therefore, must be viewed as a primary component of the literacy process (Bloome, 1985; Bloome & Green, 1992).

Progress Report Form

Student: _Kevin Jourdain_ Teacher: _N. Cox_

Time Period: From: _July 10_ To: _____

Area (Check one or more) Comprehension _✓_ Composition ____

Vocabulary ____ Independence ____ Other _____

What I can do	What I need	My teacher's job
July 10 – Identified and wrote "Right There" questions "How many bread crumbs do you feed the ant?"	Continue to develop further awareness of "Right there" questions	From another reading – Have Kevin write other "Right There" quest
Retelling of the 3 Wishes included – character episodes	Develop stratagies for retelling that best show his comprehension Develop sense of story structure to aid in recall and comprehension Self monitor to see what he needs to include	Have Kevin complete an unguided oral retelling from reading
Write a prediction including reason why – "let on the cover" Included a more definitive reason for prediction	Explain what on the cover gave him clues to aid in his arrival of his prediction	Confer and Prompt.

Figure 6-13. Kevin's Progress Report Form

In the past, discussions between children and teachers resembled the traditional testing model. Teachers initiated discussion generally by asking questions. Students' responses to questions were evaluated by the teacher and further questioning resumed. Cazden refers to this type of discussion (1986) as I-R-E (Initiate-Respond-Evaluate) participatory structure. If, for example, a child had just read *Cinderella,* a teacher might ask the following.

Teacher: How did Cinderella spend most of her time?

Child: Cleaning the house, and cooking, and washing clothes.

Teacher: She cleaned, and cooked, and washed clothes, yeah. What else did she do?

In such situations students react to issues important to the teacher. Answers are either "right" or "wrong," with little or no room for reciprocal discussion. Frequent experiences with this format leads children to believe that there is always a "right" answer.

Productive discussions promote social interactions and also provide the opportunity to observe the use of higher levels of cognitive processing (Vygotsky, 1978). Opportunities to practice social exchanges illustrate, for students, how those conversing work together to collaboratively construct meaning.

The following student-initiated conversation about *It's Too Noisy!* by Joanna Cole (1989) illustrates such a discussion. The story is about a poor farmer who complains about his overcrowded, very noisy house and seeks advice from a wise man. The suggestion to fill the house with animals leads the man to appreciate, once the animals are removed, the usual, much quieter family noise. The teacher's supportive role in the discussion facilitates the development of children's comprehension. Each child's response is followed by an identification for the response.

Child 1:   Boy, that was a little house for all of those people. (evaluation)

Child 2:   Yeah, but not as filled as when all the animals were there. That was really a lot. (compare and contrast and an evaluation)

Teacher: Why did you say that was "really a lot?" (requests justification for response)

Child 2:   Because, see the pictures! There are so many animals that the kids are being bad. (supports response with concrete data from text)

Teacher: What do you mean "being bad?" (seeks justification for response)

Child 2:   Well, they're having pillow fights. See it in the picture. (supportive picture data offered)

Child 3:   And the kids are playing with the animals and that makes it noisy.

Child 1:   When there are a lot of people the kids get bad! (analyzes data from pictures)

Teacher: Why *do you suppose lots of people in the house make the kids bad?* (fa-
           cilitates interpretive thought)

Child 1:   Well because there are so many that the mother can't help them be good!
           (goes beyond the text to interpret data)

Child 3:   And there was no room to play so they got in trouble. (reasons to hy-
           pothesize)

Child 4:   He should have been happy with only his family there because it was less
           people than when the animals were in. (extends and analyzes)

Child 2:   Yeah, and it probably smelled from all of the animals, and there wouldn't
           be that smell with just the people. (hypothesizing based on prior knowledge)

Child 1:   What does the smell have to do with the story, anyway?

Child 2:   Well, it makes the room stink and then the man won't think that his
           family makes it crowded, because they don't stink like the animals.

The dialogue portrays how one student response leads to another, how a teacher's
inquisitive facilitation supports the development of conflict and resolution. Dialogue
also helps students to see ideas beyond their own.

Descriptive interpretations of conversations by the teacher ought to be included
in the reporting process (see Chapter 9, pp. 300–313). This provides students with
the information necessary to understand how they interpret text. The following are
only a few of the skills developed when students converse.

Discussions and Conversations	
Teaches	**Assesses**
• listening skills	• students' abilities to recall points of view of peers
• comparing and contrasting skills	• use of prior knowledge as it relates to new data
• extending information	• ability to hypothesize
• almost anything the talk provokes	• the same

Graphic Organizers for Retellings and Other Comprehension Activities

The way one stores knowledge has a considerable effect on students' accessibility to
information (Pittelman, Heimlick, Berglund, & French, 1991). Systematic storage of

knowledge increases comprehension. Graphic organizers, sometimes referred to as semantic maps, require students to analyze the features of text. They provoke comparisons and contrasts, developing meaningful relationships among significant ideas in print (Bos, Anders, Filip, & Jaffe, 1989). We compare and contrast new data, basing perceptions of that data on familiar information. Interestingly, the way we perceive new information depends on how we categorize and ultimately comprehend it (Rosenfield, 1988). Graphic organizers provide the frameworks necessary for categorizing and accessing information easily. They enhance the classification of information, which plays a key role in guiding students to connect new to already existing knowledge. Semantic maps seem to be keyed to the categorical nature of memory (Pittelman, Heimlick, Berglund, & French, 1991).

Most of the literature has supported organizers and maps as instructional tools (Anders & Bos, 1986; Anders, Bos, & Filip, 1984; Nagy, 1988; Searfoss & Readence, 1989; Tierney, Readence, & Dishner, 1990). We have found them to be extremely useful as self-monitoring tools, especially in content area studies.

Teaching Children to Use Maps for Learning and Self-assessment   When Robin Hepp's third graders compared aspects of stories, it spurred heated discussions. Her assessment of the conversations led her to decide to use the Venn diagram (Figure 6-14) the next time she noticed students comparing ideas.

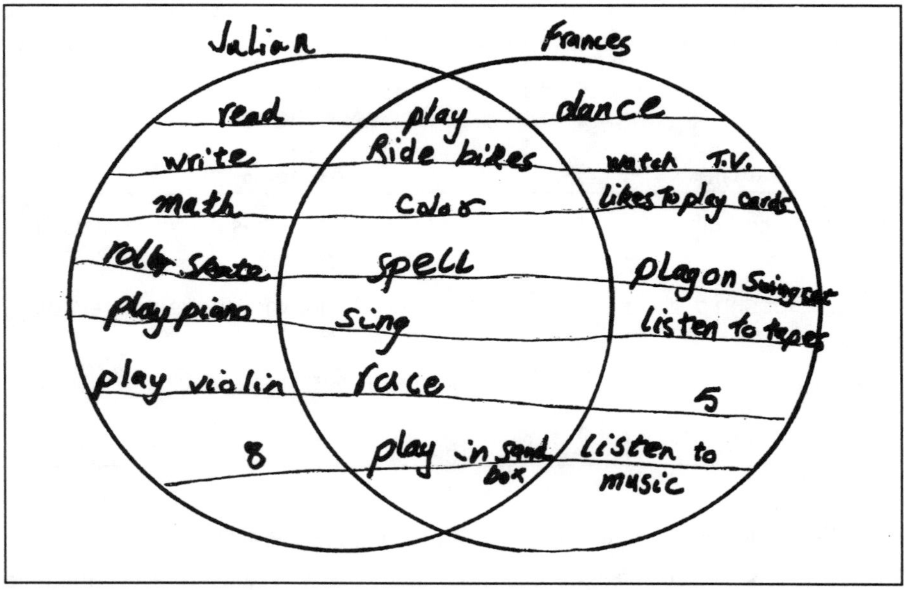

Figure 6-14.   Julian and Frances's Venn Diagram

Julian and Frances discovered they liked to do similar things. When the two were engaged in a discussion which identified similarities, Robin put a Venn diagram in front of each, pointed to the center section and said, "Write all of the things both of you like to do in this middle section. Why do you think you should write in the middle?" "Because you said to do it," replied Frances. "You're right," responded their teacher. Continued discussion led to an understanding that things alike share the middle section of the Venn diagram. When the teacher suggested that Julian's preferences be written on the left side, Frances said, "I'll write mine here (pointing to the right) because the middle circle is for both of us," he remarked. "Right on," responded their teacher.

The Venn diagram is a wonderful self-monitoring tool, especially for content areas. Some of the skills the Venn diagrams and other maps teach and guide students to self-monitor follow.

Graphic Organizers and Maps

Teach	Assess
• organizational skills	• ability to categorize content studied
• comparing and contrasting	• ability to see relationships
• frameworks "around" which to recall	• content area information
• visual ways to manage data	
• systematic frameworks for learning (by rehearsing) information	• students' ability to use frameworks to recall

Comprehension of Content Materials

Many teachers of science, social studies, math, and even composition find it difficult as part of their responsibilities to teach reading skills. This puzzles me, for it is difficult to use subject area texts without teaching the specific reading skills necessary to read specialized materials. Separating the teaching of reading from content areas has probably occurred in part because educators, like other professionals, specialize. Reading specialists, for example, take responsibility for literacy and language studies. Social studies specialists attend to content specific to the field. Segmenting literacy activities apart from other curriculum areas has always been a concern.

It behooves all teachers to know the specific literacy skills important for reading content materials and teaching these skills when necessary. Content area texts are unique, and reading and writing strategies for learning information from these texts are also unique. Many strategies are effective for guiding students to learn content area studies. My good friends Jo Anne and Rich Vacca (1993) have written a wonderful text that includes many of these. Two of the strategies seem to be used again and again with our children. These include (1) text pattern checklists, and (2) a content reading strategy.

Frameworks for Assessing and Learning about Text Patterns

Most content materials, because they are expository text, pose many challenges for students and teachers. The text patterns that predominate include sequencing, comparisons and contrasts, cause and effect relationships, and problems and solutions. The ease with which students handle these texts depends a great deal on an author's ability to represent relationships (Vacca & Vacca, 1993). Students often find it easier if they know the explicit signals that indicate text patterns. We used Vacca and Vacca's (1993) "reading signals" to create self-monitoring frameworks. Once students know the signal words they can identify the types of text. After using the checklists again and again, they learn the vocabulary necessary for identifying texts independently. The checklists in Figures 6-15, 6-16, and 6-17 guide students to determine text patterns. These encourage student self-monitoring and guide identification of text patterns students use in their writing. (See pages 141–143).

Content Reading Strategies

Content journals (Chapter 4, pp. 56–60) are wonderful for recording and reflecting upon information from content area reading. Julian filled his with observations of a hermit crab that lived in his classroom. (See Figure 6-18.)

Maps guide students to organize information. The circle map (Figure 6-19), especially, is effective for assisting students to recall and remember all sorts of content. The Venn diagram (see page 138) works "naturally" for comparing content.

The strategy suggested for developing self-monitoring consists of a series of four self-monitoring questions. The **Reading Content** strategy sheet provides the questions for students (Figure 6-20). We put them in our strategy bins (see page 68) and remind students to take and use them when they read a new piece of content material.

Comprehending the Relationship of Questions to Text

Tony Manzo (1968) developed and Taffy Raphael (1982) refined the Request Procedure. This strategy guides students to identify the different types of information usually sought by questions. "Right there" questions require that one find the answer and read it "right there" in the text. You point to and read the answer "right there."

Some questions require information from the text that is in more than one place.

Comparison-Contrast Checksheet

Check to see if some of the following words are included in the text. That means that the text pattern—

compares and contrasts

Comments

however	
but	
as well as	
on the other hand	
not only . . . but also	
either . . . or	
while	
although	
unless	
similarly	
yet	

Other words I added _____

_____

Text patterns: _____

Text: _____ my own, _____ a book. Project: _____

My name: _____ Date: _____

Figure 6-15.   Comparison-Contrast Checksheet

Cause-Effect and Problem-Solution Checksheet

Check to see if some of the following words are included in the text. That means that the text is—

cause-effect or **problem-solution** material

	Comments
because	
since	
therefore	
consequently	
as a result	
this led to	
accordingly	
if . . . then	
thus	

Other words I added _____

_____

Text: _____ my own, _____ a book. Project: _____

My name: _____ Date: _____

Figure 3-16.   Cause-Effect and Problem-Solution Checksheet

Sequence Checksheet

Check to see if some of the following words are included in the text. That means that the text is a—

sequence pattern

Comments

on (the date)	
not long after	
now	
as	
before	
after	
when	
first	
second	
next	
then	
finally	

Other words I added _____

_____

Text patterns: _____

Text: _____ my own, _____ a book. Project: _____

My name: _____ Date: _____

Figure 6-17.   Sequence Checksheet

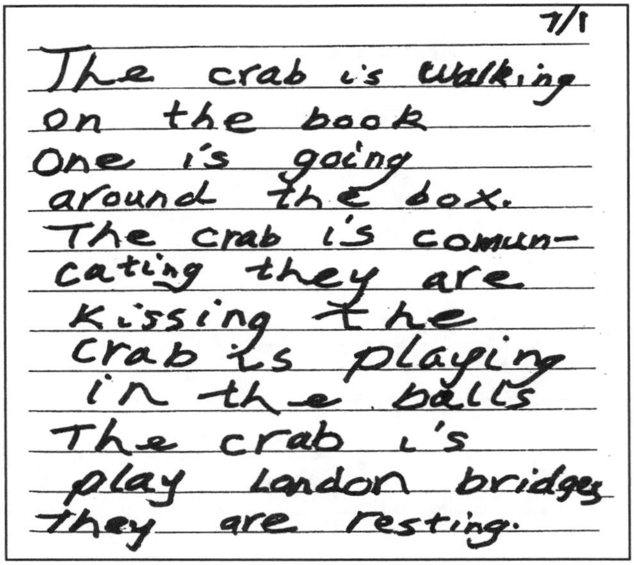
7/1
The crab is walking
on the book
One is going
around the box.
The crab is comun-
cating they are
kissing the
crab is playing
in the balls
The crab is
play London bridges
they are resting.

Figure 6-18. Julian's Content Journal

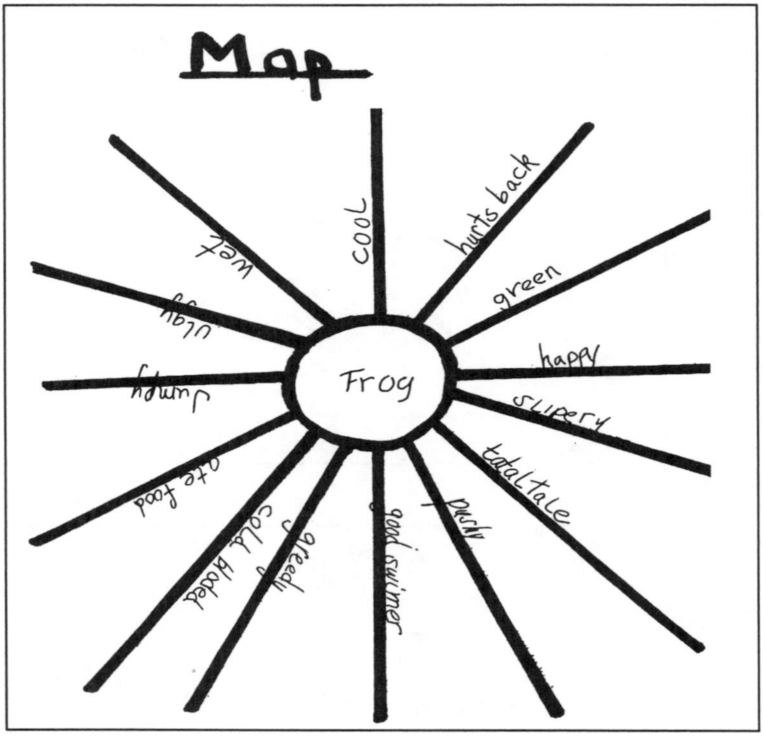
Map
Frog
cool
hurts back
green
happy
slipery
tataltale
pushy
good swimer
greedy
cold bladed
ate food
jumpy
ulgy
wet

Figure 6-19. Circle Map

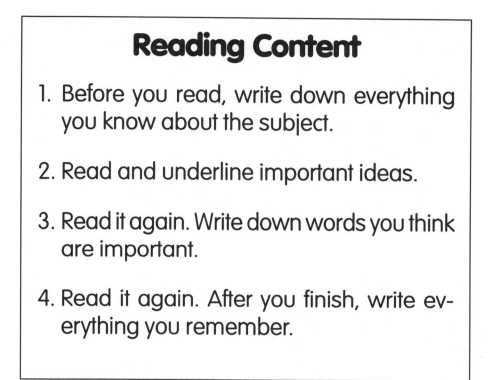

Figure 6-20.   Reading Content Strategy Sheet

To find the answers you look in several places in the text. The answers appear "right there," and "right there," and maybe even "right there." When answers are in several text locations, one "thinks" about the information sought and "searches" for it. When answers are in several places, the questions are "think and search" type questions.

Answers to "on my own" (OMO) questions cannot be found in the text, for the text does not include them. The answers are inferred, created from past experiences, hypothesized based on one's current and prior knowledge about information in the texts. Answers must be created "on my own." I recall reading an article about TWA flight 800, the jet that crashed shortly after take-off from New York's Kennedy Airport. The questions in the article focused on probable reasons for the disaster. I found myself attempting to answer the questions based on my frequent flying experiences. "Maybe," I thought, "the landing gear malfunctioned. No," I said to myself, "they were taking off, not landing." And the process continued. Children hypothesize all the time. Their imaginations coupled with their experiences help them produce many answers on their own.

Teaching Students to "Request" Information from Text

Begin by providing each student with a copy of a short, concise, complete, and appealing piece of written text. The following dialogue ought to support your efforts to guide students to use the request strategy on their own.

Teacher: We are going to learn about the kinds of questions you usually are asked on tests. Boys and girls, this strategy I am going to share will help you answer questions on tests. So, let's begin by reading this short story (distribute a copy to each student in the class). When you are finished, write a question about the story. The trick to writing the questions is to be sure that you can read the answer "right there" in the story. All you need to do is to point to where the answer is and read it. Now, who can tell me what you are supposed to do?

Anthony: Well, first read the story.

Teacher: Right, read the story and then . . .

Anthony: Read the story and then write a question and read the answer.

Teacher: Read the story and write a question that you can answer by reading the answer. Where, Anthony?

Anthony: Read the answer in the story.

Teacher: Read the answer "right there" in the story. Say it with me.

Anthony and
Teacher: Write the question and read the answer "right there" in the story.

Teacher: Right. (The teacher asks several other students what is supposed to be done, and guides them to respond as she did with Anthony in order to be sure that they hear the directions several times and that they understand the expectations). Write your "right there" question in this space (pointing to the correct line on a copy of Figure 6-21 that is displayed on an overhead projector).

As the students begin to read, the teacher reads the passage, too. When she finishes reading and notices that most of the children are about finished, she passes out a copy of the worksheet still projected on the overhead screen. When all students are finished writing their "right there" questions, the following discussion begins.

Teacher: O.K. who will share a "right there question?" O.K. Carol, (after the student raises her hand) read your "right there" question.

Carol: How many children did the family have?

Teacher: Now point to the "right there" answer in the story.

Writing Questions:
Right There, Think and Search, On Your Own

Write a "right there" question. _____

_____

_____

Write another "right there" question. _____

_____

_____

Write a "think and search" question. _____

_____

_____

_____

Write an "on your own" question. _____

_____

_____

_____

Write another "on your own" question. _____

_____

_____

_____

Figure 6-21.   Request Question Worksheet

Carol: Here —

Teacher: "Right there." Where is it?

Carol: Here, no, "right there."

Teacher: Right, the answer is "right there." Now read your "right there" question again.

Carol: Not the answer?

Teacher: No, the question.

Carol: O.K., how many children did the family have?

Teacher: Now, read your answer "right there" in the text. Where is the answer?

Carol: (pointing with her finger to the place on the page) Right there. "The family had ten children."

Teacher: Where is the answer?

Carol: (checking) It's "right there."

Using the appropriate language to guide the student is of utmost importance. The specificity with language builds appropriate expectations. It also provides consistency so that all the children are able to discuss the strategy the same way. The above dialogue includes a four-step process summarized as follows:

1.   Read your "right there" question.

2.   Now, find the answer to your "right there" question, "right there" in the text.

3.   Read your "right there" question, again.

4.   Now, read the answer to your "right there" question.

The same four-step process can be used for developing "think and search" and "on my own" questions, as well.

Using Request as Assessment

Once students understand the kind of information requested, they are ready to assess the type of questions included in their textbooks and in test items. Many teachers with whom I've worked have taken questions from both content textbooks and tests. They've created lists of these, and attached the questions to a passage or short selection for which the questions were developed. They asked students to identify the type of information that the questions are "requesting." When a student identifies a "think and search" question, he/she underlines or highlights the answers in the text itself. Children ages nine and older seem to like to find the answers and mark them in the text. Many of our children use highlighters. Others underline or circle answers. I suggest that children use a different color highlighter to identify each type of answer. One child, for example, marked "right there" answers in yellow, "think and search" in orange, and "on my own" in pink. The graphic organizer identifies some of the skills taught and assessed when using the request procedure.

Request Procedure	
Teaches	**Assesses**
• how to seek information	• ability to access appropriate inform-ation
• how to identify type of information sought	
• framework for discussion, type of information to acquire	• ability to use framework in several settings
• vocabulary to use the strategy	• ability to use vocabulary to identify and create questions

Self-Monitoring, Request, and Other Content Procedures

It is important for students to talk and then write about what they've learned and what they still need to know. The Progress Report Form (see Figure 6-5), illustrated throughout this text, works for writing about how each student uses comprehension strategies. The more students write about their progress, the more they learn about the strategies, and also about their own learning. Writing about progress MUST be incorporated in all studies.

Assessing and Teaching Good Reader Strategies

The procedure most effective for observing and assessing students' comprehension is referred to as think-alouds. Brown and Lytle (1988) define think-alouds as "a means of gathering information about individual readers' ongoing thinking processes and metacognitive behavior. Used flexibly, [think-alouds] can provide a framework for assessment integrated with instruction" (p. 96). Since assessment and instruction are integrated processes, the procedure is wonderful for determining how students make meaning of text. Then teachers can strategically plan appropriate instruction for students whose reading comprehension, or lack of it, is perplexing.

Using Think-Alouds to Assess Comprehension

The think-aloud process is an individual activity. The processes involved ask a student to read a portion of a text, usually one sentence at a time, and then voice his/

her thoughts, thinking out loud. The student's thoughts are analyzed and the processes used during reading are identified.

Sixteen-year-old Rachel wandered from subject to subject in conversations. Her written compositions also reflected the same lack of focus that was demonstrated when the child spoke.

Rachel's teacher, Margaret, decided to carry out a think-aloud in an attempt to find out what was keeping her from accomplishing tasks. The teacher selected a science passage from *Writing to Learn* by William Zinsser (1988) because it seemed to replicate the style of the text used in the student's science class. Before beginning, Margaret said, "I am interested in what you think about as you read. So, read a sentence out loud and then say out loud what you are thinking." Unlike many students, Rachel began to speak immediately. If students are silent, say, "What are you thinking about now?" or "Think out loud so I can hear your thoughts." The following passages include five sentences and accompanying think-alouds made by Rachel. These represented the type of responses she made throughout the seven-sentence passage. The sentences in bold type are the text. The regular type following each bolded sentence are Rachel's think-alouds after reading each sentence.

> **Water snakes are often classified as "pugnacious" by people who have tried to capture them.** "Right now going through my head I am thinking of my SAT course which taught me that pugnacious means eager to fight . . . water snakes bring me back to camp hide-away when I was five—or however old I was . . . and we used to go in the stream there and find crayfish and stuff, umm and then for some reason *Raiders of the Lost Ark* comes in too." **As with many forms of wildlife, these snakes will not hesitate to defend themselves.** "Many forms of wildlife, that spurs the image of Africa . . . Dr. Azoy and one of those like Nova channels . . ." (She reads aloud again . . .) **these snakes will not hesitate to defend themselves . . .** "I kind of missed that because I was thinking about the other thing . . . umm I don't know I see a coiled snake going 'hiss' (she makes a hissing noise)." **If grabbed by a person, a water snake will thrash about violently, reach around and bite, and also smear a foul smelling musk from glands in the base of the tail.** "Well, the smell kind of reminds me of church camp in the summer when there was a skunk going around and it wrecked everything and it reminds me of going to the bathroom in that buggy thing . . ." **Contrary to popular belief, water snakes can and do bite while underwater. . . .** "Oh gosh, that reminds me of being in the water and the 40-foot tress underneath the water cause it was like a glacier underneath and there were all these trees in the lake and if something happened you wouldn't find the body for days"— (she reads again, **water snakes can and do bite while underwater**) "and nothing ever bothered me in the ocean until my Mom

said Ewww just think about what is underneath there. And so I always get scared . . . and then at Church Camp—gee, a lot of Church Camp images—when we were trying to swim out to the sail boats whatever . . . there was a rail, an old dock and we saw some water moccasins two years ago, makes me shiver" . . . (re-reads, **can and do bite while underwater**). "Yeah! Oh I see a heron snatching up a fish" . . . **either to defend themselves or to catch prey. In all cases, however, the bite caused by a water snake produces mild scratches and nothing more.** "Oh yeah, right, I can see this hugh swollen cut with someone trying to suck the venom out and spitting it out . . . I think that was in a movie" . . .

Rachel is obviously inattentive to the subject matter. She focuses on past experiences unrelated to the text. She does this by selecting one word, phrase, or idea from the passage and finding something in her memory that relates to each. Rachel forces the information in the passage, twisting the data so that it fits her schemata. She certainly uses prior knowledge, but from her egocentric point of view. Her discussions include personal events or specific information spurred by the words she selected in the text. She strayed so far from the text ("I kind of missed that because I was thinking about the other thing" . . .), however, that she had to reread sections. Her explanation and the way she relates these to the phrase or word selected from the text is her starting point for understanding. Since none of her meanings connect to the content of the materials, she has little comprehension of the subject matter. Rachel used "um," pausing several times, but this is to be expected (Kucan & Beck, 1996) since she was having difficulty making meaning of the material. Rachel jumped from one topic to another almost as if she was hoping to "hit upon" the right answer.

Researchers have found that certain text materials influence the processes readers use to construct meaning. Fareed (1971) concluded that history texts sway students to make inferences, evaluate information, and summarize it when doing think-alouds (p. 525). Biology and other scientific materials spurred students to focus on literal meanings. Informational type texts caused students to provide more examples and sensory images as well as add more details than other types. Olshavsky (1975) identified inferencing and hypothesizing as processes used frequently when students read stories, especially high school students. Alvermann (1984) found that younger children related ideas in stories to previous personal experiences. Rachel's responses seem characteristic of a younger child. Certainly she seems unaware of the strategies she is using to process the informational data in the text. Figure 6-22, adapted from Glazer and Brown (1993), was used to guide Rachel to observe her thoughts during reading. Conferences with the student helped her realize that her attention to individual words and phrases hindered comprehension. The following conversation began a series that guided Rachel to "think along" (the instructional adaptation of think-alouds) in order to focus attention and comprehend.

Record of Think-Aloud		

Child's Name **Rachel**   Age **16**

Text Read **Writing to Learn**   Date _____

Directions: Place a check, tally, and/or write down examples of student's use of these reading-thinking behaviors.

	Frequently	**Sometimes**
Restates text ideas: — paraphrases		
— summarizes		
— uses own words		
Adds own ideas	✓ always finds a way to put her ideas into text.	
Recognizes when doesn't understand: — words		
— sentences		
— larger ideas		
Rereads		✓
Recalls prior knowledge	Yes, but does not connect it to text.	
Notices writing of text		
Hypothesizes, predicts, or reasons about text ideas		
Forms opinion about ideas or writing		
Other	Pushes meaning into text. Selects a word or phrase, & forces her meaning into it.	Meaning are often unrelated to text.

Figure 6-22.   Rachel's Record of Think-Aloud

Teaching "During Reading" Strategies to Enhance Comprehension

Several educators have adapted think-alouds for instructional purposes (Eddy & Gould, 1990; Farr, 1990; Wilson & Russavage, 1989). Farr (1990) has named the procedure "think-alongs" because readers "think along," attempting to look into ideas in their minds as they read. The research supporting the teaching of these strategies (Fareed, 1971; Langer, 1990; Lytle, 1982; Olshavsky, 1975; Ryan, 1985) suggests that the strategy should be helpful in guiding students to:

- **elaborate** using prior knowledge to make connections to text;
- **paraphrase and summarize** to signal understanding of information;
- **reason** in order to make inferences, predictions, or form hypotheses;
- **draw associations** using prior knowledge or experiences.

The following procedure, part of which was taken from a previous publication (Glazer, 1992) was adapted from the works of several educators (Eddy & Gould, 1990; Farr, 1990; Russavage & Arick, 1988; Wilson & Russavage, 1989).

Modeling Think-Alongs for Younger Children

Hold the book in front of the children. Put your finger to your forehead indicating that you are thinking. Imagine, for the sake of this description, that you are using the book *Cinderella.* Say, "I am thinking that this book is about, let me think. Well, the picture on the cover makes me think that it is about a poor girl. I think she's poor because her dress is made of rags. The girl is looking at a castle at the top of a hill. Maybe she is dreaming about living there." Continue **predicting** and telling **why** you make each prediction until you feel they are ready to listen to the story. As you read, stop to share ideas that come into your mind. Do this by:

- predicting what comes next (reasoning and drawing associations);
- questioning indecisive ideas (paraphrasing to signal understanding);
- rereading to clarify ideas (reason in order to hypothesize);
- rereading to seek meaning of words for which you are unsure of the meaning (reason to hypothesize and summarize in order to signal meaning);
- personalize aspects of the story by relating ideas to things in your life (draw associations using prior knowledge);
- make a picture in your mind (visualizing to reason and hypothesize).

Predicting from Text What Comes Next   At the opportune time, perhaps the moment Cinderella's fairy godmother is introduced, stop and think out loud, "I can predict what will happen next. I bet the fairy godmother will get Cinderella a new dress because she has a magic wand."

Questioning Text   Where there might be several alternatives for the direction of the story's plot, ask yourself a question, out loud, just before the event occurs. As Cinderella dances with the prince, for example, say, "I wonder if Cinderella's clothes will turn back to rags at midnight?" Then, proceed with reading the story.

Reread to Clarify Ideas   Often ideas in stories need to be clarified for understanding to occur. Rereading the text several times helps to make some of the ideas clear. The fairy godmother's ability to change mice into horses and rags into a beautiful dress illustrates concepts that might need clarification. As you read these parts, you might stop, point your finger to your forehead and ask, for example, "I wonder why she's called a fairy godmother and not just a godmother?" After asking, reread sections that help infer such an unusual happening.

Reread to Secure Word Meanings   Predicting meanings of words from text is one of the best ways to increase vocabulary. Demonstrating this strategy of thinking out loud provides the model that helps children understand "how to do it." When you approach a word during reading that might be new—for example, the word "necromancer"—say, "Hmmmm. That's a new one. I think I'll reread this sentence to figure out what the word means."

After rereading once or several times, say, "A-ha, I've got it. It must mean magical because the fairy godmother makes magic with her wand and great things happen." Then continue to read on.

Personalizing Text   Connecting one's ideas to those in a text personalizes the information. It provides readers with a way to make associations. Stop when there is a section of story that has personal meaning. Say, for example, "My Mom always said that I had to clean my room before I could go to a party. The difference is that she always kept her word. Cinderella's stepmother didn't let her go even though she did all of the cleaning."

Making Pictures in the Mind   Imagine, as you are reading, that the text says, "Cinderella looked beautiful even though her clothes were made of rags." Point to your forehead and say, "That's a funny picture. I can see pretty hair and a face, but I can't picture her raggedy clothes looking pretty at all."

It takes several demonstrations for children to learn how to use think-alongs to self-monitor their reading. Teachers suggest that biweekly modeling is the way to begin.

Involving Young and Older Students in Think-Alongs   Once young children realize what you are modeling, they will begin to tell you, "I know what you are doing. You are talking about the story." This voluntary response is similar to information secured on a test. It informs you that children are ready to learn to use the strategies. When students are ready for the instruction, find a short, complete, interesting story. Provide a copy of the story for each child. Say, "I am going to read this story as you follow along in your copy of the text. When I get a thought about the text, I will stop, and put my finger to my forehead. The finger tells you that I am thinking about the text. Watch me as I think out loud."

After the group has followed along, say, "Tell me what I did as I thought out loud. I will write what you saw on this chart (point to an easel)." Write the list of think-alongs on a worksheet in their words. Reproduce the list in worksheet form for the students. Use the list as soon as possible, preferably the next day. Select a short story to read to the students. Hand out the worksheet and ask them to check the think-alouds you use during your oral reading session. Ask for volunteers, after you've finished, to share the think-alongs they saw you use, encouraging discussion.

At the next session, group children in pairs. Provide each with a story and a copy of the checklist. Have peers take turns, one reading the story and the other noticing and checking the think-alongs he/she uses. Then have the others repeat the process.

Thinking along takes more time to learn than most other strategies. Once students learn how to use the strategy, their ability to stay on task will improve. Children ought to self-monitor their use of think-alongs weekly. A final thought: *Thinking along breaks the natural flow of language when reading. It can also break the flow of comprehension, as well. This activity, therefore, should be an addition to, not a substitute for, reading to students* (Glazer, 1992, p. 71).

Summary

We are never certain about the causes of reading comprehension problems. We do know, however, that interest, motivation, experience, and the ability to see points of view other than one's own increase understanding of text. We know, too, that concepts about comprehension have changed instructional strategies. The changing nature of instruction demands alternative assessment strategies in order for students to learn about their educational strengths and needs. Frameworks, used consistently to support the teaching of strategies, guide students to learn from reading, and also to assess their accomplishments. The essential element in all activities related to comprehension is students' self-monitoring of their own progress. Regularly writing about what they've learned using the language of the frameworks helps them learn the language of content. Most important is the fact that students MUST talk about their reading, reason with peers, rereason, reread, and rework their ideas, thinking along in order to become insightful, happy, productive readers.

CHAPTER 7

Composition

"Children want to write," says Don Graves. "They want to write the first day they attend school. This is no accident. Before they went to school they marked up walls, pavements, newspapers with crayons, chalk, pens, or pencils . . . anything that makes a mark. The child's marks say, 'I am'" (1983, p. 3).

Evaluations of children's writing begin from the time they make marks. There seems to be an aura about the writing process that seduces adults to question, critique, and even insult children's attempts to write. "What are you making?" asked one adult as she observed a five-year-old child drawing. "It's my house," replied the child. "Oh," continued the adult, "you need to put a chimney on the house so the dirty air can get out." The five-year-old continued to draw, ignoring the adult's suggestion. "The chimney goes right here," said the adult putting her finger on the specific spot in the child's drawing. "I'm done," asserted the child, as she got up and walked away from the table.

Probably without recognizing her behavior, the adult informed the youngster that her work was either incomplete or unacceptable. The youngster stopped drawing, indicating that she was either rejecting the suggestion, viewing the comment as criticism, or experiencing feelings of uncertainty. Withdrawing avoids rejection.

I abhor this type of adult communication to children. If one has a burning desire to comment, at least be honest. "My house has a chimney on it because I have a fireplace" provides the child with a rationale for drawing a chimney. Justifying the need to change the drawing supports an option without intimidation.

When children talk, we listen. Their cooing, babbling, echolalic vocalizations, their overgeneralizations and telegraphic language function to inform their worlds about their wants, needs, and desires. We accept children's initial attempts to communicate using oral language without criticism. Sometimes we expand their attempts, informing them about how to create clear text so ideas can be easily shared (Menyuk,

1963). When a toddler says, for example, "Mommy up," the mother's response may be, "Sally wants Mommy to pick her up." Adults usually find delight in children's early attempts to pronounce words and spontaneously model acceptable oral text. Criticism almost never happens in these instances.

When children write, often adult intervention becomes fierce. Educators and laypersons scrutinize spelling, punctuation, capitalization, segmentation, and neatness all too often. The appearance of the writing seems to be more important than its content (Petty & Finn, 1981). Laypersons, especially, notice these items first, and many often say something like, "If he can't spell correctly, how can he be in the business world?" Teacher's marks on student papers have caused them to minimize their written productions (Petty & Finn, 1981). I recall receiving the reviewed copy of my first manuscript. The copy editor's red marks looked like bloodstains to me. Imagine how students, especially those who have difficulty with writing, view these "bloody" marks! Compositions will always be evaluated, for evaluation is part of learning.

Unfortunately, grades are a fact of life in school, but parents and teachers of young children don't have to "grade." You can be sure that as the children grow someone will grade their creations. We most probably agree that a letter or number grade certainly can't summarize the work that students produce. The one-letter grade hinders, rather than serves as a tool for learning how to do better.

Linda Rief (1992) says, ". . . I can evaluate [my students'] growth . . . as a writer and reader, if I have to. I have all the evidence in front of me in their drafts of writing from rough to final, in their response to what they're reading, in their self-evaluations of themselves as writers and readers, and in my responses to them on their writing and in their reading [journals]" (p. 143).

Linda is correct! Each of us has the evidence for evaluating students' writing in meaningful ways. The products students produce provide the data for assessing strengths and also for guiding them to do better. The perpetual problem, however, is HOW. How do we judge? What do we judge? How often must judgments be made? There have been as many answers to these questions as there have been teachers of writing, and inconsistencies and often misunderstandings about evaluation procedures have evolved. Assessment of writing in schools has, therefore, been a source of consternation for teachers (Searle & Dillon, 1980). When assessment goes beyond sentence construction and mechanics, and when elements such as ideas, organization, tone, and audience awareness are reviewed, teachers become anxious (Fantauzzo, 1996). All the confusion occurs because evaluations of students' compositions are as unique as each of the teachers who assess them.

What Are We Assessing? What Are We Teaching?

Students' oral and written responses to reading, experiences, events, and the organization and structure of their work are what we are assessing. We also assess students' perceptions of the writing process, for these influence their productions. Observing children's developmental stages of writing needs to be part of the assessment process, as well. Unfortunately, consideration for each student's development as a writer has not been as important as it ought to be.

In recent years, educators have begun to view the writing process developmentally, much like oral language. Professionals have guided the public to understand that writing develops with experiences. The more students write, the more prolific they become. There are two types of discussion in the literature concerning written language development: (1) the development of the ability to create the written forms that make letters and words and, (2) the development of the ability to compose ideas.

Making Written Forms

Piaget and Inhelder (1969) described a sequence of changes in children's ability to copy forms from the ages of 2.6 to 7.0. They found this ability varies widely. Young children first create gross approximations of letters which later become refined (Clay, 1975). Crude letter formations result in accidental discoveries of correct letter formations. Unusual letter forms, invented words, and make-believe sentences are children's precursors for traditional formats. Clay (1975) indicates that recoding children's writing would probably not reveal any set pattern or sequence of letter discovery because of individual experiences. These early attempts, however, indicate that the youngsters are searching for the principles of written language by experimenting.

Early drawings and scribbles are precursors for later writing behaviors. Clay (1975) notes that early writing attempts are characteristically gross approximations of later refinements, but are also very specific. She cites the child "Ian" who rejects the writing of his name as such, insisting that "IAN" (not Ian) is the correct way to write it.

Experimenting and learning to write the forms that create written language happen gradually. Children begin to experiment with written forms from the moment they realize that they have the power to control the writing tool. They discover elements of print, some in their toddler years and others not until the age of six. Clay's (1975) research has resulted in a series of principles that provide a framework for examining the development of children's handwriting. These principles, based on the kinds of marks young children create on paper, are summarized in Figure 7-1. This framework, adapted from Glazer and Burke (1994), can be used to note the principles preschool children use to create marks resembling print. The framework provides language for describing writing behaviors.

Differences in development can be due to general intelligence, but they can also occur because of the experiences, or lack of them, in children's lives (Clay, 1975). There is doubt that there is a specific sequence of development through which all children pass as they become writers.

Principles of Early Writing Development	
	Comments
Recurring Principle	
Child repeats the same moves creating "recurring" marks. Example: *[handwritten recurring marks]*	
Directional/Flexibility Principles	
Child moves head or hand, from left to right indicating understanding of print direction.	
Child points to left side of texts first then right when reading pictures or attempting print.	
Child draws first on left side of paper then directs movements to the right.	
Child's drawings appear to be "creative" attempts at making letters and words.	
Generating Principle	
Child seems to use letters in patterns. Example: *[handwritten: SSM2SSM2SSM2 SSM2]*	
Child uses series of consistent patterns. Example: *[handwritten: 88● 88● 88● 88● 88●]*	
Child uses consistent pattern over and over, changing one element of text. Example: *[handwritten: I like cats. I like you. / I like cake. I like candy. / I like me. I like milk.]*	
Inventory Principle	
Child writes and rewrites groups, series, or bunches of words or letters as if taking inventory of her/his writing. Example: *[handwritten: ab2tiou2xwmndprsBF]*	

Figure 7-1. Principles of Early Writing (Page 1 of 2)

Contrastive Principle	
Child writes "contrasts" (i.e., lower case next to upper case letters; letters made with circles next to those made with lines).	
Abbreviation Principle	
Child's drawings and pictures represent ideas. Example: SOS	
Child's drawings and writing stand for things other than what they appear. Example:	
Written attempts resemble familiar signs available to child (i.e., billboards, advertisements, etc.). Example (shell)	

Figure 7-1. Principles of Early Writing (Page 2 of 2)

Composing Text

Children's letter formations inform us about growth in writing. But, without knowing what children think and feel about their creations, we know only about their ability to make marks on paper. Making marks is writing, creating ideas is composition.

Children of the same age vary greatly in their abilities to compose text. Robyn, age eight-years-seven-months (Figure 7-2), and Julie, age eight-years-five-months (Figure 7-3), exhibit different composing abilities. Robyn uses varied sentence patterns throughout her text, this determined by using the Assessing Sentence Construction checksheet (Figure 7-4). She writes with purpose, focuses, spells using conventional patterns, and uses punctuation (determined by using the Stages of Writing Development tool, Figure 7-5). Julie, on the other hand, uses the same sentence pattern throughout. She makes minimal additions to sentences. Robyn's text is more interesting to read, due mostly to the variety of sentence patterns used, and also to the additional interesting words added to the text.

Differences between these children who are about the same age are expected. Because of the differences (see Chapter 3), the assessment of writing must be as individual as the children themselves. The creative nature of the artistic process spurred the emergence of the use of alternatives to traditional assessment for writing. Portfo-

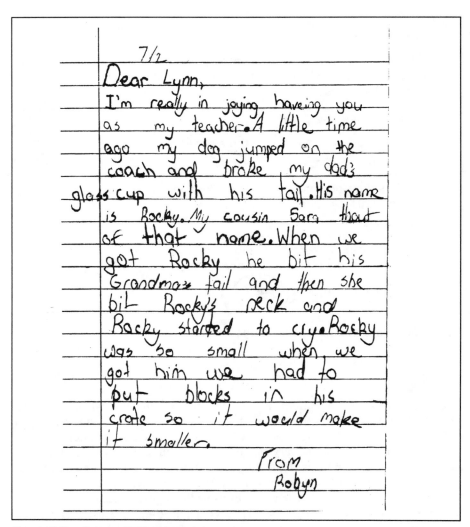

Figure 7-2. Robyn's Writing Sample

lios that include over-time collections of student products permit both planned and spontaneous comparisons and contrasts of students' work. The products are authentic and also available for continuous surveillance by students, teachers, and parents. The evidence is in front of everyone, reducing the likelihood that individual teacher and parent perceptions will control student impressions. "As teachers," says Linda Rief, "we must listen first to the perceptions our students have of themselves and address what they think they can and cannot do" (1992, p. 143).

Dear Danielle,
I have a anther friend named Danielle. Do you like the show Rugrats. It is on Nick. I will put you on my best friend list.

From
Julie

PS. Do you like me?

(Yes) or NO.

cool

Figure 7-3. Julie's Writing Sample

Assessing Sentence Construction	
Child's Name_____ Age _____	
Description of Sentence	**Comments**
Connects strings of ideas with "and." ("I love you and I have a dog and I go to school.")	
Uses the same words to begin sentences. ("I like candy. I like apples." or "I have a sister. I have a brother. I have a bike.")	
Writes additions at the beginnings of sentences. ("Today I went.")	
Writes simple sentences. ("I went") with an addition ("to the park"); ("I ran after my friend")	
Uses dialogue. ("He said, 'I don't think they're hungry.'").	
Uses dependent clauses in sentences. ("I like to eat candy when I am hungry.")	
Combines sentences. ("We went backstage and met them.")	
Uses coordinates in addition to "and" to connect sentences. (but, or, so, yet, etc.) ("We rented a video but it was boring.")	
Uses descriptive words.	
Uses pronouns to identify people. (clearly; unclearly: "Mary and Jane were playing and she had to leave.")	
Uses a variety of sentence types. ("Why are they singing?" "Go home!")	

Figure 7-4.   Assessing Sentence Construction

Stages of Writing Development

Child's Name: _____ Age: _____

Behavior   **Comments**

STAGE 1: PREWRITING

Scribbles without preconception
Shows interest in words and letters   _____
Preplans writing and drawing projects   _____
Spends long periods on these projects   _____
Shows space relationships and cri-   _____
  tiques own work
Recognizes and names letters   _____
Writing of words lacks sound/symbol   _____
  relationship
                                                       _____

STAGE 2: THE BEGINNING WRITER

Labels drawings
Makes lists of same-pattern sentences   _____
Develops a sense of story   _____
Includes personal experiences in   _____
  writing
Overuses structure   _____
Invents spelling   _____
Requests help with spelling   _____
Uses some punctuation   _____

STAGE 3: THE EMERGENT WRITER

Writes with purpose
Can focus thoughts through writing   _____
Uses varied sentence structures   _____
Spells using mostly conventional   _____
  patterns
Uses correct punctuation   _____
                                                       _____

Summary Statement: _____

_____

Stage: _____

Figure 7-5.   Stages of Writing Development

What About Students' Perceptions?

A six-year survey of 1500 children indicates that students' perceptions of themselves is greatly influenced by what they actually do in literacy classrooms (Glazer & Fantauzzo, 1993). Most (see Figures 7-6, 7-7, and 7-8), unfortunately, are over-cautious about expressing their ideas, fearing that they may conflict with those of their teachers. In a survey of children ages 5 to 17, students describe their abilities in terms of behaviors. Responses were sensitive to anticipated adult expectations. When asked to describe their reading abilities, 93 percent of the responses were noncommittal and indecisive. Children seemed to be waiting for teachers' ideas before expressing their own.

Name some things good readers do when they read.

Good readers read silently so they don't disturb other people reading.

Name some things poor readers do when they read.

They mumbul when they try to read a book.

What kind of reader are you?

I'm a good reader but I mess ups some times.

Your name: *Anit*

Your age: *8*   Date: *Sept 22*

Figure 7-6. Anit's Good Reader Sheet

Name some things good readers do when they read.

read alote of chapters.

Name some things poor readers do when they read.

read slow and get stuck on words.

What kind of reader are you?

not to bad but a little bad.

Your name: *andy*

Your age: *9*   Date: *2 - 15 - 93*

Figure 7-7.   Andy's Good Reader Sheet

Adult expectations and perceptions of children's achievements have always played a part in children's ideas about themselves as learners. Children will usually accept adult evaluations, and discard their own, at least in school. It is important that students develop their own perceptions about their reading and writing abilities using guidelines for justifying their judgments. Children's perceptions of their literacy activities provide valuable insights about the learning. Their real perceptions, however, may not always match those of adults (Glazer & Fantauzzo, 1993; Michael, 1994).

```
Name some things good readers do
when they read.  I think after
they read they would
tell someone what they
read.

Name some things poor readers do
when they read.  I think after
they read they would forget
what they read.


What kind of reader are you?  When
I finish a book I some-
times forget what I
read.

Your name: Gregory Jackson
Your age: 11   Date: 10/15/9•
```

Figure 7-8. Gregory's Good Reader Sheet

Evaluating Writing: How to Begin

It is essential to determine students' perceptions of themselves as writers from the moment we meet them. Pete's Good Writer Sheet identifies specific characteristics about his writing, justifying his perception. He has, however, vacillated, putting himself in between "good" and "not perfect" (Figure 7-9). His perceptions, as well as those of other children, will determine how to plan for instruction. I suggest that you use the Good Writer Sheet at the very beginning of the school year.

Good Writer Sheet

Name some things good writers do when they write.

I think a good has opening sentence that well pursade you to read on in the story. He or she also understands what they are writing about.

Name some things poor writers do when they write.

A poor writer's work is asllay choppy. They also will jump from topic to topic.

What kind of writer are you?

I'm in be twian because I'm not perfect.

Name: Peter Foster   **Age** 11 **Date** 11/20

Figure 7-9. Pete's Good Writer Sheet

Once we know how students feel about themselves as writers, their writing stage (Figure 7-5) ought to be assessed. Since writing is a developmental process, several student samples must be collected over time and reviewed. The checklist provides descriptive language for identifying and discussing students' development. Describing behaviors and using the same language for all children provides consistent and authentic benchmarks for defining growth.

Seven-year-old Elizabeth's story (Figure 7-10) illustrates the developmental aspects of writing and the importance of experiences for learning to compose. Although her handwriting is inconsistent, irregular, and difficult to read, she knows about words and sentences. She knows the difference between lower and uppercase letters. She was aware of the fact that sentences began and ended, this indicated by the fact that she began her second sentence on a new line. She is aware of the sounds of the English language. This is evident by the repeated "LST" at the beginning of

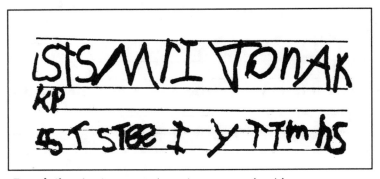

Translation: Last summer I went on a camping trip.
Last spring I went to my house

Figure 7-10.   Elizabeth's Story

each of the sentences. She told her teacher, "This is how I spell 'last.'" Elizabeth is able to write with purpose, as well. A look at Elizabeth's writing using the Stages of Writing Development checklist in Figure 7-5 (Glazer & Searfoss, 1988) indicates that she uses the same sentence pattern, creates text by using personal experiences, invents spelling, and writes without using punctuation. These characteristics place her in Stage 2. We can refer to her as a "beginning writer." Several months of writing at least five different times daily without critiques helped Elizabeth's development. A dialogue journal entry pictured in Figure 7-11 includes purpose, focus of thought, and punctuation, indicating that she is moving into the emergent writer stage. A journal entry (Figure 7-12) seven weeks later shows dramatic change. Handwriting is clear and regular; varied sentence patterns and more conventional spelling also characterize her text. The daily routine (see Chapter 4, pp. 45–63) writing activities and

Dear Betsy,

kTN U TOK me
WT U BE for
Halloween
Love, LIZ

Dear Liz,
I went trick-or-treating
with my son Ricky on
Halloween Night. I met
your Uncle Mike on Parents'
Night. He is a nice man.
Love,
Betsy

Figure 7-11. Elizabeth's Dialogue Journal Entry

teacher encouragement provided the necessary support for Elizabeth's composing abilities to soar. She wrote, and her teacher responded to her journal entry. Her audience, the teacher, spurred a desire, interest, and purpose for producing text. When the writing became legible, growth occurred rapidly. Elizabeth grew from a beginning to an emergent writer, whose text created laughter and delight for her audience. As Vygotsky wrote, ". . . as the child gains proficiency, task demands are raised until the child is functioning independently and the teacher functions as a supportive observer" (1962, p. 101).

I had a good Thanksgiving. My Mom wasn't in the mood to make a turkey. She was too tired. She only made baked ziti and spaghetti.

Elizabeth, age 7.

Figure 7-12.   Elizabeth's Later Dialogue Journal Entry

What Is Assessed Next?

How students write, what they write, the value of their writing to themselves, the audiences for whom they write, and the mechanical aspect of writing are only a few of the elements that we need to review. My teachers have compiled and revised checklist after checklist of things important to writing assessment over the years. The checklists have been cumbersome, all-encompassing or scant, but always changing. The creative and developmental nature of the writing process confuses most educators, for the changes disrupt the professional decisiveness used for assessment in other content area subjects.

I suggest, therefore, that you begin by assessing the environment you create for supporting and enticing students to compose. Table 7-1 includes some guidance for this assessment.

Teacher Behavior	Comments
I talk about what good writers do when they write, whenever it is appropriate, and in all content areas.	
I model writing, by engaging in activities as a learner in the classroom.	
There are many different kinds of paper available for students to select from in order to write.	
Students talk about their topic before they write.	
Students write about ideas based on their realities.	
Students always realize a functional purpose for writing, this indicated in conversations.	
Discussions about style and formats occur.	
Students engage in functional and recreational writing at least five times daily, without critiques.	
Peer evaluation is encouraged by engaging in this activity as a class member.	
Discussions about using language appropriately for the audience occurs regularly.	
Self-monitoring frameworks are used consistently across content areas.	
Collections of written products are reviewed over time and observations guide instruction.	

Table 7-1.

Children need to learn how to construct texts. More important, students and their teachers need to know how to inform each other about what each knows and what each needs to learn. The strategies that guide them to self-monitor also instruct. Authentic assessment is part of an authentic instructional process.

Learning and Assessing Composition

Frameworks for assessing writing are also the frameworks for guiding students to create products. The frameworks "flip" and "flop" between serving as assessment tools and acting as instructional strategies for creating writers. Selecting instructional strategies, therefore, that can be "flipped-flopped" from instructional to assessment tools is important.

We have developed a series of guidelines that seem to facilitate the development of writers, especially reluctant writers. Observations of hundreds of children in our Center for Reading and Writing and elsewhere have supported the efficacy of these guidelines:

- students need to write without critiques at least five times daily;

- written products must be accepted, NOT corrected, unless they are to be published and shared;

- adults and students need to look at "what each knows" first and "what each needs" next;

- children's writing will reflect but be less advanced than their oral language unless there is an articulation problem. Then they will speak as they can, rather than how we'd like them to;

- handwriting is NOT a reflection of writing ability but rather of motor coordination or visual spatial abilities.

Writing Five Times Daily Without Critiques

I suggest that children write at least five times daily without intervention. You might begin by using the daily routines—dialogue journals, literature and content journals, and mail described in Chapter 4—as vehicles for natural writing. Additional spontaneous writing can occur when children caption their drawings, or write narrative or explanatory text in reference to these drawings.

Leaving notes for students encourages them to leave notes for you and their peers. Children often ask when they've completed an assignment, "What should I do now?" The routine writing activities and those mentioned below are perfect and productive "time users."

Instructional Frameworks That Entice

Many wonderful books about the teaching of writing have been published (Atwell, 1987; Bissex, 1980; Calkins, 1994; Elbow, 1981; Graves, 1983; Graves & Sunstein, 1992; Harwayne, 1992; Moffett and Wagner, 1992; Shaughnessy, 1977; Wilde, 1997). Working with reluctant writers has provided me with some information to add to the literature.

Students who have received inappropriate or more-than-necessary evaluations have made the decision that the assessments are painful. It is easier for them to be nonwriters than poor ones. Instruction for reluctant writers, therefore, must be camouflaged. A positive, supportive environment is essential. Structured, foolproof frameworks to entice them to compose, focusing on the content rather than the mechanics of writing, has proven to be successful.

These foolproof strategies work when my teachers follow two rules:

> Do NOT interrupt children during writing times. Let them write.
> Do NOT evaluate these products.

The strategies are meant to "turn them on" to writing. They permit students to tell "what they know." They must be used to prove to reluctant students that they can write!

Getting Them Started

Fourteen-year-old Jason had many negative experiences with reading and writing in school. "It's not that I don't like to read," he commented. "It's that I lose interest really fast and I'd rather be outside playing ball." Jason spent most of his elementary school years in remedial classes. He resisted teacher-direction due to agitation from teachers who lacked sufficient knowledge to satisfy the needs associated with his learning disability. It was not until Lee Bennett Hopkins, the children's poet, author, and anthologist, visited his school that he began to change. Jason, who chose not to attend the assembly, was given no choice by the principal. Lee talked about his difficult childhood and failures in school. Jason's facial expressions indicated surprise and interest. A one-on-one conversation with Lee and an autographed book led Jason to read, without coaxing, several of Lee's books. He had discovered poetry. Poems were short, interesting, and easy to read quickly. During the presentation, Lee shared his poem "Good Books, Good Times!" (1995) with the students and his strategy for writing this poem.

> Good book.
>
> Good times.
>
> Good stories.
>
> Good rhymes.

Good beginnings.

Good ends.

Good people.

Good friends.

Good fiction.

Good fact.

Good adventures.

Good acts.

Good stories.

Good rhymes.

Good books.

Good times.*

"All I did to write that poem," Lee explained, "was to take the word 'good' and write it sixteen times down the left side of the page. Then I picked sixteen other words and wrote one next to each 'good,' and zap, there's my poem." The audience of adults and children were excited with the "framework" for creating a poem, which was evident by their attentive postures during Dr. Hopkin's one and one-half hour presentation.

    Later that week, Jason's teacher used the "Make a Poem" framework (Figure 7-13) and modeled the creation of her own poem to the entire class using Lee's strategy. She asked for suggestions for words, in addition to "good," that might be used. Margot suggested, "happy;" Billy, "sad." Devon said, "lovely;" Trisha, "exciting." Helen came up with "love;" Brigitte, "blue." The teacher wrote the words on the chalkboard as the suggestions flowed from the children. Then she put the "Make a Poem" framework with the composition strategies in the wall bins, and suggested that the children use them when they had some time to write. Excited children created individual poems using the structured framework presented by the wonderful author. Children, including Jason, joined the nouveau poets. "I never knew," volunteered Jason, "that it was so easy to write a poem." The visual representation of the poem's structure provided by the worksheet (Figure 7-14) provided the framework or outline for creating the poem. Students who need specific structure to create text find this easy, relaxed, and supportive. It is a way to build secure feelings about their products. One youngster followed the poem-writing activity with the Progress Report Form (Figure 7-15) without teacher direction. He had been "hooked" into poetry writing by using a formula, and was able to identify his accomplishments and needs.

---

*Copyright © 1985 by Lee Bennett Hopkins. Reprinted by permission of Curtis Brown, Ltd.

Lee Bennett Hopkins List Poem

Pick a word. Write it sixteen times on the left. Then put a different word next to it to make a poem.

_____	_____
_____	_____
_____	_____
_____	_____
_____	_____
_____	_____
_____	_____
_____	_____
_____	_____
_____	_____
_____	_____
_____	_____
_____	_____
_____	_____

Figure 7-13.   Lee Bennett Hopkins List Poem Framework

Lee Bennett Hopkins List Poem

Pick a word. Write it sixteen times on the left. Then put a different word next to it to make a poem.

Good	morning
Good	day
Good	afternoon
Good	group
Good	grades
Good	report card
Good	info
Good	ant farm
Good	breakfast
Good	butterflies
Good	team
Good	boy
Good	girl
Good	teacher
Good	boy
Good	name

Figure 7-14. Student List Poem Using Framework

Progress Report Form

Student: **Jason**   Teacher: **Beth**
Time Period: From:_____To: _____
Area (Check one or more) Comprehension____ Composition____
         Vocabulary____ Independence____ Other_____

What I can do	What I need	My teacher's job
Use good describing words. Write good poems.	I need to write more often. Write different kinds of poems.	To help me write different poems.

Figure 7-15.   Jason's Progress Report Form

"I guess," he commented, "I know how to make a poem because I can use the 'make a poem' sheet." This, dear readers, illustrates how assessment IS in fact instruction. The framework used to create the poem and the self-assessment provide a way for students to take charge of their learning. Jason, whose reluctance to write permeated his classroom agenda, independently wrote "Ants" (Figure 7-16) while researching and writing a science report about ants. What a wonderful example of how frameworks guide text production! The pleasure and success from their products guide students to believe that they are in control of both the writing and its evaluation.

Ants

Ants dig.

Ants might like to eat a fig.

Ants bite.

Ants fight.

Ants like to sleep at night.

Ants crawl.

Ants bawl if they fall.

Ants like the mall.

Ants die.

Ants cry.

I hope they fly to heaven.

Figure 7-16.   Jason's List Poem

The following strategies help students play games with words. These may be carried out in sequential order, or randomly, as you feel appropriate. The activities provide structure, format, and security for those who "think" they can't do it.

Structured Frameworks for Reluctant Writers

Writing Lists

This activity is a good one for students whose perceptions about writing are so negative that they just won't compose. Lists can be made for content area studies where categorizing information is important. If, for example, students are studying insects, children could each take a pad (or clipboard with paper), and walk around the school building identifying and writing the names of as many insects as they can find. I have found that limiting time in these activities provides that competitive edge that students seem to enjoy. For the sake of these directions, hypothesize that you are taking the children outside. When the students are gathered outside, say, "Before we begin, write 'crawlers and flyers' at the top of your paper." Then share the directions which might be as follows:

When I say GO, search for insects that crawl.

Write the names of insects that crawl on your list.

You have five minutes. Ready! GO!

Inform the children when five minutes have passed. Gather together and begin a discussion that guides them to compare and share lists. I have found that students enjoy discovering that others have included the same words in their lists. These children, when grouped together, begin to talk and, with teacher encouragement, oral texts are created. One reluctant student talked for seven minutes about her list of favorite foods. Her teacher incidentally (but, on purpose) left on a tape recorder and transcribed her text that night. She presented the child with her composition about favorite foods the next day, and the child was amazed at her production. The incident helped the student realize that:

- when you talk about a topic you are writing about it;

- writing is easier when you write about what you know;

- you don't have to handwrite in order to produce text.

Encourage students to keep lists of everything—their assignments, their spelling words, words associated with content area studies, and more. The format is consistent, the contents vary, but the results are always successful.

Writing Descriptive Riddles

Riddles are wonderful for developing descriptive writing. We have found that our framework provides the constraints needed to spur interest and more and more riddles. Begin by saying something like the following:

I am going to describe something. Here are three clues. At the end
I will write, "Do you need another clue?" Ready!

Write your clues, one at a time, on the chalkboard or easel saying them as you write.

It is gray.

It has wrinkled skin.

It is very big.

Do you need another clue?

If children indicate another clue is needed, write one. Create several riddles, building momentum and a desire in students to write their own. You may begin by asking the children to write their own riddle following your model. You might also want to pair children, and have each write and then ask his/her partner to solve the riddle.

Place the riddle framework (Figure 7-17) in the location with other composition frameworks. This, like the Lee Bennett Hopkins poem and the cinquain which follows, become one of the many independent activities students will engage in during the language arts time block. It also resembles the format of currently used standarized reading tests (see Chapter 1).

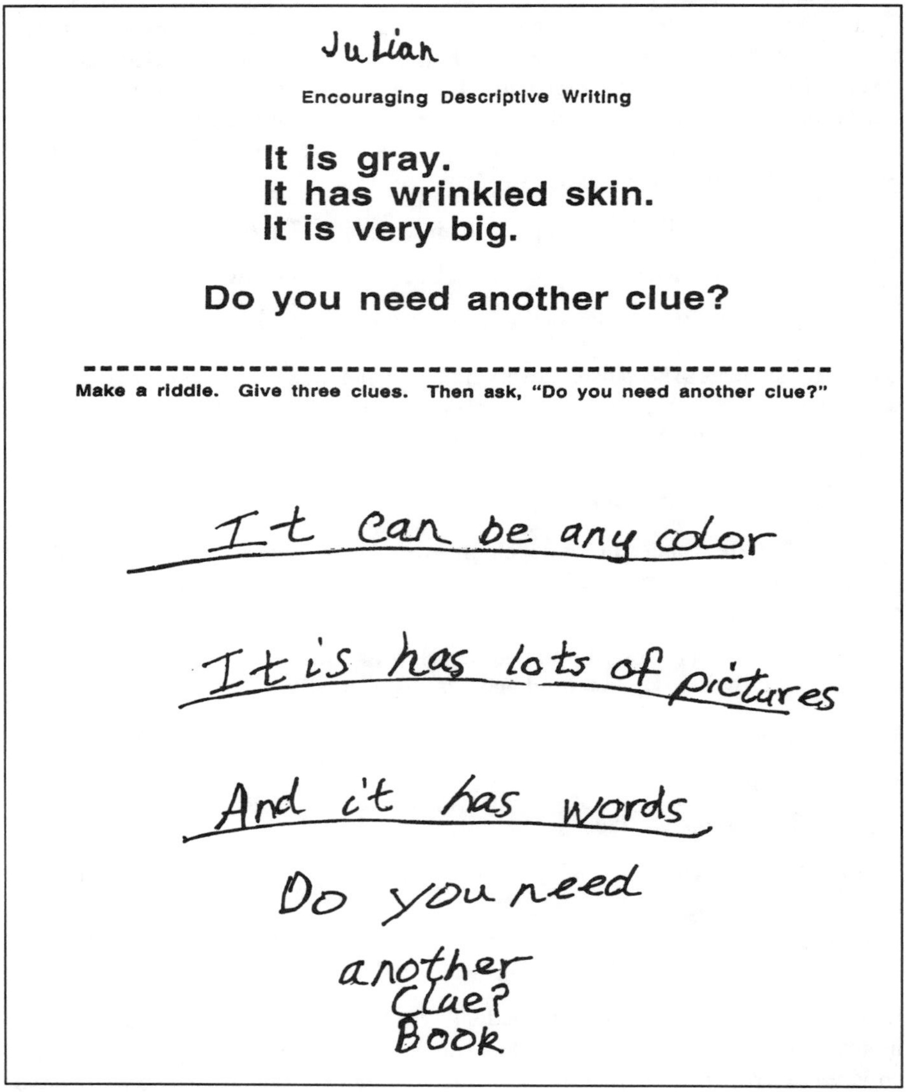

Julian

Encouraging Descriptive Writing

It is gray.
It has wrinkled skin.
It is very big.

Do you need another clue?

Make a riddle. Give three clues. Then ask, "Do you need another clue?"

It can be any color

It is has lots of pictures

And it has words

Do you need another Clue? Book

Figure 7-17. Julian's Descriptive Riddle

Writing Cinquains

A cinquain is a five-line poem with two, four, six, eight, and two syllables in each line, respectively. The cinquain shown in Figure 7-18 was written by a ten-year-old. Provide the structured framework in Figure 7-18 for students to use. This, like those above, will become part of their writing repertoire.

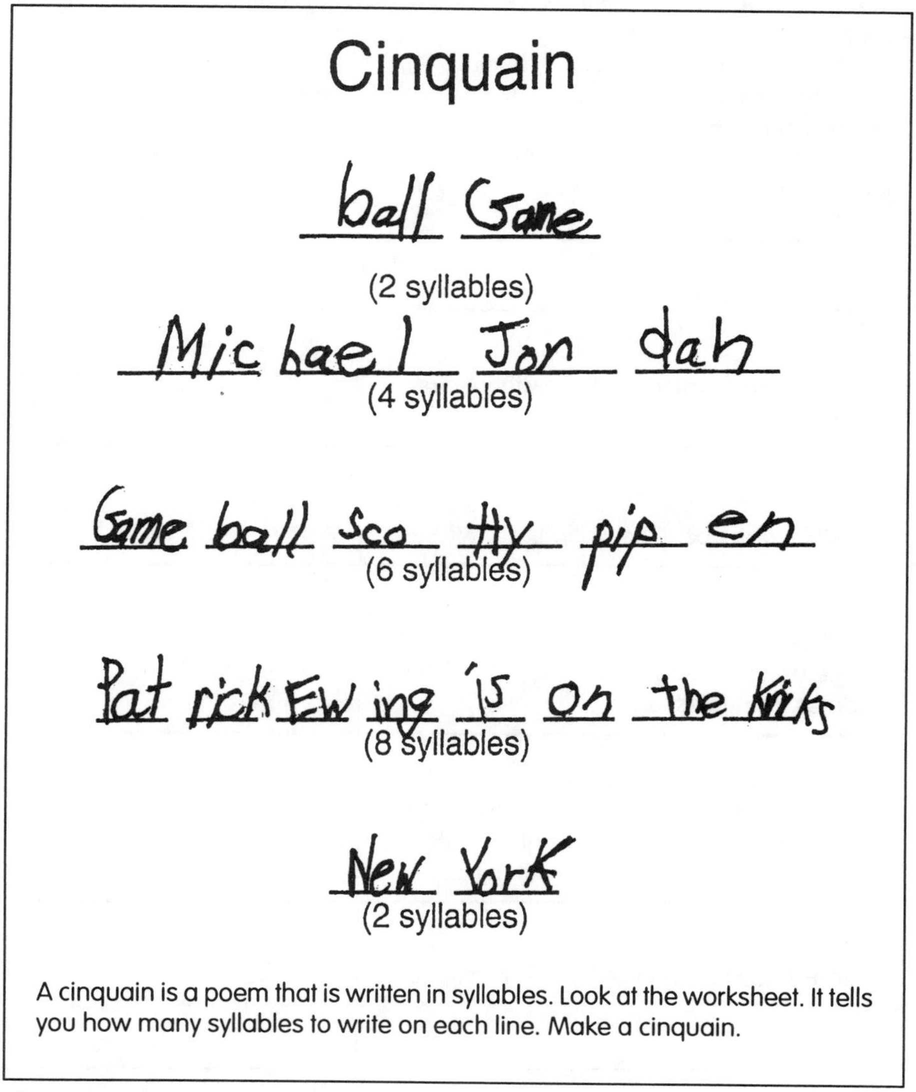

Cinquain

ball Game

(2 syllables)

Michael Jordah

(4 syllables)

Game ball Sco Hy pip en

(6 syllables)

Pat rick Ewing is on the Knks

(8 syllables)

New York

(2 syllables)

A cinquain is a poem that is written in syllables. Look at the worksheet. It tells you how many syllables to write on each line. Make a cinquain.

Figure 7-18.   Student Cinquain Using Framework

Assessing Beginning Efforts

The frameworks in Figures 7-16, 7-17, and 7-18 are themselves evaluation as well as the instructional tools. Each time a student writes using the framework, she/he has demonstrated her/his ability to use the tool successfully. Discussing, in small groups and individually, how the student carried out the activity is important. The Progress Report Form can be used following discussions, so learners are able to write "what I know," and "what I need to learn" (Figure 5-2).

Teacher assessment is most effective when a progress report form is used to keep over-time observations of actions and products. This may be difficult with a large number of children in a classroom. I've created the checksheet in Table 7-2, which can be used as a quick check of growth.

Behaviors	Comments
He/She uses strategies daily without direction.	
She/He talks about the writing.	
He/She writes more interesting vocabulary since using the strategies. (lists, list poems, riddles, cinquains, etc.)	
She/He seems enthusiastic about writing when using frameworks. (i.e., talks about products, shares products, wants to write often, gets peers interested in writing).	
She/He uses framework(s) with content areas.	

Table 7-2.

It's important to notice students' use of frameworks. The frequent use of the frameworks in varied content areas informs us that they have incorporated frameworks into their repertoire. They create lists, poems, riddles, and cinquains about their social studies and science materials. They also begin to create these without using the worksheet. Structure frames that guide children to make lists, make a poem, write riddles and cinquains teach and assess the following:

Structured Writing Frameworks

Teach	Can Assess
• visual structures for creating text	• ability to use structure
• self-confidence for writing	• vocabulary to describe the framework
• relationship of written to oral text	• spelling
• independence	• ability to follow frameworks and directions
	• effectiveness of framework for each student

Moving Toward Composing Narratives

Writing Stories

Dialogue, literature and content journals, and mail provide vehicles for students to compose narrative text. Intimidated writers, however, are often fearful of writing narratives, for these products are usually longer, and often more complicated than the formats discussed previously. Frameworks for creating narratives provide structure for the process, relaxing and enticing reluctant writers to produce.

Phyllis Fantauzzo, the Center's psychologist, discovered that writing three-sentence stories is one way to provide systematic guidance for students. It limits the quantity of writing, eliminating the often heard, "But how much do I have to write?" It also provides structure through the framework (Figure 7-19), and entices novice writers with fun.

The following dialogue illustrates one way to approach the activity.

Teacher: You know, boys and girls, I can write a story with only three sentences.

Child: I don't believe it. Stories are long.

Making A Story

Here is a story in three sentences.

A monster lived in a forest.

(Character) (is where)

He wasn't scary.

(Character's problem)

He got a scary mask.

(How the problem is solved)

Write a story in three sentences here.

(Character)   (is where)

(Character's problem)

(How the problem is solved)

Figure 7-19.   Three-Sentence Story Framework

Teacher: I bet you I can. Watch. Now stories have a main character. So I think that my main character will be a mouse. (The teacher writes, "The mouse . . . " on the chalkboard). Now, the mouse lives somewhere. Where do you want him to live?

Child: In the kitchen.

Teacher: O.K. (She writes and says, "The mouse lives in the kitchen.") Now main characters have problems in stories. The mouse's problem is that a cat is chasing him (she writes as she talks) "The mouse lives in the kitchen. A cat is chasing him.") In order to solve his problem, he has to get away from the cat. So, he runs into his mousehole and the cat can't get him. (She adds to her story and writes, "The mouse ran into his mousehole and he solved his problem.") And that's my story. O.K., boys and girls, who is the main character?

Child: The mouse.

Teacher: Right! And, where does he live?

Child: In the kitchen.

Teacher: Right, and what was his problem?

Child: A cat is chasing him.

Teacher: (Enthusiastically) Right! And how did the mouse solve his problem?

Child: He ran into his hole.

Teacher: You got it. Now let's do another. Who has a main character?

Continue in this way, creating at least three short stories for the children. The modeling creates something magical, and children will begin to write. Figure 7-20 illustrates one child's story, which was created independently during a free-time period.

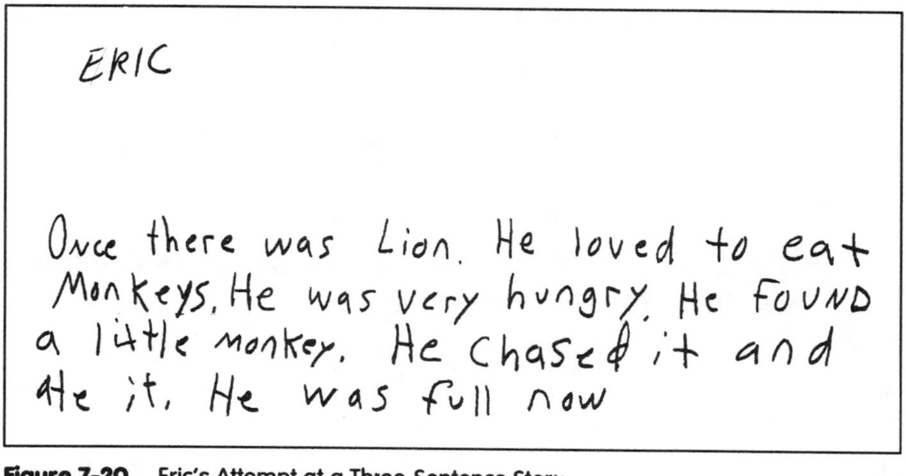

ERIC

Once there was Lion. He loved to eat Monkeys. He was very hungry. He found a little monkey. He chased it and He it. He was full now

Figure 7-20.   Eric's Attempt at a Three-Sentence Story

Extending Three-Sentence Stories

It is important for students to understand that episodes help main characters solve problems. So, I model story writing, as above, but this time extend the activity to include episodic structure. Let me demonstrate.

Teacher: O.K., who has a suggestion for a main character.

Child: A monster.

Teacher: All right (she writes "A monster"). Now, where is the monster?

Child: In the forest.

Teacher: (writes and says, "A monster lives in the forest.") Now, what is the monster's problem?

Child: No one thinks he's scary.

Teacher: (writes and says, "There once was a monster who lived in a forest. No one thought he was scary.") Now, boys and girls, what is one thing this monster can do to solve his problem?

Child: He can make scarier faces.

Teacher: (writes, adding to the text already on the easel, "He made scarier faces." Turns to the children and then says) But that didn't help so he—

Child: Put on a scary Halloween mask.

Teacher: (writes, adding this to the already written text, "Then, he put on a scary Halloween mask, but that didn't work.") So, what's the next episode that helps the monster solve the problem?

Child: He went to school to learn to be scarier.

Teacher: (writes, adding the above to the text and then says) This didn't work, so we need another episode.

Child: The monster got his big brother who was scarier.

Teacher: (adds the above to the text and writes and says) And his big brother was so scary that he frightened everyone.

Child: Yeah, and that's the end.

Teacher: You're right, Michael. The monster solved his problem, and the story ends. So boys and girls, the main character is—

Children: The monster.

Teacher: And where did he live?

Children: In the forest.

Teacher: And what was his problem?

Children: He wasn't scary.

Teacher: So, what was the first thing he did to try to solve his problem?

Children: He made a scarier face.

Teacher: But that didn't work, and in the next episode he—

Child: He put on a Halloween mask.

Teacher: Right! But that didn't work so—

Child: Then he got his big brother who was scarier.

Teacher: Correct! And he solved his problem because—

Child: Because his brother scared everyone.

Teacher: O.K. And, how did the story end?

Child: The little monster was scary like his brother.

Teacher: O.K., so there was a main character (coaches the children to say this with her), who had a problem, and there are three episodes to solve the problem, and then the story ended.

The discussions and group activities described here will encourage children to independently create stories.

Retellings and Story Writing: An Over-Time Process

Students realize the connection between retelling and story writing after using the retelling checksheet several times. This was illustrated by eight-year-old Eric, who came to me one day holding the story retelling sheet in his hand. "I'm going to cheat," he whispered. "What do you mean," I responded. "Well," continued Eric, "Well I wrote a story and I left out a lot of stuff." Eric and his teacher met for a conference concerning his story after he'd begun (Figure 7-21). His teacher read the story out loud, and as she did, she wrote on the rewriting sheet, "I wonder where the lion lives?" She continued and wrote and said, "Where did the lion find the monkeys?" Eric used the questions to rewrite his story (Figure 7-21). After completing a second draft, he took the retelling sheet and put it next to the computer and reviewed his story to be sure all of the elements were included (Figure 7-22). "This retelling sheet works for writing, too!" Rewriting helps students develop a sense of how they write

REWRITING

Write here	Things to change and add
① What type of monkey	c himpanzees
~~Whe~~ ⊗ Male or feml?	both
What were the monkeys like?	the Monkeys were fast, they got away
Who got away?	The Lion
Who had another adventure?	The Lion

Figure 7-21. Eric's Writing Conference

text. Eric's teacher read his story out loud. He used the checksheet as both an assessment and instructional tool. Eric reviewed his final draft using the Editing My Writing tool (Figure 7-23) and then produced his final draft (Figure 7-24). His teacher knew that the product was important, but that the processes he used to create his story were even more important. The processes will be used again and again each time he

STUDENT'S (COMPOSITION) AND RETELLING CHECKLIST

NAME _Eric SM_ _____ DATE _____

NAME OF COMPOSITION OR BOOK _____

AUTHOR _Eric SM_ _____

	YES	NO

SETTING:
I began my composition/~~retelling~~ with an INTRODUCTION   ✓
I told WHEN the story happened   ✓
I told WHERE the story happened   ✓

CHARACTERS:
I told about the main character   ✓
I told about the other characters   ✓

PROBLEM:
I told about the story problem or goal   ✓

EPISODES:
I included episodes   ✓

SOLUTION:
I told how the problem was solved or the goal was met   ✓
I told how the story ended   ✓

THEME:
My story has a theme   __ __

When I compose/~~retell~~ on my own, I included _the introduction,_
where the story happened. Main charrecter,
omer chirecters, Goal, episodes, solution, theme

The next time I compose/ retell, I need to remember to include these things:_____
When the story happened. How the
story ended.

Figure 7-22.   Eric's Composition Checklist

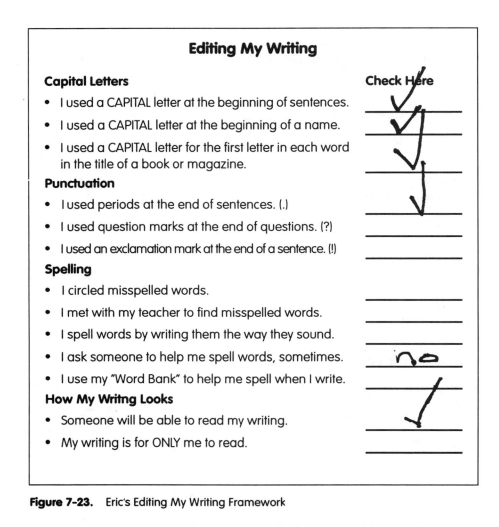

Figure 7-23. Eric's Editing My Writing Framework

creates a story. The Processes I Use When I Compose tool (Figure 7-25) was used often in order to guide Eric and his classmates to realize "HOW" they moved through a series of activities in order to compose. This most important monitoring sheet guides students, when coached with conversations, to understand that knowing how to use the steps to create a product is the key to doing it successfully. Understanding the process helps students produce a wonderful product, and also guides them to justify reasons for their actions. Responding to questions concerned with the processes used to create text demonstrates Eric's ability to reflect on his actions. Self-monitoring has helped him to become self-aware.

Once there was a Lion who lived in the deepest part of the jungle. It was a late afternoon. He was very, very hungry, and he loved to eat little monkeys. He set out to find some. When he got to a river, he saw a family of Chimpanzees. He charged but the little one was too fast for the lion. The little Chimpanzee jumped, the lion hit a tree. The monkeys scattered away, laughing. He was starving now, and ashamed. The lion went on. He found another Chimpanzee. It was all alone, he swallowed it with one gulp. But another Lion chased him. The lion got away. He was not hungry anymore. The lion had an adventure himself.

THE END

By: Eric Su

Figure 7-24.   Eric's Final Draft

Teaching and Assessing Research and Report Writing

I recall loathing content area studies in school. In most cases I loved the topics. What stopped me from diving into the books were the reports I was expected to write.

Research and report writing are essential parts of learning at all levels of learning. Finding a way for students to enjoy learning to use these skills is challenging.

How to Begin

My teachers have elaborated on the KWL strategy conceived by my good friend Donna Ogle (1989). They use Donna's model as the basis for developing a series of activities that guide students to learn research and report writing skills. The strategies also enhance their desire to read content-specific materials and report the information for others to enjoy.

PROCESSES I USE WHEN I COMPOSE

Name Eric Su

Date 11-20-96

Title of My Writing The Lion and the Monkeys

1. What helped me to get the idea for this writing selection?

I like adventure stories. Lynn also made up a story about monkeys.

2. How long have I been working on this piece of writing?

2 weeks

3. What gave me trouble while I was writing?

Adding details gave me trouble while I was writing because I seem to always forget when the story happened, where.

4. What strategies did I use to revise drafts?

A Composition sheet, and rewriting with a buddy.

5. What would I like to add or take away to make my writing better?

I would add information on important parts. I would take away non-important words.

6. How will I know when my writing is finished?

when I have my editing done I feel Great when I finish because I get something done

7. Who is my audience for this writing?

My friends, my parents, and whoever likes to read adventure books

Figure 7-25. Eric's Processes I Use When I Compose Framework

One of our reading specialists, Carol Satz, has created the three-part pocket folder and calls it "Research Project." (See Figure 7-26.) The first pocket is labeled **K,** and "What I **K**now" is written underneath the letter. The middle pocket is called **W** and "What I **W**ant To Know" is written beneath it. The third is titled **L** and captioned "What I **L**earned." An envelope is fastened to the back of the middle panel

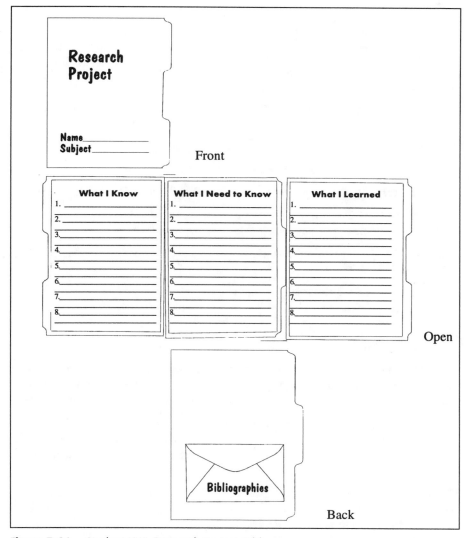

Figure 7-26.   Student KWL Research Project Folder

(the one called **"W"**) and labeled "Bibliography." Carol makes a folder for each of the children working on a research project, and makes one for herself, as well. Since Carol, like the rest of our teachers, considers herself a learner in the classroom, she teaches by modeling the use of this framework for completing her own research project. She uses Don Holdaway's (1979) learning model (see Chapter 5, pp. 83–84) as a guide for instruction. The following illustrates her introduction for guiding her students.

Carol: I've always loved dancing. I used to dance when I was little. My mother took me to dancing school, and I liked tap the best. So, I learned a lot about tap dancing.

Patricia: My Mom takes me to tap dancing too.

Carol: Let's see. I know that Bill Robinson is the father of tap dancing in America. His name was really Bill, but I know that everyone called him "Bo Jangles."

Patricia: My Mom takes me to tap lessons.

Teacher: Do you know any famous tap dancers, Patricia?

Patricia: Yeah, I know about Shirley Temple. She tap-danced in the olden times.

Teacher: Shirley Temple was a child star in the 1940s and Bo Jangles taught her how to dance. They were in a lot of movies together.

Sally: Oh, yeah. I saw a movie and there was this little girl, and this man tap dancing.

Carol: Sometimes tap is called the "black man's dance." My dad's favorite tap dancer was Fred Astaire. My favorite was Gene Kelly. Both of them were white.

Leonard: Sammy Davis, Jr. was a tap dancer, and he was black.

Each time a fact was offered, Carol wrote it on a large piece of paper titled, "What I Know." She had a second piece of easel paper posted and labeled, "What I Want To Know." The following dialogue includes information written on the second sheet.

Teacher: I'm not sure why tap is called the "black man's dancing." I think if I find how tap dancing was invented I could find out how it got that name. That's what I want to find out. **"I want to know** how tap dancing got invented."

Carol said and wrote this on large easel paper. She continued, "I want to know where the first tap dancers lived. I want to know, too, did they get paid to tap-dance?" Each time she inquired, she wrote the request on the second chart paper labeled, "What I Want To Know."

Children should select their own topics for research projects, especially during language arts periods. In schools with mandated curricula, self-selection of research topics is difficult. Children, in these instances, might be able to choose a topic within a topic, especially in content area studies. If, for example, the class is learning about the country of Mexico, in a discussion use a map (see Chapter 6, Figure 6-19) to designate subtopics. The word "Mexico" would be written in the circle of a map projected from an overhead projector, or drawn on the chalkboard. You might begin by saying, "I am interested in finding out about the foods of Mexico." You would write the words "Mexican foods" on one of the spokes of the map. Then say, "Let's see, what else would I like to know? Oh yes, sports. I wonder what sports they play there?" Begin to ask children what they are curious about, and write their ideas on the spokes, as well. Children who offer specific ideas can be asked to research that aspect of the main topic being studied.

Doing the Research

Carol put at least five different resource books concerned with each of the student's topics in the classroom library. During the language arts period, she selected one of the books about dance, and searched for answers to her questions, one at a time. She used 5- × 7-inch index cards for recording information from the texts. As she worked, she spoke out loud to herself, or to a child working nearby about her activities. She wrote the name of the book she used to gather specific information, its author and publisher on each index card that included the data. She slipped it into the pocket labeled "Bibliography" on the back of the three-part folder. The teacher chose to use and guide the children to use the American Psychological Association (APA) (1994) style of referencing. Some of the children observed their teacher working on her report, and began working on theirs. Others needed to be coached to begin. Still others asked questions.

Writing a First Draft

Learning to organize in order to write the first draft is a major step. I have found that creating categories by organizing index cards into categorical piles is extremely helpful. So before actually writing, model the actions by putting all of the cards on which information has been gathered on your desk. Provide each student with a copy of the following directions. Guide students to put the directions next to them on the table.

1. Take out the cards.
2. Spread them on the table.
3. Put cards that seem to go together in a pile.
4. Name each pile and place it on the table next to your folder.

Gather students in small groups (not more than eight) in a circle or around a table with their KWL folders. Read the directions using the choral reading technique cited on page 116. Choral reading relaxes reluctant and new readers, providing the collegial support necessary in order for them to take a risk, and write. Our teachers begin by moving their own cards into categories, and labeling each with a name and writing that name on an index card. Discussion will guide students to realize that each group might be a paragraph, or even a chapter of a report. Once children have organized their cards into categories and labeled each, they can take the first pile and begin to write.

Rewriting or Revising

First drafts are usually the most difficult but, when completed, they are a source of great satisfaction. The Writing Drafts guide sheet (Figure 7-27), which has been used successfully with children ages 6 to 17, is wonderful for revisions. This strategy, used with all content areas, becomes part of the students' repertoire for future independent writing. When rewriting is complete, students need to edit their work since

---

Writing Drafts

Comments

Reread your writing. Think, "Will my audience like it?"

_____

Reread it out loud, again. Circle things that you want to change.

_____

Reread it again. Write words or ideas that you want to add or change.

_____

Ask a friend to read and tell you what can be added or changed.

_____

Rewrite to add and make changes.

_____

Reread your writing.

_____

Ask your friend to reread it.

_____

If you are happy with this draft, edit it. If not, change and add, again.

_____

P.S. Use the "Edit My Writing" sheet to edit.

Figure 7-27. Writing Drafts Framework

the product is meant to be shared. Figure 7-23 guides youngsters to edit independently. The editing sheet defines for students the elements of text that must be "cleaned up" for sharing. It is straightforward, easy to read, and appropriate for all genres. I suggest that you introduce students to this format the following way.

1. Begin by picking one item on the sheet.
2. If you pick "I used a CAPITAL letter at the beginning of sentences," read what you've written.
3. Check to see if all of the sentences begin with a CAPITAL letter.
4. Read the whole thing and look ONLY for one thing at a time.
5. When you've finished reading to check for capitals at the beginning of sentences, go to the next item (I used a CAPITAL letter at the beginning of a name).
6. Read your writing again, and this time look for the next item.
7. Do each item, one at a time, until you've edited your piece of writing.

This tool is appropriate for editing research projects, and all other types of writing, as well.

Assessing Progress in Research and Report Writing

The framework specifically designed for research and report writing serves as a guide for completing steps in the process (Figure 7-28). It also provides benchmarks for each student, who charts his/her own progress with the step-by-step guide.

Teaching and Assessing Explanatory Writing

Demonstrating and involving (not explaining and directing) is the way to guide students to explain in writing. Our students, especially those eight years and older (including teens) love the following introductory activity.

Barbara's twelve-year-olds agreed to make a "power drink" to celebrate the Thanksgiving holiday. They brainstormed foods (as their teacher recorded the ideas on the circle map, Figure 6-19) to include in order to create the "most nourishing." Each student in the class agreed to bring one of the ingredients to school. Barbara brought in a blender. She divided the students into groups of six, and directed each student to write directions for making the drink. The small-group setting encouraged the children to talk to each other about the directions.

The ingredients had been placed in the center of the room on a table. The agreement with the children was that once the drink was made, each one would taste it. Karli named his drink "acolade," and volunteered to read his directions (Figure 7-29) to the class. The teacher followed the directions as Karli read. This twelve-year-

About My Research

Comments

I selected _____ to re-search. _____

I wrote everything I know about the topic. _____

I wrote questions that I want to research. _____

I found books to help answer my questions. _____

I recorded the names of books using APA style. _____

I read information to answer my questions. _____

I organized the information into categories. _____

I wrote my first draft. _____

I revised my draft. _____

I asked a friend, or my teacher to read to see if I need to revise again. _____

I wrote my final draft. _____

I edited my final draft. _____

The illustrations and the writing match. _____

My research is published and ready to share. _____

The most important thing I learned by doing this project is _____

_____

_____

Name _____ Date _____

Figure 7-28. About My Research Framework

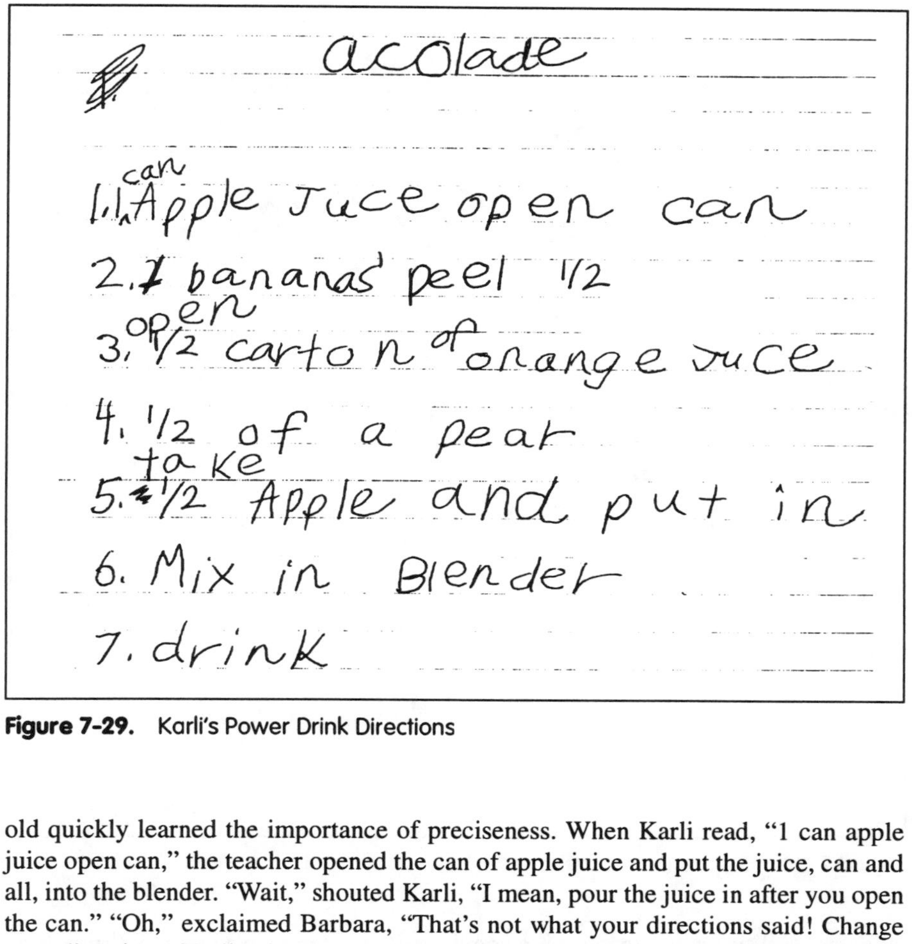
acolade

1. 1 can Apple Juce open can
2. bananas peel 1/2
3. open 1/2 carton of orange juce
4. 1/2 of a peat
5. take 1/2 Apple and put in
6. Mix in Blender
7. drink

Figure 7-29. Karli's Power Drink Directions

old quickly learned the importance of preciseness. When Karli read, "1 can apple juice open can," the teacher opened the can of apple juice and put the juice, can and all, into the blender. "Wait," shouted Karli, "I mean, pour the juice in after you open the can." "Oh," exclaimed Barbara, "That's not what your directions said! Change your directions, Karli, when you rewrite them." Karli continued to read and Barbara followed his directions. Laughter and oral editing by peers made the importance of preciseness evident.

The "test" of clear explanatory text was the drink, itself. Suggestions to rewrite the directions came from ALL of the students in the room.

Understanding Students' Knowledge about Persuasive Writing

Tracy's class was focusing on learning how to get someone to do something you really wanted them to do. The teacher paired the children so that they'd have a functional purpose for writing a piece of persuasive text. Her purpose was to assess the

Figure 7-30. Stephen's Persuasive Letter

students' abilities to use language to convince others. Stephen's letter to Tracy (Figure 7-30) illustrates his understanding that persuasion must "shout." He repeats the word "now," illustrating an impatience and demand for vanilla wafers. His persistence is further illustrated by the very large "now" at the end of his letter. It is evident from the sample that Stephen is begging for techniques that will make his text assertively persuasive.

The teacher began a lesson by asking the children to make a list of all of the words that they would use to try to persuade someone to do something. Lists included words and phrases such as: "please, oh please, pretty please, it is important, I must, I need, I can't live without," etc. Using single words and phrases seems to be easy for children. Guiding them to negotiate, however, in order to persuade seems necessary.

Discussion followed, with the purpose of demonstrating to students the need to justify their requests by telling "why." The teacher modeled requests and said, for example, "I need a new car, but my husband doesn't want me to spend the money. I will tell him WHY I need one. First, I need a new car because mine doesn't start when it is cold outside and then I'm late for school. Next, I need a new car because the old one doesn't always start when it is cold, and then . . ." The teacher paused, and looked at the children for suggestions. As they volunteered these, she wrote them on the easel paper.

A third approach for guiding students to persuade in writing is bartering. "I will let you drive the new car if I get one," illustrates this approach. There are many ways to guide students to convince. The self-monitoring checksheet in Table 7-3 confirms, and also guides students to use the strategies to write convincingly.

Things I write to persuade

Comments

I use words like "please, I must," and

_____

_____

_____

I tell "why" I need or want something
when I persuade.

_____

_____

_____

I say, "If you do it, I will

_____

_____

_____

I tell what will happen if I do not get
what I want or cannot do what I
want.

_____

_____

_____

Other things I do to persuade are

_____

_____

_____

Table 7-3.

Other Assessment Techniques

The impact of self-monitoring on both learning and learning to assess is well illustrated in the following incident (Glazer and Burke, 1994).

"Look, Mrs. Fantauzzo! I made the longest sentence in the world," exclaimed seven-year-old Samantha. "It has 42 words in it." "Really?" responded the teacher, raising her voice in question, encouraging further explanation. "Yeah," replied Samantha. "I always make little sentences. See this story?" (Figure 7-31), she said,

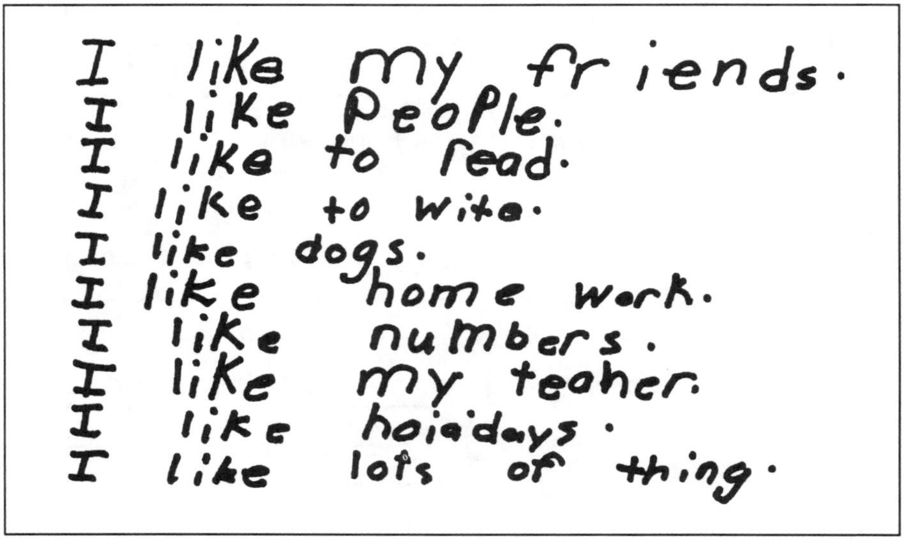

I like my friends.
I like people.
I like to read.
I like to wite.
I like dogs.
I like home work.
I like numbers.
I like my teaher.
I like hoidays.
I like lots of thing.

Figure 7-31. Samantha's Story: A First Draft

confirming her statement by pointing to her text. "How do you know that you always write little sentences—short ones?" asked her teacher. "Well," Samantha continued, "I used the About My Writing sheet and it told me that (Figure 7-32). It says, 'I write short sentences' right here." The child pointed to the sheet, moving her finger under the words as she read. "I look at the About My Writing sheet and it tells me about my writing. Then I look at my writing, and I know what my writing is like." "Oh, so the About My Writing sheet helps you look at your story and to decide what you want to change?" asked Mrs. Fantauzzo. "Yeah," replied the child, "and then I decided I wanted to write a long sentence so it'll look like a grown-up wrote it." "Samantha," began her teacher, " I would love to hear you read your sentence." "O.K.," replied Samantha. And joyfully the child read her story (Figure 7-33).

About My Writing

	Comments
I am writing fiction.	No
I am writing nonfiction.	Yes
I get ideas for writing from_____ _____.	Books
I am writing a story.	No
I use pictures to help tell about my writing.	No
I am writing an autobiography.	Yes
I begin sentences the same way.	Yes
I begin sentences differently.	No
I write "and" a lot in my compositions.	No
I write short sentences.	yes
I write long sentences.	No
I use different words when I write.	No
I write best by hand.	No
I write best with a computer.	Yes
I write best when I dictate to someone.	Yes

Name: _Samantha_ Date: _11-20_

Figure 7-32.   About My Writing Framework

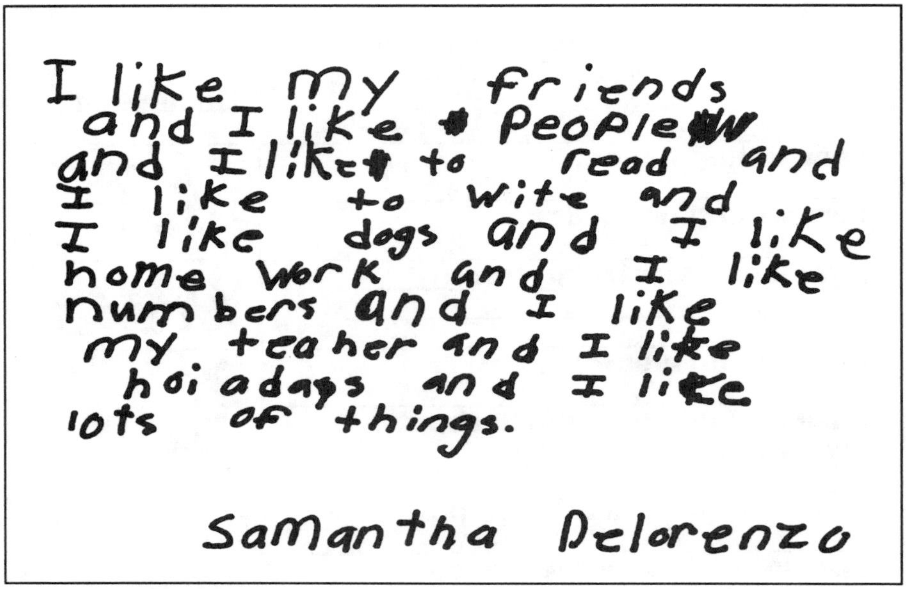

I like my friends and I like people and I like to read and I like to wite and I like dogs and I like home work and I like numbers and I like my teaher and I like hoiadays and I like lots of things.

Samantha Delorenzo

Figure 7-33.   Samantha's Revised Story

Although the change was uncomplicated, Samantha created new sentence structure independently and deliberately. The self-monitoring sheet permitted the student to observe, take stock, and make a decision about change. The delight on Samantha's face supported the fact that self-monitoring frameworks used for assessments are instructional tools, as well.

Figure 7-34 is successfully used with beginning and new writers. Those more experienced find this, as well as others, helpful. They draw attention to specific elements of the English writing system. Students, when using these tools, assess the type of sentences, words, phrases, or syntactic structures they use to write stories, letters, compositions, research reports, and journals. They learn to ask themselves, "What makes the text interesting?" They provide youngsters with the vocabulary to describe their writing. These tools permit students to deliberately take control of their academic actions.

Introducing Self-Monitoring

Story writing, language experience charts, or recording events on large easel paper with groups of students are perfect activities for modeling the use of the About My Writing and other self-monitoring tools. You might even use a piece of your own writing to model the use of the sheet.

About My Writing

	Comments
I am writing a story.	
I am using description in my writing.	
My writing persuades someone to_____ .	
I explain something in my writing.	
I use pictures to help tell my story.	
I use illustrations to explain my topic.	
I write short sentences.	
I write long sentences.	
I write "and" lots of times in my sentences.	
I use adjectives (descriptive words) when I write.	
I use pronouns (I, me, he, you, them, they, she) when I write.	
Someone can follow my written directions.	
Someone can read my writing, and tell what it is about.	
My writing is the best when I write by hand.	
My writing is best when I use a computer.	
My writing is best when I dictate to someone.	
The writing I am doing now is good because_____	

Name: Date:

Figure 7-34.   About My Writing Framework

Project a copy of the sheet onto a screen using an overhead projector. Say, "I am going to read my story and check to see how I wrote it." Read the story through. When you've finished, point to the sheet projected on the screen and read the first line ("I am writing fiction"). Comment appropriately and record your comments in the appropriate section on the sheet. Continue, moving from the first to the last item on the list. When you've completed the sheet, summarize. You might summarize by saying the following:

> I am writing fiction. I am writing a story. I didn't use pictures to help tell my story, but I'm going to make some. I began all of my sentences with "I." I think I want to change that. I write a lot of short sentences. I want to make some longer ones. I write best when I use the computer, that's why I don't think this story is so good.

Some students may need to work with you, one-on-one, the first time the sheet is used. The purpose is to guide students to learn how to further develop, enhance, or create more effective text. One eight-year-old said, after using the sheet many times, "I like my story just like it is. I write long sentences, and I write short ones too. I use a lot of different words and I don't use 'and' a lot. I like to write a biography because I like to write about myself."

What a wonderful way to guide students to explain *why* they create what they do.

Assessing Spelling

Spelling is assessed in students' writing during the editing process. The purpose for such activity is to "clean up" the text for sharing. So when children learn to edit their texts, they are simultaneously editing, and also learning how to notice their needs (or errors). Teachers and students might also want to discuss specific instructional spelling needs that would be carried out at a separate time (see Chapter 8).

Kim's teacher assessed the spelling trends in her story (Figure 7-35) using the Spelling Trend Assessment sheet (Figure 7-36). The information would be used to plan a spelling lesson in the future. Her immediate purpose for using the sheet was to show Kim how to look for and identify misspelled words so that her writing could be published. Justeen's Spelling Self-Monitoring Sheet guided her to identify and then determine needed corrections (Figure 7-37). Often a second look can make the difference.

Narrative Self-Monitoring

Mark came to the school very insecure about his ability to write (Figure 7-38). He was not quite sure, either, about what writing was and what were the mechanics used to write. When he wrote about his writing, he focused first on his mother's perception of good writing habits (holding the pencil appropriately). The fact that he refocused

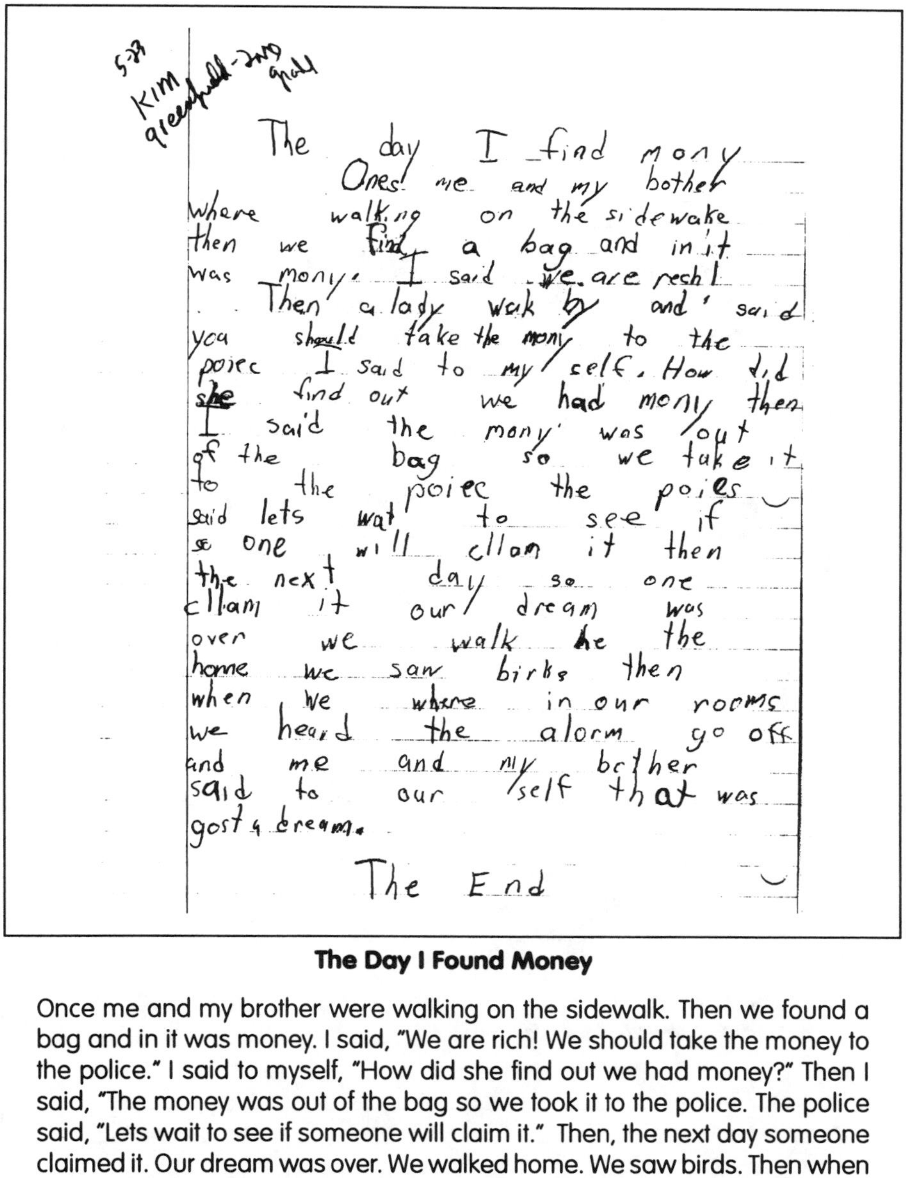

The day I find mony
Ones! me and my bother
where walking on the sidewake
then we find a bag and in it
was mony. I said we are rech!
Then a lady wak by and said
you should take the mony to the
poiec I said to my self. How did
she find out we had mony then
I said the mony was out
of the bag so we take it
to the poiec the poies
said lets wat to see if
so one will cllam it then
the next day so one
cllam it our dream was
over we walk he the
home we saw birks then
when we where in our rooms
we heard the alorm go off
and me and my brother
said to our self that was
gost a dream.

The End

The Day I Found Money

Once me and my brother were walking on the sidewalk. Then we found a bag and in it was money. I said, "We are rich! We should take the money to the police." I said to myself, "How did she find out we had money?" Then I said, "The money was out of the bag so we took it to the police. The police said, "Lets wait to see if someone will claim it." Then, the next day someone claimed it. Our dream was over. We walked home. We saw birds. Then when we were in our rooms we heard the alarm go off and me and my brother said to ourselves, "That was just a dream."

Figure 7-35. Kim's Story

SPELLING TREND ASSESSMENT

Student's Spelling	Correct Spelling	Patterns Noted
find	found	Vowel confusion
ones	once	spells as it sounds one + s
bother	brother	br blend – missed "r"
where	were	
mony	money	Silent letter at end of word
rech	rich	Vowel confusion
Wakl	walk	unexpected consonant reversal
polies	police	needs to see & trace word
my self	myself	Compound word rule
take	took	tense confusion
cllam	claim	two vowel rule needed
so one	someone	Compound word rule
alorm	alarm	Vowel confusion "or" for "ar"
our self	ourselves	Compound (glue together) word rule
gost	just	Use letter name as letter sound

Comments: Knows some spelling conventions; NEEDS – now – two vowel rule; compound word rule; ar, or, ur sound lesson; lots of oral conversation using present and past words that match (ie find and found, foot and feet, etc.).

Spelling is: Mostly invented_____ Somewhat correct ✓ Mostly correct_____
Student writes: Using known words (seldom risks)_____
　　　　　　　　 Using new words (risks)_____
Sources of words: Story_____
Student's Name: Kim_____ Date: 5/23____

Figure 7-36. Kim's Spelling Trend Assessment

Spelling Self-Monitoring Sheet

My Spelling	First Try	Correct Spelling	Differences
till	until	until	typo
emba resing	embaressing		
surprizes	surprised	surprised	typo
pushes	pushes	pushed	typo
anout	about	about	typo

Comments: There ~~wthe~~ were really no mistakes, just typos.

Sources of words: My story

My name: Justeen   Date: 11/22

Figure 7-37. Justeen's Spelling Self-Monitoring Sheet

his evaluative narrative to discuss topics for writing provided his teacher with the "inkling" that he might have lots of abilities locked up inside of him. Adult expectations seem to have played a major role in his performance.

When I write my mom yells at me because I hold my pencil to tite and because I hold my pencil tip instiad of holding the pencil and I like writing storys about my brother and me but I don't like writing about other thing.

Figure 7-38. Mark's First Narrative Self-Evaluation

His teacher was determined to help him gain confidence, but also to have him describe his writing and justify the description. Figure 7-39 was written three weeks after the self-evaluation process was initiated. The student tells about his writing, and then says **WHY** he's described it in such ways. Justifying responses means taking responsibility for one's actions with reason.

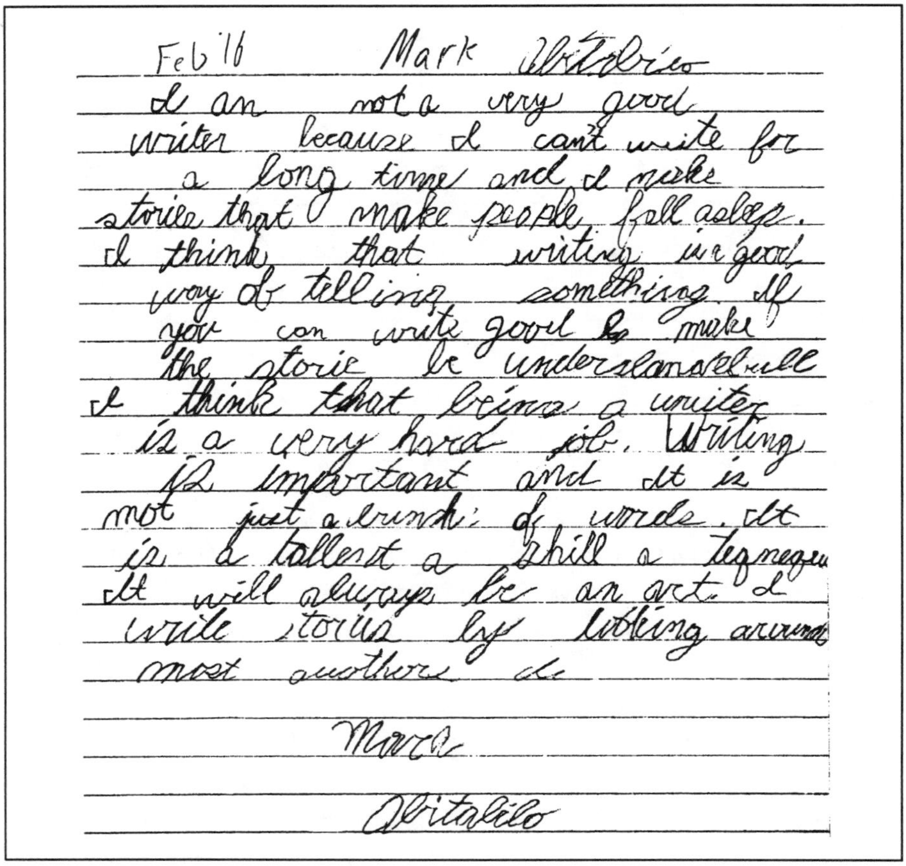

I am not a very good writer because I can't write for a long time and I make stories that make people fall asleep. I think that writing is a good way of telling something. If you can write good so make the stories be understandable. I think that being a writer is a very hard job. Writing is important and it is not just a bunch of words. It is a talent, a skill, a technique. It will always be an art. I write stories by looking around [at what] most authors do.

Figure 7-39.   Mark's Later Narrative Self-Evaluation

The most exciting self-monitored narrative I've found over the years is Claire's (Figure 7-40). She is witty, creative, and honest about her writing challenge. Her experiences have permitted her to be uninhibited, relaxed, and honest in a most delightful way.

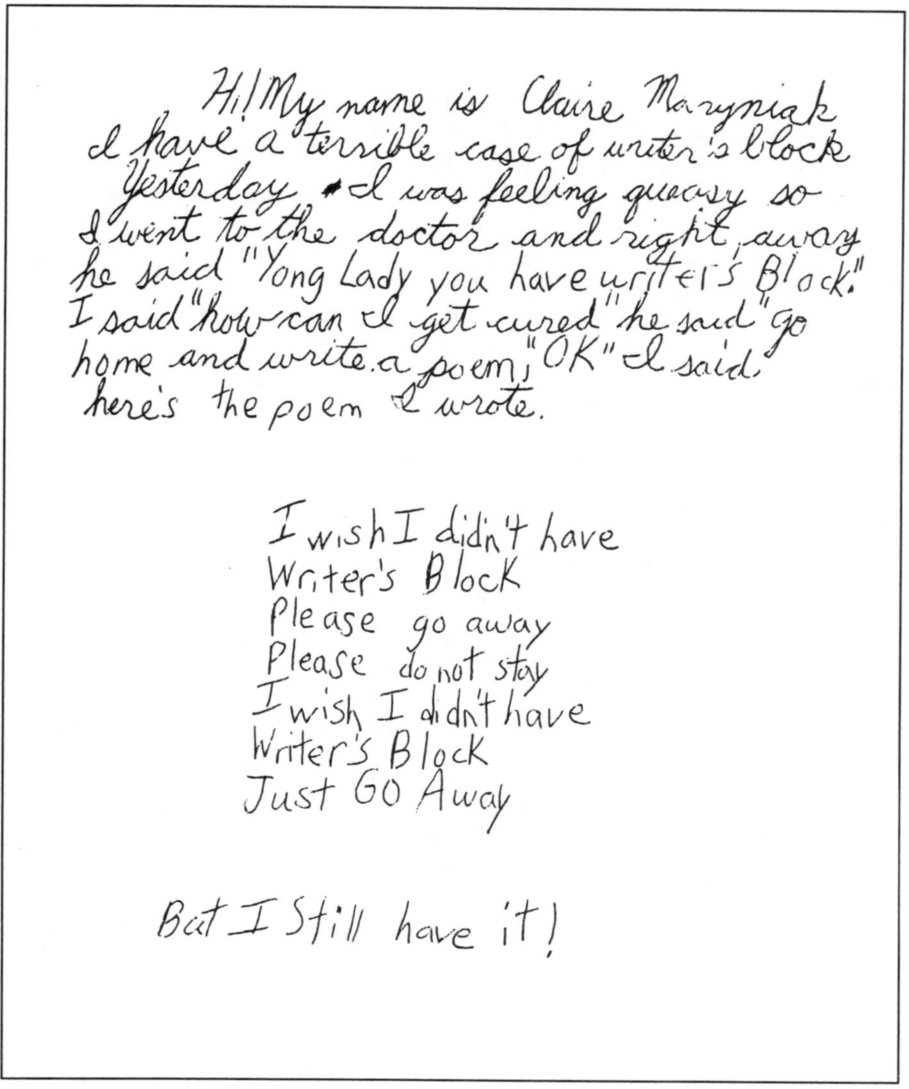

> Hi! My name is Claire Maryniak I have a terrible case of writer's block Yesterday • I was feeling queasy so I went to the doctor and right away he said "Yong Lady you have writer's Block." I said "how can I get cured" he said "go home and write a poem," "OK" I said. here's the poem I wrote.
>
> I wish I didn't have
> Writer's Block
> Please go away
> Please do not stay
> I wish I didn't have
> Writer's Block
> Just Go Away
>
> But I Still have it!

Figure 7-40.   Claire's Self-Evaluation

Self-Monitoring and Composition: A Summary

The assessment of writing is tricky, subjective, and often carried out inappropriately. I am suggesting the following outline, based on this chapter, for guiding students to become self-assessing, productive, creative, and excited writers.

To Begin, assess—

- students' stage of writing using several over-time samples;

- students' understanding of the writing process;

- students' perceptions of themselves as writers.

The purpose of these activities is to begin to develop a plan for guiding students to grow to understand the writing processes, and to view themselves as writers.

Next—

Guide students to be writers by using self-monitoring sheets, FUNCTION-ALLY. When, for example, a student has written a story (or is immersed in a research or content area report), guide rewriting using the following self-monitoring tools. Notice what each has learned during the self-monitoring activities. Provide students with these tools, when they are needed, one at a time, and over a period of time. These tools teach the students:

- HOW to review their written productions;

- WHAT to review in their writing;

- consistent language for assessing writing in content areas;

- questions to ask of themselves about their writing;

- how to assess what needs to be rewritten and edited;

- how to assess spelling errors;

- the effectiveness of persuasive, explanatory, narrative, and descriptive writing.

As the students use the tools to assess their writing, they also learn. The tools included in this chapter that facilitate self-assessment and instruction in writing follow.

Self-Monitoring Tool	What It Teaches Students
Make a Poem (Figure 7-13)	Structure for creating text; writing can be fun.
Progress Report Form (Figure 7-15)	Language of content; summarizing; organization; vocabulary associated with content.
Encouraging Descriptive Writing (Figure 7-17)	Structure for descriptive and riddle writing; writing can be fun.
Cinquain (Figure 7-18)	Structure for writing; writing is fun; descriptive vocabulary, etc.
Making a Story (Figure 7-19)	Structure for beginning story writers.
Rewriting (Figure 7-21)	How to find places in text that need rewriting.
Student's Composition Checklist (Figure 7-22)	Identification of elements needed to write a story.
Editing My Writing (Figure 7-23)	Elements of text that require editing.
Processes I Use When I Compose (Figure 7-25)	What a student does in order to start, continue, and complete a piece of writing.
Writing Drafts (Figure 7-27)	Procedure for rewriting.
About My Research (Figure 7-28)	Steps for writing a research report.
Things I Write To Persuade (Table 7-3)	Language to convince, persuasively.
About My Writing (Figures 7-32 & 7-34)	Noticing HOW he/she constructs text; the type of text produced.
Spelling Trend Assessment (Figure 7-36) (Usually used by teachers)	Determine where instruction is needed.
Spelling Self-Monitoring Sheet (Figure 7-37)	Words to correct; where instruction may be necessary.

There is nothing more effective for growth and change than self-monitoring. The process provides the language for describing writing. Self-monitoring tools also provide safe vehicles for students to look at themselves objectively, consistently, and purposefully.

CHAPTER 8

Phonics, Spelling, and Word Study

My graduate students and I often talk about the "rituals" we encounter before solving a difficult challenge in our classrooms. We equate this with the "rituals" we experience before settling down to write the first draft of a paper. Some take a second cup of coffee. Others prepare the evening meal. Still others, like myself, make a series of unnecessary telephone calls to avoid the inevitable quandaries that accompany the initial creation of text. I have gone through more than the usual series of procrastinating rituals before beginning this chapter and the reason is quite clear: How to teach aspects of language including (1) phonics, (2) spelling, and (3) word study, phonics particularly, has caused strife and anxiety for millions of good teachers. As a result, this chapter has taken as much time to write as the rest of the text.

Phonics

The study of language has many aspects, but phonics is discussed the most. To paraphrase Hamlet, "To phonic or not to phonic, that is the question."

As a young teacher of very young children, I struggled with explicit phonics instruction. I knew, even three decades ago, there were political undertones to phonics instruction and I'd "better" do it. I discovered that some children know that phonics was supposed to help them learn to read, but most didn't understand how. The children had a difficult time connecting explicit phonics instruction to word meaning. So, I found ways to incorporate the teaching of phonics through content area and literature studies, play and recreational activities. We studied phonics (phonemic awareness) in a scientific way, got data about the sounds of language, and assessed the idiosyncrasies. The children used the school district's adopted phonics series that I was told to use, but not in the way prescribed by the authors. The required weekly lesson plans were submitted to the principal in a traditional format, however. I knew I had to disguise my classroom activities, or I'd be reprimanded. Since the activities were successful for more children, I continued to use them. Many of the children found ways to understand how sounds and symbols are used to facilitate the decoding process. So, I continued to camouflage lesson plans so that they appeared like those expected for phonics instruction.

Years of experience have taught me that there is no one way for children to learn. There is also no way to separate phonics from reading, or even to take it away. Astuteness cultivated through the years has guided me to understand that public figures have used phonics as a tool for gaining notoriety.

I've attempted, in this chapter, to provide ideas for teaching and testing phonemic awareness and analysis, spelling, and word study in healthy, productive ways. There are ideas for those of you who believe that implicit instruction is the way. There are also ideas for teachers who believe that explicit, teacher-directed instruction is most effective.

What Is Phonics?

Phonics, says Sandra Wilde (1997), is the relationship between the sounds of language and the letters used to represent them. Phonics, in classrooms, is instruction that guides children to decode words using these relationships, in order to learn to read. Many agree that, in order to read and also write successfully, learners must be aware of sound/symbol relationships. Understanding the principles of our coding system (the alphabet) is important in the reading/writing process, as well.

What's Important?

There are two distinct areas of instruction important for success in reading and writing: (1) phonemic and morphemic awareness, and spelling and, (2) increased vocabulary for reading and writing. Understanding the meanings of words and how to use them in appropriate contexts is essential for both good readers and writers. What and how to teach children to spell and decode words, and how to guide children to increase their knowledge of word meanings continues to be controversial. Most argue about the importance of learning to decode words using a phonics approach. Still others debate how much phonics instruction is needed. These aspects of language study have been at the root of the continuous debate—how to teach our children to read.

Why Controversies?

The belief that phonics instruction is THE most important variable for teaching beginning and unsuccessful learners to read has distorted the public's understanding of the reading/writing process. Even quality research in the area of phonics has often been misinterpreted to please the public, which seems to want to hear that "phonics works." In addition, education concerning the history of the English language is rare in professional development activities. Lack of knowledge about how we can craft American English, with all of its glitches and idiosyncrasies, results in inappropriate instruction about how language works to make words and their meanings.

Phonics, Phonemic Awareness, and Reading and Writing

The predictable resurgence of the notion that phonics is the key to success in reading has detracted the public from considering other important aspects of language and learning to read. I agree with many (Perfetti & Zhang, 1996; Routman, 1996) that phonics is important for children to learn. But the focus on phonological skills has "over-blown" its importance for success in reading and writing. Even children, when asked what they do when they don't know a word, respond, "I sound it out." Although there are many strategies for decoding words, "sounding out" and "asking someone" seem to be the two known to most children and adults (Routman, 1996).

Reading tests assessing phonics skills are, in part, responsible for the "over-blown" importance of phonics, especially when scores are low. The sounds become the important content, exaggerating their role in the reading process. The quiet, unnatural environments in which children usually take these tests casts a spell of caution for youngsters, for these times feel very different than instructional sessions.

This exaggerated thinking about reading instruction is not new. So much media "hype" existed in the early 1950s about reading instruction that the United States Office of Education (USOE) launched a study involving twenty-seven individual projects whose goal was comparing and contrasting the effectiveness of alternative approaches to teaching beginning reading. According to the findings, approaches that in one way or another included systematic phonics instruction consistently exceeded the straight basal program in word recognition achievement scores. The approaches that included both systematic phonics and considerable emphasis on connecting reading and meaning surpassed the basal-alone approaches on virtually all measures. In addition, the data indicated that exercise in writing was an important component of beginning reading instruction (Bond & Dykstra, 1967). The notorious volume *Becoming a Nation of Readers* (1985) includes a summary of research concerning early phonics indicating that children who had received intensive phonics instruction in kindergarten or first grade performed better in the third grade than a comparison group of children on both a word identification test and a comprehension test. By the sixth grade, the group that years earlier had received intensive phonics instruction still did better than the comparison group on a word identification test. However, the advantage in comprehension had disappeared. The fact that an early phonics emphasis had less influence on comprehension as the years passed is probably attributed to the increasing importance of knowledge of the topic, vocabulary, and reasoning ability on advanced comprehension tests. Follow up research in the

1970s suggests that instructional models emphasizing basic skills (phonics) tended to elicit the best achievement scores, especially in the first and second grades. Evaluations were weaker in third grade as well as fourth (Becker & Gerstein, 1982). This occurred because of the shift from decoding to comprehension needs as children progress upward in the grades.

Editors Readence and Barone's (1997) insightful reprinting of the first grade studies reflects their keen insight into history's lessons. Their sensitivity to the past coupled with their insights into the current resurgence of interest in phonics had to be an impetus for the marvelous issue of *Reading Research Quarterly, 32* (4).

Conclusions from scholarly works indicate that phonics instruction is important for many children in the earliest grades. I, as well as others (Perfetti & Zhang, 1996), agree that the ability to understand phonological (the sound system) concepts associated with our language is important for reading. When children can identify words and say them, comprehension improves, especially when word identification is quick and automatic (Perfetti, 1992). Even skilled readers sound out words they don't recognize. They recode printed words into the sounds they represent so effortlessly and automatically that they don't realize it's happening (Tannenhaus, Flanigan, & Seidenberg, 1980).

Often skilled readers recognize words by taking "sophisticated guesses" (Adams, 1991). This occurs when there is information about how words are spelled in the readers' memories. Skilled readers have acquired the ability to scan words, identifying them without attending to every detail (Adams, 1991). The automaticity with which they are able to do this results because written English is redundant, and often predictable. When, for example, you see the letter **"q"** you will predict that it is followed by a **"u."** When you see a **"z, h, or y"** you take a sophisticated guess, predicting that a vowel most probably comes next. You've learned, from interacting with the language, that **sl** is a letter combination that starts words, but **ls** is not.

Phonemic awareness is more than knowledge about sounds. It requires one to have a well-developed visual memory, which increases one's ability to use phonics and spelling correctly. Children need to be able to picture letters and words and hold these in their memories.

Even when phonemic and visual memory skills are well developed, youngsters may still have problems. The fact that there are twenty-six letters and some don't represent the sounds of the language in consistent ways is usually the cause. It was George Bernard Shaw who said that the word *fish* might as well be spelled *ghoti—gh* as in *rough, o* as in *women,* and *ti* as in *vacation.* New young writers spell fish **FS, FES, FESHE** and sometimes **FX,** but never **GHOTI.** The children's spellings and also Mr. Shaw's are both incorrect, confirming the fact that matching letters with sounds can have several results. Mr. Shaw's extensive experience with the sounds of language justifies his creative spellings.

Understanding sound-symbol relationships is important, but it is not enough. Learners must also be able to expand their vocabulary and knowledge about the

English language. Information about the derivations of the American English language, and how language works, improves comprehension. We need to know the foibles of the English language and what causes them.

The Study and Foibles of the English Language

Some historical knowledge about the American English language helps to explain why aspects of the language can be confusing. The history puts the importance of phonics in a more realistic perspective.

English reflects the various languages from which it has been derived. We have been scavengers, borrowing words from languages including German, Danish, Norman French, Church Latin, Classical Latin, and Greek (Henderson, 1985). We've also taken words from Arabia, India, the Americas—both native and Spanish, Polynesia, Russia, and even Tibet. These have been absorbed into American English in order to have the words necessary to communicate effectively. Ralph Waldo Emerson once defined English as "the sea which receives tributaries from every region under heaven" (McCrum, Cran, & MacNeil, 1992, p. 1). The inclusive *Oxford English Dictionary* lists over 500,000 words and an additional half-million technical and scientific terms. German has about 185,000 words and French fewer than 100,000. Of the world's approximately 2,700 languages, English is the richest in vocabulary (McCrum, Cran, & MacNeil, 1992).

The amazing thing about English is how the language has spread. Over the past one hundred years, at least three to four hundred million people have learned to speak it as a second language. English today is spoken by about 750 million people. Three-quarters of the world's mail, telexes, and cables are in English, and so are half the world's technical and scientific periodicals (McCrum, Cran, & MacNeil, 1992). It is the official voice of the air and sea, and 80 percent of the information stored in the world's computers is in English (McCrum, Cran, & MacNeil, 1992).

A Very Brief History of English

English did not exist when Julius Caesar landed in Britain a little over 2,000 years ago (McCrum, Cran, & MacNeil, 1992). When first used 500 years later, it was incomprehensible to most and spoken by only a few.

Old English (600 to 1100 A.D.)

The earliest spoken form of English, referred to as Old or Saxon English, emerged between 500 A.D. and 600 A.D. and continued until about 1100 A.D. Modern English, which is what we read and write today, evolved during the 1400 and 1500s.

The following points from the period of Old English seem important for teachers today.

1. English was the first of the modern European languages to attain a standard written form.
2. The written form was used for functional as well as artistic purposes.
3. English originally had a more regular spelling system with Latin letters (Baugh, 1983).

Old English was spelled the way the language sounds. New writers spell that way as exhibited by the sign written by a five-year-old.

B ki t i m rkeee.

Translation: Be quiet I am working.

Middle English (1100 to 1500 A.D.)

Old English was an oral language. The need for a written code emerged with Middle English. Words dealing with social dress (**garment, attire**), law (**jury, evidence**), church (**religion, sermon**), arts and medicine (**painting, physician**), and government (**royal, mayor**) were words borrowed from French. Borrowed words altered English pronunciations, creating interesting, complex spellings. Words were often respelled from one language to another. Alterations from English to French forms such as **is** for **ice** and **mys** for **mice** caused confusion. Combinations of words from Latin and English resulted in replacing the vowel letter **u** with the letter **o**. Because **u** was used so often, the English adopted the French spelling **ou**, which is the reason for the spellings of the words **loud, through, wound,** and **soup.** Combining Anglo-Norman-English spelling led to different vowel sounds represented by the digraph **ea** (**ease, measure**) and to variations of the long **e,** as spelled in **piece, people,** and **meet.**

The merging of many oral and written conventions disrupted the relatively consistent relationship between the letters and the sounds used in Old English. When immigrant workers began to set type at the time the printing press was invented in the 1400s, their crude knowledge of English turned into curious spellings. Since spellings went unmonitored, spellings were printed and became part of the language. However, forces were at work altering the language so that it took the form of the modern English of Shakespeare, basically the language that is in use today (McCrum, Cran, & MacNeil, 1992).

From Middle to Modern English

Because of the communication demands of the information age, Latin and Greek words and spellings were melded to French and English. Within a hundred years, the pronunciation of English changed. This "great vowel shift" caused long vowels to change so that one vowel sound began to take the place of another. Long **a,** for example, originally pronounced **ah** as in **father,** became **a** as in **name. E** "stole" the old sound of long **i.** When young children try to guess what vowel letter to use for short **i,** as in **tin,** they choose **e** as in **ten.** They also spell **pet** as **pat** (Henderson, 1985). So, vowels were disjuncted from their normally paired relationships whose sounds were consistent. The time line in Figure 8-1 provides a terse overview of the critical points in the history of the English language.

Time, People, and Their Influence on the English Language

Year	Event
55 B.C.	Julius Caesar attempts to conquer Britain and is unsuccessful.
50 A.D.	Celtic and Latin coexist when Claudius I colonizes Britain.
450	Teutonic tribes invade Britain and Romans leave.
600	Old English acquires written code when England divides.
750	The Danes invade England, bringing their language with them.
1066	Norman French becomes the language of the state when William of Normandy conquers England. English remains the language of the people.
1350	Middle English is made the official language of the English Parliament during the Hundred Years War (Edward III's reign).
1420	Middle English is first used in his correspondence by Henry V.
1476	English borrows words from classical languages of the Renaissance, and the first printing press is used.
1603	Modern English is used by Elizabeth I and William Shakespeare in their writings.
1755	First comprehensive dictionary is compiled by Samuel Johnson.
1828	Noah Webster compiles the first dictionary of American English.

(Henderson, 1985; McCrum, Cran, & MacNeil, 1992).

Figure 8-1. Dates of Events That Influenced the English Language.

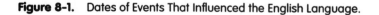

The English language system was further confused by social and political issues, especially the concept that there are many "Englishes." There's the "Queen's" English, American English, dialects of American English, and Englishes spoken as a second language. The "Englishes" one speaks establishes who one is, and what one may become. I remember hearing a friend say, "Oh, he talks like he's had an Ivy League education." Humans see themselves as members of particular groups based on how they use language (F. Smith, 1995).

If you have come to the conclusion that modern English is dreadfully confusing, political, and complex, you are correct. Children, however, have learned to use English for centuries. This is possible because the system is complex, but not chaotic.

So, Who Should Learn Phonics, Spelling, and Aspects of Word Study?

How children acquire knowledge about letter-sound relationships, and how that knowledge is facilitated, is central in the development of word concepts (Perfetti, 1992). It is well known that many school failures are the result of inappropriate instructional procedures. How we guide children, therefore, to use strategies and the context in which skills are acquired makes a difference in what and how they learn.

Phonics, Morphemic Analysis, and Spelling: Understanding Sound–Symbol Relationships

Fred Fedorko, a colleague in our field, shared a story about a six-year-old who, when asked if he was going to fall in love replied, "No, I won't. If it's anything like phonics, I don't want to have anything to do with it." Well, for some children phonics is like falling in love with the wrong person. It just doesn't work. But for others it is wonderful. It's our job, as teachers, to make the decisions about the appropriateness of teaching and using phonics or anything else.

Children's needs must be assessed before instruction begins. I consider assessment part of the instructional process. So, assessment occurs while children are engaged in all activities. As children work in literacy activities—listening or reading, and then responding to stories, poems, word games, and more—listen and look in order to determine each's propensities for using phonics to decode words. I've hesitated to create Figures 8-2 and 8-3, but they have been helpful (when used cautiously) for deciding who can and cannot use phonics as a word recognition tool.

Some children intuitively understand relationships between sounds and symbols. They rhyme words and play with sounds even in the toddler years. Some children—as early as three-and-a-half—write, matching letters with sounds. There are some whose ability to match letters and sounds are not as well developed, nor will they ever be. These children, no matter what activity is used, respond inappropriately or in unexpected ways to instructional approaches. These children are very often poor spellers in the elementary grades, and even into high school and college. They're

Who CAN (Most Probably) Use Phonics			
Phonics is probably appropriate when the child—	**Yes**	**No**	**Not sure**
Picks out letters and says their names.	☐	☐	☐
Notices, without prompting, letter/sound matches.	☐	☐	☐
Rhymes easily.	☐	☐	☐
At times, confuses initial consonant sounds with rhyming. When asked, "Tell me another word that starts with 'r' like in 'rat,' may say, 'cat.'"	☐	☐	☐
Says "I know what letter it starts with" at an early age (older threes and four-year-olds) when long vowels and consonants appear at the beginning of words.	☐	☐	☐
Sometimes uses pictures to guide decoding of words.	☐	☐	☐
Creates her/his own logical spellings based on the sound-symbol relationships of our language.	☐	☐	☐
When writing, can be seen "sounding out" words.	☐	☐	☐
Attends to one letter in a word, when writing. Needs strategies for attending to others.	☐	☐	☐
Demonstrates confidence when "taking risks" and spelling words as they sound.	☐	☐	☐
Although they may not be correct, uses vowels in words illustrating an awareness of spelling conventions.	☐	☐	☐
Spellings seem to become conventional the more she/he writes.	☐	☐	☐
Rereads and self-corrects some spellings of words.			
Enjoys talking about how to make (spell) words.	☐	☐	☐

Figure 8-2.   Who CAN (Most Probably) Use Phonics?

sometimes those "inbetweeners" who can make sense of some of the regularities and irregularities of the coding system, but find other aspects of the language difficult.

Who CANNOT (Most Probably) Use Phonics

Phonics is probably inappropriate when the child—   Yes   No   Not sure

Seems to be unable to make any sense of sound-symbol relationships.

WILL NOT attempt to use word attack skills.

Has difficulty pronouncing words accurately.

Reverses letters at the age of 8, or older.

Spells words as if they were spelled differently.

Confuses consonant sounds.

Uses physical more often than verbal expressions.

Responds inconsistently to sounds.

Handwriting is often illegible due to an inability to remember letter shapes.

Has difficulty rhyming words.

Can copy something almost perfectly, but without copying, writing is illegible.

Figure 8-3.   Who CANNOT (Most Probably) Use Phonics

Children who have difficulty using phonics exhibit combinations of many of the behaviors described in Figure 8-3. REMEMBER, some of the characteristics are present in all of us. But children with difficulties exhibit many of them. Children with severe problems usually produce products (drawings, stories, etc.) that are significantly different from those of others in the classroom. Often, their excessive inability to remember stands out. Experiments with alternative strategies suggested for these students are included later in this chapter. If the youngster is still unsuccessful, and exhibits an excessive number of the characteristics included in Figure 8-3, seek guidance from a reading specialist, school psychologist, and other appropriate specialists.

Teaching and Assessing Phonemic and Morphemic Awareness, and Spelling

We've asked children to look at mismatches between letters and sounds—the irregularities. We ask them to understand about the coding system as if their experiences were numerous. For example, many teachers explain about letters and their sounds. They discuss these aspects in isolation. The sounds and letters become the content, rather than a tool for recognizing ideas. Children are expected to notice minimal sounds and visual contrasts between words including **bed** and **bad, tin** and **ten, went** and **want, farm** and **from.** If they use the oral code for something that is represented in print, confusion is even greater. When teachers tell without modeling the behaviors they expect of youngsters, children are often frightened away from examining language. Some are virtually paralyzed, causing them to memorize rather than decode words.

Many children have a natural affinity for phonics and spelling. Beginning writers exhibit this affinity with their crude, but nearly perfect phonetic correspondence between letter sounds and the symbols representing the sounds (see Figure 8-4). This natural (often referred to as "invented") spelling is wonderful, but can distort, even obliterate the basis for and meanings of many words. So, it makes sense to guide children to study the regular, reliable, and manageable sounds and meaning units of English, first.

Assessing Awareness of Sound/Symbol Relationships

Description of Behavior	Yes	No	Needs more practice
Knows letter names, and identifies them, in lower and upper case formats.	❑	❑	❑
Points to letters, says their names without prompts.	❑	❑	❑
Rhymes words in conversations without request.	❑	❑	❑
When writing, attempts to sound letters for writing. May say "p-p-p-p-p-p-pap-p-p-per," for example.	❑	❑	❑
Talks about the sounds of letters (i.e., "This is an e, see! It says eeeeeeeeeee.").	❑	❑	❑

Figure 8-4.   Assessing Awareness of Sound/Symbol Relationships

Although not supported by other research, we have found that approximately 900 children between the ages of five and eight have defined sounds of language during explicit instruction as summarized below (Glazer, 1980–1997). The explanations follow, for the most part, the alphabetic principles.

1. Some letter sounds say their names as long as your breath will last. These letters include all of the long vowels (**a** as in **ape; e** as in **eat; i** as in **ice; o** as in **ocean; u** as in **unicorn**).

2. Some letters do not say their names, but you can still hold onto the sounds as long as your breath lasts (**a-apple, e-egg, i-insect, o-octopus, u-umbrella, c-circus, f-fish, h-hot, l-love, m-mom, n-nurse, r-read, s-sun, v-vanilla, w-warm, z-zoo**).

3. You can figure out some sounds because of the way you say the letter names. These include the long vowels (see #1 above) and also **b** as in **ball, c-circus, d-dad, f-food, g-giraffe, h-hello, j-jelly, k-kite, l-lamb, m-milk, n-noodle, p-puppy, q-quack, r-ring, s-snake, t-tiger, v-violin, x-x-ray,** and **z** as in **zebra.**

4. Some letters have more than one sound. These are **c** sounds like **k** in **cake, s** in **is** borrows the sound from **c** in **circle,** soft **g** borrows the sound from **j** as in **giraffe, s** sounds like **c** in **facade, y** as in **yes** or as in **happy.**

The collection of childrens' comments are practical, sensible, and easy to understand. It's clear that talk about language and games that instigate cognitive awareness guide all children to become phonemically aware.

So, How Should Phonics Be Taught?

The continuous controversies over the order and method for teaching the sounds of language need to stop. We must compromise for the sake of children and their parents, and consider both (1) implicit and, (2) explicit instruction. We need to begin by realizing that quality instructional outcomes result in students questioning themselves about issues. The self-questioning is self-assessment, and also instruction. The process of self-assessment is ongoing. A person asks himself questions, then searches for data to support an answer. Students "flip-flop" back and forth between the two. They ask questions about their accomplishments—that's the assessment. Then they collect data and answer the questions. Especially when instruction is implicit—that is, happens within the context of content areas—assessment must also be implicit. Figures 8-2, 8-3, and 8-4 are guides for observing each child's readiness for phonological instruction. I suggest that you concentrate on observing two children at a time. I also suggest that you notice the child carrying out these behaviors at least three times, in several different activities, in order to make a judgment concerning readiness.

Although traditional testing approaches are less desirable for assessing readiness, if you must (for whatever reason), use them to determine readiness. If you do, you need to create role-play situations prior to administering the tests that replicate the test-taking experience. The children will become familiar with the testing environment, and will be less stressed during testing.

Assess children's ability to use aspects of phonics. Continuously "listen and look" at each child's behaviors. When you hear or see children using each phonic skill at least three times daily in functional settings, they own those skills. Describe their interactions with and knowledge about phonemes by using the descriptors in Figures 8-5, 8-6, 8-7, and 8-8. Review children's products—things they write—to notice the following:

- when "natural" (invented) spellings reflect the sounds;

- when children talk frequently about sounds and are correct.*

Make a photocopy of Figures 8-2 to 8-8, one for each child. Use them to guide your observations of children's phonemic awareness as well as knowledge of letter sounds.

Do not use these figures to create tests that require youngsters to select the "right answer." Use them when observing children as they write, read, and play phonic games. Check "yes" when the child uses a phonic element at least three times independently. Then you can be fairly sure that they have conceptualized the specific sounds of letters as they are used in words.

Implicit assessment—looking and listening within the context of all school activities—can also be used for determining children's ability to use and understand the following:

- consonant blends at the beginning and endings of words;

- consonant digraphs at beginnings and end of words (**ch, sh, th, wh**);

- phonograms (usually a vowel sound plus a consonant sound). These are the families that make rhyming games fun. Some phonograms include **at**—as in **cat, all**—as in **tall, air**—as in **hair.**

Figures 8-6, 8-7, and 8-8 provide parameters for noticing children's competence with blends, digraphs, and some phonograms.

---

* The following was used to identify phonic elements. Develop additional observation guides that include other phonic elements using this helpful resource—Fry, E., Kress, J., & Fountoukidis, D. (Eds.) (1993). *The Reading Teacher's Book of Lists.* New York: The Center for Applied Research.

Listen, Look, and Assess Knowledge About Phonics

Analyzing Sounds of Words: Phonics	Yes	No	Not sure
Recognizes single letters that say their names as long as their breath lasts and makes the correct sound or writes the correct symbol representing the sounds.	☐	☐	☐

These include:
a as in ape, **e** as in eat, **i** as in ice, **o** as in open, **u** as in uniform.

Recognizes and makes or writes the sound/symbols for letters that do not say their names but you can still hold onto the sound as long as your breath lasts. These include some letters whose sounds you can figure out by the way you say the letter name (see the next item).	☐	☐	☐

These include:
a as in apple, **e** as in egg, **i** as in insect, **o** as in octopus, **u** as in umbrella, **c** as in circus, **f** as in fish, **h** as in hot, **l** as in love, **m** as in mom, **n** as in nurse, **r** as in red, **s** as in sister, **v** as in vampire, **w** as in wash, **z** as in zebra.

Figures out the sound because of the way you say the letter name.	☐	☐	☐

These include:
b as in boy, **c** as in circle, **d** as in dad, **f** as in fairy, **j** as in jelly, **k** as in kite, **l** as in lamb, **m** as in mitten, **n** as in nest, **p** as in potato, **q** as in quiet, **r** as in rooster, **s** as in sneaker, **t** as in toast, **v** as in violin, **x** as in x-ray, and **z** as in zipper.

Recognizes some letters have more than one sound because they borrow sounds from other letters.	☐	☐	☐

These are:
c as in cake, and **c** as in circus; **g** as in giraffe, and **g** as in gadget; **y** as in yes, **y** as in happy.

Figure 8-5.   Listen, Look, and Assess Knowledge About Phonics

Consonant Blends

Directions: Observe children's unguided written products. Notice their use of each consonant blend. Include children's spellings on appropriate line. Prepare instruction for those who seem to "have an idea" about a blend, but need guidance. When a child uses a blend three times without intervention, he/she has mastered that phonemic element.

r family blends

br _____

cr _____

dr _____

fr _____

gr _____

pr _____

tr _____

wr _____

l family blends

bl _____

cl _____

fl _____

gl _____

pl _____

sl _____

s family blends

sc _____

sk _____

sm _____

sn _____

sp _____

st _____

sw _____

no family

tw _____

3 letter blends

scr _____

squ _____

str _____

thr _____

spr _____

spl _____

shr _____

sch _____

Figure 8-6.   Consonant Blends

Consonant Digraphs, Exceptions, Rare Exceptions, and Silent Consonants

Directions: Observe children's writing. Listen and look as they speak. Notice if oral pronunciation and writing match (writing represents the way the child says phonemes).

Consonant Digraphs: beginning & endings of words

ch _____

sh _____

th (voiced) _____

th (voiceless) _____

wh (hw blend) _____

Rare Exceptions

ch = /k/ as in "character"

_____

ch = /s/ as in "chef"

_____

ti = /sh/ as in "attention"

_____

s = /sh/ as in "sure"

_____

x = /gz/ as in "exact"

_____

Exceptions

qu = /kw/ as in "quick"

_____

ph = /f/ as in "phone"

_____

c = /s/ before i, e, y, as in "city"

_____

c = /k/ before a, o, u, as in "cap"

_____

g = /g/ before i, e, y, as in "gem"

_____

g = /g/ before a, o, u, as in "good"

_____

x = /ks/ as in "vex"

_____

s = /z/ at end of some words as in "is"

_____

Silent Consonants

gn = /n/ as in "gnat" _____

kn = /n/ as in "knife" _____

wr = /r/ as in "write" _____

Student demonstrates knowledge about phonics to create the following words: _____

Figure 8-7.   Consonant Digraphs, Exceptions, Rare Exceptions, and Silent Consonants

Recognizing Two-Letter Combinations

Directions: Notice students' use of these in written products. If used three times incorrectly, provide explicit instruction. When used three times correctly, use of two-letter combination is probably learned.

a-e vowel sound	**Other two-letter combinations**
ate _____	**e** as in "hose" _____
final **e** as in "ace" _____	**ai** as in "rain" _____
final **e** as in "life" _____	**au** as in "author" _____
	ar as in "stare" _____
	ar as in "start" _____
	ee as in "see" _____
	ea as in "seat" _____
	ea as in "dead" _____
	er as in "her" _____
	ng as in "sing" _____
	oa as in "coat" _____
	or as in "ore" _____
	ow as in "cow" _____
	oy as in "toy" _____
	oi as in "coil" _____
	ou as in "out" _____
	oo as in "look" _____
	oo as in "zoo" _____

Student uses knowledge represented above and creates the following words:

_____

_____

Figure 8-8.   Recognizing Two-Letter Combinations

Implicit Phonics Instruction

When children begin to notice and talk about language naturally, teachers and caregivers need to seize that moment of readiness,* and begin a discussion. When six-year-old Shana said, "Teacher, the poem has letters that all say the alphabet names," the child is indicating that it's time for instruction.

When the Opportunity Arises: Implicit Instruction

I recently overheard a four-year-old say to his mother, "Look," as he pointed to the sign above the counter in a physician's waiting room, "Look, Mommy. It has a **P** like my name." Peter's mother had been reading a magazine, but she seized the teachable moment, responding, "You are right, Pete. That word, **pay,** starts like Peter. Look," she said, pointing to a captioned picture in the magazine, "this is a picture of a picnic. See, here's **picnic**" (pointing to the word in the magazine). "This looks like a family, like ours, on a picnic. Picnic starts like Peter, too. And your sister's name, **Patty,** does too."

On the car ride home, Peter and his mom played the game of finding all of the things that started with a "P" like his name. She coached the child, providing clues by making her lips into the formation used before saying, "Peter," and also naming many objects. Transactions between the mother and child illustrate the following:

Child's Behaviors	Mother's Behaviors	Interpretations
Notices and makes connection between what he knows (his name) and the environmental print.	Seizes the teachable moment, and provides additional examples of words that start like Pete's name.	Mother knows how to observe and notice child's need and readiness for a concept. Uses child's language as a starting point for instruction.
Demonstrates ability to match and describe the initial sound of "p" by providing a word that begins with "p."	Coaches by using body language to encourage the child to participate.	Teaches by contributing as a learner, so child will model her behavior.

---

*"Readiness," usually used to describe the preparedness of children in the beginning school years, refers in this text to one's preparedness to cope with tasks at all ages.

In conversation with this mother, I learned that she and Peter played the game often. Peter usually began the game, and his mother followed. At times, Peter asked his mother to write words that were of personal interest to him. These included his name, Peter, and his sister's name, Patty. On one occasion he asked her to write Misty, his dog's name. The request was followed by, "I know it doesn't have a 'P'." The child provided data confirming that he understood how "P" sounded. This is the ultimate test. The child was able to differentiate, without prompting, the sound of "P" in a real setting.

I recall hearing my nephews, nieces, and godchildren playing with language as toddlers. "La—dee, la—dee, la—dee" or other rhyming type words were repeated over and over again. As they grew, I had the pleasure of taking them on day trips. Once when walking, I began to say, "Billy silly, nilly, whilly, hilly." The three-year-old looked at me with a smile, as I repeated "Billy, silly." Then I paused, bent down next to him using body language that said, join me, and began again. "B-i-l-l-y, s-i-l-l-y," and he began with me, "ch-i-l-l-y, n-i-l-l-y," until we exhausted the "illy" word family.

Playing with Words

Rhyming books, poetry, and books with repeated language are adored by children. Authors like Dr. Seuss, Lee Bennett Hopkins, Paul Galdone, and others (see Appendix A) have written enticing poetry and story books using repetitive language. Spelling patterns (*at*, as in *fat, bat, cat*, etc.), repeated sentences (I'll huff and I'll puff and I'll blow your house down!), and rhyming words catch children's fascination, luring them to want to hear and produce more of the same. It's fun, when reading these to children, to leave out the rhyming word at the end of each sentence after they've heard that pattern several times. Children will "partially participate," and automatically rhyme, saying the final word correctly.

Language plays—those tricky, sticky, lickity split oral and written language games—present language opportunities and also help children discover the complexities and fascinations of language. Jim Moffett (Moffett & Wagner, 1992) defined word play as the category of discourse that entices children most of all. They include tongue twisters, puns, word puzzles and games, pictographs and cryptograms, brain teasers, concrete and typographical poetry, lighthearted verse and songs in this category. We know about these wonderful "language plays" because of authors like Dr. Seuss, Lewis Carroll, Ogden Nash, and the lyricist and composer Tom Lehrer. There are so many plays with words and authors who created them. These fascinating language arrangements are referred to by students in our Center for Reading and Writing at Rider University as "stuff" that's just for fun (JFF). The examples included here thus far have been implicit in their instruction in phonics. They are immersed in the contexts of literature and poetry.

Explicit Instruction

The following activities are designed for those children who need or might like direct instruction. They receive support and comfort from small-group strategies. They also may need to hear about the aspects of language they may already know implicitly.

Language Play

Our youngsters call some language play JFF (Just For Fun). The activities can serve as guides for creating more language plays and games in both formal and informal settings.

Tongue Twisters

Tongue twisters, such as *those **thrilling thermal thrashing thrilling thumping thin thesis,*** can be created with blends and digraphs that appear at the beginning or the ending of words. Any words that start or end with the same letter combinations lend themselves to JFF exercises. The following are examples.

Same Beginning, Different Ending

Snoring sneaky snails sniff snakes' sneakers.

Flying flags flank flowering floats.

Splashing splitting splatting splattering splinters splendidly splice splints.

Same Ending, Different Beginning

A bath and math wrath my path.

A slick quick thick chick named Rick tricked sick Nick.

A Model Lesson for ALL Phonic Skills

I like to use a learning model to create activities. Don Holdaway's (1979) four-step instructional model is one of my favorite frameworks. His four steps to learning—(1) observations of actions to be learned; (2) partial participation with a mentor who is engaged in the actions; (3) role-play or rehearsal independently; and (4) performance— the time to share with others the accomplishments—follow the learning model human beings use naturally from birth.

The following format for instruction can be used for all phonics instruction as well as other content learning.

Session #1. Bombard Students with Correct Answers: Model So They Can Observe

1. Use the element (word family, blend, etc.) to be learned or as much as you naturally can in your oral language.

2. Find poems, tongue twisters, riddles, and jokes that use the element again and again. Read or tell them to children (more for children to observe).

3. Repeat, tell, or read the language plays, encouraging children to say the words that begin or end with the blend, digraph or other phoneme, encouraging partial participation.

4. Once children partially participate, create charts with the blend, digraph, initial or final consonants, etc., printed at the top. Write two or three words that include the phoneme or letter combination and post the sign. Be sure there is a marker nearby. This will serve as a tool for children to rehearse using elements.

5. Gather the children who need explicit instruction (not more than six at once) around the chart with the letters to be studied written at the top.

6. Repeat one of the stories, poems, riddles, or other language plays that include lots of words with the letters of focus.

7. Each time you say a word that uses the letter, write it on the chart. Underline or highlight the letters of focus.

8. When you finish repeating the language play and have written the words, ask the following questions, one at a time:

   What letters are at the top of the chart? Where else do you see these letters? Where else?

9. Then say, "Let's read the words together." After the words are read by the group, ask, in a tone of voice that implies that you are repeating the same questions again and again, "What's the same about each word?" This step involves partial participation with students.

These questions sometimes guide children to attend to specific phonemic characteristics. I've rationalized the use of questions by fitting them into Holdaway's first step—things to observe. Children are being asked to look as you model behavior at the easel.

Session #2. Partial Participation and Rehearsal

Until this point, you have been providing children with the correct answer. Now it is their turn to "partially participate" and contribute.

Begin by gathering children in front of a posted easel paper with the phonemic element being studied written, in large font, at the top of the paper. Say, "Watch what I am doing so you can tell me what I did." Write words, saying each one at a time. If the letters at the top were "sh," for example, I'd write four to seven words, matching my voice to the speed of writing, "shoe, shop, ship, shepherd," etc. As I was about to complete the last word, I'd say, "O.K., who has a word that begins like 'ship'?" Encourage children to contribute, but do not restrict them from spontaneously "calling out." When they do call out, say in a lighthearted, fun way, "Hold your horses,

I'm writing as quickly as I can." When you're finished, post several charts around the room with the letter combination written at the top of a blank sheet of paper. Casually, during work or play times, write a word on a chart. Encourage children to write words that belong, too. Some will copy yours, others may use a dictionary, or ask another child to suggest a word. The purpose of the activity is to get them to "feel" the experience of writing, categorizing the words appropriately. It is helpful, therefore, for reluctant learners to have words that include the phoneme posted around the classroom. This permits children to look for answers in their immediate environments.

Session # 3. Provide Choices: A Game to Assess Effects of Instruction

I'm not sure Dr. Holdaway would agree with using the next activity. I'm suggesting something rather unorthodox, and against my better professional judgment. But, it works to excite and invite children to participate in an activity. This is the time that we "sort of" test the children by creating a game. In this game, children select and match letters with pictures of objects whose names begin with that letter combination. I suggest that you do the following:

1. Create enough cards with the letter combination in focus for the number of children you want to play the game together. Young children do best in pairs. Eight-year-olds and older enjoy a foursome.

2. Collect pictures of objects whose names, for example, begin with those letters. Make cut-out letters, or the phonemic element being studied, for as many as there are pictures. If, for example, there are twenty pictures that include objects whose initial consonants are "cr," make twenty cards with "cr" written on them, one on each.

3. Cut as many pieces of tagboard as there are pictures into the same size rectangle. Cut tagboard for mounting the letters, as well.

4. Pair the children using one table or desk for each. Tell, while demonstrating, how to cut one picture at a time and paste onto a piece of tagboard. Do it again, and ask the children to do it with you. Move at the children's pace.

5. Demonstrate, with a partner, how to match a picture with the letter(s) that represents the beginnings of each word.

Children will discuss what they are doing during the construction activity. Listen and look to hear what each knows about letter/sound relationships. You will be assessing as they create materials. The game encourages children to make correct responses, for all objects begin with the letters of focus.

Session #4. Children Become Teachers and Create and Share

This is the fun part for children. They become teachers, sharing and bragging about their accomplishments. It usually happens when a child says, "Ms. Susan, look what I did!" Several ways to increase children's excitement while building vocabulary include:

- making a personal dictionary;
- making individual word charts with each youngster;
- writing words on cards and creating a personal word wallet;
- cutting words that include the letters studied from newspapers and magazines and then pasting each on a card for the word wallet;
- collecting names of animals, foods, toys, friends, relatives, or fun things to do, and more.

Provide an enthusiastic environment with activities that require children to rehearse using the letters and letter combinations in different positions in words. Post blank charts with the letter combination written at the top. Leave a writing tool near the chart, as means of suggesting that the children write a word for the appropriate word group on the chart.

These few sample formats for instruction can be used appropriately for many skills. Combining implicit and explicit instruction with phonemic analysis provides children with a way to discuss sounds of language and to create words. They react to print, and also create that print. They learn from the strategies how to solve decoding problems independently.

CAUTION: Like cutting teeth, children must be ready to understand how to use phonemes to decode and construct words. Readiness precedes learning. Remember, too, that some children can learn phonetically and some cannot (these children will be discussed later in this chapter).

Back to Assessment

The phonemic skills that early and new readers are usually expected to learn are included in Figures 8-3 to 8-8. Remember, you can tell if a child has most probably mastered a skill when you've observed or heard the skill used in at least three functional, independent situations. These checklists are not meant to be prescriptive. They are prepared only to supply teachers with an example of how to prepare a list of skills to use for monitoring children's growth.

Children's Self-Monitoring Tool

Self-monitoring (see Chapter 5) helps children learn how to take charge of their learning. It is necessary, in environments that respect students, to provide a self-assessment tool, even for phonics. I suggest the following:

1. Have children use the Progress Report Form (Figures 5-2, 5-3, 5-4, 5-5) to record "What I know," and "What I need to learn" about the sounds of language.

2. Prepare games that provide rehearsal for using phonemic elements. Board games where children are expected to identify and select the correct blends, word families, and more, are fun. Use the formats of commercial games such as *Monopoly* or *Wheel of Fortune*, for example, to create these.

There continues to be much controversy over explicit instruction with specific sounds of our language. I find, for example, that consensus is never achieved during professional discussions about how or if to teach single and double vowel sounds. Although double vowel sounds, especially within words, are almost impossible for most of us to learn, some children can't learn these sounds, or any other sounds of language. Phonics instruction, for these learners, could complicate the use of other word recognition strategies. This is especially true if the children are pushed and struggle with this type of instruction.

The lack of capacity or inability to use phonics to decode occurs for reasons mentioned earlier in the text (page 226), but also because our language does not have enough single letters to represent sounds for words. We've had to create combinations of letters to represent the sounds needed. This has made both phonics and spelling difficult for many. In addition, there are some youngsters who just don't have an aptitude for phonics.

So, What About Explicit Phonics Instruction?

As in traffic jams, "proceed with caution." Continuously assess by listening and looking at how children decode words when reading; how they respond to poems, tongue twisters, and other language plays that focus on letter/sound relationships. Read literature that plays with sounds (see Appendix A), and play with sounds as you talk to the children. Use the formats for instruction shared earlier to create lessons. Think about the purposes for knowing about and learning phonics. Ask yourself the questions I've pondered for more than three decades:

- Until what age or stage do children need to use phonics (Figure 8-3)?
- What do I do with the children I've assessed as nonphonic learners?
- What is the difference between phonics and spelling?

What to Do With the Child Who Can't Learn Phonics Either Implicitly or Explicitly

When hearing the sounds and using them to unlock symbolic representatives of these sounds does not work, alternative word recognition strategies must be used. I have found four such strategies to be successful with many children. The first, and most important, is to read, read, and read some more to children of all ages. Read stories, poems, fables, fiction, and nonfiction at a "reading-to-class time" daily. This increases a sensitivity to the sounds of language, word meanings, genres—everything! In addition, try the implicit activities that include: (1) environmental print activities, (2) listening to literature (especially poetry) that includes lots of single and multiple letter combinations, and (3) explicit strategies for remembering words for both reading and writing.

Environmental Print Activities

Opportunities to play with and become aware of phonemic relationships exist all around us. Peter's mom (page 234) seized a propitious moment and used a doctor's waiting room for a learning. The interactions also directed Peter to observe the relationship between his name and "p" at the beginning of words in his environments. This helped to bring what Peter already knew to the new information. Teachers in classrooms need to seize moments for explicit instructional sessions. Group lessons make information important, and provide peer support for reluctant learners.

Explicit Activities Using Environmental Print to Teach Phonics

Activity #1.   Conduct an explicit teaching experience focusing on one phonemic element. For example, use Session #1 of the lesson format on pages 236–237 using the letter **"f."** Be sure to hang the charts developed in the lesson around the classroom. It is also helpful to photocopy an individual replica of the chart for each child.

Activity #2.   Take a walk with your class. Be sure that each child has either a pad, or clipboard with paper, and a writing tool. Whatever the letter of focus may be, say to the children before the trip, "We are going play a phonics game. First there have to be two teams. So, this half of the class is team _____ (give it an appropriate name). This half is team _____. We are going to play the game in the school halls." Line the children up inside your classroom. Say, "Now, when I say go, walk QUIETLY around the first floor of the school. Write down the names of all of the things you see that start with the letter **f** like **fish, farm, flat,** and **fox.** The team that writes the most words is the winner."

This second activity is most effective when it follows from the first. It is, in a sense, a combination of sessions 2 and 3 of the phonic lesson format on pages 237–238.

There are many other activities in which children can "hunt for words" that fit the topic of the lesson. I am sure that after children are "bombarded" with correct responses, select from choices, and finally collect words, they will know the phonemes and the graphemes the letters represent.

Literature for Learning Phonics

Almost every word in Stanley and Janice Berenstain's *The Berenstains' B Book* (1971) begins with the letter "B." The authors' ability to use humor, repeated language, and rhyming formats make this and many of their books delightful, enticing, and alluring, especially for reluctant readers. *Four Famished Foxes and Fosdyke* by Pamela Edwards (1995), an adventure about four "foxy" brothers who make fun of Fosdyke because he likes fried figs, fennel, and French bread, incorporates at least 60 words that begin with the letter "F." These and other books, including those in Appendix A, challenge children's thoughts about how language works, and whets their appetite for literature.

Some reluctant readers resist reading anything, especially when they are skill-related materials. Luring, by involving peers, is often necessary with these youngsters. I suggest, therefore, that you label a shelf in your classroom library, "Books for Buddies." Rubberband two copies of at least six different titles, with all the books related to the sounds of language. Introduce the concept, implicitly, by asking a child to be your reading buddy, and together select and then read a book. During a group discussion time, even show-and-tell, you and your buddy share the activity, and retell the content of your paired reading. This models shared reading for the youngsters and other students will follow your lead.

Additional books for developing phonemic awareness while enjoying great literature are included in Appendix A.

Reading wonderful literature that emphasizes letter sounds enhances phonemic awareness. Search for and read children's literature that focuses on the sounds of language to and with children. Notice children's responses to the literature. Notice, too, if they produce their own words following spelling and rhyming patterns used by the authors. Use the assessment tools in Figures 8-2 through 8-8 to determine each student's strength and needs, and record your observations on the Progress Report Form (Figure 5-2).

Explicit Strategies for Recalling Words for Reading and Writing

I know that some of you believe that explicit phonics instruction is necessary for ALL children. I disagree with the notion. It's like prescribing aspirin for anyone who has a headache. It's unrealistic. I agree with my friends Regie Routman (1996) and Sandra Wilde (1997) that children don't need explicit instruction in phonics, or even spelling. Phonics can be taught and reinforced during shared reading and writing, and assessed and taught during writing times. When phonics is an outgrowth of these activities, the implication is that phonics is naturally part of the reading/writing process. Most children learn phonics tacitly, without realizing it. When tacit learning occurs, children are learning to use phonics, or anything else, because the skills are needed in order to function as a reader or writer.

I often find myself writing ideas in sentences and phrases, and then rewriting them when trying to figure out what I want to write about. I discovered that I write like this in order to figure out what I know. Then, I write lectures, speeches, or articles learning about what I know by writing about it. Kids have ideas in their heads about how words ought to be spelled and written. They get these ideas from immersion into language from the beginning of their lives. They learn it from hearing stories, poems, and conversations. They learn it by observing adults read, talk, and write, and from parental interactions. They incorporate what they know into their memories, using the information to solve language problems in and out of school. They solve code breaking when reading, and that's phonics. If writing is involved, and it surely is, then where does spelling fit in?

Our teachers always use children's writing to glean information about needed phonics instruction. They examine children's spelling and listen to shared oral readings to make decisions concerning instructional needs. They use instructional strategies mentioned earlier and later in this text. We even prepare strategy sheets so children are able to manipulate the phonemes independently. One such sheet was prepared for several children who needed to learn that they could manipulate letters and letter patterns and create many words. Figure 8-9 is an example of one of the many prepared using the same format. The important things about this worksheet include:

- the reason to make "at" pattern words developed because the student spelled "sat" three different ways in her writing (st, set, sot);

- the worksheet is void of written directions because the materials are designed in such a way that the student knows how to proceed;

- the words are presented as a whole unit, the way children read them, and then broken into phonological units.

The more typical worksheet begins with the parts, and expects the child to create the whole word. A frequently seen format looks somewhat like the following:

Make a word. Add the first letter to "at."

c + at = cat
f + at = fat
m + at = _____
r + at = _____
h + at = _____
b + at = _____

This format, unlike Figure 8-9, includes written directions, and words are built from parts to whole. Although the differences may seem minimal, they are important. Children, who find reading or following written directions confusing, could be hindered by the above word-making activity.

				at			
cat	c	+	at	=	cat	
fat	f	+	at	=	fat	
sat	s	+	at	=	_____
rat	r	+	at	=	_____
hat	__	+	__	=	_____
nat	__	+	__	=	_____
bat	__	+	__	=	_____
mat	__	+	__	=	_____
zat	__	+	__	=	_____

Figure 8-9.   Whole to Part "at" Worksheet

What About the Relationship Between Phonics and Spelling?

Children must know something about the spelling (orthographic) system in order to use phonics. They must know that:

- English has twenty-six letters;

- sometimes we use a letter twice—one next to the other—to represent differences in vowel sounds in words (lose and loose, for example).

When I reread, dear educators, what I've just written, and ask myself, "Is there really a difference between spelling and phonics?" conclusions are unclear, confusing, and puzzling. It's like asking, which comes first, the chicken or the egg? I've come to believe that the processes for learning and using phonics and spelling are similar and interchangeable for many children. Charles Read (1975), in his work with preschool writers who used invented spelling,* found that the spellings represented the regular consonant sounds very consistently.

There is a fine line between phonics and spelling. Seven-year-old Tawanda taught me lots about how children think about both. Her mom had informed us that she insisted that her child learn to read the "right" way, with phonics. Tawanda concluded, during a long discussion involving her mother, myself, and her, "I write words the way they sound to me. I just sound them out and know how to spell words. So, I don't have to know phonics."

When Do Children Need to Be Taught Explicit Phonics?

I have observed thousands of beginning readers and writers over the years. When youngsters write phonetically, producing spelling that represents the rational sounds of language, they're demonstrating that they understand sound/symbol relationships. They already know how phonics is used! Some children's spellings reflect knowledge of some letter sounds, and not others. These children attend to the letters whose sounds are familiar. This is indicated by the fact that the specific part of the word that includes the letter(s) makes sense phonically. These children might benefit from direct instruction, and yet they may not. When children's writing and interactions with literature illustrate that they have no sense about how the sounds of letters work to make words, phonics will, most probably, be inappropriate. Some children need to learn spelling rules. The fact that spelling rules guide decoding implies that there is a crossover between spelling and phonics. I am not sure, but I'd say that the strategies that follow guide children to make the transition from learning phonics to spelling.

From Phonics to Spelling

Assessing and Teaching Spelling

Instructional and assessment procedures most often used in schools have infuriated me since the beginning of my career. Poor spelling has often been equated with inadequate writing ability. My own report cards always showed "poor" in spelling. Low grades were aggravated by a high school teacher's comment, "Susan, you should not pursue a college career. You can't write." Supportive parents' and friends' encouragements were stronger than the recurring teacher's remark in my mind, and I made it through.

---

*The term "invented spelling" is used to describe those who spell a word without knowledge of the rules that govern the irregular sounds and spelling of our language. Donald Graves in a personal communication (1996) has referred to this as "temporary spelling." Since learning to spell is a developmental process, "temporary" seems logical.

Hundreds of thousands of students suffer from the same fate. This happens, I believe, because of (1) the over-emphasis on the importance of spelling, (2) the reasons for spelling problems, (3) a lack of knowledge concerning reasons for failure, and (4) inappropriate instruction and assessment procedures.

How Important Is Spelling?

Spelling is very important. Knowing how to spell enables authors to write quickly, easily, and correctly. It is not as important, however, during initial writing efforts. Before the advent of computers, good handwriting habits were necessary elements in the writing process. Poor spelling habits often resulted and were equated with poor handwriting habits. In today's sophisticated computer age, one is no longer required to struggle to perfect handwriting. The importance of handwriting to the spelling process, therefore, is minimal. The importance it had when students were creating written text has been replaced by expectations that quality writing be produced.

Reasons for Spelling Problems

The nature of spelling, itself, often creates spelling problems. By the time a child begins to spell, she/he has learned to speak and understand the meanings of words. When she learns to spell, she must begin with symbols that make up the word. It isn't sufficient to recognize words as one does when reading. The child must grasp the word in sufficient detail to make it possible for her to reproduce it correctly. It's like recognizing a person when you see her, and paying enough attention to her in order to produce a portrait.

Spelling failures are due, in part, to bad habits that were forced upon children when adults attempted to teach them to spell. This was true of many past practices, and even today some teachers in schools and some parents

1. continue to use inappropriate instructional strategies, insisting that children who spell incorrectly write, and rewrite the same words again, and again;
2. test under timed conditions, and before students have developed automaticity for writing the words;
3. discard or lack knowledge about well-established theories of learning;
4. arouse negative emotions due to assigned, out-of-context word-learning expectations, and then treat the child in uncomfortable ways because of failures.

Strategies and Circumstances That Often Produce Poor Spellers

There is no better way to produce poor spelling habits than to dictate prescribed spelling words to children. Students are asked to study these dictated words usually as homework. More often than not, they are not provided with strategies that guide them to learn the words. Many teachers tell children to memorize, without saying how. Others tell children to use flash cards and don't say how or why. Testing their ability to spell words generally comes once a week. Children who have difficulty spelling words out of context in particular, or have difficulty due to time constraints often panic, get confused, and can't help but misspell words. Attempts to correct misspelled words often fail. Some classroom teachers even prohibit correcting words during testing. These insensitive teachers move on to the next word, the child begins to write the word late, becomes confused, gets it wrong, knows he's wrong, and the nightmare continues.

The teacher corrects the child's paper by marking the misspelled words in ways that draw the child's attention to misspellings, rather than correct spellings. This devastating horror is often topped with a poor grade that convinces the child that he is stupid. Handing back the paper enhances poor self-esteem, especially when the student is told to write and rewrite the words correctly a given number of times.

If that's not enough, some teachers require that children stay after the regular school hours to write and rewrite the words. Sometimes a note is sent home, which results in anything from a parent offering a prayer that this "dummy" might learn how to spell, to a severe or even violent punishment.

This monotonous, repetitious writing, and rewriting, causes poor attention. Students become disinterested in the meanings of words because of the boring and sometimes hypnotic nature of repetition. They often withdraw rather than continue to suffer when teachers use their errors as the basis for class discussion and instruction. Try and write your own name between 25 and 100 times and reflect on your feelings. I bet that even your own name becomes a bunch of meaningless symbols. One youngster shared his strategy. "You know what, Susan," he commented, "when my teacher asks me to write a word 25 times, I write the first two letters 25 times, and then the next two letters 25 times, and the last letters 25 times, and it's not so boring." Unfortunately, all this outrageous activity occurs without ever providing students with strategies for learning how to spell and recall the words. They aren't learning HOW to spell and remember words. What they're really learning is that spelling is a boring, tedious, unpleasant, frustrating exercise.

Spelling Techniques Often Used

Teachers usually select one technique for ALL students. The activities generally ask students to: (1) form images in the mind, (2) learn from oral spelling, and (3) copy words. When any single strategy for learning is forced on an entire class of children, some will fail to learn.

Visual Images and Memory

Students with an aptitude for spelling generally picture words in their minds. Poor spellers seem to be unable to use their visual memory effectively to do this. The images they produce are vague and indistinct, preventing them from receiving the details necessary to reproduce the word. Some learners are unable to form any image. There are some who can recall a bit of the word's image, at first. They visualize the rest of the word with rehearsal, over time.

Students who are unable to develop visual images absolutely cannot use visual imagery to learn to spell. They generally respond to auditory stimuli (hearing sounds of the word) and kinesthetic stimuli (using hands, tongue, throat, lip, or eye movements), which takes the place of visual learning. The student needs to feel himself say the word, think the sound, and feel the movements his hand makes when writing the word. It's a commonly used practice to say, "Boys and girls, close your eyes and try to make a picture in your mind of the word." Children who can't "get the image" cannot produce the right answer with this "picture in the mind" approach.

Oral Spelling

Nonvisual learners also have difficulty spelling words one letter at a time. The image of the word as a whole unit is lost as they concentrate on a one-letter image. When they begin to spell the word, they attend to the "letter of the moment," losing all idea of the word itself. These same children have difficulty finding words in a dictionary. Focusing on finding the word by looking at the first letters helps them forget how to pronounce the rest of the word. The usual practice for helping the hard-to-teach, kinesthetic speller has been to spell the word out loud. The ridiculous thing about this is that it's impossible for them to learn this way.

Copying Words

Copying words is discussed in connection with asking students to write words from memory. Children who are auditory-kinesthetic learners have difficulty copying words. The eyes move back and forth from the copy written on paper or a chalkboard at the front of the classroom to the paper. Auditory-kinesthetic learners say each letter as it's copied; they too focus on each letter as a whole, and forget the word.

If hard-to-teach learners with spelling problems are given correct spellings of words each time they need to write them, they will learn how to form the letters. Children who have difficulty spelling, and ask how to spell words when writing, MUST be provided with a written copy of the WHOLE word. Spelling it out, making a picture in their mind, or copying it letter for letter just won't work.

Strategies That (Most Probably) Work

The Modified Ashton-Warner/Fernald Strategy

Grace Fernald (1943) believed that professionals needed to develop ". . . remedial, and preventive techniques that will result in a satisfactory adjustment of the individual to his environment" (p. 1). Dr. Fernald supported the idea that students with learning disabilities, developmental lags, and other anomalies needed adjustments in instructional strategies in order to maximize their learning. One of her many techniques designed for students with disabilities in reading and spelling words seems to work for ALL learners. This kinesthetic (type of hands on) approach was first instigated by Plato who lived between 427 and 347 B.C. In discussions concerned with early stages of writing, Plato wrote in the *Protagoras,* "When a boy is not yet clever in writing, the masters first draw lines, and then give him the tablet and make him write as the lines direct." Seneca (3 B.C. to 65 A.D.) suggested that the teacher place his hand on the child's to guide his fingers (Freeman, 1908). Quintillion, a scholar active in the year 68 A.D., recommended, "As soon as the child has begun to know the shapes of the various letters, . . . have them cut as accurately as possible upon a board, so that the pen may be guided along the grooves. Thus mistakes . . . will be rendered impossible, for the pen will be confined between the edges of the letters and will be prevented from going astray." Quintillion advised "learning the sound and the form of the letter simultaneously . . ." (Haarhoff, 1920, pp. 58–59). These philosophers knew, even then, that alternatives were necessary in order for some to learn.

Sylvia Ashton-Warner wrote in *Spinster* (1959), that children don't need "foreign stuff . . . plastered on at all when there's so much inside already. If only I could draw it out. . . . If I had a light enough touch, it would just come out under its own volcanic power" (p. 1). Sylvia found that when she talked to children, she drew out their thoughts, the desire to discuss events, ideas, and things in their lives. As described in *Teacher* (1963), she guided children using the hundreds of words already inside them, thus spurring their desire and comfort to read and write.

I have found in years of working with children and teachers that aspects of Sylvia Ashton-Warner's "key word" approach, coupled with Grace Fernald's methods, are just about foolproof for learning to recognize and write* words. My staff and children in our Center have named our version of the method, The Modified Ashton-Warner/Fernald Strategy.

Our melded strategy needs to be taught to children one-to-one when a child asks, "How do you spell a word?" My teachers go to the children's tables, and teach them the strategy because they need it THEN.

Each student needs a legal-size envelope, or a ring holder that can be opened and closed. Words are written on cards, about 3 × 5 inches in size. The word cards are stored in each child's envelope labeled, "Katie's Words," or on the ring holder with holes punched in one corner. Older children like to file their word cards alpha-

---

*The word "spell" not "write" would normally be used in this context. "Write" implies that the words are whole units, with parts, rather than parts (the letters) forming the whole. "Write" describes what students are actually doing.

betically, or by content, or even based on where they were used. Many prefer to write the words in a notebook designated for that purpose. Use this technique when:

- children find a special word associated with content, discussions, etc.;

- children ask to spell a word needed for their writing;

- several pieces of their text, written independently, indicate instruction.

Katie learned to use this technique in the Center after her teacher realized that this was more effective than any other for writing words. She often wrote without a care about the correct spelling of words. Other times, she knew that she wanted to share her writing and therefore had to spell correctly so others would be able to read it. "How do you spell elephant?" Katie shouted spontaneously one day while writing about her favorite topic. Her teacher pulled a 3- × 5-inch word card from her pocket and placed it in front of Katie. She wrote "elephant," matching her voice to the flow of her written language and holding onto the sound of the vowels until the next consonant was written. After writing the word, the teacher placed her hand over Katie's writing hand, and holding onto the index finger said, "Katie, say the word and trace it with me." The teacher moved both of their hands together, tracing and saying the word simultaneously. The first few tracings were done this way to guide the child in how to use the procedure. After several times, the teacher said, "Do it again yourself, Katie," as she lifted her hand from the child's. Katie traced the word three times. Her teacher watched to be sure that she was using the procedure correctly. Only when tracing is done from left to right, slowly, and the hand moves over every part of each letter, is this procedure effective. The teacher asked if she thought she could say and write the word without looking at the card. Katie responded affirmatively, and the teacher continued, "Katie, turn the card over so you can't see the word, and write your word on a piece of paper." After Katie wrote the word, the teacher directed her to refer to the word card to check for correctness. Katie forgot to include one letter, so she was directed to say and retrace and try again.

The teacher observed Katie for three weeks to be sure that the strategy was effective for her. If the procedure had not been effective, she would have found another.

Generally, this procedure works with almost everyone. It does not work when tracing and saying are incorrectly executed, or when youngsters have severe emotional or social problems (Fernald, 1943). As places where children can practice their words, you might create columns, one for each child in your classroom, on chalkboards or easel paper posted on the walls. Some children prefer to leave their desks to test writing and saying their words. Be sure to inform children that they need to say and trace, without referring to their cards. Most children are able to learn two to four words daily. They ought to write all the words they have learned, one after the other, without their cards.

Some words are not as power packed as others. Students' interest influences learning, as well. If some words pose learning difficulties, the option of trying again or disposing of that word must be built into the process. When the process for using this strategy becomes part of students' repertoire, words relevant to children's lives will be added by them, and learned.

Children who are able to do so can use their word envelope or word box to learn alphabetizing skills. Categorizing by alphabetizing follows naturally.

Some Cautions   The scientific nature of this strategy requires that it be carried out exactly as described. Teachers must observe to be sure children do the following:

- trace and say the word simultaneously;

- trace and say the word slowly and with care;

- never spell out the word, always say and trace;

- review by tracing, saying, and writing the words, daily.

Although Grace Fernald (1943) and Sylvia Ashton-Warner (1963) developed their techniques for children who had difficulty learning, I, and others, have used it to remember statistical formulas, technical spellings, and more. It works with special needs students, those average, and those considered gifted. It is most effective when children learn words they select because they need them for their writing.

Self-Questioning Strategy

Self-questioning guides students to focus attention on word elements. I've prepared a self-questioning guide sheet that children use independently. With practice, most children remember how to write the word from memory because they've asked themselves these questions. The following strategy sheet should be placed with other spelling strategies for easy access for children of all ages. Again, written directions for using the self-questions are necessary.

> What letter begins the word?
>
> What letter ends the word?
>
> What vowels are in the word?
>
> What little words are in the word?
>
> What spelling pattern is in the word?

All of these questions may not be appropriate for all students to remember words. Some of the questions are helpful only for some words. You need to decide with a student, which helps him/her to recall spellings.

Spelling Workshop Strategy

Imagine looking for a telephone number in a phone book and not having paper to write it on. I get frustrated, but then I say the number, repeating it again and again until I've dialed and reached my party. Repetition and rehearsal are strategies for recall. They are the basis for the Spelling Workshop created for middle- and upper-grade students. The unique part of this strategy is that students are able to move through the workshop independently. All of the strategies for learning to remember how to spell words are present throughout.

We make these available to students as they want to use them. The workshop combines a series of strategies that guide students to learn to write words from memory without teacher intervention (Figure 8-10). It also includes self-testing throughout. Third-grade teacher Katrin Rooman gives each of her children the workshop at the beginning of the school week. She structures the use of the workshop as follows:

> *Monday:*   Student and teacher, together, develop a personal list of words for the week. The words are taken from their Spelling Trend Assessment sheet (Figure 7-36) which includes those from content area and writing projects. The number of words for each child depends on his/her capacity.

> *Tuesdays, Wednesdays,* and *Thursdays:*   Children, individually or in pairs, use the spelling workshop as it self-directs. Word games that include at least two, but preferably four players, are wonderful activities for repetition and rehearsal activities. They are "sort of" quizzes monitored by peers.

> *Fridays:*   At the end of the week, Katrin uses a student buddy system for children to self-test. They find a spot congenial for two, and give each other a make-believe spelling quiz in the traditional format. Since each child's words are personalized, the tester is rehearsing reading the peer's words. Peer testing is usually game-like, creating a relaxed, nurturing environment for learning.

Katrin conferences briefly with each of the twenty-two children in her classroom during the week, as they work through the activities. She checks for habit building, and spelling errors. Her goal is to find the trends that cause the spelling errors, and teach appropriate strategies.

Assessing Spelling

Three things seem to be most important when assessing spelling: (1) today's concept of spelling; (2) spelling development; and (3) characteristics of good spellers.

Today's Concept of Spelling

The last ten years have changed our view of the spelling process. In earlier years, good spellers were students who "mastered" large numbers of words (Hodges, 1987). Sandra Wilde (1992) tells us that today, "children's spelling is not only [considered] a reflection of children's exposure to and knowledge of words but an indication of their understanding of the system of complex and varied patterns" (p. 19).

Spelling Workshop

STEP 1 Read your spelling words. Look at them for a few minutes. Have some-one dictate them to you.

_____

_____

_____

STEP 2 Write the words you spelled correctly.

_____

_____

_____

Write the words you misspelled, correctly.

_____

_____

_____

STEP 3 Write your spelling words here.

_____

_____

_____

Write the small words that you see in each spelling word.

_____

_____

_____

STEP 4 Write your spelling words.

_____

_____

_____

Write words that rhyme with your spelling words.

_____

_____

_____

STEP 5 Write your words from memory.

_____

_____

_____

STEP 6 Write the words you spelled correctly.

_____

_____

_____

Write the words you misspelled, correctly.

_____

_____

_____

Figure 8-10. Spelling Workshop (Page 1 of 2)

STEP 7   Find the word card with the correct spellings for misspelled words.

Take ONE word card.

Say the word to yourself or out loud.

Trace the word with your finger saying the word as you trace.

Keep saying and tracing the word until you think you can write it from memory.

Turn the word card over so you can't see it.

Write the word from memory.

Do another word.

Write it from memory.

Do another word.

Write the word from memory.

Trace and say, and write three words correctly.

Take A Break!

After you trace and say and write five words, put all the word cards on the table. Look at them, then...

Make believe you are taking the test. Write these five words from memory.

STEP 8   Give the words you learned to a friend. Ask your friend to dictate the words you learned. Write them here.

_____

_____

_____

STEP 9   Write the words you spelled correctly.

_____

_____

_____

Write the words you misspelled, correctly.

_____

_____

_____

STEP 10   Trace the words you still need to learn. Write them here when you think you can write them from memory.

_____

_____

_____

10-Step Approach to learning to spell is copyrighted by S.M. Glazer

May be reproduced for classroom use only with citation: S.M. Glazer, Rider University

Figure 8-10.   Spelling Worksheet (Page 2 of 2)

Children learn about how words are spelled and why. The concept of spelling has changed from a static to an active process because we've learned a lot about children's cognitive development as it relates to literacy.

Spelling Development

Children acquire information about our spelling system long before they come to school (Clay, 1975; Gentry, 1987). They discover and experiment with lines, curves, circles, and other forms that make letters. As they play, they learn that (1) print represents talk, and (2) that print always looks the same. We also know by observing very young children that their scribble moves from left to right. This indicates that they've discovered, very early, that writing is horizontal.

When children are able to distinguish characteristics of written forms, they begin to write lines characteristic of letters, and then letters themselves. The discovery that children have made when they write is that there is a system for writing. This is the beginning of spelling development. Gentry and Gillet (1993) divide the development of spelling into five stages, as defined in Figure 8-11.

Stage	Child's Writing	Translation	Age
Precom-municative	SOPLOVS	Says, "It's a story about my sister."	3 years, 3 months.
Semiphonetic (captions or labels)	fon col	phone call	5 years, 11 months.
Phonetic	Lus tok a mos to ski	Luis took a mouse to school.	6 years, 3 months.
Transitional	I won't a fon be cus mi friends hav won.	I want a phone because my friends have one.	7 years.
Conventional	Monday I went to my aunt Nancy. she gave me a kitten.		7 years, 9 months.

Figure 8-11.   Spelling Development

Characteristics of Good Spellers

Good spellers are able to visualize a word in their minds. They can store the image of the word and access that image when they need to write the word. Most poor spellers are unable to do this. Words that include letters that have different sounds—such as "g" in giraffe, which has the sound of "j"—cause much difficulty for these learners. Without a picture in their minds of the word, a "j" would be used at the beginning, for that's the sound one hears.

There is little research explaining why some can and others cannot visualize a word, but it is important to notice the behaviors of children as they write words, and take note of how they produce words. When the letters used replicate only sounds, not irregularities in spellings, students most probably have difficulties with visual imagery.

Children write from the time they are able to hold onto and control a writing tool. Their markings reflect the writing formats of their language and culture. The more children write, the more they learn about the spelling system. It is important, therefore, to keep continuous records of their spelling habits so that you can determine their development and an instructional plan.

Teacher Assessment of Spelling Development

Eight-year-old Quaeenkqua had difficulty spelling. Her teacher decided that she had to focus on her writing for two weeks. This would help her to get a sample of her spellings, so that she could study her spelling habits. Kristine, her teacher, collected the child's spellings of words and recorded them on the "Spelling Trend Assessment" sheet (Figure 8-12). The words were taken from routine writing activities, as well as other written products. The child's spelling trends were summarized so that appropriate instruction could be planned based on Quaeenkqua's needs. The analysis showed that Quaeenkqua spelled words the way they sounded. She seemed to attend to specific sounds within the word, lost attention, and stopped noticing specifics about spelling in the middle of words (i.e., zeez for zebra; pround for pronounce, Satday for Saturday). It was evident that she understood spelling conventions by her use of the double (ee), Zebra (zeez), "tion" in Trenton (Treltion), and "le" in report (repole). Causes for misspellings may be multiple. Some possibilities include (1) an inability to attend to task for more than a few moments, (2) poor memory for visual images of words, or (3) inappropriate or inadequate instruction. The reversed "d" for "b" in Job, and "form" for "from" might indicate some perceptual problems, since Quaeenkqua is more than eight years old. The section labeled "instructional needs" at the bottom of Figure 8-12 provides suggestions for instruction.

SPELLING TREND ASSESSMENT

Student's Spelling	Correct Spelling	Patterns Noted
jod	job	reversal of "b"
Trelion	Trenton	phonetic
write	writes	didn't pluralize
frown	from	phonetic -
tocck	tooth	phonetic -
frown	from	phonetic -
zeez	zebra	initial consonant & vowel sounds
sken	skin	phonetic - vowel sub.
fishs	fish's	possessive rule
beuse	because	initial consonant & vowel sound & ending missing middle 2 letter blend.
to	two	homophone - confusion
dog	dogs	pluralize
form	from	transposed "ro"
happie	happy	phonetic (- y - sound)
frpound	pronounce	initial consonants & vowel sounds
woke	work	phonetic - omission of "r" extra "e" sound
wat	what	phonetic - omission of "h" - wh
repole	report	initial sounds
satday	Saturday	phonetic
to	too	homophone
borb	board	phonetic - reversal of b for d

Spelling is: Mostly natural (temporary) ✓   Mostly conventional_____

Source(s) of words: unguided writing, retell, reading log, journal, & sentence projective

Instructional Needs: Fernauld technique, encourage to take time when spelling - seems to rush - point out careless errors (missing letters) Explain/model - use of possession & pluralizing words, direct praise for taking risks, continue using word bank/cards, make word cards for words that are repeatedly spelled in a temporary format -

Student's Name: Quaeenkqua Woods   Date: 3/5

Teacher's Name Kristine Kaufman

Figure 8-12. Quaeenkqua's Spelling Trend Assessment

Student Self-Assessment of Spelling Development

My goal for students of all ages is to provide them with self-monitoring tools so they are able to discuss their strengths and needs. Most children, with rehearsal, are able to learn to self-assess. Self-assessment involves the ability to look at one's own work, but also to feel confidence about oneself as a learner. It is very difficult for an insecure student to look at and find errors. The first thing, therefore, that teachers need to do is to support student efforts in everything they do in order to build their self-confidence. Direct praise (see page 41) must be used immediately, when teachers observe children's personal critiques. Praise must come for all self-monitoring, even those nonacademic, social, and physical efforts. Discussion and analyses with children in order to guide them to look at their efforts also helps develop this skill. One of our teachers created the "Spelling Self-Monitoring Sheet" with her children. It has proven to be an important tool for building self-confidence and spelling skills, as well. Children often find their errors and correct them. When they are unable to detect misspellings, instruction is probably needed. Imagine how important a ten-year-old feels when she corrects and points out her own errors (Figure 8-13). Once she is able to describe her needs, she's automatically making corrections. So, assessment is, in fact, the instruction when self-monitoring spelling.

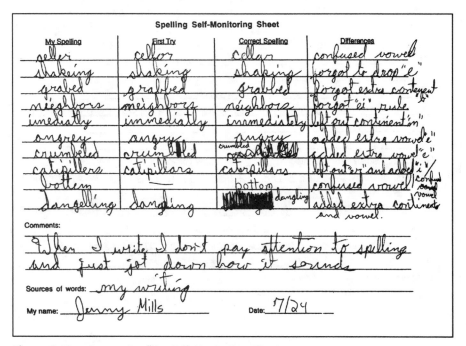

Figure 8-13. Jenny's Spelling Self-Monitoring Sheet

Spelling Instruction Driven by Assessment

Danyell discovered from several writing products that Ross continuously misspelled words that included "ir." She developed the worksheets based on the first and second sections of the four-part lesson based on Holdaway's learning model (page 83–84). Her goal was to first bombard Ross with words that included "ir" over and over again, correctly (Figure 8-14). A close look at Ross's work indicates that he attended

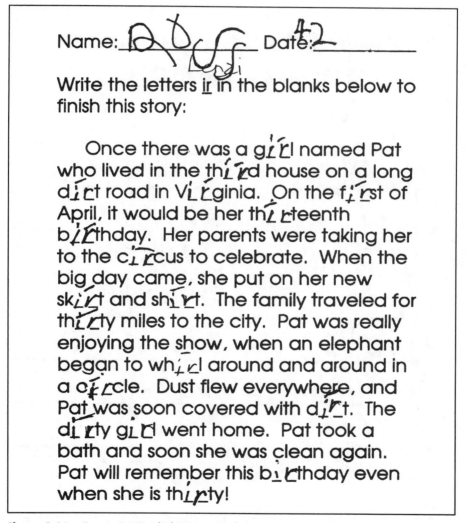

Name: _____   Date:_____

Write the letters <u>ir</u> in the blanks below to finish this story:

Once there was a girl named Pat who lived in the third house on a long dirt road in Virginia. On the first of April, it would be her thirteenth birthday. Her parents were taking her to the circus to celebrate. When the big day came, she put on her new skirt and shirt. The family traveled for thirty miles to the city. Pat was really enjoying the show, when an elephant began to whirl around and around in a circle. Dust flew everywhere, and Pat was soon covered with dirt. The dirty girl went home. Pat took a bath and soon she was clean again. Pat will remember this birthday even when she is thirty!

Figure 8-14.   Ross's "ir" Finish the Story Worksheet

to the task by going through the story and marking the spaces that were to be filled in with "ir." Then he went back and wrote "ir" in the appropriate spaces provided. The second step in the lesson, after bombarding, was to provide Ross with rehearsal space (Figure 8-15). This forced him to review his first efforts, and rewrite the words, focusing on the common element, "ir."

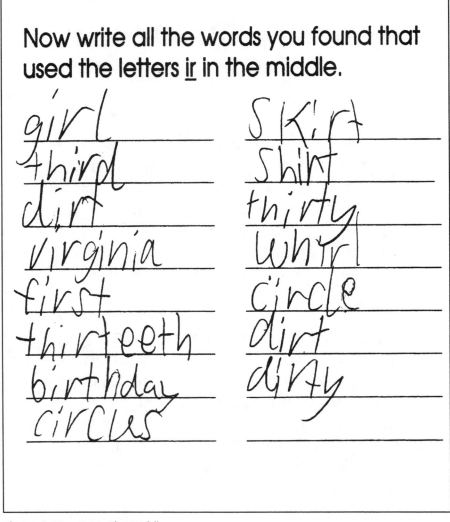

Figure 8-15. "ir" In The Middle

Her third (Figure 8-16) task forced Ross to correctly write "ir" within words. A close examination of Figures 8-14, 8-15, and 8-16 illustrates how even the teaching of phonics needs to be personalized.

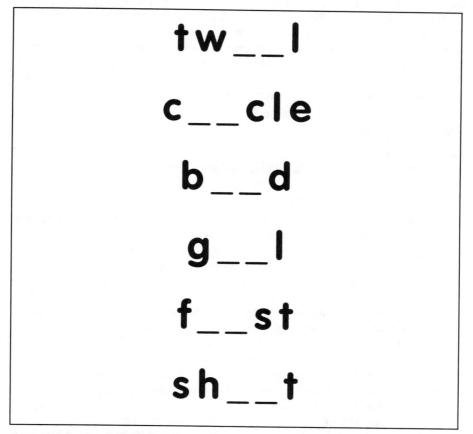

Figure 8-16.   "ir" Cloze Worksheet

Spelling instruction is as controversial as phonics. The only relevant way to make spelling meaningful to students is to use students' misspellings found in their written products as the basis for teaching. If you choose to do this, you are making spelling functional by

- teaching, based on student needs;
- making instruction relevant to the student;
- teaching spelling through content area studies.

Word Study

A reasonable and sensible solution to combining the learning of spelling and meaning is to explore our language system. Observations and a bit of history (see the section on the history of English earlier in this chapter) about the development of language guide students to draw conclusions. Knowledge about word origins and groups helps increase students' vocabulary. Knowing that people control aspects of language in order to "make it do something" guides students to love their language. This knowledge also provides them with control over the spelling process. Most important, it expands their vocabulary for reading, writing, and talking.

Expanding Vocabulary

Spelling and phonics is confusing, to say the least. Learning the meanings of words in a logical manner by studying word groups and origins makes the process easier.

How Words Get Their Meanings

American English grew as the result of contributions from many other languages. The names of places and people demonstrate that so well. Twenty-seven of our fifty states—more than half—have names of native American origin (McCrum, Cran, & MacNeil, 1992). These include Arkansas and Dakota, which are the names of tribes. It also includes Mississippi, which means "big river," and Alaska, meaning "mainland." Names of some of our states originated because of confusions. When, for example, the native American chief of the Choctaw people was asked the name of his land, he said "red people," which in his language translated as Oklahoma.

All of our state names and many city names were derived from other languages. Chicago means "the place of strong smells." Several French explorers who found the Moingouena people living at the mouth of a river called the place Riviere des Moingouenas. The name des Moines (the monks) eventually evolved. Other places, like New Mexico, New Hampshire, New Jersey, and New York were named by the British who remembered a place in England that resembled the new lands.

Hackensack and Hoboken, as well as Brooklyn and Harlem, take their names from the Dutch. Philadelphia is derived from classical and biblical lore and means "city of brotherly love." The town names King of Prussia, Blue Balls, and Intercourse are derived from tales of the frontier and are still being used today (McCrum, Cran, & MacNeil, 1992).

Using Word Origin Information in Language Study

I suggest that you begin with third graders and up, and with younger children who seem to be able to make connections between derivations and words. Post a list somewhere in the classroom similar to the one following.

Words Created from People's Names

Adam's apple—Adam, the first man, ate the forbidden fruit, an apple.

cardigan—Earl of Cardigan, a British officer whose soldiers wore knitted sweaters.

graham crackers—Sylvester Graham, an American who worked to improve diets for diabetics and vegetarians.

sandwich—John Montagu, Earl of Sandwich, England, who invented the sandwich so he could gamble without stopping to eat a regular meal.

sideburns—Ambrose Burnside, a Civil War general who had thick side whiskers.

teddy bear—named for Teddy Roosevelt, president of the U.S. who spared the life of a bear cub on a hunting trip.

Modify lists to make them age, grade, and interest appropriate for the children you teach. My teachers have begun discussions surrounding derivations of words in other implicit situations. While children were decorating the classroom for a class play based on the storybook, *Reuben Runs Away* (Galbraith, 1987), Lynn began to discuss the derivation of the phrase "teddy bear."

Lynn: This teddy bear looks just like Reuben.

Child: Yeah. And it looks like my teddy bear at home.

Lynn: Do you know how the bear got the name Teddy?

Child: I thought that's what all bears were called.

Lynn: They are now, but they never were before Teddy Roosevelt was president of the United States.

Child: Oh, they named the teddy bear after the president?

Lynn: Yeah, but they did it because when he was on a hunting trip, he refused to shoot a baby bear. So, he saved all baby bear cubs, and after that baby bear toys were all called teddy bears, after the president's name "Teddy."

Child: So, teddy bears are named after a president.

Lynn: Yep. And Adam's apple, you know that bump that is right here (points to her throat) in a man's neck. Well, it's named after Adam, the first man on the earth. He ate the apple, and the lump in his neck is part of the apple

> that was supposed to have gotten stuck in his throat. Adam's Apple. It is the lump that sticks out. Other objects get their names from other things. I could call the mobile that you made for your science project, Sophia, a Sophia Mobile.

Child: Cause Sophia is my name and I made it?

Lynn: You're right! So any mobile that is like yours will always be called a Sophia mobile. Do you know the shot—the vaccine you get so that you don't get polio?

Child: Yeah, I hate shots.

Lynn: Well, it's called the Salk vaccine because Dr. Salk invented it.

Child: I had the German measles. Did a German invent it?

Lynn: I don't know, but I bet somebody in Germany discovered that it was a sickness.

Implicit instruction through casual one-on-one conversation during other activities provokes thoughts about derivations and meaning. It also spurs children to talk about words outside of the classroom. Sophia's grandmother told me that the child insisted that they go through the dictionary to find words that were names. How great it was to discover that the teacher's "teachable moment" guided Sophia in how to explain the process to her grandfather and initiated further investigation of things named for people. The interest was high, the enthusiasm outstanding. Think of how often children create homework and carry it out without it being assigned!

There are many categories of word origins. These include:

- **clipped words**—words that have been shortened or clipped (limo for limousine, exam for examination, bus for omnibus, etc.);

- **portmanteau**—words blended together to make a new one (blot + botch = blotch, flutter + hurry = flurry, smack + mash = smash, twist + whirl = twirl);

- **compounds**—words glued together that sometimes take on a new meaning (back + yard = backyard, wrist + watch = wristwatch);

- **contractions**—words where an apostrophe is used in place of one or more letters (I'm for I and am, you'd for you and would, we'll for we and will);

- **acronyms and initializations**—first letters of each word used to represent a name (ABC = American Broadcasting Company, CEO = chief executive officer, DA = district attorney);

- **onomatopoeia**—words borrowed from sounds resembling the real sound that it refers to (arf arf, crash, kerchoo, tap);

- **phobia words**—words derived from the Greek word *phobos,* meaning "fear" (aerophobia means fear of flying, pyrophobia means fear of fire);

- **ology words**—used as a suffix meaning "the science of" (biology means the science of life, criminology means the science of crime).

Knowing the meanings of prefixes, suffixes, and roots helps vocabulary for reading, writing, and oral language to grow. When students know, for example, that the prefix **quadra** means four, they are able to discover the meaning of words including **quadrangle, quadrant, quart,** and **quarter.** The suffix **or,** for example, means "one who." When the meaning of this popular word ending is shared, youngsters easily understand that an actor is *one who* acts, and a donor, *one who* contributes. Teachers with whom I've worked have created exciting and fun ways to guide children to understand concepts these categories generate about words. The following are examples of activities.

Using Interesting Words

I suggest that you select a word category, choose one word daily belonging to that category, and use it in your daily talk. Post the word on a chart labeled "Interesting Word of the Day." You might also want to create a mobile for the category of words, making and hanging one card for each word on the structure.

Ingrid selected the category "phobia" to use for a one-week period of time. She picked five words, using one each day in order to spark interest, and teach the meaning of words functionally. She chose to begin with the word *nyctophobia,* which means "fear of darkness." This seemed timely, for it was the middle of October, and the word fit easily into the Halloween scheme. She used the word as often as possible in daily activities. She used it as soon as they entered the classroom.

"It's so dark outside today, I'm worried about my mother," remarked Ingrid to several students. "Is your mother sick?", asked a child. "No, not really," replied Ingrid. "She has nyctophobia, so when it's dark out like it is today, she gets scared." "Oh," responded another child without further comment or questions. Later in the morning when a child shared her Halloween picture, Ingrid remarked, "Oh my goodness, if my mother were in a house as dark as the one you've drawn, she'd be scared stiff." "Why?" asked the child. "Well," continued Ingrid, "she has nyctophobia. She's afraid of the dark." Ingrid continued to use the word as often as appropriate. She wrote it on the word chart, and also made a card for the mobile that hung from the ceiling. Children will figure out what you are doing after several days, even on the first. One six-year-old said, "You used that word a lot today." This comment indicates that this strategy is working with this child. Ingrid's response, "You are right. I am using the word a lot today. I like the way it sounds, and it is good for today, because it is dark outside. My mother is afraid of the dark, and the word nyctophobia means afraid of the dark," supports the child's attention to her instruction.

I've encouraged children to create their own "phobia" words. Some written by children ages 7 through 12 include:

assignaphobia—meaning fear of homework

mediphobia—meaning fear of medicines

sisaphobia—meaning scared of my little sister

blindaphobia—meaning fear of a blind date

Modification of this procedure works for guiding children to learn compound words and portmanteau words. Youngsters get excited about gluing words together to form new words. Exhibiting a list of blend-together words, and casually discussing these with children, much as Lynn did with word origins, spurs students to create their own. *The test of understanding is students' own word creations.* Instruction has led children to perform, demonstrating their learning. The following list is a collection of words that were created by children between the ages of six and nine.

Barbjo = <u>Barb</u>ie dressed in G.I. <u>Jo</u>e's clothing

mudo = <u>mud</u> that looks like dog <u>do</u> (excretive waste)

Jupto = a new plant formed from pieces of <u>Jup</u>iter and Plu<u>to</u>

compable = a <u>tab</u>le for a <u>comp</u>uter

Discussions result in word inventions that make language study at times fascinating and at other times, comical.

There are many opportunities to use words from different groups in functional yet natural conversations. Using real and students' created words meaningfully is the most effective way to teach word meaning and their origins. When children use the words in their oral language and writing, and understand how words are created, they've taken and passed the test of understanding.

Using Word Roots to "Decode" Meaning

"My word is *microdermazitz*," shouted fourteen-year-old Stacy. "It's simple. Micro means small, derma means skin, and," pointing to a pimple on her cheek, "this is a zitz. If you put it all together, you've got *microdermazitz*, a small pimple on my skin." Wow! What a wonderful test of comprehension!

The following procedure seems to work for guiding students to understand how roots affect word meanings, and how they help humans create words.

Teacher: Each of these words in my list has something the same. Who sees it?

bicycle	bimonthly
bicolor	biennial
bidentate	bicentennial

Melanie: I do. They all have "bi."

Teacher: Right! They all have "bi" at the beginning. Let's say them together (she points to bicycle first, and moves from left to right as she and the children read them in unison). Now what is a bicycle?

John: It's a two-wheel bike and I have a new one that I got for my birthday.

Teacher: Right, John, it's a bike with two wheels. What about bimonthly?

Joshua: Well, I guess it means two months?

Teacher: Why?

Joshua: Because there is "bi" in the front. And "bi," bicycle was a two-wheeler, so it means two months.

Teacher: Close. The actual meaning is, every two months.

Joshua: Oh, yeah, but it could mean two months, too.

Teacher: You're right, Josh. Very creative! That's how words get meaning; people thinking of meanings of words because of their parts.

Mandy: I know what bicolor means. It means two colors.

Teacher: Cool. You got it. Why does it mean that, Mandy?

Mandy: Because "bi" means two like in bicycle, and it has "bi" at the beginning.

Teacher: And biennial means every two years.

Steven: How did you know that one?

Teacher: Well, "bi" is two, and then I know that annual means every year, so the rest of biennial is like annual, so I just guessed it from those two things.

Steven: Cool! You don't even need a dictionary to find out what it means.

Rachael: I think I know what bidentate means. It could mean two dentists because "dent" is the first part of dentist.

Teacher: Wow! I'm impressed with how you're all discovering out the meanings of these "bi" words.

Kristin: It's easy because of the "bi." All the words mean something about two.

Teacher: What about bicentennial?

Larry: I know what it means. It means something that happens every 200 years.

Teacher: How'd you know that, Larry?

Larry: My grandma had a party when America was 200 years old. My Mom told me about it. It was on her balcony and you can see the water there, and there were all the tall ships, too.

Teacher: So you figured out the meaning of bicentennial because you remember the experience you had at the bicentennial celebration of America.

Larry: Yeah!

Teacher: So, "bi" means (raises her voice waiting for the children to respond)—

Children: Two.

The following words were created by a five- and six-year-old after several discussions similar to the one above.

Homobono—meaning good man

homoderma—meaning man's skin

bihomo—meaning two men

I suggest posting root charts with the root, labeling the chart and a list of words including the root following. You might want to write the meaning of the root at the bottom of the chart AFTER the students discover it. This sort of activity can be done with any Greek or Latin roots.

Word Groups for Meaning Making

The study of word groups is more often seen than other types of language study. These include synonyms, antonyms, analogies, similes, metaphors, idiomatic expressions, word idioms, and also proverbs, and euphemisms. Children's books that use these word groups entice, enhance, and encourage children to understand their concepts (see Appendix A). Teachers have used elements of these groups in creative and whimsical ways so children can learn about them. Board games, especially, are wonderful for guiding students to understand word groups. Basic rules from popular games (including *Password, Monopoly,* and *Scrabble,* for example) provide recreational activities that facilitate learning. Dizzy is a natural for synonyms, antonyms, and analogies.

Using Word Groups in Conversations

One way to guide children to understand that synonyms are words that have similar meanings is to use synonyms in daily conversations as much as possible. Switching from one word to the next several times will guide students to "catch-the-fact" that more than one word means the same thing. The following dialogue between a teacher and a child during a free work and play time illustrates this procedure.

Teacher: *Gee, Kim. You're so able with creative writing.*

Kim: *Yeah, I like to write a lot.*

Teacher: *I see that. Being capable makes you like it.*

Kim: *I love to write in my diary the best.*

Teacher: *That's because you're a competent writer who can write like she talks.*

When we do something competently, we usually like it.

Assessing Students' Knowledge of Word Groups, Origins, and Expanded Vocabulary

There are several ways students' knowledge can be assessed. The checksheet in Figure 8-17 is one observational guide for determining students' growth and instructional needs.

Student Self-Monitoring of Word Knowledge

Using words functionally is the "test" of learning. When students create words using word roots, prefixes, suffixes, and word groups and families in their creative writing, diaries, and journals, they've demonstrated that they understand the meanings of the parts, and how words are created. Students need to discover that they have incorporated new words and origins in their knowledge base. I suggest that students use the Progress Report Form to chart their growth. I also suggest the following:

A notebook can serve to catalog new words by organizing those learned (1) alphabetically, (2) into categories based on word origins or groups, or families, and (3) into content area categories, or any other organizational system selected by each student. They might also list new words they've created on a wall chart, or at the back of a notebook. It is best for students to select for themselves their monitoring system. I suggest, however, that all children continue to record their progress.

Word Study Observation Guide

Observed Behaviors

Uses word(s) in the following kinds of conversations

    Uses word(s) for writing.

_____   _____   _____

_____   _____   _____

_____   _____   _____

    Can discover meaning from the word root(s)

_____   _____   _____

_____   _____   _____

_____   _____   _____

    Discovers word meaning from prefix

_____   _____   _____

    Discovers word meaning from suffix

_____   _____   _____

Creates new words using prefixes. The words are

    Word _____, meaning _____

    Word _____, meaning _____

    Word _____, meaning _____

    Word _____, meaning _____

    Word _____, meaning _____

Creates his own words using suffixes. The words are

    Word _____, meaning _____

    Word _____, meaning _____

    Word _____, meaning _____

    Word _____, meaning _____

    Word _____, meaning _____

Figure 3-17. Word Study Observation Guide (Page 1 of 2)

Creates words using word origins including roots, prefixes, suffixes, and word groups.

Word _____, origin _____

Word _____, origin _____

Word _____, origin _____

Word _____, origin _____

Student knows the following word origins and how to originate her/his own words in each category:

clipped words_____

portmanteau words_____

compound words_____

contractions_____

acronyms and initializations_____

words borrowed from names_____

onomatopoeia_____

phobia words_____

Evidence of student mastery_____

Knows about, and uses in oral language and writing the following word groups:

synonyms_____   metaphors_____

antonyms_____   idiomatic expressions_____

analogies_____   similes_____

Evidence_____

_____

_____

Student talks, spontaneously, about word studies during free time, lunch, playground activities, etc.

Figure 8-17.   Word Study Observation Guide (Page 2 of 2)

Summary

The content of this chapter says that phonics, spelling, and word study are important for reading and writing. Students need to know that there are logical descriptions, definitions, and instructional practices for learning the sounds, spellings, and origin of words. The chapter promotes teacher assessment practices, and student self-monitoring activities that are integrated into daily classroom activities and content area studies. I hope the content is used to simplify students' understanding of our complicated language.

CHAPTER 9

Reporting Progress: Engaging Parents

Reporting progress has been through a metamorphosis in the past decade. The surge to create a reporting system that replicated, as much as possible, instructional settings has been the focus. This has occurred because many children who perform well during instructional activities do not do well on formal, standardized type tests. The environments in which children learn and those for testing are different. In spite of the more than thirty years of concern about testing instruments, and criticism of test scores and A, B, and C grading systems, these indicators are still being used as proof of achievement. Society has made grades magical, and students and parents seem to be mesmerized by the magic. Bumper stickers on cars that read "My son's an honor student" suggest that hierarchal grades are important for building students' and parents' self-esteem. Since grades continue to be important, our schools MUST provide instructional activities that guide students to be successful in this system. Because scores represent a "point-in-time" assessment, grades cannot be the only means of connoting growth. Continuous, ongoing classroom reporting procedures illustrating short- and long-term achievements need to supplement grades to add depth of meaning to synthetic test scores.

Reporting Progress Meaningfully

Reporting progress meaningfully for students consists of integrating evaluation procedures with instruction throughout the school day. Instruction and assessment become interchangeable, and assessment becomes a natural part of instruction. This needs to happen because human beings interchange these activities naturally in all of their activities.

When we receive information, our minds attempt to incorporate the data into existing ideas. We ask ourselves questions, talk about the ideas with a colleague, or write them down in an attempt to make them our own. We automatically test our ability to understand the ideas by asking ourselves questions and using information from prior experiences. Since human beings move from getting information to testing their understanding of the ideas (by self-questioning), it seems natural that these actions be included in daily learning routines. Reading, writing, and vocabulary activities in this text "flip-flop" back and forth between assessment and instruction. Students are exposed to strategies, ask themselves questions about how to use them, and then answer their own questions with actions. Once familiar with these strategies, they can share achievements with parents as an integral part of parent conferences. Specific guidelines for establishing a classroom environment where assessment and instruction are naturally integrated are shown in Figure 9-1. Work with thousands of teachers and students has indicated that the guidelines facilitate concurrent development of student self-monitoring practices.

Assessment Settings

Assessment settings ought to replicate instructional situations in order for students to feel comfortable. If standardized test formats are administered regularly, classrooms should be arranged in rows, quiet, and test-like some of the time. This permits students to become familiar with this environment, reducing or alleviating the anxiety usually experienced in unfamiliar situations. In these "stiff" environments students get used to identifying and selecting items with definitive expectations.

These formats are quite different from interactive discussions, debates, and conversational instructional times. But, settings and materials change in many classrooms several times during a school day. Students listen to lectures, work in pairs, in small groups, and individually. Desks are often in rows, and sometimes arranged in small groupings. Some rooms are carpeted for sitting, others have soft chairs. Often, hallways accommodate small group work. All the settings in which assessment takes place must be experienced during instructional times in order to reduce student anxiety.

Dancers, athletes, and equestrians rehearse their skills and demonstrate achievements in the same setting. They practice on stage, in a gym, and on a horse farm. They perform in these same kinds of spaces, as well. Many students in school are expected to learn in one setting, but demonstrate growth in another. Just imagine asking an ice skater to take a pencil and paper test to demonstrate her ability to become a member of the United States Olympic Ice Skating Team. The thought is absurd! Yet, children are asked to read a passage, and then demonstrate their reading achievement by selecting from several predetermined answers. When environments change, expectations and behaviors change. Change without practice elicits feelings of discomfort, inducing hesitancy and cautiousness.

	Check Here
Settings for assessment are the SAME as settings for instruction.	_____
Students are provided with tools that guide them to observe and describe their achievements.	_____
The "words" used to describe achievements are "words" used during instruction.	_____
Individual, small group, and class discussions include what each student knows and what he/she needs to learn.	_____
Students talk and write about observations of achievements as part of daily instruction.	_____
Students, with teachers, share progress, interact with and respond to questions during parent conferences.	_____
Concrete evidence of progress is shared by students and teachers with parents.	_____
Progress reports replicate daily classroom management and instructional practices.	_____
Assessment IS an instructional process in the classroom.	_____

Figure 9-1.   Classroom Settings

I suggest you develop a series of ongoing role-playing activities that provide students with the time to role-play how to deal with traditional testing episodes. Prepare mock tests. Facilitate student preparation so that students will be familiar with mock tests of all formats: multiple choice, true-false, questions, essay exams, and whatever standardized testing formats are used. Review commercial programs designed to help students learn test-taking skills, and use these, too, when appropriate.

In addition, establish ongoing discussions and record keeping routines. The routines establish consistent expectations which become authentic and natural classroom behaviors.

How to Begin Daily Assessment for Reporting to Parents

Begin by making it a pattern to review daily classroom activities. The steps in Figure 9-2 have been used again and again to guide teachers and students to observe, review, and then establish ways to continue instruction in classrooms. The steps move you and your students from teacher-centered assessment to rich self-monitoring experiences.

Activity	Check Here
I routinely ask students, "What do you know?" "What do you need?"	_____
I model by telling students what I know as the result of a lesson, and what I need to learn.	_____
When student reviewing has become routine, I post a chart with two headings: "What I know," and "What I need." I review by writing each of my achievements in the appropriate column on the chart.	_____
I reproduce a 9 × 11 copy of the chart for each student. During routine reviews I ask each to record, on the Progress Report Form, his/her accomplishments for the day. I write mine, as a model, on a chart or transparency and project it.	_____
There is a permanent place for Progress Report Forms in the classroom.	_____
I discuss with children, individually, or in small or large groups, reasons for routine reviews. I might share, for example: When I write what I learned, I remember it better;	_____
The Progress Report Form reminds you what you've learned.	_____
Each Progress Report Form describes an activity to which it is attached and filed in the portfolio.	_____

Figure 9-2.   Collegial Self-Monitoring Classroom Assessment Guide

Accumulating Achievement Data for Periodic Reporting to Parents

The daily progress report forms (appearing throughout this text) include the data necessary for writing reports for sharing over-time achievements. The information provides supportive materials supplementing traditional letter and number grades. The data turns ambiguous, nondescriptive test scores and letter grades into meaningful descriptors. Probably the most important aspect of daily progress recordings is the development of student self-monitoring skills. The students study their products, using self-monitoring guide sheets included throughout this text. These provide language that describes and defines elements of their work. Then they write about their observations of their products on their Progress Report Form.

A review of Figures 9-3 to 9-6 illustrates students' growth in assessing their achievements over time. Younger children tend to write general statements that are global in nature (Figure 9-3). Kendra, age six years, four months, used the language on the form as a place to start. She attempted to make the language her own, this indicated when she crossed out the column headings. As young children become familiar with the self-monitoring process, the content studied becomes the focus of the report. Chris (Figure 9-4) recorded information about his Indian studies and cinquains. Jessica, at nine, has grown to record "what" she can do—the strategies she uses to learn (Figure 9-5). Unlike less experienced children who use broad concepts and focus on content, Jessica has realized that strategies facilitate learning. Eleven-year-old Tony (Figure 9-6) has grown even further and includes the action he needs to take to grow even more. Tony is actually writing his teacher's lesson plans. In the column labeled, "My Teacher's Job" (Figure 9-6), he indicates that he can identify and use several strategies to improve his performance. He needs no help from the teacher (editing his own work, i.e., "reread—find where quotes go"; locating information, "use thesaurus or interesting word cards"; extending ideas in writing, "use a story map, try different endings"). Tony is truly self-monitoring and self-directing his work.

Learners of all ages adore talking about their accomplishments. The more they talk about learning, the easier it is to write about strengths and needs. Learning to identify needs is a difficult skill for children and adults to learn. Talking about one's accomplishments is often difficult because it is such an uncommon practice.

Steps to Student Self-Monitoring

Most students will feel comfortable recording their accomplishments if teachers model the practice. Lots of discussions and conversations about student products which include descriptors defining characteristics support self-monitoring actions. Some students need prompting individually, or with one or two other students. Many teach-

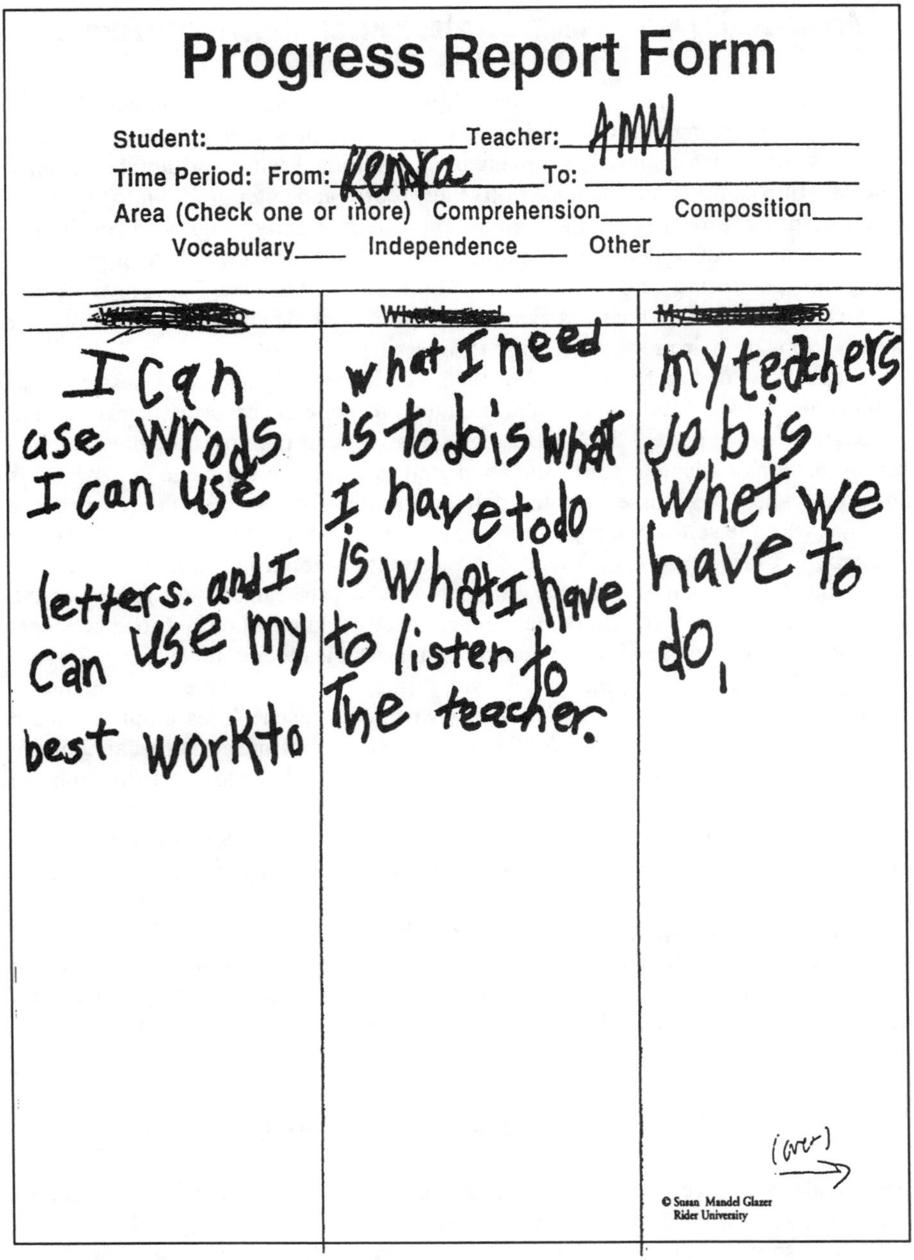

Progress Report Form

Student:_____ Teacher: *AMY*_____

Time Period: From: *Kendra*_____ To: _____

Area (Check one or more) Comprehension____ Composition____

Vocabulary____ Independence____ Other_____

~~What I know~~	~~What I need~~	~~My teacher's job~~
I can ase wrods I can use letters. and I can use my best workto	what I need is todois what I havetodo is whatI have to lister to The teacher.	my teachers jobis whet we have to do,

(over) →

© Susan Mandel Glazer
Rider University

Figure 9-3. Kendra's Progress Report Form

Progress Report Form

Your Name: _C h r i s_   Today's Date _7/2_

Your Teacher's Name _a m y_   Your Age: _8_

Check area(s) of focus:

Comprehension___   Composition___   Word Study___   Independence___

I know... _somthing about the linope indians_

I need to know... _How to write a cinguain_

My teacher's job is... _Show me how to write a cinguain_

Amy B. Kroberger
Advanced Practicum '97
Rider University

Figure 9-4.   Chris's Progress Report Form

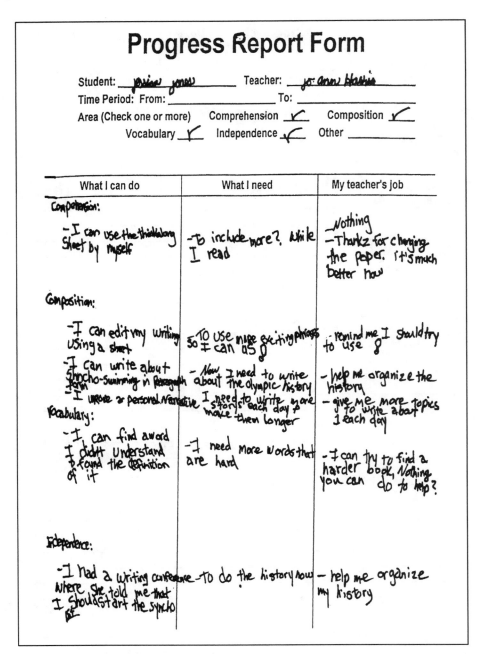

Progress Report Form

Student: ___jessica jones___   Teacher: ___jo ann hashim___

Time Period: From: _____ To: _____

Area (Check one or more)   Comprehension ✓   Composition ✓

Vocabulary ✓   Independence ✓   Other _____

What I can do	What I need	My teacher's job
Comprehension:		
— I can use the thinkalong sheet by myself	— to include more? while I read	Nothing — Thankz for changing the paper. It's much better now
Composition:		
— I can edit my writing using a sheet	So to use more exciting phrases so I can use 8	— remind me I should try to use 8
— I can write about syncho-swimming in paragraph form	— Now I need to write about the olympic history	— help me organize the history
— I wrote a personal narrative	I need to write 3 stories each day & make them longer	— give me more topics to write about 3 each day
Vocabulary:		
— I can find a word I didn't understand & found the definition of it	— I need more words that are hard	— I can try to find a harder book. Nothing you can do to help?
Independence:		
— I had a writing conference where she told me that I should start the syncho	— to do the history now	— help me organize my history

Figure 9-5.   Jessica's Progress Report Form

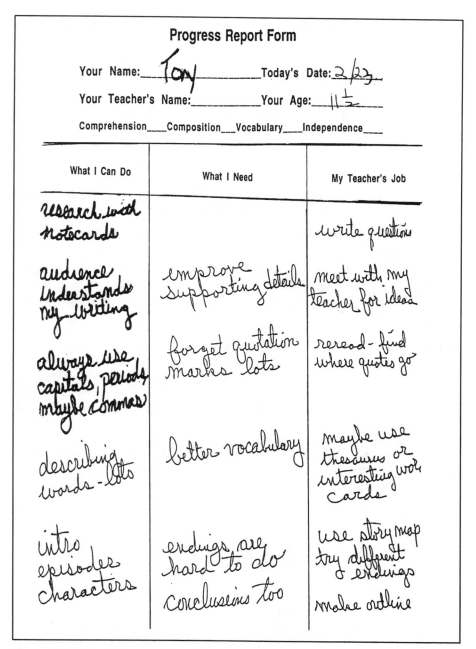

Figure 9-6.   Tony's Progress Report Form

ers with whom I've worked proceed through this prompting process using the following procedure:

1. engage students, not more than three together, in daily conversations about "what I know" and "what I need to learn," making sure each student talks about his/her activities;

2. discuss growth and needs with concrete evidence (their portfolios) at their fingertips;

3. use direct praise immediately following the student's observation (i.e., "Amy, you noticed that you need periods. That's great. You really know how to self-monitor your work!");

4. repeat student's language describing the observation, and simultaneously write comments on a Progress Report Form (Figure 9-7).

5. talk and write, encouraging the child to read the writing with you.

Continue to mentor, coaching students to talk and write about their progress. Teachers, like Alissa (Figure 9-8), direct children to write immediately following an activity. They discuss student products with the progress report form in front of each child. When, for example, Nicky said, "We did the fist full of words," Alissa immediately responded in a lively voice, "Write it on your progress report form, now!" Nicky wrote it the first time he was introduced to this procedure. Clear directions, teacher modeling, and students' oral repetition of teacher directions helps develop self-monitoring skills.

Some teachers keep individual progress report forms for children. They are resources for developing an instructional plan. Figures 9-9 and 9-10 were completed by teachers Brigitte and Fran before school began. They'd gathered the information from data in the children's accumulative school files. They also discussed the child's performance with previous teachers. Fran completed Figure 9-11 after meeting with Gregory the first week of school. She continued keeping progress records, noticing change and growth over time. The Progress Report Forms serve as data for reporting progress and lesson planning. Fran shared the forms with students for whom they were written. This provided models that further guided her students to complete their own progress reports.

Engaging Parents

Parent conferences and report cards are the usual vehicles for getting information about children to caregivers. Report cards are sent home with children for parents to read. Conferences are held and parents are told about their children's progress.

I've always been concerned about these reporting procedures. Parents and teachers confer with each other discussing the student's performance. Often ambiguous

Progress Report Form

Your Name:_Christopher_____Today's Date:_5/6____

Your Teacher's Name:__Amy_____Your Age:__7_____

Comprehension____Composition___Vocabulary____Independence____

What *~~I~~ you* Can Do	What *~~I~~ you* Need	My ~~Teacher~~'s Job
You can write in your journal every-day.	You need to read what I write to You. It makes me feel happy	Write to you everyday and answer your questions about my stamp collection.
you can retell a story after you hear me read it to you. You retell into a tape recorder	you need to retell after YOU read your own book.	Have a retelling conference to help You get started.
you can put all of the library books back on the shelves.	you need to get other kids to help you.	Remind you to get kids to put books away, too!

Figure 9-7.   Christopher's Progress Report Form

Progress Report Form

Your Name: Nicky   Today's Date: 10-14

Your Teacher's Name: Alissas   Your Age: 7

Comprehension____Composition___Vocabulary____Independence____

What I Can Do	What I Need	My Teacher's Job
we bib The Fist- Ful- fo words Journal	Journal	being a 2ND grad teacher

Figure 9-8. Nicky's Progress Report Form

Progress Report for Jonathan Kim			
9/27	**What I Can Do**	**What I Need**	**Plans**
written retelling	summarized episodes	Is this consistent with his own writing style and topics?	observe
	mirror repetitive pattern of story		
	used sequence indicator (next)		
	included main character, 4/7 episodes. 4/5 characters. And ending	need to include introduction, setting, problem, solution, theme, more episodes	story structure minilesson/ observe/retelling checklist
		Did writing mode effect length and detail of retelling?	retell orally/compare
writing	wrote own autobiography	How does self selected writing differ from directed writing?	Have Jonathan choose his own topics, observe writing
	one topic per sentence		
	maintained topic focus		
	used sequence indicators		
	used story language in autobiography	Is this consistently done?	observe/direct praise
	used personal & possessive pronouns		
	used coordinates		
	used additive words and prepositional phrases to vary sentence structures (ending) in declarative sentences	Does he use interrogative and exclamatory sentences in oral language or self directed writing?	observe, if not provide models, observe over time, if not add, revision conferences for tone
	wrote in complete sentences		
	used similar sentence beginnings	Does he vary beginnings with self selected topics?	have him choose own topic/observe
	used caps for first word, proper nouns, initial letter in random words	Is this consistent? After given models and capitalization rules does J. self correct	observe/minilesson cap when conferring
	printed legibly		
writing vocabulary	conventional + temporary spelling (based on sound-symbol, sounds heard)	Does he continue to take risks in spelling	observe/word bank/ Fernald
	asked for word cards	Does he add these words to his sight word vocabulary?	observe/Fernald
vocabulary	used simple and compound sentences	Does he use complex sentences in speech?	observe, provide written and oral models of complex sentences conversationally
	listed 5 multisyllabic words as words that he can spell	Does he use these words when writing?	observe, writing analysis
gates	Vocabulary- used initial and ending sounds regular vowels	Is this accurate? Does he do this when reading self selected books?	observe oral reading.
	Comprehension - beginning and ending context, prior knowledge, vocabulary clues	Is this accurate measure of his comprehension strategies for self selected reading?	ThinkAloud
general observations	seemed familiar initially quiet		
	join group at board voluntarily	Is he most comfortable in group or solo projects?	observe, provide option of single/paired/group work
	helped peer find object		
	ask for more info/spelling	Is he confident in his abilities?	observe direct praise
	I am a good reader		

adapted from Susan Mandel Glazer by Bridgette Nevola, Rider University, 1998

Figure 9-9.   Teacher's Progress Report for Jonathan

Progress Report Form

Your Name: Gregory Gray   Today's Date: July 7

Your Teacher's Name: Fran   Your Age: _____

Comprehension____ Composition____ Vocabulary____ Independence____

What I Can Do	What I Need	My Teacher's Job
<u>Comprehension</u> Gregory can sometimes use beginning context clues, prior knowledge and key words to help him choose his answer. Gregory can retell a story by summarizing the details. He included some story elements - He named myself and 5 other characters. ① He partially described the problem that He gave away all his food - did not say who/troop was still hungry. ② He summarized 5 of 7 episodes out of sequence	Strategies to deal w/ test taking strategies Gregory needs to include ① resolution of problem ② ending of story ③ theme ④ proper sequence of episodes	-provide modelling + instruction in "right there" questions in the context of a research project -In conference provide Gregory w/ modelling for complete retelling and modelling of all elements of story
<u>Composition</u> Alex can write to convey information in both a narrative and an expository format. He used similar sentence construction (mostly simple sentences) He used and as a connective to join 2 thoughts.	-needs to further develop expository writing -needs to use different sentence constructions	-provide different model of expository text.

Figure 9-10.   Fran's Progress Report for Gregory (Page 1 of 2)

His writing has a sense of story and audience awareness.

It includes personal experiences

He uses temporary spelling to help him convey meaning

He uses capital letters to begin a sentence

He capitalizes "I" and proper nouns (words in story + words in vocab. list)

— develop more conventional spelling

(Under Vocab)

Vocabulary

Gregory uses interesting words in his compositions

Gregory used consonant sounds, regular vowels + spelling patterns to guide his selections.

Gregory chose 2 words using letter transposition

WATCH THIS

— play/develop word games/patterns to help expand Gregory's written active vocab.

— Use Spelling Workshop to develop more conventional spelling

Independence

Gregory worked w/ diligence. Occasionally distracted by noise levels in room.

Returned to task when reminded

needs strategies to self monitor own behaviors

Introduce concept of a contract and other self-monitoring sheets

Figure 9-10. Fran's Progress Report for Gregory (Page 2 of 2)

Progress Report Form

Student: Gregory Bray   Teacher: Kay

Time Period: From: _____   To: _____ July 9

Area (Check one or more)   Comprehension ____   Composition ____

Vocabulary ____   Independence ____   Other _____

What you can do	What you need	My job
Comprehension Gregory can listen and begin a written retelling — He can do as oral retelling Gregory can use prediction sheet to predict before reading a story	— Complete a written retelling — conference w/me about retelling a story — needs to continue practicing and justifying predictions	— schedule conference to discuss Gregory's retelling, using retelling / sheet. — provide modelling & monitoring of this strategy
Composition — Gregory can write to convey information in his content journal — Gregory can write a list poem	— needs to expand/ develop writing for information/ observation — share poem w/ group teacher & discuss	— model expanded writing to convey information in content journal. — practice creating another/same type of poem

Figure 9-11. Gregory's Progress Report Form by Teacher (Page 1 of 2)

Vocabulary

Gregory pushed the group to help discover "ist" words

Gregory continues to take risks w/ his spelling

- to continue to explore "ist" words

- needs instruction in double consonants silent e rule ēa double vowel er ending

- more opportunities to explore word families
- instruction in other word patterns
- provide instruction do I spelling?? in conference

Independence
Gregory can begin to use the progress report form

- continue to develop strategy to use P.R.F. to monitor own learning

- conference again w/ Gregory to let him explore all that he has accomplished so far and let him write about it

Figure 9-11.   Gregory's Progress Report Form by Teacher (Page 2 of 2)

phrases (including "very good," "shows growth," etc.) are used to define progress. These phrases often mean different things to parents than they do to teachers, causing some concerns or confusions. Just image your boss sending home a "report card" and writing "did better" without your consent. I get outraged at a system that perpetuates the creation of student dependence, especially when this dependence relates to evaluation of growth. Predicting students' responses to "Are you smart?" is easy. Most say, "I think so." When asked, "Why?" most respond, "Because I got 'As' on my report card."

Learning how to know about one's performance by discussing it in oral and written forms is empowering. Football coaches, but also dance, piano, and creative arts teachers coach, thereby empowering their students. Teachers of literacy and content areas must do the same.

Parent, Student, Teacher Conferences

Several educators (Glazer, 1990; Harp, 1996; Hill & Ruptic, 1994; Santa, 1995) have explored parental, teacher, and student involvement in the conferencing process. I have become aware of several different styles of student and parent activities. These include (1) parental involvement through communication and activities outside of the classroom; (2) parental involvement in progress activities in the classrooms.

Parental Involvement Outside Classrooms

Nothing is more important than gaining parental support. When parents are happy, so are their children. Informing parents about programs at parent education meetings, through mailings, and with positive notes home about children's actions entices parents into the school experience. Letters explaining programs and activities from their own children are effective for engaging parental interest, support, and participation. Hill and Ruptic's (1994) questionnaires for parents are one way to engage caregivers. These ask parents to observe their child's behaviors at home, share family activities, the child's feelings about school, his/her interests, what they write and read about, and about family activities that involve reading and writing. Caregivers need also to be asked about children's successes in previous school experiences; their hobbies; favorite kinds of home activities; interactions with peer friends, siblings, and older people; how they solve problems; self-esteem; and more. Engaging parents in discussions, informal information sessions, and telephone or e-mail conversations strengthens ties and encourages collaborative efforts on behalf of the children. Parent education meetings might focus on topics similar to the following:

- helping with homework;

- the importance of talking for becoming a writer;
- discipline, when and how;
- ways to get your children to crave books;
- "tricking" your reluctant writers to write;
- the relationship between phonics and spelling; and more.

These sessions should be used ONLY to provide education for caregivers.

Parental Involvement in Classroom Reporting Activities

I recall, as a child, having a "discussion" with my parents after they attended a parent conference with my first-grade teacher. The inquisition still rings loud and clear. "Why can't you sit still, Susan?" they'd ask. "Do you have ants in your pants? I was embarrassed when your teacher told me that you didn't sit still. It sounded almost as if you were disobeying her directions!" My parents' perception of the teacher's discussion was that their sweet child was an inattentive, distracted, sometimes disobedient child. Not paying attention was the reason for less-than-expected beginning reading behavior. I am, till this day, infuriated by those recollections. The infuriation comes from the fact that I had not been privy to the conversation between my parents and my teacher. I still feel as if I'd been chastised and undermined by the three most important adults in my world, my mother, father, and teacher. I, like many youngsters, was frustrated because my folks shared nothing but what they perceived as failures. You see, my parents, although well meaning, decided that I should read out loud every day after school in order to improve. This meant that I had to give up playing outdoors with friends. I made an agreement with myself in response to what was, for me, a punishment. The experience resulted in a vow that once I became a teacher, I would make sure that (1) the child would always know beforehand that I would be speaking to the parent, and (2) I would never speak to a parent without the child being present. Years of experience have made me aware of the fact that children must be involved in the conferencing process. These youngsters know about their learning, and need to share it, as well. Their portfolios (folders containing their products) guide them to explain, demonstrate, and brag about their accomplishments. Often parents come to conferences without their children. We reschedule the meeting with the understanding that the child must be present.

Preparing for Student-Led Conferences

Two kinds of activities prepare students to lead parent conferences: (1) student portfolios, which are systematic collections of children's products over time; (2) a student progress letter to parents.

The portfolios discussed in this text are used as the basis for preparing for conferences. Their organization is specific, the data progressive. Progress reports are based on products from the first to the last day of the reporting period. The same type of data is included all year. Other formats can be found in the literature (Calkins, 1994; Graves, 1983; Harp, 1996; Rief, 1992; Routman, 1988). Those providing specific data collection and reporting techniques are best for creating self-assessors. A letter to parents precedes the conference, preparing them to ask questions. When students write these letters, we often hear, "I don't believe you learned so much!"

Writing the Letters

Discussion between students and the teacher is the way to begin letters to parents. The letter becomes an extension of the talks. Teacher prompts guide students to use the portfolio and identify progress. Our letters are organized like the sections of the portfolio. The progress report forms guided Christopher to determine what he wanted to share. Chris volunteered ideas, and his teacher at a computer recorded his statements. His teacher coached him when necessary by suggesting words and phrases for sharing (Figure 9-12). The letter is most effective when written as a running log describing the child's accomplishments and the materials used to achieve goals. Information offered by students is always specific because of the accumulated products (the data). Specificity can easily be learned when data is so readily available.

It is sometimes expedient, although less effective, for teachers to write letters. Teacher-written letters should be directed to the student. This option to write to the child is suggested when cooperative writing becomes laborious. A teacher letter is discussed with the child prior to being sent home. The portfolio is reviewed to support statements and comments. The teacher-written letter has impact when the student has opportunities to alter, edit, add, or suggest changes before it goes home. Once home, students explain contents to parents before attending the student-led conference.

July 16

Dear Mom and Dad,

I am writing this midterm progress letter with my teacher. It is to review what I have been working on and what I am going to keep working on at the Center for Reading and Writing at Rider University. The letter is in four parts, just like my portfolio. The parts are comprehension, composition, word study and independence.

Comprehension:

A retelling is something you write after you read a book. You write what you read from a book. I know how to write retellings of stories on the computer. I included an introduction, when the story happened, where the story happened, main character, other characters, problem, episodes, solution, story ending, and theme. I included everything in my retelling. Retellings help you remember what you read. The retelling checklist helps you check if you wrote the retelling correct.

After I read the Keeping Quilt by Patricia Palacco, I wrote the first word that my sister and I said. It tells what happened a long time ago. My literature journal is for remembering about me.

A reading log is for writing something about the book I read. The things that I write on the reading log are the date, title, author, genre and notes. A reading log is so I can remember the books I read.

Your prediction is just predicting what the story is about. When you predict, you guess what the story is about. Predicting helps you guess what the story is about before you read.

Composition:

In my dialogue journal, I write letters to my teacher. Then, she writes letters back. We write about anything. It helps me to write better letters.

In my content journal, I write about interesting stuff like butterflies and ants. I write the time and I write the date. This is so you know when that happened. This helps me write better and make observations.

I wrote a cinquain poem. A cinquain is a poem with the syllables. This is my poem:

Chris Lim

He is quite nice

Likes to play on his bike

He likes to play with his sister

A lot

Figure 9-12. Christopher's Progress Letter to His Parents (Page 1 of 2)

For spelling, I find a word that I think is misspelled. Then I write it in the spelling self-monitoring sheet. I write the word that I think is misspelled and I try to spell it again. I hand it to my teacher and she writes the correct spelling for me. This helps me spell better.

My research topic is about snakes. There is three parts that I have to write in my research project. They are: what I know about snakes, what I want to know about snakes and what I learned about snakes. I want to make a poster. Research helps me learn more about everything.

On the first day of school, I wrote about myself on a map. The map is a plain piece of paper with a sun shaped thing in the middle. The middle of the map is where I put my name. I wrote about my pet guinea pigs and things about myself around the circle in the middle. A map is good for knowing other people.

I use a checklist for editing my writing. I edit capital letters, punctuation, spelling and how my writing looks. This helps me edit my writing by myself.

Word Study:

My word bank is kind of like my self-monitoring sheet. This is because I get spellings of words from my teacher and I put them in my word bank. If I put a word in my word bank, I can just look back there again for the spelling.

Our interesting word wall is for interesting words. We get the words from work and things we do. We share the words. This helps me learn them.

Independence:

My contract is for checking if I did things. If I need to know what to do next, I look at my contract. My contract is helping me to be independent.

On a progress report form, I write what I know, what I need to know, and I write what my teacher's job is. This tells my teacher what I need to learn and what I know for the next day. It tells me what I know and what I need to know.

My portfolio helps me organize my things.

I use the fist-full-of-words when I'm looking for a book somewhere. You make a fist and you look at the first page of the book. If a word is too hard for you, you put one finger up. If another word is hard for you, then you put another finger up. If you put up five fingers, then the book is too hard for you to read by yourself. This helps me to pick a book.

My favorite thing to do here is go to the library. Reading a book is almost like watching T.V., except you're just reading it and the pictures aren't moving.

Love,
Christopher.

Figure 9-12.   Christopher's Progress Letter to His Parents (Page 2 of 2)

Carol Santa (1995) suggests that children create a list of questions they predict that their parents might ask during the conference. These questions are best developed in response to reviewing the letters. Questions projected by many of our children follow.

Students' Predictions: Questions Parents Might Ask

Reading

1. Read a part of your reading journal.
2. What books have you read?
3. Read me a page from your hardest book.
4. When do you do a retelling?
5. What's the retelling checklist?

Writing

1. Show me your research writing.
2. What are you writing now?
3. Do you write correct grammar? Show me.
4. When do you correct your spelling mistakes?

Social Studies/Science/Art

1. Which science experiments did you do?
2. What is the topic of your research?
3. Do you use the KWL folder in Science?
4. Show me some notes you wrote about the insect report.

Math

1. Show me what you learned about multiplication.
2. Show me a sample of graphing. Tell me about it.

Our portfolios are an accumulation of student products from the earliest to the latest. Students don't choose their "best" pieces. Students select sample work from the beginning of a marking period, the middle, and close to the time of a student-led parent conference. Observing growth and change over time certainly demonstrates students' achievements. Listening to students share their achievements and their needs with parents is exciting and satisfying for the student and parents, as well. Evaluations are "built in" because the discussions involve self-monitoring, making the assessment discussion part of instruction.

The Student-Led Conference

A conference monitoring sheet (Figure 9-13) has been developed and continuously altered based on use with children. It follows the portfolio format, and includes strategies used in the classroom. Students are provided with the conference guide early in the year in order to become familiar with it. They learn the language and grow comfortable with the format. By the time parents attend the student-led conference, they have mastered the language and are comfortable using it to guide their parents through their learning.

A maximum of forty-five minutes is suggested for each conference. A round table is best for creating an equitable feeling among the participants. The youngster is best positioned between the teacher and one parent. Copies of the guide sheet systematically take parents through the data. The portfolio is positioned in front of the child and used to reference the student's statements and confirm parents' comments.

Teachers inform children that their copy of the conference guide sheet will be completed prior to the conference. After the child reads an item on the sheet, tells about and shows parents evidence of growth concerning that item, and writes her accomplishments, the teacher shares the comment concerning that item immediately. It is important that the child NOT change his/her comments to match the teacher's. It is important, however, that students justify their comments in support of their contributions. Fostering independent ideas about performance is essential, as long as those ideas are supported with portfolio data. Figure 9-13 illustrates one child's conference guide completed during a conference. A copy of the child's guide sheet is taken home, and the original stays in the portfolio.

Students often demonstrate strategies used for learning during the conference. This is welcomed by parents, who are often astonished to see that their child is able to identify and evaluate their own growth. Often parents want to discuss matters further without their child present. Speaking with parents about the child in their absence usually results in distrust.

Conferences may be scheduled prior to or following distribution of report cards. When you are ready, use the letters as replacements for the innocuous letter and number grade reporting system. Do away with written phrases like, "tries hard," "does well sometimes," "all the time," and "not at all." Students interpret these as mere substitutes for As, Bs, and Cs.

Two More Reporting Strategies

Joanne Harris writes a final report in the form of a letter to each of her students (see Figure 9-14). It is an extension of the letters written either by the student or the teacher during the school year. Although time consuming, the letter provides an invaluable record of a student's performance. The teacher's narrative and the student's work samples draw a picture of the student's abilities, achievements, and adaptability to classroom life. No other reporting system is as effective.

CONFERENCE GUIDE - Fall

THINGS I'VE LEARNED   **COMMENTS**

Independence

I use a contract to organize my work.

Yes

I self-monitor my work by using the progress report form
to tell "What I Know" and "What I Need To Learn."
I also use self-monitoring sheets for comprehension of
story, editing my writing, and other activities.

Yes, but I didn't need it

I use a strategy to select literature to read.

Yes, I use fist full of words,

Composition: Rhetorical

My favorite kind of writing is fiction, information,
writing for a purpose, and others. Write it here.

fiction

The prewriting strategies I use for creative writing
and research are:

taking notes, read books, wrote questions

I revise by using the following strategies:

spelling, punctuation, reread, self monitoring sheet.

After I've revised my writing, I edit using the following strategies:

//

I use a journal to communicate ideas with my teacher.

Yes

Other things I want to tell about my writing:

reading respose log

Figure 9-13. Conference Guide (Page 1 of 3)

Composition: Research

I use questions to begin research and, then, follow
by looking for books that answer the questions.

Yes

I know how to paraphrase information from the
book in order to answer the questions.

Yes

I am able to write a first draft and revise that
draft in order to write a research report.

Yes

I know how to create a bibliography using APA style
of referencing (American Psychological Association).

No

Vocabulary

When I miss a word when reading, I:

Start again, or asks

I learn to spell words by tracing them and, then, writing them.

Yes

I learn to write words by using the following spelling patterns:

No

I've learned the following word origins, roots, prefixes, suffixes,
and anth, bi, di, tri, micro, mono, phobia, ology
to increase vocabulary.

Other word studies that help me understand words meaning are:

dichonary

Figure 9-13.   Conference Guide (Page 2 of 3)

Comprehension: Fiction and Nonfiction

I like to read:

Fichon

Some of the genres of the books I'm reading include:

Fichon, mystary, Mysary, biography, adventure

_I use the following strategies to demonstrate
comprehension after I read (for example, retellings)._

retellings, reading, respose log

_I use self-monitoring sheets to record "What I Know"
and "What I need to learn."_

Yes, but not needed

Research and Study Strategies

_Request questions - "right-there," "think and search,"
and "on-my-own - are used to help me identify the kind
of information I need to answer questions. These are
important when I take tests in school._

Yes

I can use think-alongs to aide reading comprehension.

imagine, predict, guess, & reread

_I use think-alongs to increase my comprehension.
Those think-alouds include:_

//

My suggestions for making the program better are:

longer computer time

Name: Natalie Morten

Teacher's name: Elena

Today's date: 11/12

Figure 9-13.   Conference Guide (Page 3 of 3)

April 9, 1996

Dear Jessica,

It is a pleasure to have you as a student. You seem to have a real desire to learn and do well. You always pay such close attention to what we talk about during conferences. Then you try to use my suggestions when you are writing on your own. Your focus, along with your confidence in yourself, helps you to be successful.

This letter is a progress report for the third marking period. I will review the strategies you have used and the growth you demonstrated in using them. I will also discuss areas on which you need to continue working during the rest of the year. Like your portfolio and other letters you received from me this year, this report is divided into four categories: Comprehension, Composition, Vocabulary, and Independence.

Comprehension

Comprehension strategies, such as prediction and retellings, provide you with ways to understand and remember what you read. Some of the strategies you used and what they showed about you as a reader follow.

Prediction

When you predict, you connect what you know to the new information you are reading. You used prediction in several ways during this marking period:

1. **Look, Think, Predict: (Before Reading)**

    Before you read a book, you looked at the cover, the illustrations, and the jacket. You also read a page or two. You made a prediction before you started reading *The New Boy* by R.L. Stine. You predicted that it was about **"a girl who likes a boy, but he is a killer."** I like how you consistently justify your predictions. For example, you wrote, **"I looked at the cover and read the back of the book,"** before you began reading *The New Boy*. Using parts of the cover, illustrations, and reading the back of a book or the inside cover helps you focus. It starts you thinking about the story you are about to read. It also helps you choose a book that you will enjoy.

2. **Reading the Pictures: (Before Reading)**

    You read the pictures in *Pink and Say* by Patricia Polacco before reading the text of the story. You, Robyn, Joe, and Jenny used each picture to make decisions about the story episodes and the plot. You used the different

Figure 9-14. Final Report to Jessica

colors of the soldiers' uniforms to help you decide that the setting of the story was during the Civil War. When you disagreed with Robyn's idea that the soldier was taking a rest, you used that very small spot of blood on the soldier's knee to justify your belief that he was wounded rather than resting. That was great! You also used the expressions on the faces of the characters to predict what was happening. Your attention to the details of the illustrations helped you make predictions that were logical and quite accurate.

Reading pictures and talking about possible story episodes is a powerful way to make predictions, and you do this. Your group had a lively discussion that got you thinking about the things you already knew about the Civil War. This also made you think about what life was like during that time period in American history. Your predictions led you to tell a story about how the lives of Pinkus Aylee and Sheldon Curtis were connected.

Thinkalongs (During Reading)

We talked about becoming more aware of what good readers do to comprehend text using the thinkalong strategies. I modeled several of the thinkalong strategies when I read the article about sneezes. You identified all the things I was doing while thinking aloud as I read. You jotted them down on your copy of the article. You wrote:

Mrs. Harris:
- **thinks about questions she has**
- **relates what she's reading to people that she knows**
- **relates what she's reading to herself**
- **reads over a part if it's confusing**
- **adds to the story with her stories.**

You tried using the thinkalongs on your own. When you read the story "The Telltale Will," you made a prediction as you read. When Mrs. Crabb and the uncle left Helen's room, you wrote: **"I bet she drinks the milk."** You learned as you read on that this prediction was wrong, but it was a valid prediction, especially since Helen actually picked up the glass. When you made this prediction during reading, two things happened:

1. **You found out that your prediction was partly right.**

2. **Your prediction was also partly wrong, though, so you had to change your ideas.**

You jotted down other comments as you were reading. Then you used the Thinkalong Self-monitoring Sheet. It helped you identify the strategies you use to comprehend. Your written comments: **"nice and cozy; I love that",**

"Who's Mrs. Crabb?", "Wow, I would say no!", "Where did he come from?", and **"Where did she meet him?"** showed that you:

1. connect ideas in your head to new ideas you are reading
2. ask questions
3. make predictions
4. visualize ideas in your mind
5. personalize the text by connecting ideas in the story to things in your life.

ReQuest

My son Ryan has to read sections of his science or social studies textbook for homework at least twice a week. Then he has to answer four or five questions about the material. He has found out that some of the questions are easier to answer than others. The ReQuest strategy helped Ryan learn to recognize what kind of question is being asked and where he needs to look to answer it. The three types of questions, "right there," "think and search," and "on my own," are often seen in textbooks from content area subjects, such as science.

We used the ReQuest strategy with an article about octopuses. You wrote and answered the three types of questions after reading the octopus article. You knew **"Why does an octopus change color?"** was a "right there" question because the answer was stated right in the text. Some of the key words in the question (an octopus changes color) were in the text, and that helped you find the answer. You wrote **"How is an octopus mischievous in captivity?"** as a "think and search" question. You showed me that the answer to that question was found in several different places in the article. Finally, in an "on my own" question, you asked: **"Why do you think an octopus gets scared?"** You knew this was an "on my own" question because the answer was not found in the article. You needed to use ideas from your experience and background knowledge to answer your "on my own" question.

Retellings

You have grown a lot since September in demonstrating your comprehension through retellings. In your recent retellings of the folktales *Swallowed Alive* and *The Haunted House*, retold by Robert D. San Souci, you used the Retelling Checklist to review what you remembered in your written retellings. In our conference, you showed me that you remembered the introduction, part of the setting, all the characters, the problem, most episodes, and the resolution. The Retelling Checklist helped you notice that you left out "when" or "where" the story happened. You and I talked about using clues from the story to decide "where" or "when" the story took place. For example, in *The Haunted House,* the author wrote about a haunted house "in his settlement." We discussed the idea that most people do not live in settlements today, and this information indicated that the story probably took place long ago. Looking for clues like these help you identify story settings.

You also discovered that the themes in some stories are not directly discussed in the text. Stories usually include hints in the episodes that indicate the theme. It's almost like answering "on my own" questions; the theme is not "right there" in the story. The hints in the story and what you already know help you to recognize the theme on your own. You showed you understood themes by telling me about the themes of familiar stories, like *Pinocchio* and *The Tortoise and the Hare.* This helped you to understand and identify the theme in the story you read.

In a talk, we discovered that our Retelling Checklist needed something added. It was, "Is the theme stated or not stated?" We added that to the checklist. When you used the new checklist for your retelling of "Snowbound," you indicated that you like the new checklist better because **"it really works"** for you. Impressive, Jessica! You have improved a self-monitoring tool.

Literature Response Journal

After you read independently, you respond in the Literature Response Journal. Your first journal writings were a summary of what you were reading. One of those responses was about *The New Boy* by R.L. Stine. You wrote:

> **"I started a new book by R.L. Stine called *The New Boy.* It's all about this girl and how she's shy. She saw this new boy that she wants to meet, but her friends, who already have boyfriends, are all over him. Janie feels left out when Eve and Kathy always make fun of her. They are her best friends."**

I asked you questions when I wrote back. They were: "How did you know Janie was shy? What do you think about her friends? Have you ever had a friend who made fun of you? What was it like? How did you handle it?" I was asking you to give evidence from the story to support what you wrote. I wanted you to personalize the story and expand your responses to what you read.

In a journal entry about *The Babysitter* by R.L. Stine, you wrote that when a girl named Jenny was babysitting, someone was calling her and breathing into the phone. You wrote:

"Jenny thinks that a boy named Chuck is the person, but he swears he only called her once to talk. [Then] he got nervous, so he hung up. Now she found a note. She's really scared. I would be scared, too. But I would tell the mother right away, and I would babysit Danny at my house."

I like that you put yourself in this character's place (you personalized) and thought about how you would feel and act. You said you would be scared, and you wouldn't just keep it to yourself like Jenny. You would take steps, like talking to an adult and babysitting at your house. I would definitely want you, not Jenny, to watch my children. During this final marking period, you need to continue reflecting on stories by telling what the text makes you think about. Include "why" you feel the way you do in your journal responses. When you do this, you demonstrate how you connect what you read to your life and feelings. Your recent responses to literature, including how you would handle the unknown caller, show that you are beginning to do this. Keep it up, Jess!

Composition

You wrote for many purposes during this marking period. I reviewed the composition file in your portfolio to see what your writing shows you can do and what you need to work on during the rest of the year.

Research

Research is what we do to find out about information related to a specific topic. You will need to do research to complete many projects in high school and college. I still use the research process as a graduate student.

The first step in research is choosing a topic. You chose to do your research project on the Olympics because of the trip to Atlanta that your family has planned for the summer. You also chose to focus part of your project more specifically on one Olympic event, synchronized swimming. As a longtime fan of the Olympics, I was very interested in what you would discover in your research.

KWL is the strategy you used to construct your research project. The strategy guided you to organize the information you found. KWL means:

K: Things I already **know** about the Olympics.

W: What do I **want** to find out about the Olympics?

L: What I **learned** about the Olympics from my reading.

When you began using the KWL strategy, you listed everything you knew or thought about the Olympics and synchronized swimming. This included:

What I Know

- started in ancient Greece (Olympia)
- the first prizes were olive leaves
- they sometimes fought till death
- sometimes the Olympics were failures
- kept adding new events each game
- synchronized swimming can be solo, duet, or groups
- there are many different positions to hold [in synchronized swimming]
- timing is very important in synchronized swimming

You then created a number of questions about your topic. You wrote:

What I Want to Know

1. What is some more history about the Olympics?
2. When did synchronized swimming start in the Olympics?
3. Who were the synchronized swimmers in the past?
4. How do synchronized swimmers train?
5. How long do the synchronized swimmers train each day?
6. What are the chances of this year's synchronized swimming team?

These questions guided your research as you began to read and gather information. We talked again about the three types of questions. You thought that **"When did synchronized swimming start in the Olympics?" and "How long do the synchronized swimmers train each day?"** were "right there" questions whose answers would be found "right there" in one place in the text. All your other questions were "think and search" questions that would have answers in several places in the texts you read.

We both found books about the Olympics in the library. You brought in magazines from home that included articles about synchronized swimming. You got some information to answer your questions. You used the KWL strategy, made notes, and used these notes to answer each specific question. For example, your sixth question was: **"What are the chances of this year's synchronized swimming team?"** You found the following facts related to that question and listed them under "What I Learned" on the KWL chart:

- **This year there is an 8-woman team competition.**

- **The U.S.A. is a synchronized swimming powerhouse, ranked #1 in the world since 1991.**
- **The team is led by triple world champion Becky Dyroen-Lancer.**
- **Becky's sister, Suzannah Bianco, is also on the team.**
- **In the qualifying event, U.S. was flawless, earning the first sweep of perfect 10's.**
- **The other 7 teams are silver medal contenders—Canada, Japan, Russia, France, China, Italy and Mexico.**

The KWL strategy helped you organize the information you read before you wrote a first draft.

We had several conferences to review your progress. At one, I asked you to close the book and talk to me about what was in it. This helped you paraphrase the information; that is, put it into your own words. When you finished, you edited your rough draft by using the Editing Sheet. You discovered some spelling errors and corrected them on your own. During our final conference, I noticed some words crossed out and others written in their place. You revised and edited what you had written after rereading and having a writing conference, on your own. Hurray for you, Jess!

We discovered that you needed to add commas in compound sentences or make run-on sentences into two shorter sentences. We found out that reading what you write out loud helps you find errors. You heard what you wrote as a reader would, and that's when you could fix it. I too reread and reread my rough copies, sometimes out loud, to improve my writing. This is a tricky part of the writing process because as a writer you know what you want to say. You have to consider whether your audience, the reader, will be able to understand your message. It takes a lot of practice to do this. The more you reread, the more errors you'll notice in spelling, punctuation, and capitalization. A final rereading will help you to check that your ideas are expressed clearly. Even though I am a teacher, I always reread my writing or have a friend check my final copies.

For the final step in the research process, we wrote bibliographies. I gave each of you a model of a bibliography using a magazine, encyclopedia, book, or the Internet as a source. You used this model to help you write a bibliography for your project.

It was a lot of work, Jess, but your final report shows it was worth the effort. You organized the information you found about the Olympics chronologically, noting years in which significant events happened that changed the games. This traced the history of the Olympics. I like how you chose one event to research in more depth because it made your project more interesting and also reflected your love of dance and choreography.

Dialogue Journal

You have told me that you really enjoy writing to me in your dialogue journal. In one of my responses in your journal, I talked about how much I enjoy teaching science. You wrote back:

> Mrs. Harris,
>
> You would probably enjoy speaking to my mom. She is also very interested in science. In one of the elementary schools, she started a neat science program. Now the program is in all 6 of the elementary schools. She enjoys science and she's really good at it.
>
> Jess

I found that interesting, but I didn't have enough details from what you wrote to really understand what your mom had accomplished. I wrote back and asked what the science program was all about and how your mom became involved with it. Details, details, details—I want them all!

In another entry, you wrote:

> Mrs. Harris,
>
> On Saturday, I babysat. I made $25. I'm saving up for the Olympics and Florida. So far I have $90. I'm going to mow the lawn today if it doesn't rain and I'll get $20. for that. Then I'm babysitting on the weekend again. And I'm going to mow again next week. I'm going to be RICH!!!
>
> Jess

This second entry included more details. You wrote about the two ways you were earning money, when you worked, and when you would be working again. I certainly look forward to reading your dialogue journal.

Content Journal

You used your content journal to write observations of the butterflies and ants that we recently had in our classroom. Observations help improve descriptive writing. In an entry about the butterflies, you wrote:

> There are 5 caterpillars. They look like they are starting their chrysalises but they are not. They are not very large yet but I'm sure they'll get bigger.

You used what you saw, describing the size and stage of the caterpillars, to write this.

In a later entry, you wrote:

> One [chrysalid] hatched (the one that fell). The other four all got really, really dark. The one that hatched has four legs and has orange and gray and black spots on it. It is a painted butterfly. The ants look about the same with the tunnels. There [are] a lot on the top right now.

This time, you described what you saw in more detail. You included color and other factual information.

In a final entry, you wrote:

> All the butterflies hatched, and they all have four legs. They are really pretty, and we're going to let them go later on today.
>   The ants are still digging away. There are some little tunnels on the back and one big one. Now the ants are building tunnels on top of the platform. I can't believe they are still digging. They are pretty fun to watch.

You again increased the number of details you wrote. You mixed factual information about the butterflies and ants with your opinions in this journal entry. You could extend what you wrote even more by adding, for example, the reasons you think the butterflies are pretty and the ants are fun to watch.

You used a comma in the compound sentences you wrote in the last entry above. You also placed the information about the butterflies and ants in separate paragraphs in this same entry. This is how I know that you are applying what we talk about in writing conferences when you work independently. Good for you!

Persuasive Writing

You wrote two persuasive pieces during this marking period. The first was related to doing homework assignments.

> I think there shouldn't be any homework allowed to be taken home after school. Kids are in school for seven hours. They shouldn't have to take work home. Kids need to do other things besides schoolwork. It is unfair to make kids do this, especially if it's really

hard. Yes, they do learn, but isn't that what seven hours of school is for?

You used the Editing My Writing checklist to review your writing, and then met with me. I told you this paragraph probably would not convince me to stop assigning homework. **"Kids need to do things besides homework."** That is the beginning of a strong argument, but you need to back up your ideas with supporting details and discussion. We talked about adding information about what activities kids, and you in particular, are involved in during the week. Writing about how much time these activities take up and why they are important to you would have made your writing more effective.

In your second attempt at persuasive writing, you did present more support for your ideas. Your argument was more convincing. You took a stand against wearing uniforms in public schools and explained how kids need to be different from each other.

I think that uniforms in public schools should not be allowed. Kids like to express themselves in different ways. One way they do that is dressing differently than others. Kids shouldn't be the same. They shouldn't have to dress the same, look the same, or act the same.

Kids have different personalities, and teens really need to find out who they are in these years. They need to see what they want to be, how they want to act, and [in which type of] dress they want to present themselves. Don't take away their different personalities.

After you stated your opinion that uniforms shouldn't be allowed in public schools, you gave a reason for your opinion (**"Kids like to express themselves in different ways."**). You explained that you felt the way teenagers dress is their chance to figure out who they are. Your final sentence (**"Don't take away their different personalities."**) states your belief that clothing reflects a teenager's individuality. This piece of writing made a lot of sense to me, especially since I spent many years of school wearing the same uniform everyone else was wearing.

The next time you want to convince your parents or a friend to do something, consider rehearsing your argument by first putting it in writing. One of the most effective pieces of persuasive writing I've ever read was done by the daughter of a friend of mine. She wanted desperately to have a bunny. She listed every argument her dad had against getting a bunny, and then she wrote about how she would handle each aspect. Guess what! She now has a bunny of her own.

Poetry

Lee Bennett Hopkins' poem, "Good Books, Good Times", inspired you to write a poem in a list framework. You just "listed" the word "happy" sixteen times and found sixteen other words to go next to each "happy."

happy smile
happy birthday
happy Easter
happy Hanukkah
happy bug
happy sister
happy mom
happy dad
happy brother
happy bird
happy meal
happy brownie
happy cookie
happy happy joy joy
happy shoes
happy sad

This activity was fun because it gave you an opportunity to play with words. You also learned a structure for writing that you can use again to compose such things as birthday and holiday poems.

Vocabulary

Interesting Words

When we started the year, I used an interesting word that was new to most of you each day. Soon you and the other students in our class began posting interesting words on the bulletin board. Everyone used these words in conversations or noticed them while reading. Interesting words used during this marking period include: ironic, onomatopoeia, chrysalis, skeptical, intrepid, and aversion. You added several words to the classroom display, too. You contributed **decathlon** and **synchronized** because you learned them during your research about the Olympics. You also added two interesting words you found while reading, **anesthesiologist** and **regrettably**. It's important to increase your vocabulary, especially since you are planning to go to college.

Spelling Workshop

There are some words I hated to spell when I was in school, Jess. I just couldn't seem to find a way to remember how to spell them. You and I found out that you learn to spell words best by finding the little words in the bigger words you are trying to learn. You also use the Modified Fernald strategy, saying and tracing the words simultaneously. The Spelling Workshop includes the Fernald strategy, as well as a section on finding the little words in bigger words. It combines all of the strategies you might use to learn to spell words. You do best, however, when you use these two parts of the Spelling Workshop:

- **finding little words in bigger words**
- **using the Fernald technique to learn to spell.**

Word Study

Prefixes

You studied prefixes related to numbers and generated lists of words beginning with these prefixes. You and Robyn worked on the prefixes tri- and quad-. You both created the following list of words:

tricycle	**triangle**	**Triceratops**
triceps	**trilogy**	**triplets**
triple	**tripod**	

Wow, what an easy way to increase vocabulary. We talked about the meaning of each of these words, and how the prefix tri- helps us understand that all the words have something to do with the number three.

You did the same thing for the prefix quad- to discover words that were somehow related to the number four. You wrote these words for the prefix quad-:

quadruple   **quadruplet**   **quadrilateral**

What a great way to make new words!

Homophones

I noticed that you, like so many other people, sometimes confuse words that sound alike. You mix up **there** and **their**. Homophones can be confusing, so we decided to make a list of homophone pairs. Your group wrote the following:

so–sew	**ant–aunt**	**blew–blue**
close–clothes	**brake–break**	**horse–hoarse**
pain–pane	**pray–prey**	**peace–piece**
plain–plane	**sun–son**	**stair–stare**
some–sum		

A master list of the homophones our class discussed are now on our word wall. How about trying to write a story filled with homophones? That's one way to keep a reader awake!

Onomatopoeia

Onomatopoeic words, like pop, fizz, and quack, are fun! Our class thought of many words that belong in this category. Our list of onomatopoeic words included: **drip, cluck, thump, crunch, meow, squish,** and **splat.** I brought in a pile of comics from Sunday newspapers, and we discovered that cartoonists often use onomatopoeic words in their work. We added the words cartoonists use to our list, and I'm sure we'll find even more before the year is over.

Besides onomatopoeia, watch for similes, metaphors, and alliteration in the books you read. (If you don't remember what these are, ask me.) I love finding onomatopoeia, similes, and metaphors in novels and poems. They really paint pictures with words, and I've shared some of my old favorites and new-found treasures with you this year. When you notice how authors use these devices, you can give them a try in your own writing.

Independence

As you know, being independent is important. You have really become independent this year. You use a contract to guide you from one activity to another. At first you asked, "What do I do now?" when you finished an activity. In a few weeks, you were comfortable with the routines of our class. You now check your contract right away when you arrive. You decide what you want to do first, and you understand how one activity leads to another. For example, after you read what I write in your Dialogue Journal, you write back to me.

You know that after you read independently, you should make an entry in your Literature Response Journal.

You use the Progress Report Form to monitor your learning. It helps you recall and review the activities you complete. When I look back at your Progress Report Forms, I notice a change from the beginning of the year. When you first used this form, you wrote that you could **"listen to a story and rewrite it from my memory."** On a recent Progress Report Forms, you were much more specific: **"I'm good at [including] introductions, telling about characters, telling about the problem, retelling episodes, solutions, and how the story ends."** You also recognized what you needed when you wrote: **"I need help in telling when and where the story takes place and [fitting] in a theme. My teacher needs to help [by] showing me how to fit these two problems into my writing."** Recognizing your abilities and needs really shows how much you are growing, Jess. You told me you enjoy being in charge of these aspects of your program, and you are very clearly taking responsibility for yourself.

You seem to prefer working on you own, and that works well for you in many instances. However, working with a partner or group does have advantages at times. It gives you the opportunity to hear and consider other points of view.

You made the strategies your own, Jessica, by using them again and again in all areas of your studies. Be proud of what you have accomplished this year. You know how to use KWL for research and ReQuest in the W part of KWL. You should boast about the fact that you know that Fernald and Spelling Workshop are best when you want to learn to spell words. You are able to select strategies to help you get your work done. Remember, I'm here to help you make decisions about what strategies to use in each subject area project.

I am looking forward to the rest of our time together this year. I'll be waiting to hear more details about your trip to the Olympics this summer. I will certainly watch the synchronized swimming with more interest because of you. I wonder if you'll be lucky enough to be there when the Americans go for the gold. I know they'll be quite a challenge to the other teams.

Your teacher,

JoAnn Harris

Nations change their ideas about what is and is not quality education for children. The debates, controversies, and conclusions vary as much as the ideas. In order to make this book appropriate for most current, past, and future beliefs, I have included a generic checklist of literacy and related skills that can be used to "check off" students' accomplishments (Appendix D). The language is familiar, consistent, and comfortable for most schools of thought. I suggest that you photocopy one for each of the children in your classroom. Observe his/her behaviors. When the student exhibits evidence of mastery of a skill or strategy by using it independently, write a check next to the item. Mastery suggests that a student is able to tell you about the skill or strategy, how it is used, and why.

These mastered skills can be listed in the letters to parents. The checklist format can also serve as the written reporting tool. I cautiously give this checklist to you and warn that without conferences where students demonstrate knowledge and without narratives about performance, checklists, letter grades, and other designated symbols representing performance are insufficient for reporting students' growth.

Summary

Report cards, grades, and conferences are extensions of daily routines. They are ongoing, and therefore familiar. What students learn, and what each needs to know is the core of the activities. Responsibility for demonstrating achievements and needs belongs to the learners. Guiding students to observe their products (what they produce) and the process they use to solve problems is our goal. When assessment activities grow from learning experiences, Assessment IS Instruction.

EPILOGUE

A Final Note

Samuel Johnson once wrote, "The two most engaging powers of an author are to make new things familiar and familiar things new." This textbook was written using approximately 180,000 words. The book is really a rearrangement of the same 180,000 words used in my earlier books. The text, however, synthesizes my experiences as an educator to the date of its completion. The content is based on pertinent ideas, notions, research, and practices in literacy education. I have attempted to make new things familiar and old things somewhat new in my word arrangements. The 180,000 words and their meanings, however, are as Louise Rosenblatt (1978) writes, "simply paper and ink until a reader evokes from it a literacy work—sometimes, even a literary work of art" (p. ix). The book will, hopefully, guide you to visualize and feel the healthy classrooms created by the many wonderful teachers with whom I've worked. It is impossible to create the experience you'd have if you actually visited the rooms where these teachers and students live and work harmoniously. The words are meant to spur your desire, curiosity, enthusiasm, fortitude, and interest. It is up to you to take responsibility for putting the words into actions, and create change. Search for ways, dear educators, to create environments that will enable your students to receive many invitations to read and write. I hope that the invitational environments are enticing enough to develop bibliomaniacs who think of books like the chocoholic thinks of chocolate. I pray that your students become so addicted to literacy that they find anything that is between covers as irresistible as a candy kiss. May the desire for the language that creates text be savored by all!

Susan

APPENDIX A

Literature for Developing Readers and Writers

Phyllis DiMartino Fantauzzo

Stories for Retelling

Books for retelling must be strong in story structure: contain a definite problem and solution; have an easily identifiable introduction, setting, main and secondary characters, and a satisfactory ending. For assessment purposes, they should take no more than ten minutes reading time. They cannot be encumbered with too many episodes, details, or descriptive passages.

Ages five through seven

The day the teacher went bananas. (1984). James Howe. Lillian Hoban (Ill.). New York: Puffin Unicorn.

> The children in the class do not see a problem when a gorilla is sent by mistake to be their new teacher. They learn unique ways to play, draw, and do science. When the real teacher (who had been sent to the zoo) is finally switched by the principal, he finds his class belongs in the zoo.

Geoffrey Groundhog predicts the weather. (1995). Bruce Koscielniak. Boston, MA: Houghton Mifflin.

> Pandemonium breaks loose and all weather reports are cancelled when the groundhog doesn't predict the length of winter one February second. Popular for predicting how long winter will last, Geoffrey Groundhog finds himself in so much of a spotlight he can't see the ground let alone his shadow.

Just a little bit. (1993). Ann Rompert. Lynn Munsinger (Ill.). Boston, MA: Houghton Mifflin.

When a mouse and elephant play on a seesaw, the mouse can't go down despite help from other animals, as each lands on the mouse's side of the seesaw. The problem is solved when a brown beetle lands on top, proving that just a little bit can help. **(appropriate for picture reading)**

The monster bed. (1986). Jeanne Willis & Susan Valey. New York: Lothrop, Lee & Shepard. (Great Britain: 1987. Andersen Press Ltd.).

In a story told with humor and rhythm, a little monster is afraid to go to bed, for a human might get him. He sleeps under the bed to be safe, when a boy, lost in the woods, stops in the cave to rest. He checks under the bed for "monsters." The boy and the monster see each other; both scream and run away.

Old Winter. (1996). Judith Benet Richardson. R. W. Alley (Ill.). New York: Orchard.

Old Winter's feelings are hurt when the townspeople complain about the cold weather. He retires to a meat locker to sleep for an extended nap. When winter keeps getting worse and is neverending, a young girl called Spring finds him and convinces him to head south. **(weather study)**

Ages eight to ten

Dog breath: The horrible trouble with Hally Tosis. (1994). Dan Pilkey. New York: The Blue Sky Press, an imprint of Scholastic Inc.

This is a hilarious tale and play on words about Hally, the dog, whose bad breath causes leaves to fall from plants and visitors to stay away. Taking Hally to a breath-taking view, a film, or roller coaster so that he would be left breathless, does not solve the problem. When burglars pass out from Hally's breath, the family knows that life makes "scents" with him.

Lost. (1996). Paul Brett Johnson & Celeste Lewis. Paul Brett Johnson (Ill.). New York: Orchard.

When a girl's beagle is lost in the desert, she trusts he will return. Left-hand page illustrations show the dog surviving loneliness, the elements, and predators. The right-hand page drawings depict the girl's memories and the efforts she and her father use to find the worn-out, weak and hungry dog.

The man who tricked a ghost. (1993). Laurence Yep. Isadore Seltzer (Ill.). New York: Troll Medallion (Imprint of Troll Communications Inc.).

People fear traveling the road at night because of "the ghost" who has made people disappear. One brave man sets off fearlessly to the city. When he meets the ghost, he tricks him into helping him through the woods and into telling him how to get rid of "the ghost" forever.

Wayside School gets a little stranger. (1995). Louis Sachar. Joel Schick (Ill.). New York: William Morrow.

> Children can select a short story from this newest Wayside School collection. When Wayside School closed down to get rid of the cows, the children had to spend 243 days in horrible schools. Each story is complete in itself for retelling, as are the old favorites: *Sideways stories from Wayside School* and *Wayside School is falling down.*

Ten year olds and up

The Apprentices. (1978). Leon Garfield. New York: Viking Press.

> Any short story can be selected for retelling from the historically authentic tales that describe the problems encountered when young children are apprenticed out to learn a trade in nineteenth century England.

Connections: Short stories by outstanding writers for young adults. (1989). D. R. Gallo (Ed). New York: Delacorte Press.

> Young adults can select a story for retelling from this marvelous collection of seventeen contemporary short stories by well-known writers of adolescent literature. Writers include such notables as Todd Strasser, Richard Peck, and Jerry Spinelli.

Favorite Greek myths. (1989). Retold by Mary Pope Osborne. Troy Howell (Ill.). New York: Scholastic. (Blue Ribbon Press).

> The problems and solutions that helped explain man's beginnings are briefly retold in twelve beautifully illustrated myths from ancient Greece.

Tongues of jade. (1991). Laurence Yep. David Wiesner (Ill.). New York: HarperCollins.

> Yep captures magic, mystery, and human relationships in his retelling of the ancient folk tales in this collection of seventeen Chinese American stories.

Picture Reading

The cow who wouldn't come down. (1993). Paul Brett Johnson. New York: Orchard.

> Cows don't usually fly, but Miss Rosemary's cow has a mind of her own. After hilarious attempts to get her down fail, Miss Rosemary advertises for a cow and then creates a fake cow. The jealous flying cow then swoops down to crush the fake cow. **(also appropriate for retelling)**

The hall of the beasts. (1994). Mark Shasha. New York: Simon & Schuster.

> Through spectacular illustration, the animals on the wall murals come to life when a boy and his dad visit the house which had been closed for many years.

Reuben runs away. (1987). Richard Galbraith. New York: Orchard.

> When Reuben the teddy bear gets fed up with his mistreatment by a little girl and her dog, he runs away. He finds the big city is more scary than his home was, winding up in a trash can and a store for used toys.

Three young Pilgrims. (1992). Cheryl Harness. New York: Bradbury.

> Illustrated with rich, detailed pictures, early Pilgrim experience is shown through the activities of three young Pilgrims. From setting sail on the Mayflower, through busy and hard times, changing of the seasons, the young Pilgrims reach the first Thanksgiving feast.

Modified Request Activities

Accidents may happen: Fifty inventions discovered by mistake. (1996). New York: Delacorte.

> Fifty amusing yet interesting true stories behind the discoveries of inventions that came about because of a mistake.

Cat mummies. (1996). Kelly Trumble. Laszlo Kubinyi (Ill.). New York: Clarion.

> A fascinating and well-researched information book answers questions about ancient Egypt's mummification of animals, particularly cats. Written in a narrative format, the book begins with an Egyptian farmer unearthing thousands of previously undisturbed cat mummies.

Grandfather Four Winds and Rising Moon. (1994). Michael Chanin. Sally J. Smith (Ill.). Tiburon, CA: H. J. Kramer, Starseed.

> A young Native American boy learns lessons of courage and faith as well as respect for the natural environment from his blind grandfather. Illustrations are stunningly beautiful.

The strength of these arms: Life in the slave quarters. (1997). Raymond Bial. Boston, MA: Houghton Mifflin.

> This timely informational book presents the brutality experienced by the slaves from their kidnapping in Africa to their harsh treatment on the plantations. Photographs depict their living conditions and social customs.

Journal and Letter Writing

Letters from Felix. (1994). Ann Langen & Constanza Droop. New York: Abbeville.

Felix, the stuffed rabbit, disappears, and soon letters arrive as he travels from London, Paris, Italy, Cairo, and Kenya to New York. (**appropriate for social studies as well as letter modeling**)

Felix travels back in time. (1995). Ann Langen & Constanza Droop. New York: Abbeville.

When the stuffed rabbit, Felix, disappears, no one can find him but soon letters come from his visits to the Stone Age down through Greece and the Middle Ages to a settlement in the New World as each letter describes the surroundings with historical accuracy. (**also social studies**)

Kate on the coast. (1992). Pat Brisson. Rick Brown (Ill.). New York: Bradbury.

When Kate's family moves to the Pacific Northwest, they travel through several western states to get there. Kate's letters to her best friend chronicle her travels through Hawaii, Canada, and Alaska. (**also appropriate for geography**)

The long, long letter. (1996). Elizabeth Spurr. David Catrow (Ill.). New York: Hyperion Books for Children.

Lonesome Hetta, who lives far from anyone, waits for a letter from her sister. The sister writes a letter so long it needs a thousand stamps. Hetta waits by the mailbox through all kinds of weather; the massive letter blows off the truck and pages scatter everywhere. It took fifty children to put the letter back together again.

The Magpie song. (1995). Laurence Anholt. Dan Williams (Ill.). New York: Houghton Mifflin.

Carla lives in the city and her grandfather lives in the country. She writes to granddad about her concerns and worries about her family while granddad writes back with letters containing riddles about the birds in his backyard. Through the letters, the reader realizes that the grandfather will soon die. He leaves Carla a letter to learn the secret of the magpies.

Vocabulary Development and Word Play

Antics. (1992). Cathi Hepworth. New York: G. P. Putnam & Sons.

An amusing alphabet book that focuses on the syllable **ant.** Each illustration shows an ant or ants acting out the word in an amusing way, whether it be **brilliant, jubilant,** or **immigrant.**

A cache of jewels and other collective nouns. (1987). Ruth Heller. New York: Scholastic.

Through simple illustrations, children learn that groups have different names. Whether it be a host of angels, a bed of oysters, or an army of ants, children will begin looking for collective nouns in their daily lives.

Quick as a cricket. (1982–1996). Audrey Woods. Don Woods (Ill.). Auburn, ME: Child's Play.

Woods presents a variety of animals and the adverb that describes each in lively illustrations as the animals move through their habitats.

Whatley's quest: An alphabet adventure. (1994). Bruce Whatley & Rosie Smith. Bruce Whatley (Ill.). Sydney, Australia: HarperCollins.

The beautiful pictures in this large book are suitable for all ages so that children search for and identify the items and events beginning with the alphabet letter for the page. Vocabulary expands with such words as **abacus, accountant, acorn, adversary,** and **albatross.**

Phonic and Word Patterns

Play with "a" and "t." (1989). Jane Belk Moncure. Jodie McCallum (Ill.). Elgin, IL: The Child's World.

Children have fun with the letters "a" and "t" as a boy called "t" and a girl called "a" find what out they can do and play when they join with various consonant children.

Jesse Bear, what will you wear? (1986). Nancy White Carlstrom. Bruce Degen (Ill.). New York: Macmillan Publishing.

With a lilting, predicable rhyme, many beginning word patterns are presented as Jesse the Bear decides what to wear for different times of day and in various places.

Snow dance. (1997). Lezlie Evans. Cynthia Jabar (Ill.). Boston, MA: Houghton Mifflin.

Children, wishing it would snow on a dreary, weary day, begin dancing and prancing when snow arrives. Rhyming predictable patterns flow through this lovely poem which also focuses on the "ing" suffix as the children are whirling and twirling with boots stomping and clomping in the snow.

Zug the bug: A flip-the-page rhyming book. (1988). Colin & Jacqui Hawkins. New York: G. P. Putnam's Sons.

Children will chuckle and learn word patterns as they flip the page to change *bug* into *slug*. The amusing cartoon-like pictures are accompanied by a consonant that will join with the "ug" spelling pattern as the child flips each page.

Homophones

What in the world is a homophone? (1996). Leslie Presson. JoEllen Bosson (Ill.). Hauppauge, NY: Barron's Educational Series.

An excellent reference for children and adults, this illustrated dictionary of 400 pairs of pure homophones is a must for each classroom. Each pair of easy-to-read words is presented in alphabetical order. An appendix contains homophones with contractions and near misses.

Eight ate: A feast of homonym riddles. (1982). Marvin Terban. Giulio Maestro (Ill.). New York: Clarion.

This original book of humorous homonym riddles helps youngsters understand the concept of words with the same meanings but different spellings. (They can create their own homonym riddles.)

The king who rained. (1970). Fred Gwynne. New York: Prentice-Hall.

A young girl talks about the things her parents tell her but pictures them literally (hearing the house will have two coats of paint is pictured with two giant cloth coats on the house). Each picture presents the alternate meaning for the homonym or figurative language.

A chocolate moose for dinner. (1976). Fred Gwynne. New York: Windmill Books and E. P. Dutton & Co.

In the same hilarious mixture of humor and style as *The King Who Rained.* This book presents an additional 23 homonyms and figurative language (a fork in the road shows a metal fork in the road).

Alliteration

Alligator arrived with apples: A potluck alphabet feast. (1987). Crescent Dragonwagon. Jose Aruego & Ariane Dewey (Ills.). New York: Macmillan.

This is a wonderful model for children to create their own alliterative alphabet game, story, or book. From alligators and apples, through parrots providing pumpkin pie to Zebra's zucchini, each animal brings something for the feast in his own alphabet way.

The amazing animal alphabet book. (1988). Roger & Mariko Chouinard. Roger Chouinard (Ill.). New York: Doubleday & Co.

Kangaroos kiss in a kayak, and an emu and elephant eat elegantly in this delightful alphabet book with its full-page colored illustrations. Each animal (noun) indulges (verb) in an activity in the alliterative pattern.

Animalia. (1986). Graeme Base. (1986). New York: Penguin.

> With delightful art in its creative detail, beasts and birds travel through an alphabetic fantasy world. The tongue-twisting pages entice readers to create their own alliterations. Vocabulary develops as beautiful blue butterflies, quivering quails, or ingenious iguana splash on the pages.

Six sleepy sheep. (1991). Jeffie Ross Gardon. John O'Brien (Ill.). Honesdale, PA: Caroline House, imprint of Boyds Mills Press.

> Told in rhymthic prose, six sleepy sheep slumber as the letter "s" advances the wacky text. One sheep's snoring awakens the other sleepy sheep who then try various antics (skipping, singing) to fall back to sleep.

Onomatopoeia

Do bunnies talk? (1992). Dayle Ann Dodds. A. Dubanevich (Ill.). New York: HarperCollins.

> Do quiet little bunnies talk, does everything else have a voice or sound? Animal sounds, machine sounds, human sounds and describing sounds all appear in this cleverly crafted picture book.

Ducks like to swim. (1996). Agnes Verboven. Anne Westerduin (Ill.). New York: Orchard.

> As a duck quacks for water, each animal begins making his own special sound until enough noise is made in hope that it will rain. (Quacks, oinks, neighs, etc.)

Four famished foxes and Fosdyke. (1995). Pamela Duncan Edwards. Henry Cole. (Ill.). New York: Harper Trophy.

> In a tale so filled with "f" alliterations it is almost a spoof, four foxes hunt while their brother Fosdyke fixes a vegetarian feast.

Night Noises. (1989). Mem Fox. Terry Denton (Ill.). New York: Harcourt Brace.

> As nearly ninety-year-old Lily naps and dreams of her younger days, the night noises go on, crunching in the garden, creaking in her knees, and fists banging on the door. Finally responding to the noises, she celebrates her ninetieth surprise birthday.

Similes, Metaphors, and Idioms

The dangerous journey of Doctor McPain to make the sick animals better again. (1994). Leon Steinmetz & Gaile Sarma. Krystyna Stasiak (Ill.). Littleton, MA: Sundance.

> An adaption of the classic Russian tale, the same rhythm, similes, and metaphors are kept as Doctor McPain travels through all kinds of rough terrain to rid the animals of their pain.

Mad as a wet hen! And other funny idioms. (1987). Marvin Terban. Giulio Maestro (Ill.). New York: Houghton Mifflin.

This charming book contains origins of sayings with hidden meanings, as well as over 130 common idioms. Humorous pictures accompany interesting explanations of the idioms.

Many luscious lollipops: A book about adjectives. (1989). Ruth Heller. New York: Scholastic.

With a large picture on each page, adjectives are described in rhyme in this informative word book.

Fiction with Word Play

The adventures of Isabel. (1992). Ogden Nash. James Marshall (Ill.). Boston, MA: Joy Street/ Little, Brown & Co. (original text 1963).

In this hilarious up-to-date tale of the old favorite rhyme, Isabel remains undaunted whether confronted by a ravenous and cavernous bear, a horrid monster, or a wrinkled witch.

The cat and the fiddle & more. (1992). Jim Aylesworth. Richard Hull (Ill.). New York: Atheneum.

We know that the cat fiddles and the dish runs away with the spoon, but in this rhyme, each page continues the rhyme with variations. Beautifully illustrated, the rhymes have **predictable** endings. Children will develop category awareness as the pan runs away with the pot and the key runs away with the lock.

Repetitive and Predictable Language

Walking through the jungle. (1997). Debbie Harter. New York: Orchard.

Repetitive and predictable language, and onomatopoeia fill this beautiful and colorful easy-to-read story. A young girl explores the world and meets each animal in its habitat before making it safely home for supper. The phrases "I think I see . . ." and "chasing after me" precede and end each encounter.

Brown bear, brown bear, what do you see? (1967–1983). Bill Martin, Jr. Eric Carle (Ill.). New York: Henry Holt.

Children learn "color" words and read repetitive words as each animal fills a page with its color. The words "what do you see?" and "looking at me" accompany each page. Follow with *Polar Bear, Polar Bear, What Do I Hear?* (1991). Bill Martin, Jr. New York: Holt.

I went walking. (1990). Sue Williams. Julie Vivas (Ill.). New York: Harcourt Brace.

> Real animals are seen as the repetitive lines "I went walking" follow a question and answer format (What did you see?). They provide a model for children to write their own "I went walking" stories.

Five little monkeys. (1989). Eileen Christelow. New York: Clarion.

> A predictable and repetitive favorite story of the little monkeys who jump and fall off the bed can also be used for math, as one less monkey is jumping on the bed after each one falls off and bumps his head.

Five ugly monsters. (1995). Tedd Arnold. New York: Scholastic.

> The author changes the characters from the classic five little monkeys jumping on the bed to five little monsters. Printed as a very easy-to-read, large-print, cartoon-style story about one young boy who is tired of the monsters jumping, falling, and bumping.

Poetry

Bear in mind. (1989). Bobbye S. Goldstein (Ed). William Pene DuBois (Ill.). New York: Viking.

> A specialized collection of poems about bears of every kind: polar bears, circus bears, and teddy bears that can be read aloud, read chorally, or moved to, that will entice children to write their own bear poems.

Hailstones and halibut bones. (1961–1989). Mary O'Neill. John Wallner (Ill.). New York: Doubleday.

> Powerful rhythm and rich language permeate O'Neill's poetry, with updated illustrations bringing it to a new generation of readers. Imagery and descriptive language bring color alive as each of twelve poems describes the sights and feelings evoked by that color.

Good rhymes, good times. (1995). Lee Bennett Hopkins. Frane Lessac (Ill.). New York: HarperCollins.

> This wonderful book of poems ranges in topics from city sounds to seasons to bedtime rhymes. Various shape poems, crisp rhymes, and list poems are accompanied by colorful illustrations. Poems serve as models for children to create their own poems.

The new kid on the block. (1984). Jack Prelutsky. James Stevenson (Ill.). New York: Scholastic.

> Prelutsky plays with language and rhyme in this humorous collection of his original poems. Children of all ages can relate to or laugh at the various characters portrayed in the more than 106 brief poems.

The Random House book of poetry for children. (1983). Jack Prelutsky. Arnold Lobel (Ill.). New York: Random House.

A poetry anthology of 572 poems selected by Jack Prelutsky with numerous lively full-color illustrations make this a necessary collection for every classroom. From fine poetry by Robert Frost to chuckling verse by Shel Silverstein, the variety of images covers rhyme schemes, sounds, rhythm, and word patterns in addition to topics for every occasion.

Riddles

Q is for duck: An alphabet guessing game. (1980). Mary Elting & Michael Folsom. Jack Kent (Ill.). New York: Clarion.

Readers must use thinking skills to decide why "B" is for dog and "Q" is for duck in a riddle book that uses the repetitive phrases "Why" and "Because" as each animal appears in a cartoon-like drawing.

What's a frank frank? Tasty homograph riddles. (1984). Guilio Maestro. New York: Clarion.

Children enjoy answering the more than 60 riddles and puns that are examples of homophonic homographs. Presented with one question per page and a large comic illustration, children try to guess the answer before finding it at the bottom of the page.

Glossary of Terms
Often Used When Speaking About the "At-Risk," "Diverse," or "Difficult" Learners

ability grouping—Placing students according to similar levels of intelligence or achievement.

accountability—The idea that schools or teachers are responsible for educational outcomes.

active reading—Constructing meaning from text by transforming and integrating information into one's existing networks of knowledge and experiences.

affective disorder—A disorder of emotion usually characterized by depression or elation.

alexia—Complete inability to read when reasonable vision, intelligence, and language functions other than reading remain intact.

aliteracy—Lack of reading habit in capable readers.

articulation—Movements the vocal tract makes during production of speech sounds; enunciation of words and vocal sounds.

at risk—Population whose prospects for school success are marginal or worse.

attention-deficit disorder (ADD)—A developmental disorder involving one or more of the basic cognitive processes relating to orienting, focusing, or maintaining attention.

attention-deficit hyperactivity disorder (ADHD)—Basic problems with attention, impulsivity, and deficits in rule-governed behavior, not restlessness or squirminess that have been the focus of adult's concern. Also involves problems of motivation.

auditory memory—Retention or recall of what has been heard.

automaticity—Fluent processing of information requiring little effort or attention (sight-word recognition).

behavior disorder—Disruptive conduct without an organic basis that interferes with learning or social adjustment.

bilingual education—The use of two languages as the media of instruction.

cerebral palsy (CP)—Condition characterized by paralysis, weakness, uncoordination, and other motor dysfunctions because of brain damage before it matured.

choral reading—Group reading aloud much like a chorus.

cinquain—A stanza of five lines; specifically, one that has successive lines of two, four, six, eight, and two syllables.

circle map—Semantic map showing relationships between events or concepts in a text.

cognitive deficit—A perceptual, memory, or conceptual difficulty that interferes with learning.

cognitive map—A mental scheme that preserves and organizes information about events that occur in a learning situation in a systematic way.

communication disorder—An impairment in the ability to use speech or language to communicate.

comprehension monitoring—The ability to keep track of one's own comprehension of reading materials and to make adjustments to comprehend better while reading.

constructivism—Reality constructed or interpreted in terms of one's own perceptions.

cooperative learning—Teaching approach where students with heterogeneous abilities work together.

decode—To analyze spoken or graphic symbols of language to determine meaning.

direct instruction—Teaching that emphasizes drill, practice, and immediate feedback. Instruction is precise, fast-paced, and well-rehearsed by teachers.

dysgraphia—Difficulty producing handwriting because of disease of, or injury to the brain.

dyslexia—A developmental reading disability, presumably congenital and maybe hereditary that varies in degree from mild to severe (originally called word blindness).

dysorthographia—Spelling difficulty that reflects defective cognitive processing of language.

encode—Change a message into symbols (i.e., oral language into written).

expressive aphasia—Difficulty producing syntactic patterns in speech and often in writing due to brain injury or disease.

fetal alcohol syndrome (FAS)—Abnormalities associated with the mother's drinking during pregnancy. Defects include hyperactivity.

fluency—The flow with which oral language is produced.

full inclusion—All students with disabilities should be educated in regular classrooms in neighborhood schools.

giftedness—Intellectual (cognitive) superiority, creativity, and motivation of sufficient magnitude to set child apart from the majority of age-mates and make it possible for her/him to contribute something specific to society.

graphophonic—Sound relationships between the writing and sounds of language.

homograph—A word with the same spelling as another word (i.e., bow = ribbon for hair, bow = front part of a ship).

homonym—A word with a different origin and meaning but the same oral and written form (i.e., bear = an animal vs. bear = to support).

homophone—Words that sound the same, but are spelled differently (i.e., bear and bare).

incremental repetition—Repeating, with variation, a refrain or part of a poem, parallel repetition, as, "O what will you leave to your father dear? The silver-shod steed that brought me here? What will you leave to your mother dear?"

individual education program (IEP)—PL 94-142 requires that a plan for instruction be developed by the educational team for each exceptional child.

intellectual functioning—Ability to solve problems related to academics (usually estimated by IQ test).

invented spelling—An attempt to spell a word that is not already known, based on the writer's knowledge of the spelling system and how it works.

kinesthetic method—Method in which learning takes place through a combination of senses.

language—An arbitrary code or system of symbols used to communicate meaning.

language disorder—A lag in the ability to understand and express ideas that puts the person's linguistic ability behind other areas (i.e., motor, cognitive, or social development).

learning disability—A generic term that refers to a group of disorders manifested by significant difficulties in the acquisition and use of listening, speaking, reading, writing, or mathematical abilities.

modality—Ways individuals receive information in order to learn.

morphology—Study of word formation; how adding or deleting parts of words changes meaning.

orthography—Study of the nature and use of symbols in a writing system.

peer tutoring—A method used to integrate students with disabilities in regular classrooms, based on the notion that students can effectively tutor one another. Role of learner or teacher can be taken by the disabled or nondisabled student.

perception—The extraction of information from sensory stimulation; an active, selective process.

perceptually handicapped—Persons with faulty functioning in one or more aspect of sensory, integrative, expressive, or social perception. Used VERY broadly, and often as a "catch-all" term.

phoneme-grapheme correspondence—Relationship between a sound and its representing symbol.

phonological skills—Ability to understand grapheme-phoneme correspondence, the rules by which sounds go with letters to make words (generally thought to be the reason for the reading problems of many students with learning disabilities).

phonology—Study of how sounds make up words.

picture clues—Illustrations or photographs that provide a visual clue for completing tasks.

PL 94-142—The Education for All Handicapped Children Act, which contains a mandatory provision that to receive funds under the act, every school system in the nation must make provision for a free, appropriate public education for every child between the ages of 3 to 21 regardless of how, or how seriously, he or she may be disabled.

PL 99-457—Extended PL 94-142 to include children age 3 to 5; also included a special incentive for states to institute programs for ages birth to 3 years.

prelinguistic communication—Communication through gestures and noises before the child has learned oral language.

reading disability—Reading achievement that is significantly below expectancy.

reading log—Student-kept journal of responses and reactions, as well as summaries of books the student has read.

reciprocal teaching—Students and teachers get involved in dialogue to facilitate reading comprehension.

scaffolded instruction—Teacher provides temporary structure or support while students are learning a task; support is gradually removed as students are able to perform tasks independently.

self-monitoring—Technique that requires students to keep track of their own behavior.

semantic mapping—Graphic display of clusters of meaningful words. Valuable tool for building vocabulary and for guiding recall of ideas.

semantics—The meanings of language.

social intelligence—Ability to understand social expectations and to cope in social settings.

specific language disability—Language disorder not attributed to impairments of hearing, intelligence, or physical mechanisms of speech; a language disorder of unknown origin.

standard American English—American English in which most educational texts, and government and media publications are written in the United States.

strategy—Systematic plan adapted to improve performance in learning.

subvocalization—Lip, tongue, and larynx movements during silent reading.

syntax—The structure (rules) of word order in sentences.

visual memory—Retention or recall of things seen.

word calling—Word-by-word reading.

word family—A group of words sharing a common phonic element (i.e., it, ite, ight, etc.).

word perception—Visual or auditory identification of a word.

APPENDIX C

Checklist of Characteristic Behaviors Associated With Learning Problems

Checklist of Characteristics

Children who have learning difficulties frequently show some combination of the following characteristics.

Reading

_____ holds book too close
_____ calls words
_____ always sounds out words
_____ always points to words
_____ reverses words (saw = was)
_____ sees double
_____ re-reads lines (involuntarily)
_____ oral reading is choppy
_____ always vocalizes during reading
_____ cannot tell about what he reads
_____ skips lines without knowing it while reading
_____ omits ending consonants in oral reading
_____ can make little sense of sound-symbol relationships, therefore . . .
_____ lacks the ability to use word attack skills
_____ eyes regress frequently during reading
_____ moves head when reading
_____ loses place during reading
_____ frowns and looks sad during reading activities
_____ blinks eyes excessively
_____ closes or covers one eye during reading
_____ squints

_____ eyes burn or itch
_____ rubs eyes a lot
_____ has difficulty focusing
_____ indicates difficulty reading (i.e., "I mess up when I read.")
_____ changes syntax ("He always goes." to "He be going.")
_____ uses pronouns inappropriately ("Her is here.")

Auditory

_____ seems listless
_____ frequent colds, allergies, asthma
_____ seems to depend on others visually
_____ responds to directions slowly
_____ difficulty pronouncing words accurately
_____ breathes through the mouth
_____ has or complains of ear problems
_____ complains of dizziness in the head
_____ unnatural pitch of voice
_____ blank facial expression when speaking to another
_____ watches speaker, closely
_____ uses loud voice
_____ needs excessive volume for listening to T.V., radio, VCR, etc.
_____ can follow ONLY one direction at a time

Writing

_____ inconsistent spacing between words
_____ moves body while writing
_____ reverses letters
_____ produces pressure points in writing
_____ has poor posture when writing most of the time
_____ writing appears rigid
_____ letters vary in size
_____ writes short pieces for short periods
_____ grips writing tool tightly
_____ mixes capital and small letters
_____ moves paper while writing
_____ letters extend beyond the lines
_____ does not follow margins

Spelling

_____ omits letters at the beginning and/or end of words
_____ omits letters within words
_____ can sometimes spell better orally than in writing
_____ spells word as if it sounds differently
_____ reverses letters
_____ transposes letters in words
_____ drops letters as people do when talking
_____ confuses consonant sounds

Work and Other Habits

_____ difficulty getting organized
_____ has trouble getting started
_____ has many projects going on at the same time; has difficulty following through
_____ says what's on his mind without considering its appropriateness
_____ searches for high stimulation
_____ easily distracted
_____ does not tolerate a lack of activity and feels bored
_____ often creative, intuitive, and highly intelligent
_____ trouble following "proper" procedures
_____ impatient; low tolerance for frustration
_____ impulsive verbally or actively (changes plans, spends money impulsively, etc.)
_____ tends to worry needlessly, endlessly
_____ switches moods suddenly
_____ is extremely restless
_____ older children have tendency toward addictive behaviors

Personality and Physical Characteristics

_____ has sense of underachievement, of not meeting goals (even if he does)
_____ has difficulty making and keeping friends
_____ has sense of insecurity
_____ will not (can't) conform
_____ moves about a lot
_____ difficulty exchanging conversations
_____ talks "at" rather than with peers
_____ seems uncooperative
_____ seems lazy
_____ seems careless
_____ often bumps into furniture or other large objects
_____ is referred to as clumsy

Communication Handicapped

A child who has difficulty understanding language has a RECEPTIVE language handicap. The child has MANY (not few) of these characteristics.

____ responds inconsistently to sounds or speech
____ has short attention for listening
____ sometimes looks "blank" when spoken to
____ seems frustrated during class discussions
____ has difficulty understanding abstract language
____ has problems with multiple word meanings
____ has difficulty recognizing relationships of words to concepts
____ distracted from speech and seems to listen to environmental sounds
____ has difficulty using phonics as a method of word recognition
____ often gives inappropriate answers (e.g. "What did you do yesterday?" Response might be, "It is warm outside.")
____ has difficulty learning new vocabulary
____ lacks understanding of riddles, jokes, rhymes, or absurdities
____ seems to have a poor memory for what happened during listening activities
____ has difficulty sequencing events (days of week, numbers, story episodes)
____ often repeats a question or statement rather than responding
____ makes impulsive, immediate, inappropriate responses to questions
____ has a tendency to "shadow" questions or directions (subvocally or vocally)

EXPRESSIVE language difficulties result in the child having difficulties organizing thoughts when speaking and writing. The child has some or many of the following characteristics.

____ seems unusually quiet
____ does not contribute to class discussions
____ sometimes uses words incorrectly
____ sometimes uses words in incorrect order in sentences
____ seems lethargic and unanimated
____ uses more physical rather than verbal expression
____ sometimes substitutes one word for another within a category (i.e., orange for apple)
____ has difficulty finding correct describing words (i.e., "You know, that thing we saw?")
____ uses short sentences most of the time
____ rambles on to answer a question or when telling a story or event
____ uses an inordinate amount of "ums," pauses, or repetitions
____ overuses concrete vocabulary
____ seems to be an excessive talker
____ seems hyperverbal
____ often fails to recognize social cues to stop talking

REMEMBER: Some of these characteristics are present in all of us. But students with problems will exhibit many of them. There will be many overlaps, as well. If a child has an excessive number of characteristics, you MUST seek appropriate, special services. *Children with severe problems produce products that are significantly different from those of others in class. Their excessive **inability to remember** stands out from the others.*

Skills Usually Associated With Reading and the Language Arts: A Checklist

Skills lists, because of the way they are often used, cause my blood to boil. Items are "checked" to inform parents about what children can do (or not do). Now, I ask, how can a check item tell about a student's ability to "infer from reading?"

I know it is difficult to personalize instruction for all students and write about children's progress in narrative format. I have, therefore, included a skills list initially prepared by Amy Kroberger and Aimee Patti. These graduate students, who teach in the public schools, created the format to parallel students' daily activities. The checklist style can be used (1) to supplement letters to parents, and (2) as a daily guide for children who can check items themselves, as they interact with each skill. You may add, delete, or change lists on this progress report form checklist to meet the curriculum content of your programs.

CAUTION: Some of the dangers of using a checklist for illustrating student achievements include:

1. descriptors can be interpreted in many ways;
2. some things are always (unintentionally) left out of skills lists;
3. an assumption that all students must learn all of the skills on the list;
4. the need to continuously alter and change a skills list to match curriculum content;
5. limited descriptions of student behaviors;
6. a tendency for adults to view checklists much like test scores;
7. a tendency to create grade-level equivalents for mastery of each skill.

This list is useful for students to use as a guide for identifying learning skills and strategies for reading, writing, spelling, and phonics.

Progress Report Form

Comprehension

Student: _____ Teacher: _____ Date: _____

What you can do	What you need	My job

*Retell to demonstrate story comprehension:
 oral_____ written_____
 Introduction_____
    When_____
    Where_____
 Main character(s)_____
 Other character(s)_____
 Problem
 Episodes_____
 Solution to problem _____
 Ending _____
 Theme_____
	*Retell to demonstrate story comprehension:
	 oral _____written_____
	 Introduction_____
	    When_____
	    Where_____
	 Main character(s)_____
	 Other character(s)_____
	 Problem
	 Episodes_____
	 Solution to problem _____
	 Ending _____
	 Theme_____	

*Use think-alongs to assist comprehension: Predict before reading ____ Brainstorm to predict _____ Visualize _____ Self-question _____ Reread for idea _____ Personalize test _____ Use prior knowledge ____ Reread for word meaning__ Summarize _____ Ask for help _____	*Use think-alongs to assist comprehension: Predict before reading ____ Brainstorm to predict_____ Visualize_____ Self-question_____ Reread for ideas_____ Personalize text_____ Use prior knowledge_____ Reread for word meaning__ Summarize_____ Ask for help_____	

*Identify information in questions as:
    Right there_____
    Think and search_____
    On my own_____
 *Create questions:
    Right there_____
    Think and search_____
    On my own_____
	*Identify information in questions as:
	    Right there_____
	    Think and search_____
	    On my own_____
	 *Create questions:
	    Right there_____
	    Think and search_____
	    On my own_____	

What you can do	What you need	My job
*Literature journal shows comprehension_____ uses pictures_____ writes_____	*Literature journal to show comprehension_____ uses pictures_____ writes_____	
*Picture reading aids comprehension_____	*Picture reading to aid comprehension_____	
*Benefit from peer discussions_____	*Benefit from peer discussions_____	
*Benefit from teacher discussions and literature journal responses_____	*Benefit from teacher discussions and literature journal responses_____	
*Use KWL to guide research comprehension: Self-select topic _____ Tell all you know _____ Write right there questions to research_____ Write other types of questions_____ Understand concept of a bibliography_____ Read information to answer questions_____ Skim_____ Scan_____	*Use KWL to guide research comprehension: Self-select topic_____ Tell all you know_____ Write right there questions to research_____ Write other types of questions_____ Understand concept of a bibliography_____ Read information to answer questions_____ Skim_____ Scan_____	
*Read challenging content materials: Read for important parts_____ Identify words important to subject_____ Read and then retell____	*Read challenging content materials: Read for important parts_____ Identify words important to subject_____ Read and then retell____	

Other comprehension skills and strategies:

_____

_____

My comments about my reading comprehension:

_____

_____

_____

_____

_____

_____

_____

_____

_____

_____

_____

_____

_____

_____

_____

_____

_____

_____

_____

_____

_____

_____

_____

_____

Progress Report Form

Composition

Student: _____ Teacher: _____ Date: _____

What you can do	What you need	My job

*Writing stage:
  Prewriting _____
  Beginning _____
  Emergent _____
(See descriptors,
Figure 7-5 in text).
	*Writing stage:
	  Prewriting _____
	  Beginning _____
	  Emergent _____	

*Use varied sentence constructions _____ (See descriptors, Figure 7-4)	*Use varied sentence constructions _____	
*Use retelling checklist (Fig. 6-4) to guide story writing _____	*Use retelling checklist (Fig. 6-4) to guide story writing _____	

*Write at least five times
daily without critiques:
  dialogue journal _____
  content journal _____
  literature journal _____
  mail _____
  reading log _____
  other _____
	*Write at least five times
	daily without critiques:
	  dialogue journal _____
	  content journal _____
	  literature journal _____
	  mail _____
	  reading log _____
	  other _____	

*Benefit from writing
frameworks:
  List poems _____
  Riddles _____
  Three-sentence stories _
  Cinquains _____
  Labels and captions ____
  No prompt journal _____
  writing _____
  other _____
	*Benefit from writing
	frameworks:
	  List poems _____
	  Riddles _____
	  Three-sentence stories ___
	  Cinquains _____
	  Labels and captions _____
	  No prompt journal _____
	  writing _____
	  other _____	

What you can do	What you need	My job

*Research and report writing
    Use KWL independently
    without prompts _____
	*Research and report writing
	Use KWL independently
	without prompts _____	

*Understand the writing process _____	*Understand the writing process _____	
*Use graphic organizer(s) circle map _____ Venn diagram _____	*Use graphic organizer(s) circle map _____ Venn diagram _____	
*Know how to redraft a paper _____	*Know how to redraft a paper _____	
*Use the "About my writing" sheet to redraft _____ (Figures 7-32 & 7-34)	*Use the "About my writing sheet" to redraft _____	
*Use "Editing my writing" sheet to proof and correct for publication _____	*Use "Editing my writing" sheet to proof and correct for publication _____ (Figure 7-23)	

Other things about writing include

_____

_____

_____

_____

_____

_____

_____

Progress Report Form

Phonics, Spelling, and Word Study

Student: _____ Teacher: _____ Date: _____

What you can do	What you need	My job
*Phonics _____ (Figures 8-2 & 8-3)	*Phonics _____	
*Learn phonics with explicit___implicit___ instruction.	*Learn phonics with explicit___implicit___ instruction.	
Know these: letter names_____ _____ initial sounds for_____ _____ (Fig. 8-5)	Know these: letter names_____ _____ initial sounds for_____ _____	
blends_____ _____ (Fig. 8-6)	blends_____ _____	
consonant digraphs at the beginning of words_____ _____ at the end of words___ _____ silent consonants___ _____ (Fig. 8-7)	consonant digraphs at the beginning of words_____ _____ at the end of words___ _____ silent consonants___ _____	

What you can do	What you need	My job

a-e vowel sound_____
other two-letter
    combinations_____
(Fig. 8-8)
	a-e vowel sound_____
	other two-letter
	    combinations_____	

*Spelling Learn to spell using: Spelling workshop_____ _____ Modified Fernald_____ Self-Questioning_____ Mnemonic devices_____ Combinations of_____ _____ _____ Other things _____ _____ _____	Learn to spell using: Spelling workshop_____ _____ Modified Fernald_____ Self-Questioning_____ Mnemonic devices_____ Combinations of_____ _____ _____ Other things_____ _____	

*Word Study
Know about the
    following word groups:
clipped words_____
portmanteau words_____
compounds_____
contractions_____
acronyms and initializations
_____
onomatopoeia_____
phobia words_____
ology words_____
	Know about the
	    following word groups:
	clipped words_____
	portmanteau words_____
	compounds_____
	contractions_____
	acronyms and initializations
	_____
	onomatopoeia_____
	phobia words_____
	ology words_____	

Suffixes_____ _____ Prefixes_____ _____ Roots_____ _____	Suffixes_____ _____ Prefixes_____ _____ Roots_____ _____	
Make words using roots_____ Other_____	Make words using roots_____ Other _____	

Other things I want you to know about how I use phonics

_____

_____

_____

_____

_____

_____

_____

_____

_____

_____

_____

_____

_____

_____

_____

_____

_____

_____

_____

_____

_____

_____

_____

_____

Progress Report Form

Independence

Student: _____ Teacher: _____ Date: _____

What you can do	What you need	My job
Independence Strategies:	Independence Strategies:	
Portfolio_____	Portfolio_____	
Contract_____	Contract_____	
Progress Report Form___	Progress Report Form_____	
Fist-Full-of-Words_____	Fist-Full-of-Words_____	
Self-Questioning_____	Self-Questioning_____	
Routine Writing:	Routine Writing:	
Dialogue journal____	Dialogue journal_____	
Content journal_____	Content journal_____	
Mail_____	Mail_____	
Self-Monitoring sheets	Self-Monitoring sheets	
_____	_____	
_____	_____	
_____	_____	
_____	_____	
_____	_____	

(See monitoring sheets throughout text).

I work best independently when

_____

_____

_____

_____

_____

_____

_____

_____

_____

_____

References

Adams, M. J. (1981). What good is orthography? In O. J. L. Tzeng & H. Singer (Eds.), *Perception of print: Reading research in experimental psychology* (pp. 197–221). Hillsdale, NJ: Erlbaum Associates.

Adams, M. J. (1991). *Beginning to read: Thinking and learning about print.* Cambridge, MA: MIT Press.

Airasian, P. (1991). *Classroom assessment.* New York: McGraw-Hill.

Allington, R. L. (1994). The schools we have. The schools we need. *The Reading Teacher, 48,* 14–29.

Almasi, J. F. (1996). A new view of discussion. In L. B. Gambrell & J. F. Almasi (Eds.), *Lively discussions!* (pp. 2–24). Newark, DE: International Reading Association.

Almasi, J. F., McKeown, M. G., & Beck, I. L. (1996). The nature of engaged reading in classroom discussions of literature. *Journal of Literacy Research, 28,* 107–146.

Alvermann, D. E. (1984). Second graders' strategic preferences while reading basal stories. *Journal of Educational Research, 77,* 184–189.

Anders, P., & Bos, C. (1986). Semantic feature analysis: An interactive strategy for vocabulary development and text comprehension. *Journal of Reading, 29,* 610–616.

Anders, P., Bos, C., & Filip, D. (1984). The effect of semantic feature analysis on the reading comprehension of learning disabled students. In J. A. Niles & L. A. Harris (Eds.), *Changing perspectives on research in reading language processing and instruction* (33rd Yearbook of the National Reading Conference, pp. 162–166). Rochester, NY: National Reading Conference.

Anderson, R. (1994). Role of the reader's schema in comprehension, learning, and memory. In R. Ruddell, M. Ruddell, & H. Singer (Eds.), *Theoretical models and processes of reading* (4th ed., pp. 469–482). Newark, DE: International Reading Association.

Anderson, R. C., & Freebody, P. (1981). Vocabulary knowledge. In J. T. Guthrie (Ed.), *Comprehension and teaching: Research reviews* (pp. 77–117). Newark, DE: International Reading Association.

Anderson, R. C., Hiebert, E. H., Scott, J. A., & Wilkinson, I. A. G. (1985). *Becoming a nation of readers.* Champaign, IL: University of Illinois, Center for the Study of Reading.

347

Archbald, D. A., & Newmann, F. M. (1988). *Beyond standardized testing.* Paper presented at the meeting of the National Association of Secondary School Principals, Reston, VA.

Ashton-Warner, S. (1959). *Spinster.* New York: Simon & Schuster.

Ashton-Warner, S. (1963). *Teacher.* New York: Simon & Schuster.

Atwell, N. (1987). *In the middle: Writing, reading, and learning with adolescents.* Portsmouth, NH: Heinemann.

Avi (1989). *The man who was Poe.* New York: Orchard.

Barbe, W. (1961). *Educators guide to personalized reading instruction.* Englewood Cliffs, NJ: Prentice Hall.

Barkley, R. (1981). *Hyperactive children: A handbook for diagnosis and treatment.* New York: Guilford.

Barron, R. W. (1981). Development of visual word recognition: A review. In G. E. MacKinnon & T. G. Waller (Eds.), *Reading research: Advances in theory and practice.* (Vol. 3, 119–158). New York: Academic Press.

Bartlett, F. C. (1932). *Remembering: A study in experimental and social psychology.* London: Cambridge University Press.

Baugh, J. (1983). *Black street speech: Its history, structure, and survival.* Austin, TX: University of Texas Press.

Beck, I. L., & McKeown, M. G. (1989). Expository text for young readers. The issue of coherence. In L. B. Resnick (Ed.), *Knowing, learning, and instruction: Essays in honor of Robert Glaser* (pp. 47–65). Hillsdale, NJ: Erlbaum.

Becker, W. C., & Gerstein, R. (1982). A follow-up of follow through: The later effects of the direct instruction model on children in fifth and sixth grades. *American Educational Research Journal, 19,* 75–92.

Belanoff, P., & Dickson, M. (Eds.). (1991). *Portfolios: Process and product.* Portsmouth, NH: Heinemann.

Berenstain, S. & J. (1971). *The Berenstain B. Book.* New York: Random House.

Binet, A., & Simon, T. (1905). Upon the necessity of establishing a scientific diagnosis of inferior states of intelligence. *L'Annee Psychologique, 11,* 163–191.

Bissex, G. L. (1980). *Gyns at wrk: A child learns to read and write.* Cambridge, MA: Harvard University Press.

Bloome, D. (1985). Reading as a social process. *Language Arts, 62,* 134–142.

Bloome, D., & Green, J. L. (1992). Educational contexts of literacy. In W. Grabe (Ed.), *Annual review of applied linguistics, 12* (pp. 49–70). New York: Cambridge University Press.

Blumer, H. (1969). *Symbolic interaction: Perspective and method.* Englewood Cliffs, NJ: Prentice-Hall.

Bogdan, R. (1982). *Illiterate or learning disabled? A symbolic interactionist approach to the social dimensions of reading and writing.* Paper presented at the meeting of the International Reading Association regional conference, Syracuse, NY.

Bond, G. L., & Dykstra, R. (1967). The cooperative research program in first-grade reading instruction. *Reading Research Quarterly, 4,* 5–142.

Bos, C., Anders, P., Filip, D., & Jaffe, L. (1989). The effects of an interactive instructional strategy for enhancing reading comprehension and content area learning for students with learning disabilities. *Journal of Learning Disabilities, 22,* 384–390.

Botel, M., & Dawkins, J. (1973). *Communicating: The Heath English series.* Lexington, MA: D. C. Heath.

Bower, G. H. (1976). Experiments on story understanding and recall. *Quarterly Journal of Experimental Psychology, 28,* 511–534.

Brown, C. S., & Lytle, S. L. (1988). Merging assessment and instruction: Protocols in the classroom. In S. M. Glazer, L. W. Searfoss, & L. M. Gentile (Eds.), *Reexamining reading diagnosis: New trends and procedures* (pp. 94–102). Newark, DE: International Reading Association.

Bruno, E. (1996). Final letter/report written to Natalie Morten. Rider University Center for Reading and Writing, Lawrenceville, NJ.

Burke, E. M. & Glazer, S. M. (1994). *Using nonfiction in the classroom.* New York: Scholastic.

Burrows, A. T. (1965). *They all want to write* (3rd. ed.). New York: Holt, Rinehart & Winston.

Calkins, L. M. (1994). *The art of teaching writing.* Portsmouth, NH: Heinemann.

Camp, R. (1992). Portfolio reflections in middle and secondary school classrooms. In K. Yancy, *Portfolios in the writing classroom: An introduction* (pp. 61–79). Urbana, IL: National Council of Teachers of English.

Cazden, C. B. (1986). Classroom discourse. In M.C. Wittrock (Ed.), *Handbook of research on teaching* (3rd ed., pp. 432–463). New York: Macmillan.

Chall, J. (1967). *Learning to read: The great debate.* New York: McGraw-Hill.

Chittenden, E. (1991). Authentic assessment, evaluation, and documentation of student performance (pp. 22–31). In V. Perrone (Ed.), *Expanding student assessment.* Alexandria, VA: Association for Supervision and Curriculum Development.

Clay, M. (1975). *What did I write?* Auckland, New Zealand: Heinemann Educational Books.

Clay, M. (1993). *An observational survey of early literacy achievement.* Portsmouth, NH: Heinemann.

Cole, J. (1989). *It's too noisy!* New York: Thomas Y. Crowell.

Collins, A., Brown, J., & Larkin, K. (1980). Inference in text understanding. In R. J. Spiro, B. C. Bruce, & W. F. Frewer (Eds.), *Theoretical issues in reading comprehension* (pp. 385–407). Hillsdale, NJ: Erlbaum.

Covington, M. V. (1983). Motivated cognitions. In S. Paris, G. Olson, & H. Stevenson (Eds.), *Learning and motivation in the classroom.* Hillsdale, NJ: Erlbaum.

Crawford, L. W. (1993). *Language and literacy learning in multicultural classrooms.* Needham Heights, MA: Allyn & Bacon.

Cullinan, B. E. (1989). *Literature and the child* (2nd ed.). San Diego, CA: Harcourt Brace Jovanovich.

Daniel R. R. v. State Board of Education, 874 F. 2d 1036 (5th Cir. 1989).

Davis, F. B. (1944). Fundamental factors of comprehension in reading. *Psychometrika, 9,* 185–197.

Davis, F. B. (1968). Research in comprehension in reading. *Reading Research Quarterly, 3,* 449–454.

DeBoer, J., & Dallmann, M. (1965). *The teaching of reading.* New York: Holt, Rinehart & Winston.

Dechant, E. V. (1964). *Improving the teaching of reading.* Englewood Cliffs, NJ: Prentice-Hall.

Denburg, S. D. (1976–1977). The interaction of picture and print in reading instruction. *Reading Research Quarterly, 12,* 176–189.

Durkin, D. (1966). *Children who read early.* New York: Teachers College Press.

Durkin, D. (1993). *Teaching them to read* (6th ed.). Boston, MA: Allyn & Bacon.

Eddy, B. L., & Gould, K. A. (1990). Comprehension system 8: A teacher's perspective. *Literacy: Issues and Practices, 7,* 70–75.

Edwards, P. D. (1995). *Four famished foxes and Fosdyke.* New York: HarperCollins.

Eisenberg, L. (1962). Introduction. In J. Money (Ed.), *Reading disabilities: Progress and research needs in dyslexia* (pp. 3–7). Baltimore, MD: Johns Hopkins University Press.

Elbow, P. (1981). *Writing with power: Techniques for mastering the writing process.* New York: Oxford University Press.

Fantauzzo, P. D. (1993). Assessing writing. In S. M. Glazer & C. S. Brown, *Portfolios and beyond: Collaborative assessment in reading and writing* (pp. 47–85). Norwood, MA: Christopher-Gordon.

Fantauzzo, P. D. (1996). Using standardized tests, observations, and nontraditional assessment techniques to identify specific factors in reading. In L. R. Putnam (Ed.), *How to become a better reading teacher: Strategies for assessment and intervention* (pp. 101–112). Englewood Cliffs, NJ: Prentice-Hall.

Fareed, A. A. (1971). Interpretive responses in reading history and biology: An exploratory study. *Reading Research Quarterly, 6,* 493–532.

Farr, B., & Trumbull, E. (1997). *Assessment alternatives for diverse classrooms.* Norwood, MA: Christopher-Gordon.

Farr, R. (1969). *Reading: What can be measured?* Newark, DE: International Reading Association.

Farr, R. (1990, May). *Thinkalong strategies.* Paper presented at the meeting of the International Reading Association, Atlanta, Georgia.

Feitelson, D., Kita, B., & Goldstein, Z. (1986). Effects of listening to series stories on first graders' comprehension and use of language. *Research in the Teaching of English, 10,* 339–356.

Fernald, G. M. (1943). *Remedial techniques in basic school subjects.* New York: McGraw-Hill.

Flesch, R. (1955). *Why Johnny can't read.* New York: Harper & Row.

Flesch, R. (1956). *Teaching Johnny to read.* New York: Grosset & Dunlap.

Frederiksen, C. H. (1975). Representing logical and semantic structure of knowledge acquired from discourse. *Cognitive Psychology, 7,* 317–458.

Freeman, K. J. (1908). *Schools of Hellas.* London: Macmillan & Company.

Fries, C., et. al. (1966). *Merrill linguistic readers* (teacher's ed.). Columbus, OH: Charles E. Merrill.

Fry, E., Kress, J., & Fountoukidis, D. (Eds.) (1993). *The reading teachers book of lists.* New York: The Center for Applied Research

Galbraith, R. (1987). *Reuben runs away.* New York: Orchard Books.

Gall, M. D., & Gall, J. P. (1976). The discussion method. In N.L. Gage (Ed.), *The psychology of teaching methods* (No. 75, pt. 1, pp. 166–216). Chicago, IL: University of Chicago Press.

Gallup Organization (1984, 1988, 1994). National Survey sponsored by Phi Delta Kappa. Princeton, NJ.

Gambrell, L., Pfeiffer, W., & Wilson, R. (1985). The effects of retelling upon reading comprehension and recall of text information. *Journal of Educational Research, 78,* 216–220.

Gearheart, B. R., Weishahn, M. W., & Gearheart, C. J. (1992). *The exceptional student in the regular classroom* (5th ed.). New York: Macmillan.

Gentry, R. (1987). *Spel... is a four-letter word.* New York: Scholastic.

Gentry, R., & Gillet, J. W. (1993). *Teaching kids to spell.* Portsmouth, NH: Heinemann.

Glaser, R. (1981). The future of testing. *American Psychologist, 36,* 923–936.

Glazer, S. M. (1990). *Creating readers and writers.* Newark, DE: International Reading Association.

Glazer, S. M. (1992). *Reading comprehension: Self-monitoring strategies to develop independent readers.* New York: Scholastic.

Glazer, S. M. (1994, March). Self-monitoring: Taking control as a writer. *Teaching, K–8, 91–*92.

Glazer, S. M. (1998). *Children's perceptions about reading and writing the first day of school, 1980–1997.* Unpublished manuscript.

Glazer, S. M., & Brown, C. S. (1993). *Portfolios and beyond: Collaborative assessment in reading and writing.* Norwood, MA: Christopher-Gordon.

Glazer, S. M., & Burke, E. M. (1994). *An integrated approach to early literacy: Literature to language.* Boston: Allyn & Bacon.

Glazer, S. M., & Fantauzzo, P. D. (1993). *Students understanding of the reading process and perceptions of themselves as readers.* Unpublished manuscript.

Glazer, S. M., & Searfoss, L. W. (1988). *Reading diagnosis and instruction: A C-A-L-M approach.* Englewood Cliffs, NJ: Prentice-Hall.

Goodman, K. S. (1965). A linguistic study of cues and miscues in reading. *Elementary English, 42,* 639–643.

Goodman, K. S. (1969). Analysis of oral reading miscues: Applied psycholinguistics. *Reading Research Quarterly, 5,* 9–30.

Goodman, K. S. (1986). *What's whole in whole language?* Portsmouth, NH: Heinemann.

Goodman, Y. (1985). Kid watching: Observing children in the classroom. In A. Jagger & M. T. Smith-Burke (Eds.), *Observing the language learner* (pp. 9–18). Urbana, IL: National Council of Teachers of English.

Graves, D. H. (1983). *Writing: Teachers & children at work.* Portsmouth, NH: Heinemann Educational Books.

Graves, D. H., & Sunstein, B. S. (1992). *Portfolio portraits.* Portsmouth, NH: Heinemann.

Gray, W. S., Monroe, M., & Artley, A. S. (1940). *Think-and-do book: To accompany the new fun with Dick and Jane.* Fair Lawn, NJ: Scott, Foresman.

Greer v. Rome City School District, 950 F. 2d 688 (11th Cir. 1991).

Haarhoff, T. (1920). *Schools of Gaul.* New York: Oxford University, Press.

Halliday, M. A. K. (1975). *Learning how to mean: Exploration in the development of language.* London: Edward Arnold.

Hallowell, E. M., & Ratey, J. J. (1994). *Driven to distraction.* New York: Pantheon.

Harp, B. (1996). *The handbook of literacy assessment and evaluation.* Norwood, MA: Christopher-Gordon.

Harris, T., & Hodges, R. E. (Eds.). (1995). *The literacy dictionary: The vocabulary of reading and writing.* Newark, DE: International Reading Association.

Harwayne, S. (1992). *Lasting impressions.* Portsmouth, NH: Heinemann.

Heath, S. B. (1983). *Ways with words: Language, life and work in communities and classrooms.* Cambridge, England: Cambridge University Press.

Henderson, E. (1985). *Teaching spelling.* Boston, MA: Houghton Mifflin.

Henry, M. (1993). *Album of horses.* New York: Aladdin Books.

Hiebert, E. H., Valencia, S. W., & Afflerbach, P. P. (1994). Definition and perspectives. In S. W. Valencia, E. H. Hiebert, & P. P. Afflerbach (Eds.), *Authentic reading assessment: Practices and possibilities* (pp. 6–21). Newark, DE: International Reading Association.

Hill, B. C., & Ruptic, C. (1994). *Practical aspects of authentic assessment: Putting the pieces together.* Norwood, MA: Christopher-Gordon.

Hodges, R. E. (1987). American spelling instruction: Retropect and prospect. *Visable language, 21,* 215–234.

Holdaway, D. (1979). *The foundations of literacy.* Exeter, NH: Heinemann.

Holland v. Board of Education, 786 F. Supp. 874 (9th Cir. 1994).

Hopkins, L. B. (1995). *Good rhymes, good times.* New York: HarperCollins.

Hopkinson, D., & Ransome, J. (1993). *Sweet Clara and the freedom quilt.* New York: Alfred A. Knopf.

Huey, E. B. (1968). *The psychology and pedagogy of reading.* Cambridge, MA: M.I.T. Press. (First published by Macmillan Company, 1908).

Hunt, L.C. (1957). Can we measure specific factors associated with reading comprehension? *Journal of Educational Research, 51,* 161–172.

Irwin, P. A., & Mitchell, J. M. (1983). A procedure for assessing the richness of retelling. *Journal of Reading, 16,* 391–396.

Jagger, A. M., Carrara, D. H., & Weiss, S. E. (1986). Current research: The influence of reading on children's narrative writing (and vice versa). *Language Arts, 63,* 292–300.

Johns, J., VanLeirsburg, P., & Davis, S. J. (1994). *Improving reading: A handbook of strategies.* Dubuque, IA: Kendall/Hunt.

Johnson, J., & Immerwahr, J. (1994). *First things first: What Americans expect from the public schools.* A report published by Public Agenda, New York, NY.

Kerfott, J. F. (1968). Problems and research considerations in reading comprehension. In M. A. Dawson (Ed.), *Developing comprehension including critical reading* (pp. 38–44). Newark, DE: International Reading Association.

King, S. (1989). *The tommyknockers.* New York: Penguin.

Kintegen, E. (1985). Studying the perception of poetry. In C. Cooper (Ed.), *Researching responses to literature* (pp. 128–155). Norwood, NJ: Ablex.

Kintsch, W., Mandel, T. S., & Kozminsky, E. (1977). Summarizing scrambled stories. *Memory and Cognition, 5,* 547–552.

Koretz, D. (1991, April). *The effects of high-stakes testing on achievement: Preliminary findings about generalization across tests.* Paper presented at the annual meeting of the American Educational Research Association, Chicago, IL.

Kucan, L., & Beck, I. L. (1996). Four fourth graders thinking aloud: An investigation of genre effects. *Journal of Literacy Research, 28,* 259–288.

Lesgold, A. M., DeGood, H., & Levin, J. R. (1977). Pictures and young children's prose learning: A supplementary report. *Reading Research Quarterly, 9,* 353–360.

Levin, J. R., Bender, B. G., & Lesgold, A. M. (1976). Pictures, repetition and young children's oral prose learning. *AV Communication Review, 24,* 367–380.

Lowry, L. (1993). *The giver.* New York: Bantam Doubleday Dell.

Lytle, S. L. (1982). Exploring comprehension style: A study of twelfth grade readers' transactions with text. *Dissertation Abstracts International, 43* (7), 2295A.

Mandler, J., & Johnson, M. (1977). Remembrance of things parsed: Story structures and recall. *Cognitive Psychology, 9,* 111–151.

Manzo, A. V. (1968). *Improving reading comprehension through reciprocal questions.* Unpublished doctoral dissertation, Syracuse University, Syracuse, NY.

Marshall, N. (1983). Using story grammar to assess reading comprehension. *The Reading Teacher, 36,* 616–620.

Marshall, N., & Glock, M. (1979). Comprehension of connected discourse: A study into the relationships between the structure of text and information recalled. *Reading Research Quarterly, 16,* 10–56.

Martin Jr., B. (1974). *Sounds of language.* New York: Holt, Rinehart, & Winston.

McCrum, R., Cran, W., & MacNeil, R. (1992). *The story of English.* London: BBC Books.

McDaniel, T. (1986). A primer on classroom discipline: Principles old and new. *Phi Delta Kappan, 68,* 63–67.

McDowell, R., Adamson, G., & Wood, F. (1982). *Teaching emotionally disturbed children.* Boston, MA: Little, Brown.

McFarland, C. (1993). *Hoofbeats: The story of a thoroughbred.* New York: Atheneum.

McKee, P. (1948). *The teaching of reading in the elementary school.* Cambridge, MA: Houghton Mifflin.

Meek, M. (1982). *Learning to read.* London: The Bodley Head.

Menyuk, P. (1963). Syntactic structures in the language of children. *Child Development, 32,* 407–422.

Meyer, C. (1992). What's the difference between *authentic* and *performance* assessment? *Educational Leadership, 49* (5), 39–40.

Michaels, P.A. (1990). What first graders think about reading. In R.W. Blake (Ed.), *Whole language explorations and applications* (pp. 41–46). Schenectady: New York State English Council.

Michaels, P.A. (1994). *The child's view of reading: Understandings for teachers and parents.* Boston, MA: Allyn & Bacon.

Milz, V. (1980). First graders can write: Focus on communication. *Theory into Practice, 13,* 179–185.

Moffett, J. (1968). *Teaching the universe of discourse.* New York: Houghton Mifflin.

Moffett, J., & Wagner, B. J. (1992). *Student-centered language arts, K–12* (4th ed.). Portsmouth, NH: Heinemann.

Morrow, L. M. (1988). Retelling stories as a diagnostic tool. In S. M. Glazer, L. W. Searfoss, & L. Gentile (Eds.), *Reexamining reading diagnosis* (pp. 128–149). Newark, DE: International Reading Association.

Nagy, W. E. (1988). *Teaching vocabulary to improve reading comprehension.* Newark, DE: International Reading Association.

Oberti v. Board of Education, No. 92–5462, slip, op. at 17 (3rd. Cir. May 28, 1993, as corrected, June 23, 1993).

Ogle, D. M. (1989). The know, want to know, learn strategy. In K. D. Muth (Ed.), *Children's comprehension of text* (pp. 205–223). Newark, DE: International Reading Association.

Olshavsky, J. (1975). An exploratory analysis of the reading process. *Dissertation Abstracts International, 36* (9), 5975-A.

Patterson, K., Marshall, J., & Coltheart, M. (Eds.). (1985). *Surface dyslexia.* London: Erlbaum Associates.

Pearson, P. D., & Spiro, R. J. (1981). Toward a theory of reading comprehension instruction. *Topics in Language Disorders, 1,* 71–88.

Pearson, P. D., & Camperell, K. (1994). Comprehension of text structure. In R. B. Ruddell, M. R. Ruddell, & H. Singer (Eds.), *Theoretical models and processes of reading* (4th ed.). (pp. 448–468). Newark, DE: International Reading Association.

Pearson, P. D., & Stephens, D. (1994). Learning about literacy: A 30-year journey. In R. B. Ruddell, M. R. Ruddell, & H. Singer (Eds.), *Theoretical models and processes of reading* (4th ed.) (pp. 22–42). Newark, DE: International Reading Association.

Pearson, P. D., & Valencia, S. W. (1987). Assessment, accountability, and professional prerogative. In J. E. Readence & R. S. Baldwin (Eds.), *Research in literacy: Merging perspectives* (pp. 3–16). Rochester, NY: National Reading Conference.

Peeck, J. (1974). Retention of pictorial and verbal content of a text with illustrations. *Journal of Educational Psychology, 66,* 880–888.

Perfetti, C. A. (1992). The representation problem in reading acquisition. In P. B. Gough, L. C. Ehri, & R. Treiman (Eds.), *Reading acquisition* (pp. 145–174). Hillsdale, NJ: Erlbaum.

Perfetti, C. A., & Zhang, S. (1996). What it means to learn to read. In M. F. Graves, P. Van Den Broek, & B. M. Taylor (Eds.), *The first R: Every child's right to read* (pp. 37–61). New York: Teachers College.

Petty, W. T., & Finn, P. J. (1981). Classroom teachers reports on teaching written composition. In S. Haley-James (Ed.), *Perspectives on writing in grades 1–8* (pp. 19–34). Urbana, IL: National Council of Teachers of English.

Piaget, J., and Inhelder, B. (1969). *The psychology of the child.* New York: Basic Books.

Pittelman, S. M., Heimlick, J. E., Berglund, R. L., & French, M. P. (1991). *Semantic feature analysis: Classroom application.* Newark, DE: International Reading Association.

Prelutsky, J. (1990). *The new kid on the block.* New York: Greenwillow Books, A Division of William Morrow & Co., Inc.

Raphael. T. E., (1982). *Improving question-answering performance through instruction.* (Reading Education Report No. 32). Urbana, IL: University of Illinois, Center for the Study of Reading.

Read, C. (1975). *Children's categorizations of speech sounds in English.* Urbana, IL: National Council of Teachers of English.

Read, J. D., & Barnsley, R. H. (1977). Remember Dick and Jane? Memory for elementary school readers. *Canadian Journal of Behavioral Science, 9,* 361–370.

Readence, J. E., & Barone, D. M. (Eds.). (1997). *Reading Research Quarterly, 32* (4) 220.

Reder, L. M. (1980). Comprehension and retention of prose. *Review of Educational Research, 50,* 15–53.

Rhodes, L. (Ed.). (1993). *Literacy assessment: A handbook of instruments.* Portsmouth, NH: Heinemann.

Rief, L. (1992). *Seeking diversity: Language arts with adolescents.* Portsmouth, NH: Heinemann.

Rigney, J. W., & Lutz, K. A. (1976). Effect of graphic analogies of concepts in chemistry on learning & attitude. *Journal of Educational Psychology, 68,* 305–311.

Rippa, S. A. (1988). *Education in a free society.* New York: Longman.

Rohwer, W. D., Jr., & Harris, W. J. (1975). Media effects on prose learning in two populations of children. *Journal of Educational Psychology, 67,* 651–657.

Roncker v. Walter, 700 F. 2d 1058 (6th Cir.) cert. denied, 464 U.S. 864 (1983).

Rosenblatt, L. (1978). *The reader, the text, the poem.* Carbondale and Edwardsville, IL: Southern Illinois University Press.

Rosenfield, I. (1988). *The invention of memory.* New York: Basic Books.

Routman, R. (1988). *Transitions: From literature to literacy.* Portsmouth, NH: Heinemann.

Routman, R. (1996). *Literacy at the crossroads: Critical talk about reading, writing, and other teaching dilemmas.* Portsmouth, NH: Heinemann.

Royer, J. M., & Cable, G. W. (1975). Facilitated learning in connected discourse. *Journal of Educational Psychology, 67,* 116–123.

Ruddell, R. B., Ruddell, M. R., & Singer, H. (Eds.). (1994). *Theoretical models and processes of reading* (4th ed.). Newark, DE: International Reading Association.

Ruddell, R., & Unrau, N. (1994). The reader, the text, and the teacher. In R. B. Ruddell, M. R. Ruddell, & H. Singer (Eds.), *Theoretical models and processes of reading.* Newark, DE: International Reading Association.

Rummelhart, D. (1977). *Toward an interactive model of reading.* In S. Doric (Ed.), *Attention and performance VI.* London: Academic Press.

Rummelhart, D. E. (1980). Schemata: The building blocks of cognition. In R. J. Spiro, B. C. Bruce, & W. F. Brewer (Eds.), *Theoretical issues in reading comprehension* (pp. 33–58). Hillsdale, NJ: Erlbaum.

Russavage, P. M., & Arick, K. L. (1988). Thinkalong: A strategic approach to improving comprehension. *Reading: Issues and Practices, 5,* 32–41.

Samuels, S. J. (1970). Effects of pictures on learning to read, comprehension, and attitudes. *Review of Educational Research, 40,* 397–407.

Samuels, S. J. (1994). Toward a theory of automatic information processing in reading, revisited. In R. B. Ruddell, M. R. Ruddell, & H. Singer (Eds.), *Theoretical models and processes of reading* (4th ed., pp. 816–837). Newark, DE: International Reading Association.

Santa, C. M. (1995). Students lead their own parent conferences. *Montana State Reading Association Journal, 9,* 12–13.

Scardamalia, M., & Bereiter, C. (1984). Development of strategies in text processing. In H. Mandl, N. Stein, & T. Trebasso (Eds.), *Learning and comprehension of text* (pp. 379–406). Hillsdale, NJ: Erlbaum.

Searfoss, L. W., & Enz, B. J. (1996). Can teacher evaluation reflect holistic instruction? *Educational Leadership, 53* (6), 30–41.

Searfoss, L. W., & Readence, J. E. (1989). *Helping children learn to read.* Englewood Cliffs, NJ: Prentice-Hall.

Searle, D., & Dillon, D. (1980). The message of marking: Teacher written response to student writing at intermediate grade levels. *Research in the Teaching of English, 14,* 233–242.

Sharp, Q. (Ed.). (1989). *Evaluation: Whole language checklists for evaluating your children.* New York: Scholastic.

Shaughnessy, M. P. (1977). *Errors and expectations.* New York: Oxford University Press.

Shepard, L. A. (1990). Inflated test score gains: Is the problem old norms or teaching the test? *Educational Measurement: Issues and Practice, 9* (3), 15–22.

Singer, H. (1994). The substrata-factor theory of reading. In R. Ruddell, M. Ruddell, & H. Singer (Eds.), *Theoretical models and processes of reading* (4th ed.). Newark, DE: International Reading Association.

Slavin, R. E. (1992). *Educational psychology* (3rd. ed.). Englewod, NJ: Prentice Hall.

Smith, F. (1971). *Understanding reading: A psycholinguistic analysis of reading and learning to read.* New York: Holt Rinehart.

Smith, F. (1975). *Comprehension and learning: A conceptual framework for teachers.* New York: Holt, Rinehart & Winston.

Smith, F. (1978). *Reading without nonsense.* New York: Teachers College Press.

Smith, F. (1983). *Essays into literacy.* London: Heinemann.

Smith, F. (1995, April). Let's declare education a disaster and get on with our lives. *Phi Delta Kappan,* 584–590.

Smith, F. (1995). *Between hope and havoc: Essays into human learning and education.* Portsmouth, NH: Heinemann.

Smith, J. A. (1967). *Creative teaching of reading and literature in the elementary school.* Boston, MA: Allyn & Bacon.

Smith, N. B. (1963). *Reading instruction for today's children.* Englewood Cliffs, NJ: Prentice-Hall.

Spiro, R. J. (1977). Remembering information from text: The state of schema' approach. In R. C. Anderson, R. J. Spiro, & W. E. Montague (Eds.), *Schooling and the acquisition of knowledge.* Hillsdale, NJ: Erlbaum.

Stallman, A. C., & Pearson, P. D. (1990). Formal measures of early literacy. In L. M. Morrow & J. K. Smith (Eds.), *Assessment for instruction in early literacy* (pp. 7-44). Englewood Cliffs, NJ: Prentice-Hall.

Stanton, J. (1980). Writing and counseling: Using a dialogue journal. *Language Arts, 57,* 514–518.

Stein, N. L., & Nezworski, T. (1978). *The effects of organization and instructional set on story memory* (Tech. Rep. No. 129). Urbana, IL: University of Illinois, Center for the Study of Reading.

Stein, R. L. (1993). *Goosebumps* New York: Scholastic.

Swanson, B. B. (1985). Listening to students about reading. *Reading Horizons, 22,* 123–128.

Tannenhaus, M. K., Flanigan, H., & Seidenberg, M. S. (1980). Orthographic and phonological code activation in auditory and visual word recognition. *Memory and Cognition, 8,* 513–520.

Teale, W. H. (1984). Reading to young children: Its significance for literacy development. In H. Goelman, A. A. Oberg, & F. Smith (Eds.), *Awakening to literacy.* London: Heinemann.

Templeton, S. (1986). Literacy, readiness and basals. *The Reading Teacher, 39,* 66–82.

Thorndyke, P. (1977). Cognitive structures in comprehension and memory of narrative discourse. *Cognitive psychology, 9,* 77–110.

Tierney, R. J., Carter, M. A., & Desai, L. E. (1991). *Portfolio assessment in the classroom.* Norwood, MA: Christopher-Gordon.

Tierney, R. J., & Leys, M. (1984). What is the value of connecting reading and writing? (Reading Education Rep. No. 55). Champaign, IL: Center for the Study of Reading.

Tierney, R. J., Readence, J. E., & Dishner, E. K. (1990). Reading strategies and practices: A compendium (3rd ed.). Boston, MA: Allyn & Bacon.

Tinker, M. A., & McCullough, C. M. (1952). *Teaching elementary reading.* New York: Appleton-Century-Crofts.

Vacca, R., & Vacca, J. L. (1993). *Content area reading* (4th ed.). New York: HarperCollins.

Valencia, S. (1990). A portfolio approach to classroom assessment: The whys, whats, and hows. *The Reading Teacher, 43* (4), 338–340.

Valencia, S. W., & Pearson, P. D. (1987). Reading assessment: Time for a change. *The Reading Teacher, 40,* 726–732.

Valencia, S. W., Pearson, P. D., Peters, C. W., & Wixson, K. K. (1989). Theory and practice in statewide reading assessment: Closing the gap. *Educational Leadership* (April), 57–63.

VanLeirsburg, P. (1993). Standardized reading tests: Then and now. In J. L. Johns (Ed.), *Literacy: Celebration and challenge* (pp. 31–54). Bloomington, IL: Illinois Reading Council Publication.

Veatch, J. (1966). *Reading in the elementary school.* New York: Ronald Press.

Vygotsky, L. S. (1962). *Thought and language.* Cambridge, MA: MIT Press.

Vygotsky, L. S. (1978). *Mind in society: The development of higher psychological processes.* (M. Cole, V. John-Steiner, S. Scribner, & E. Souberman; Eds. and Trans.). Cambridge, MA: Harvard University Press.

Wallace, G., & Kaufman, J. M. (1986, 1990). *Teaching students with learning and behavior problems* (3rd & 4th eds.). Columbus, OH: Merrill.

Weinstein, C. S. (1977). Modifying student behavior in an open classroom through changes in the physical design. *American Educational Research Journal, 14,* 249–262.

Weiss, J., & Hagen, R. (1988). A key to literacy: Kindergartners' awareness of the functions of print. *The Reading Teacher, 41,* 574–578.

Wells, G. (1986). *The meaning makers: Children learning language and using language to learn.* Exeter, NH: Heinemann.

Wilde, S. (1992). *You kan red this! Spellng and punctuation for whole language classrooms, K–6.* Portsmouth, NH: Heinemann.

Wilde, S. (1997). *What's a schwa sound anyway?* Portsmouth, NH: Heinemann.

Williams, G. (1958). *The rabbits' wedding.* New York: Harper & Row.

Wilson, R., & Russavage, P. (1989). Schoolwide application of comprehension strategies. In J. D. Coley & S. S. Clewell (Eds.), *Reading issues and practices* (pp. 45–46). Maryland: State of Maryland Reading Association.

Yerkes, R. M. (Ed.). (1921). *Memoirs of the National Academy of Sciences: Psychological examining in the United States army* (Vol. 15). Washington, DC: U.S. Government Printing Office.

Zabrucky, K., & Ratner, H. H. (1992). Effects of passage type on comprehension monitoring and recall in good and poor readers. *Journal of Reading Behavior, 24,* 373–391.

Zemach, M. (1986). *The three wishes: An old story.* New York: Farrar, Straus, & Giroux.

Zinsser, W. (1988). *Writing to learn.* New York: Harper & Row.

About the Author

Susan Mandel Glazer is director of the Reading and Writing Center and Professor of Education at Rider University. A past President of the International Reading Association, she is the 1998 recipient of the IRA Outstanding Teacher Educator in Reading Award. She is the author of numerous articles and books, among them *Portfolios and Beyond: Collaborative Assessment in Reading and Writing,* also published by Christopher-Gordon Publishers. A popular presenter, Dr. Glazer is also a Teaching Editor for *Teaching Pre K–8*. She received her Ed.D. from the University of Pennsylvania.

Author Index

Subject Index